JOHN BRA

A BIRDWA

GUIDE ⊤ᴜ

MALAYSIA

Waymark

First published in 1993 by Waymark Publishing

Designed by Quick Brown Dog Productions
Typeset by Aimsetters, Adelaide, South Australia
Printed by Kyodo Printing Co. Ltd, Singapore

National Library of Australia
Cataloguing-in-Publication Data
Bransbury, John
    A birdwatcher's guide to Malaysia

    Bibliography.
    Includes index.
    ISBN 0 646 14559 2.

    1. Bird watching - Malaysia. 2. Birds - Malaysia
    - Geographical distribution. I. Title.

    598.07234595

This book is distributed by
Natural History Book Service Ltd
2-3 Wills Road, Totnes, Devon TQ9 5XN, UK
Telephone 0803-865913 (International +44 803 865913)
Fax 0803-865280 (International +44 803 865280)
E-mail nhbs@gn.apc.org

Cover illustrations
Main photo: Early morning in the rainforest, Kinabalu
                National Park, Sabah, Malaysia
Inset: Rhinoceros Hornbill
                (*photos: J. Bransbury*)

Contents

Acknowledgements   1
Introduction   3
      Helpful Hints   4
      Useful Addresses   7
      Further Reading   11
      Glossary of Malay terms   12
      Map of West Malaysia   13
      Map of East Malaysia   14

Sites   15
    1 Lake Gardens and Bukit Tunku   15
    2 Sungai Batu Mining Pools   19
    3 Universiti Malaya and Rimba Ilmu   24
    4 Templer Park   29
    5 Gombak Valley (Ulu Gombak)   34
    6 Genting Highlands   40
    7 Bukit Gasing and Petaling Jaya   46
    8 Taman Pertanian, Shah Alam   51
    9 Pulau Tengah, Klang   57
  10 Kuala Selangor Nature Park   61
  11 PBLS Ricefields, Sekinchan   67
  12 Tanjong Karang and Pantai Rasa Sayang   72
  13 The Gap (Semangkok Pass)   76
  14 Fraser's Hill (Bukit Fraser)   83
  15 Kuala Gula   89
  16 Penang Island (Pulau Pinang)   95
  17 Cameron Highlands   100
  18 Bukit Larut (Maxwell Hill)   106
  19 Pulau Langkawi   114
  20 Kenyir Dam (Tasik Kenyir)   121
  21 Pulau Redang   126
  22 Taman Negara   129
  23 Tasik Chini   141
  24 Pulau Tioman   148
  25 Endau-Rompin   153
  26 Pasoh Forest Reserve   160
  27 Bako National Park   165
  28 Niah National Park   171
  29 Lambir Hills National Park   177
  30 Gunung Mulu National Park   182

31 Tunku Abdul Rahman National Park   193
32 Pulau Tiga Park   198
33 Kota Belud Bird Sanctuary   201
34 Kinabalu National Park   206
35 Poring Hot Springs   213
36 Sepilok Forest Reserve   220
37 Uncle Tan's Jungle Camp   228
38 Turtle Islands Park   232
39 Danum Valley Conservation Area   235
40 Tawau Hills Park   242
41 Pulau Sipadan   245
42 Crocker Range National Park   247

Birds of Malaysia - Checklist with Site Index   249

Mammals of Malaysia - Checklist   277

Acknowledgements

It is fair to say that all authors draw on the experience of others, at least to some extent, and this is especially true for writers of site-guides. Over the past couple of years, in one way or another, many people have helped me with the site accounts for this book - for their kindness, assistance and advice I warmly thank all of the following: Roger Jaensch, formerly of the Asian Wetland Bureau, Kuala Lumpur, who assisted with writing the early drafts for sites around Kuala Lumpur and in Selangor and Pahang; Brett Lane, Asian Wetland Bureau; Dr David Wells, University of Malaya; Andrew Ponnampalam, Malayan Nature Society, Petaling Jaya; Kenneth Kee, Singapore Nature Society; Neal Nirmal and Lim Ban Beng, Malayan Nature Society, Penang; Ngu Ka Sen, Asian Overland Services, Kuching; Sylvia Alsisto, head ranger, Sepilok Forest Reserve; Joanna K-Kissey, director, Sabah Archives; Philip Lawing, head guide, Gunung Mulu National Park; members of the Danish Ornithological Society (for their excellent bird report on Gunung Mulu); Guna of Bukit Larut (for his hospitality and for sharing his knowledge of that area's bird life); Nash of Fraser's Hill (Nash is an enthusiastic birder who has played host to many an overseas visitor); Azman Said, officer-in-charge, Kuala Gula Bird Sanctuary; Clive Marsh, Sabah Foundation, Kota Kinabalu; Nigel Collar, BirdLife International, Cambridge, UK; Adrian Long, BirdLife International and Oriental Bird Club (for his helpful advice and for giving me permission to use an excellent article on the Danum Valley by Dave Showler); Linda Birch, Edward Grey Institute, Oxford, UK; and June Pellegrino, National Library of Australia, Canberra.

If possible, I like to visit the places I write about so that I can describe them from first-hand experience; also, since Malaysia is developing at a rapid rate I wanted to go to the country close to the time of publication of this book, and to gather as much up-to-date material as I could. For these reasons I visited Malaysia towards the end of 1992. In part, my trip was made possible by the generous support of the Malaysia Tourism Promotion Board (MTPB) and Malaysia Airlines (MAS). MTPB and MAS also sponsored my two companions, Edie Bransbury and Roger Jaensch. First among those at MTPB that I would like to thank for their commitment to the project are Mohd Roslan Ali, MTPB director for Australia and New Zealand, and Dennis Pile of Dennis Pile Associates, public relations consultant to MTPB Australia. Both have my sincere gratitude for their patience and support. Wendy Lee of MTPB Sydney worked hard to make things run smoothly, as did Hafiz Abdul Majid of MTPB's Kuala Lumpur office. While I was in Malaysia a number of MTPB staff provided me with a great deal of assistance - some names escape me, but Noridah Kamarudin and Abdul Halim Mohd Anuar, both of MTPB Kuching, Sarawak, are two I'll never forget. Thank you both - Noridah in particular (while escorting my group, Noridah fell from the boardwalk at Niah National Park and severely injured her back, yet she remained cheerful throughout the ordeal). Others who helped with the ground arrangements in Malaysia included Ngu Ka Sen of Asian Overland Services, Khairul Annuar of Khairul Adventures, Richard Hii of Tropical Adventure, Mimi Rodiah Abdul Rahman of Cantumas Travel & Tours, Fishol Ishak of Sala Travel & Tours, George Woo of Cherry Bird Travel, and Philip Lawing of Gunung Mulu National Park - my thanks to you all.

Malcolm Longstaff, MAS public relations consultant for Australia and New Zealand, also worked hard to ensure that our tight air schedule went without hitch - it did, in fact things went perfectly, and I very much appreciate the efforts of Malcolm and MAS's Malaysian staff, especially Elizabeth Chong of MAS Kota Kinabalu.

Books go through a great many stages - more, I think, than most people realise - and each step brings new problems and frustrations. For their support, my gratitude goes to Edie, to Marko Lahnstein and Ineke Posthumus of Aimsetters, Adelaide, to Hideyuki Suzaki and Mabel Chew of Kyodo Printing, Singapore, and to Peter Exley of the Natural History Book Service, Totnes. You may not know it, but in different ways each of you stopped me from quitting more than once. And thank you Marco for your company, and for the splendid photos used in this book.

Finally, my regards to Ray and Pat Ledger, and to Roy and Gweneth Johnson for helping me in various ways. My mother, Pat and Frits, Hilary and John, and Keith and June all have my love and deep gratitude - I'm sure I don't have to say what for.

I lovingly dedicate this book to Edie, Julian, my father, and Sally and Kyra, all now gone from my life but still in my heart and soul.

> On a windswept hillside the broken body of a
> blackbird lies cold,
> while from a nearby tree her mate pours forth
> his golden song.
> Don't expect life to be fair; there's just life,
> and life goes on, each day bringing the promise
> of love and joy anew.
>
> j.b.

Introduction

I first went to Malaysia (or Malaya as it was called until 1963) back in the late 1950s when my father was posted to the RAF base at Butterworth, near Penang. During the four or so years that we stayed there I got an unforgettable taste of life in the orient: the lush tropical vegetation, sunbirds darting about in brightly flowering hibiscus shrubs, colourful processions through Georgetown's narrow streets, the taste and smell of exotic fruits like rambutans and mangosteens - all this and much more made an indelible impression on me (I was only eight or nine years old at the time).

Many changes have taken place in Malaysia over the past few decades; it is now one of the most rapidly developing countries in south-east Asia. Despite this, Malaysia remains as alluring as ever. The sights, sounds and smells are still unmistakably oriental; the people are engagingly open and friendly; and the wildlife - though threatened like just about everywhere else - is truly breathtaking in its diversity and abundance. What's more, basics such as food and accommodation are still absurdly cheap by Western standards. And it's easy to get around in Malaysia since the country's public transport system is excellent (though admittedly a little chaotic in places) and almost everyone speaks English, except in parts of Sarawak and Sabah.

This book covers many of the best birding sites in both West (Peninsular) Malaysia and East Malaysia (Sabah and Sarawak). West Malaysia occupies roughly the southern half of the Malay Peninsula, between Thailand and the island of Singapore, while the East Malaysian states of Sabah and Sarawak lie across the South China Sea, in north Borneo. Sarawak, the largest of Malaysia's 13 states, is almost cut off from Sabah by the small independent nation of Brunei; the southern part of Borneo - Kalimantan - is Indonesian.

My main aim when selecting the sites for this book was to include as many different habitats as possible. Some sites are large and therefore offer a wide variety of habitats and birds; some are good for special birds like endemics or localised species; and others are simply very pleasant places to visit. Most of the sites are readily accessible, and the ones that aren't will probably become easier to reach over the next few years. As well, at the time of writing there are plans to upgrade the visitor facilities at a number of the sites included in this guide - Taman Negara and Kuala Gula for example - and this may well have happened by the time you go to Malaysia.

With ecotourism a growth industry in the region, especially in East Malaysia, you may soon have even more birding destinations to choose from, notably some new national parks in Sarawak. Among the proposed additions to Sarawak's reserve system are the Pulong Tau, Usun Apau and Hose Mountains National Parks, all in the remote interior of the state, and the Batu Laga Wildlife Sanctuary, which would adjoin the Hose

Mountains National Park. These are the largest of the proposed reserves - each would be around twice the size of Gunung Mulu. (With an area of 544 square kilometres, Mulu is currently the biggest national park in Sarawak.) At least 10 other areas may be added to the state's park network in the near future, thus if you are going to Sarawak it would pay to contact the National Parks and Wildlife Department in Kuching or Miri - some of the proposed parks may be open to the public by the time you get there.

In the bird lists for most of the sites in this book, species are grouped under subheadings that indicate where you should look for the birds. Difficult-to-find or rare species are grouped separately. While I've made every effort to check my facts, and to be consistent, inevitably there will be occasions when a bird listed under open areas, overhead for example turns up somewhere else. As well, there will be times when birds in the difficult-to-find group will be quite easy to get. Nonetheless, the system I've used should be of help - if you've never birdwatched in the rainforest before you may find it a somewhat daunting experience, at least at first.

In all, some 640 bird species occur as residents or regular migrants in Malaysia, and a good many of them are common to both the West and the East. West Malaysia has about 430 residents, 120 or so regular migrants and around 70 vagrants on its list - there are only two endemics, however, the Mountain Peacock-Pheasant and the Malayan Whistling Thrush. East Malaysia has slightly fewer species than the West (about 400 residents, 120 regular migrants and 50 vagrants), but it is a much better place for endemics - 31 Bornean endemics can be found there. To get the most out of your trip to Malaysia, you should of course go to both the West and the East, and you should plan your itinerary so that you visit at least one lowland and one highland site in each of the two places.

Lastly, in the bird lists in this guide 'm' indicates that the species is a migrant, while endemics are marked with an asterisk. The checklist at the back of the book gives additional information about the distribution and status of Malaysia's birds; as well, the checklist has an index to the sites where each species occurs.

If you have any information that could be used in further editions of this book, please send it to Waymark Publishing, c/o Natural History Book Service Ltd, 2-3 Wills Road, Totnes, Devon TQ9 5XN, UK. All contributions will be fully acknowledged.

Helpful Hints

This list of tips is by no means exhaustive - you'll find advice about birdwatching in south-east Asia in the field guides listed under Further Reading in this book, and any up-to-date travel guide to the region will have information about visas and so on.

• Don't take too much clothing to Malaysia; if need be, you can buy quite good clothes locally at cheap prices. Even though Malaysia is a predominantly Muslim country, in most places the wearing of shorts and T-shirts is perfectly acceptable - just keep in mind that in some situations, when entering mosques for example, you'll need to cover your legs and arms. Also, it is best to wear trousers and long-sleeved shirts in the jungle, since this will help to protect you from scratches and insect bites. In the tropics, cotton clothing is far more comfortable than nylon or polyester; and remember that in the highlands the nights can be surprisingly chilly - take along a lightweight sweater (a tracksuit would also be handy). A wide-brimmed hat is essential - buy one locally - as is a large, loose-fitting poncho for when you get caught in a downpour (it's amazing how often it pours with rain when you are miles from cover, such as when you are out in a boat).

• Leather hiking boots are not a good idea - in humid conditions wet leather takes a long time to dry out. However, for jungle trekking you'll need sturdy footwear with soles that give a good grip on slippery slopes - take a pair of lightweight boots (Hi-Tec or similar) made from material that allows your feet to breathe. Canvas sneakers are fine for general use, such as when you're walking on beaches or well-formed tracks.

• In the rainforest, mosquitoes and other biting insects are not as common as you might expect (in my experience, mangroves and coastal swamps are the worst places for mosquitoes). All the same, it is wise to have some insect repellent with you at all times; a lotion is better than a roll-on or spray - you'll probably sweat a good deal and a thick coating of lotion will give longer lasting protection. Leeches can be a real pest, and you can pick them up not just in the forest but also in damp grass, often when you least expect it. They are basically harmless - as the locals will delight in telling you - but it's no fun getting blood all over your clothes, and in any case leech bites can turn septic. Although there is no complete answer to the problem, you should wear light-coloured trousers tucked securely inside long socks; you will then be able to see the leeches more easily than if you wear dark clothes, and as they make their way up your legs you can flick them off before they reach bare skin! Soaking your boots in insect repellent helps as well - and don't forget to thoroughly check yourself for leeches (and ticks) at regular intervals during the day.

• Always carry a small but well-stocked first-aid kit. Cuts can become infected very quickly in tropical conditions - never regard an abrasion as too minor to worry about. Wash the wound immediately (use your drinking water if there's no other clean water at hand), apply antiseptic (a quick-drying spray or lotion will be better than a cream) and cover the area with a plaster. Other things to put in the kit include small scissors, tweezers, safety pins, pain killers (Panadol or similar), throat lozenges, diarrhoea tablets (ask your doctor or chemist for advice), sunblock and water-sterilizing pills. Keep the kit in a waterproof and air-tight box - a small plastic food container with a tight-fitting lid will do nicely.

• Unless you are really keen, don't be tempted to carry around lots of camera gear, particularly long lenses. Photographing birds is never easy and, generally speaking, in the rainforest you'll have few opportunities to take bird photos - the light is often poor and the dense foliage invariably gets in the way. If you do decide to give bird photography a try, you'll need a powerful flash, at least some fast film, a sturdy tripod, and plenty of time. I found it best to carry the minimum of gear and to make the most of the few opportunities I had.

- By the time you've loaded yourself up with field guides, binoculars, a water bottle and other gear, you won't feel like carrying a telescope. It is well worth taking along a telescope, however, not only when you visit coastal areas but also when you go birding in the rainforest. Although this may appear to contradict the advice about carrying long lenses, birds like falconets, hornbills, treeswifts, and even barbets quite often perch for longish periods in the tops of tall trees - a telescope will give you stunning views, whereas with binoculars you may only just be able to identify the bird. As you might expect, a telescope will be of more use in the highlands, where there are usually places where you can look out over the treetops, than in the lowlands where it is often difficult to stand back from the forest, except of course along roads and in clearings. A tape recorder will also be useful - the smaller the better.

- In Malaysia, temperatures vary little throughout the year. In the lowlands, daily temperatures range from about 30 degrees C at noon to about 20 degrees C at night, the humidity is mostly very high, and deep in the jungle there's rarely any breeze. If you are not used to such conditions, you will sweat a great deal and quickly run out of energy. Don't be tempted to rush around, birding from dawn to dusk; rather, plan your days so that you have time around midday to rest and recoup (you'll find that the birds are most active first thing in the morning and late in the afternoon anyway). As well, plan your itinerary so that you have a good mix of lowland and highland sites; at places like Fraser's Hill, daytime temperatures can be as much as 10 degrees C cooler than those in the nearby lowlands, and the nights can be quite cold. A few days spent in the highlands will therefore prepare you for another bout of lowland birding. Wherever you go in Malaysia you can expect rain at any time of the year, though over much of the country the heaviest falls occur during the north-east monsoon season - October to February.

- To help protect books, optical equipment and any other gear that you don't want to get wet, take along a supply of moisture-proof plastic bags - freezer bags are good. And don't forget a powerful torch, a whistle and a compass.

- In general, camping in Malaysia is not something I recommend, except if you are really short of money. You will probably find birding in the tropics rather exhausting, especially during the first week or so of your trip when you will still be acclimatising, and you'll enjoy your holiday much more if you sleep under a mosquito net - don't forget to take one along - and a fan. Given that in most parts of Malaysia there's a wide range of accommodation, you should have little difficulty finding something that suits your budget. In the more established national parks, you'll find overnight huts and shelters along all the popular long-distance trails; if you need camping equipment you can usually hire it from the park offices.

- Don't be shy about haggling when dealing with long-distance taxi drivers or boat owners; it's expected of you, and provided you are not rude or unreasonable you won't offend anyone. With land travel, remember that you can almost always get to your destination much more cheaply by bus than by taxi, even if the journey takes longer and entails changing bus several times. And away from the cities hitching is mostly quite easy - the people are friendly and delight in picking up foreigners (of course, the usual rules apply if you are a woman travelling alone - be careful).

• Eating out is a great joy in Malaysia; food is cheap and the variety endless. Provided you don't have an overly sensitive stomach, you should be able to eat almost anything, anywhere. Do try the sidewalk eating stalls where the food is ridiculously cheap, and authentic. The main thing is to go to places that are busy - if the restaurant is doing a brisk trade you can be fairly sure the food will not have been standing around long enough to go off. Drinking water (as well as iced drinks) should be treated with more caution; in Kuala Lumpur and some of the other major centres you should have no problems, but in the countryside and throughout East Malaysia it would be wise to stick to bottled water (available just about everywhere), canned drinks or beer. As well, in general you should not eat things like washed fruit and salads.

• A credit card is very useful, not just for buying goods but also for getting cash advances, if the need arises. Major banks throughout Malaysia will give you a cash advance as long as you have your passport with you. As a guide, 1 Malaysian dollar (ringgit) = 25 UK pence, 50 Australian cents, and 35 US cents.

• You'll find plenty of other travel tips in the Lonely Planet guide to Malaysia - see the Further Reading section of this book.

Useful Addresses

Birdwatching and conservation organisations
Malayan Nature Society
485 Jalan 5/53
46000 Petaling Jaya, Selangor, Malaysia
(PO Box 10750, 50724 Kuala Lumpur, Malaysia)
Telephone 03-7912185

Asian Wetland Bureau
c/o University of Malaya
Lembah Pantai
59100 Kuala Lumpur, Malaysia
Telephone 03-7572176/7566624

World Wide Fund for Nature
3rd floor Wisma IJM Annexe
Jalan Yong Shook Lin
46200 Petaling Jaya, Selangor, Malaysia
Telephone 03-7579192

Oriental Bird Club
c/o The Lodge, Sandy, Bedfordshire, SG19 2DL, UK
Telephone 0767 680551

BirdLife International (formerly ICBP)
Wellbrook Court, Girton Road, Cambridge, CB3 0NA, UK
Telephone 0223 277318

Bangkok Bird Club
PO Box 13, Ratchathevi Post Office
Bangkok 10401, Thailand

Singapore Nature Society
c/o Botany Department, National University of Singapore
Singapore 0511
Telephone 253 2179

Government bodies
Malaysia Tourism Promotion Board
(formerly Tourist Development Corporation of Malaysia)
Head office:
26th floor Menara Dato Onn
Putra World Trade Centre
45 Jalan Tun Ismail, 50480 Kuala Lumpur, Malaysia
Telephone 03-2935188

Northern office:
10 Jalan Tun Syed Sheh Barakbah
10200 Pulau Pinang, Malaysia
Telephone 04-620066/619067

Southern office:
4th floor Kompleks Tun Abdul Razak
Jalan Wong Ah Fook
80000 Johor Bahru, Johor, Malaysia
Telephone 07-223590/223591

East Coast office:
Ground floor Wisma MCIS
Jalan Sultan Zainal Abidin
20000 Kuala Terengganu, Terengganu, Malaysia
Telephone 09-621433/621893

Sabah office:
Ground floor Wisma Wing Onn Life
1 Jalan Sagunting
88000 Kota Kinabalu, Sabah, Malaysia
Telephone 088-248698

Sarawak office:
2nd floor AIA Building
Bukit Mata Kuching
Jalan Song Thian Cheok
93100 Kuching, Sarawak, Malaysia
Telephone 082-246575/246775

UK office:
57 Trafalgar Square
London, WC2N 5DU
Telephone 071-9307932

Australian office:
Ground floor 65 York Street
Sydney, New South Wales 2000
Telephone 02-2994441/2994442

USA office:
Suite 804, 818 West Seventh Street
Los Angeles, CA90017
Telephone 213-6899702

German office:
Rossmarkt 11
6000 Frankfurt Am Main
Telephone 069-283782/283783

Department of Wildlife and National Parks
Km 10 Jalan Cheras, 56100 Kuala Lumpur, Malaysia
Telephone 03-9052872/9052873

Sabah Parks
Head office:
Block K Sinsuran Shopping Complex
Jalan Tun Fuad Stephens
88000 Kota Kinabalu, Sabah, Malaysia
(PO Box 10626, 88806 Kota Kinabalu, Sabah, Malaysia)
Telephone 088-211585/211881/211652

East Coast office:
9th floor Wisma Khoo
Jalan Tiga, Sandakan, Sabah, Malaysia
(PO Box 768, 90008 Sandakan, Sabah, Malaysia)
Telephone 089-273453

Sarawak National Parks and Wildlife Department
Kuching office (for accommodation at Bako):
Tourist Information Centre, Main Bazaar
93000 Kuching, Sarawak, Malaysia
Telephone 082-248088/410944

Miri office (for accommodation at Niah, Lambir Hills and
Gunung Mulu):
Forest Department, 98000 Miri, Sarawak, Malaysia
(The NP&W office is situated off Jalan Kingsway, Miri.)
Telephone 085-36637

Forest Research Institute of Malaysia
52109 Kepong, Selangor, Malaysia
Telephone 03-6342633

Fraser's Hill Development Corporation
Bukit Fraser, 49000 Pahang, Malaysia
Telephone 09-382044/382248/382201

Malaysia Airlines (MAS)
MAS Kuala Lumpur
33rd floor Bangunan MAS, Jalan Sultan Ismail,
50250 Kuala Lumpur. Telephone 03-2610555
Ground floor Menara Utama UMBC, Jalan Sultan Sulaiman,
50000 Kuala Lumpur. Telephone 03-2305115

MAS Singapore
190 Clemenceau Avenue, #02-09/11, Singapore Shopping
Centre, Singapore 0923. Telephone 3366777/3366566

MAS Kuching
Bangunan MAS, Lot 215 Jalan Song Thian Cheok,
93100 Kuching. Telephone 082-246622

MAS Kota Kinabalu
10th floor Kompleks Karamunsing, Jalan Tuaran/
Jalan Selatan, 88300 Kota Kinabalu. Telephone 088-51455

MAS London
61 Picadilly, London WIV 9HL. Telephone 071-8728444

MAS Sydney
11th floor American Express Tower, 388 George Street,
Sydney 2000. Telephone 02-2315066

MAS Los Angeles
5933 West Century Blvd, Room 506, Los Angeles CA90045.
Telephone 213-6420849

MAS Frankfurt
Allianz Haus, An Der Hauptwache 7, 6000 Frankfurt Am
Main. Telephone 069-289651

Tour operators
Kingfisher Tours Sdn Bhd
Suite 1107, 11th floor Bangunan Yayasan Selangor,
Jalan Bukit Bintang, 55100 Kuala Lumpur, Malaysia
Telephone 03-2421454

Asian Overland Services Sdn Bhd
33/35-M Jalan Dewan Sultan Sulaiman Satu
(off Jalan Tunku Abdul Rahman)
50300 Kuala Lumpur, Malaysia
Telephone 03-2925637/2925622

Sala Travel & Tours Sdn Bhd
2 Pokok Assam, 07000 Kuah, Pulau Langkawi, Kedah,
Malaysia. Telephone 04-917521

Cantumas Travel & Tours Sdn Bhd
2nd floor Hankyu Jaya, Menara Perbadanan,
Jalan Tunku Petra Semerak, 15000 Kota Bharu, Kelantan,
Malaysia. Telephone 09-787437

Tropical Adventure Sdn Bhd
1st floor Beautiful Jade Centre, Jalan Maju,
98000 Miri, Sarawak, Malaysia
Telephone 085-419337/414503

Seridan Mulu Tour & Travel Service Sdn Bhd
Jalan Bendahara (PO Box 1364)
98008 Miri, Sarawak, Malaysia
Telephone 085-416066

Asian Overland Services Sdn Bhd
286A 1st floor Westwood Park
Jalan Tabuan, 93300 Kuching, Sarawak, Malaysia
Telephone 082-251162/251163

Further Reading

Essential books
Lekagul, B. and Round, P.D. *A Guide to the Birds of Thailand.*
White Lotus, Bangkok, 1991.
(An excellent field guide with many Malaysian birds illustrated in colour.)

King, B., Woodcock, M. and Dickinson, E.C. *A Field Guide to the Birds of South-East Asia.* Collins, London, 1975. (Covers West Malaysia.)

MacKinnon, J. and Phillipps, K. *A Field Guide to the Birds of Borneo, Sumatra, Java and Bali.* Oxford University Press, Oxford, 1993.
(Covers East Malaysia.)

Payne, J., Francis, C.M. and Phillipps, K. *A Field Guide to the Mammals of Borneo*. Sabah Society and WWF Malaysia, Kuala Lumpur, 1985. (Includes many mammals found in West Malaysia.)

Wheeler, T. and Crowther, G. *Malaysia, Singapore & Brunei - a travel survival kit*. 4th edn. Lonely Planet Publications, Hawthorn, 1991.

Useful books
Medway, Lord and Wells, D.R. *The Birds of the Malay Peninsula (Volume V: Conclusion, and Survey of Every Species)*. H.F. & G. Witherby and Penerbit Universiti Malaya, London and Kuala Lumpur, 1976.

Smythies, B.E. *The Birds of Borneo*. 3rd edn. Sabah Society and Malayan Nature Society, Kota Kinabalu and Kuala Lumpur, 1981.

Francis, C.M. *Pocket Guide to the Birds of Borneo*. Sabah Society and WWF Malaysia, Kota Kinabalu and Petaling Jaya, 1984. (A most useful pocket edition of the book by Smythies.)

Strange, M. and Jeyarajasingam, A. *Birds - A Photographic Guide to the Birds of Peninsular Malaysia and Singapore*. Sun Tree Publishing, Singapore, 1993.

Phillipps, A. *A Guide to the Parks of Sabah*. Sabah Parks Trustees, Kota Kinabalu, 1988.

Glossary of Malay terms

air - water	air terjun - waterfall
atap - thatch	batu - rock
besar - big (often used for islands)	
bukit - hill	bumbun - animal observation hide
gua - cave	gunung (G.) - mountain
jalan - road	kampung (Kg) - village
kechil - small (often used for islands)	
kuala - river mouth or junction	lalang - fire-resistant grass
nipah - stemless palm	padang - flat area
pulau (P.) - island	rumah rehat - resthouse
sungai (Sg.) - river	taman - park
tanjong - cape	tasik - lake
telok - bay	ulu - valley or upper reaches of a river

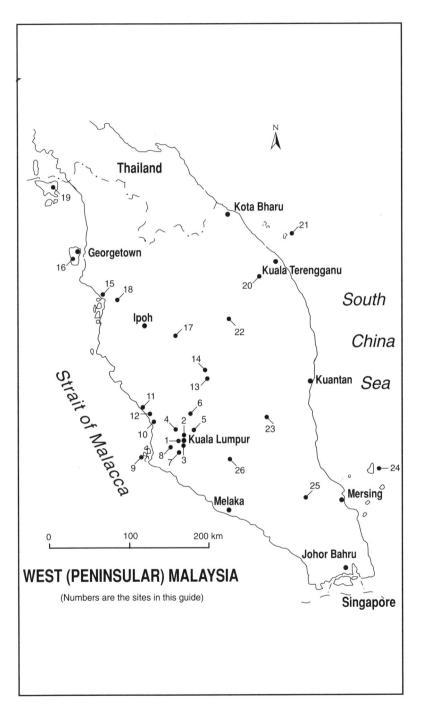

Thailand

Kota Bharu

21

19

Georgetown

16

Kuala Terengganu

20

15

18

South

Ipoh

17

China

22

14

13

Kuantan

Sea

11

6

12

4   2   5

10

23

1   Kuala Lumpur

8   3

9

26

24

25

Mersing

Melaka

0   100   200 km

Johor Bahru

WEST (PENINSULAR) MALAYSIA

(Numbers are the sites in this guide)

Singapore

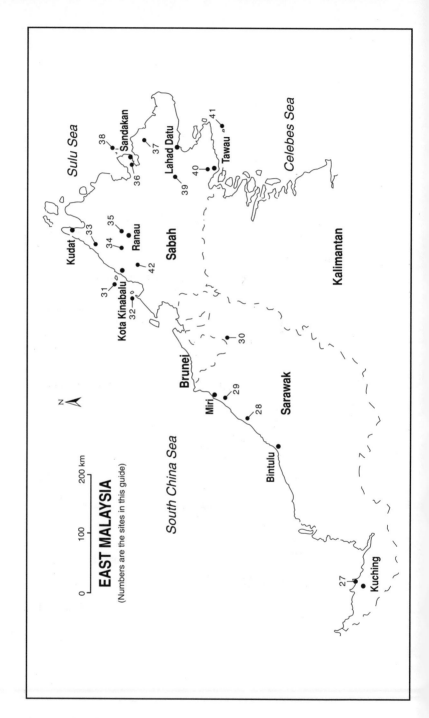

Sites

1 Lake Gardens and Bukit Tunku

Kuala Lumpur

This pleasant, hilly area - the green lungs of Kuala Lumpur - is just a short walk or taxi ride from the city centre and downtown accommodation. A visit of a few hours will introduce you to some of Malaysia's more common birds (you could see your first Large-tailed Nightjar or Greater Racket-tailed Drongo for example), as well as give you a welcome break from KL's bustling streets.

The well-established, beautifully maintained public parks and private gardens cover approximately 10 square kilometres (including houses and other buildings). There are of course extensive flower beds and lawns, but the area is dotted with many huge, mature trees, and there are also some patches of secondary forest and scrub, as well as an artificial lake (Tasik Perdana) in the Lake Gardens.

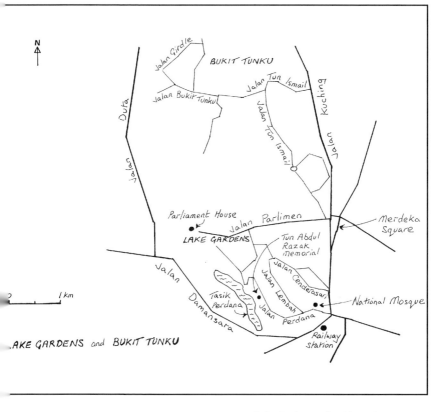

LAKE GARDENS and BUKIT TUNKU

Good birdwatching areas

The entire area bounded by Jalan Damansara, Jalan Duta and Jalan Kuching is worth exploring, but if you are short of time head west along Jalan Perdana, past the National Mosque, and try the southern part of the Lake Gardens in the vicinity of the Tun Abdul Razak Memorial. You could also try the Jalan Lembah-Jalan Cenderasari circuit, which passes through some relatively quiet, forest-like areas. In the Bukit Tunku area to the north of the Lake Gardens, the Jalan Girdle-Jalan Bukit Tunku circuit is known to be good, particularly where there are large old trees.

Birds

Open areas, overhead:
- [ ] Brahminy Kite
- [ ] Japanese Sparrowhawk m
- [ ] Black-thighed Falconet (you have a fairly good chance of seeing this sparrow-sized bird of prey - look for it perched in high bare branches)
- [ ] Large-tailed Nightjar (around street lights after sunset)
- [ ] Edible-nest Swiftlet
- [ ] White-bellied (Glossy) Swiftlet
- [ ] House Swift
- [ ] Asian Palm-Swift (look for them in the evening around tall fan palms)
- [ ] White-throated Kingfisher
- [ ] Blue-throated Bee-eater (not win)
- [ ] Barn Swallow m
- [ ] Pacific Swallow
- [ ] House Crow
- [ ] Brown Shrike m
- [ ] Common Myna

Ground, lower storey:
- [ ] White-breasted Waterhen (often in drains)
- [ ] Spotted Dove
- [ ] Peaceful Dove
- [ ] Greater Coucal
- [ ] Olive-winged Bulbul
- [ ] Abbott's Babbler (edges)
- [ ] Magpie Robin
- [ ] Common Tailorbird
- [ ] Pied Fantail
- [ ] Tiger Shrike m
- [ ] Little Spiderhunter
- [ ] Eurasian Tree-Sparrow
- [ ] Scaly-breasted Munia

Middle storey, canopy:
- [ ] Crested Goshawk (especially Bukit Tunku)
- [ ] Pink-necked Pigeon

- [ ] Common Koel
- [ ] Collared Scops-Owl (also lower storey; especially Bukit Tunku)
- [ ] Coppersmith Barbet
- [ ] Rufous Woodpecker (also lower storey)
- [ ] Banded Woodpecker
- [ ] Common Goldenback
- [ ] Grey-capped Woodpecker
- [ ] Pied Triller
- [ ] Common Iora (also lower storey)
- [ ] Yellow-vented Bulbul (also open areas)
- [ ] Greater Racket-tailed Drongo
- [ ] Black-naped Oriole
- [ ] Flyeater
- [ ] Arctic Warbler m
- [ ] Asian Brown Flycatcher m
- [ ] Philippine Glossy Starling
- [ ] Brown-throated Sunbird
- [ ] Scarlet-backed Flowerpecker

Difficult-to-find or rare species:
- [ ] Black Baza m (especially Oct-Dec)
- [ ] Thick-billed Pigeon
- [ ] Chestnut-winged Cuckoo m
- [ ] Barred Eagle-Owl (interestingly, this species bred at Bukit Tunku in the late 1980s)
- [ ] Brown Hawk-Owl
- [ ] Grey-rumped Treeswift
- [ ] Dollarbird
- [ ] Ashy Minivet m
- [ ] Yellow-rumped Flycatcher m
- [ ] Spectacled Spiderhunter

Access and accommodation

Being located close to the heart of KL, this is an easy site to get to and, of course, there is no shortage of nearby accommodation. If you are staying in the southern part of the city, at the YMCA at Brickfields for example, walk to the railway station via Jalan Tun Sambathan and Jalan Sulaiman, then into the Lake Gardens past the National Mosque. From the more central or eastern hotels go to Merdeka Square, and from there to the main entrance of the gardens on Jalan Parlimen. The northern part of the area - Bukit Tunku - can be reached on foot (it's rather a long walk from downtown KL however) or by taxi via Jalan Tun Ismail.

When to visit

April to July, and September to December are probably the best times to visit. Since you could get caught in a downpour at any time of the year, however, it would pay to carry an umbrella! February and August can be oppressively hot and hazy - and whatever the month, an early morning or evening visit would be best because roads in the area can become choked with traffic from about 8.00 a.m. onwards (except on Sundays).

Other attractions

The bird park (Taman Burung) is certainly worth seeing. Situated within the Lake Gardens, close to the Tun Abdul Razak Memorial on Jalan Perdana, it is a massive structure housing a vast array of Malaysian birds in relatively natural surroundings. Among the birds to be seen are ducks, various predators, Crestless Fireback, Crested Wood-Partridge, White-breasted Waterhen, pigeons, Blue-crowned Hanging Parrot, barbets, Maroon Woodpecker, bulbuls, orioles, Asian Fairy-Bluebird, Purple-backed Starling, Hill Myna, and munias. A number of hornbill species - Rhinoceros, Great and Bushy-crested for example - are kept in a separate section and are hand-fed each morning, allowing you to get as close as you'll ever be to these magnificent creatures, and providing you with all-too-rare photo' opportunities.

The bird park is open daily from 8.00 a.m. until 6.00 p.m., there's a restaurant within its grounds, and many of the paths are suitable for wheelchairs. Just across the road from the bird park there are orchid and hibiscus gardens that are worth a brief visit; also, you should have little trouble finding at least a few squirrels in the area, as well as the Long-tailed Macaques that roam the Lake Gardens in search of handouts - treat them with caution for they can get over-enthusiastic in pursuit of food.

2 Sungai Batu Mining Pools

Kuala Lumpur

A trip to these mining pools, only a ten- or fifteen-minute drive from central KL, is highly recommended for the chance to see three *Ixobrychus* bitterns, eight species of rail, snipe, both of Malaysia's resident ducks, plus a large assortment of open-country birds such as the handsome Long-tailed Shrike, migrant flycatchers and, perhaps, the elusive Chestnut-winged Cuckoo. Approximately 100 species have been recorded, including more than 30 migrants.

The main habitats here are a large, deep pool (created when mining for tin ended) with steep sides and little vegetation; two shallow marshes, similarly formed, one covered in lotus, the other with various low rushes, and both having patches of the tall reed *Phragmites*; scattered tiny marshes, mainly grass covered, formed in depressions left by gravel extraction; and dryland areas, including short grazed grassland and dense scrub thickets (notably prickly mimosa). The last mentioned, though quite extensive at present, are being developed for urban and industrial use. To the east of the main wetlands lies the Sg. Batu, a canalised stream (drain!) fringed by some tall trees such as acacias.

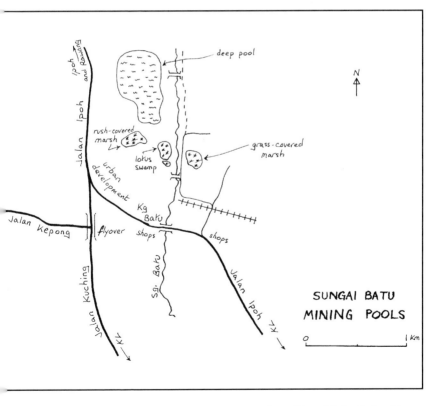

Good birdwatching areas

Spend an hour or two walking around the lotus swamp and you should see many of the species present at this site. Search the lotus carefully for ducks and crakes; quails and the shyer rails can often be found near the water's edge. The rush-covered marsh and the deep open pool are generally less productive, but they may be worth looking over for waders and birds of the open areas. As well, the many small marshes are worth checking for roosting snipe. Scrub thickets - those at the northern end of the lotus swamp for example - may harbour migrant cuckoos, warblers and flycatchers, while Long-tailed Shrikes can occur anywhere at the edge of the sparse scrub.

Birds

Wetlands:
☐ Little Grebe
☐ Purple Heron (secluded sites)
☐ Little Heron (along the Sg. Batu)
☐ Yellow Bittern (scarce in sum)
☐ Cinnamon Bittern
☐ Lesser (Treeduck) Whistling-Duck
☐ Baillon's Crake m
☐ White-browed Crake
☐ White-breasted Waterhen
☐ Common Moorhen
☐ Purple Swamphen
☐ Common Greenshank m
☐ Wood Sandpiper m
☐ Common Sandpiper m
☐ Pintail Snipe m
☐ Lesser Coucal
☐ Common Kingfisher (especially win)
☐ Great (Oriental) Reed-Warbler m
☐ Black-browed Reed-Warbler m
☐ Yellow-bellied Prinia
☐ Zitting Cisticola (hovering around wet grassland)
☐ Chestnut Munia

Open areas, overhead:
☐ Cattle Egret m
☐ Black-shouldered Kite
☐ Brahminy Kite
☐ Barred Buttonquail
☐ Asian (Lesser) Golden Plover m
☐ Little Ringed Plover m
☐ Spotted Dove
☐ Peaceful Dove
☐ Long-tailed Parakeet (passing over - listen for its harsh call)
☐ White-bellied (Glossy) Swiftlet
☐ House Swift

☐ Asian Palm-Swift
☐ White-throated Kingfisher
☐ Blue-tailed Bee-eater (absent in sum)
☐ Blue-throated Bee-eater (absent in win)
☐ Barn Swallow m
☐ Pacific Swallow
☐ House Crow
☐ Large-billed Crow
☐ Yellow Wagtail m (daytime migration may be seen in aut)
☐ Richard's Pipit
☐ Philippine Glossy Starling
☐ Purple-backed Starling m (flocks of hundreds sometimes occur)
☐ Common Myna
☐ Jungle Myna
☐ Baya Weaver
☐ Scaly-breasted Munia
☐ White-headed Munia

Scrub:
☐ Pink-necked Pigeon
☐ Plaintive Cuckoo
☐ Common Koel
☐ Large-tailed Nightjar (roosts during the day in thickets)
☐ Black-capped Kingfisher m
☐ Rufous Woodpecker
☐ Pied Triller
☐ Common Iora
☐ Yellow-vented Bulbul
☐ Black-naped Oriole
☐ Magpie Robin
☐ Arctic Warbler m
☐ Common Tailorbird
☐ Ashy Tailorbird
☐ Asian Brown Flycatcher m
☐ Pied Fantail
☐ Brown Shrike m
☐ Long-tailed Shrike
☐ Scarlet-backed Flowerpecker
☐ Eurasian Tree-Sparrow

Difficult-to-find or rare species:
☐ Chinese Pond-Heron m
☐ Schrenck's Bittern m
☐ Garganey m
☐ Cotton Pygmy-Goose
☐ Eurasian (Crested) Honey-Buzzard (especially Oct-Nov)
☐ White-bellied Sea-Eagle
☐ Japanese Sparrowhawk m

- [ ] Grey-faced Buzzard m (most likely in Oct, migrating with Eurasian Honey-Buzzards over the Sg. Batu)
- [ ] Changeable Hawk-Eagle
- [ ] Blue-breasted Quail
- [ ] Slaty-breasted Rail
- [ ] Red-legged Crake m
- [ ] Ruddy-breasted Crake
- [ ] Watercock (mostly win)
- [ ] Greater Paintedsnipe
- [ ] Oriental Plover m (bare ground)
- [ ] Common Snipe m
- [ ] Long-toed Stint m
- [ ] Oriental Pratincole m (bare ground)
- [ ] White-winged Tern m
- [ ] Little Tern
- [ ] Chestnut-winged Cuckoo m
- [ ] Greater Coucal
- [ ] Collared Scops-Owl
- [ ] Edible-nest Swiftlet
- [ ] Himalayan Swiftlet m
- [ ] Coppersmith Barbet
- [ ] Sand Martin m
- [ ] Red-rumped Swallow
- [ ] Stonechat m
- [ ] Pallas's (Grasshopper) Warbler m
- [ ] Lanceolated Warbler m
- [ ] Ferruginous Flycatcher m
- [ ] Yellow-rumped Flycatcher m
- [ ] Tiger Shrike m
- [ ] White-vented Myna
- [ ] White-rumped Munia

Access and accommodation

Ownership of this site is uncertain. However, the area is regarded as common land by local residents who graze cattle, grow vegetables, and fish and bathe in the ponds. Unfortunately, development is proceeding at such a rapid rate that the area may well be drastically changed, or even totally built upon, by the time this book is published.

The pools are situated about 7 km north-west of downtown KL and can be seen - development permitting -from Jalan Ipoh, north of the Jalan Kepong flyover. Easiest access is from Jalan Ipoh in the Kg Batu district; as you pass through Kg Batu coming from KL, take the road on the right before you reach the river (Sg. Batu). From there, continue across the railway line and turn hard left on to the bitumen, then follow along the edge of the Sg. Batu and enter the site via one of two bridges (see map). At least one bus (number 66 from KL to Rawang and Kuala Kubu Bharu - catch it at platform 20 in the Pudu Raya bus station in central KL) runs at regular intervals through Kg Batu, and the pools are a short walk from the shops on Jalan Ipoh. The nearest hotels are in KL.

When to visit

To have the greatest chance of seeing migrant species you should visit in October-November or March-April, although there are usually at least a few migrants about all winter. September, January and May are usually good months both for weather and bird variety - tracks can be boggy, and marshes over-full, from about October to December and during April. Summer (June-July) is the worst time for species variety.

Other attractions

Batu Caves, one of the best-known attractions in the vicinity of KL, are within 10 minutes of the pools by car (in good traffic). Set in towering limestone, the largest cave houses a Hindu shrine that is reached via a flight of almost 300 steep steps. Two other caves are open to the public: the 'art gallery' with its statues depicting Hindu mythology, and 'poets cave', which contains the works of the famous Hindu poet Thiruvalluvar.

Open daily from 7.00 a.m. to 9.00 p.m., the caves can be reached by bus number 69 or 70 from the Pudu Raya station.

3 Universiti Malaya and Rimba Ilmu
Kuala Lumpur

The many fine old trees and parklands of the Universiti Malaya offer quite good birding, as do the small but attractive botanical gardens (Rimba Ilmu) set within the university's grounds. Although it is not the most exciting of birdwatching sites, the area is only 10 to 15 minutes from downtown KL by bus or taxi, and a visit of two or three hours should produce at least a few interesting species. Over the years quite a sizable bird list has been compiled for the site; some 70 species have been recorded, including Schrenck's Bittern, Changeable Hawk-Eagle, Slaty-breasted Rail, Pintail Snipe, Asian Palm-Swift, Laced Woodpecker, Banded Woodpecker, Straw-headed Bulbul, Greater Racket-tailed Drongo and Baya Weaver. A raptor migration route passes over the site's eastern side, and Black Bazas and Eurasian (Crested) Honey-Buzzards are regularly seen in autumn and spring.

As you might expect, the area has extensive playing fields and lawns. Of more interest to the birdwatcher, however, are the parklands dotted with numerous trees, including casuarinas, acacias, palms and figs; the experimental agricultural areas in the eastern part of the campus, where there are fishponds, shrub-crops and lalang; and the 40 hectares of botanical garden in the north-east, which feature a diversity of Malaysian and exotic plants, together with patches of secondary forest (including abandoned rubber plantation) and a stream that feeds a small wetland.

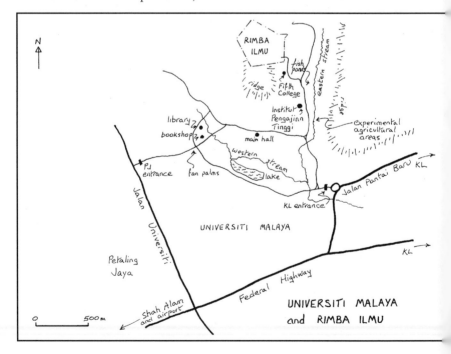

Good birdwatching areas

The eastern part of the campus, notably Rimba Ilmu and other areas within walking distance of the botanical gardens, offers the best chance of seeing a fair variety of species in a relatively short time. Access to the eastern stream (see map) is very limited, but try at the northern end, close to the bitumen road that ends at the northernmost playing fields. Western parts of the campus have rather more roads and buildings and are less 'wild'. For migrating raptors, position yourself with a good view of the two ridges shown in the map - near the Institut Pengajian Tinggi carpark for example. There are paths, some sealed, within the botanical gardens so that this may be a good spot to take a disabled friend. Note too that you may be challenged by security guards on occasion - just explain that you are birdwatching and there should be no problems.

Birds

Open areas, overhead:
- [ ] Black Baza m (best chance in Nov when small flocks pass overhead during mid to late morning)
- [ ] Eurasian (Crested) Honey-Buzzard (migrant birds can be seen in Oct soaring on morning thermals, then moving in loose flocks or single file more or less southwards)
- [ ] Brahminy Kite (irregular)
- [ ] Crested Serpent-Eagle (a resident of the quieter areas)
- [ ] Japanese Sparrowhawk m (migrates with honey-buzzards)
- [ ] Barred Buttonquail (lalang near water)
- [ ] Spotted Dove
- [ ] Peaceful Dove
- [ ] Plaintive Cuckoo (also in scrub)
- [ ] Lesser Coucal (lalang near water)
- [ ] Large-tailed Nightjar
- [ ] White-bellied (Glossy) Swiftlet
- [ ] House Swift (roosts in buildings such as the main hall)
- [ ] Asian Palm-Swift (roosts and probably nests in fan palms - e.g. those near the PJ entrance [see map])
- [ ] Grey-rumped Treeswift (clearings near trees)
- [ ] Blue-tailed Bee-eater (absent in sum)
- [ ] Blue-throated Bee-eater (absent in win)
- [ ] Barn Swallow m
- [ ] Pacific Swallow
- [ ] House Crow
- [ ] Large-billed Crow
- [ ] Magpie Robin
- [ ] Richard's Pipit (playing fields)
- [ ] Brown Shrike m
- [ ] Common Myna
- [ ] Jungle Myna

- ☐ Eurasian Tree-Sparrow
- ☐ Baya Weaver (breeds in colonies in scrub near lalang)
- ☐ Scaly-breasted Munia

Wetlands:
- ☐ Little Heron (stream beds)
- ☐ Cinnamon Bittern (vegetation beside streams)
- ☐ Slaty-breasted Rail (has regular haunts where it is mainly seen on overcast evenings after rain; breeds in or near wet lalang)
- ☐ White-breasted Waterhen (breeds on campus; wanders far from water)
- ☐ Common Sandpiper m (stream beds)
- ☐ Pintail Snipe m (marshy areas with short, cut grass)
- ☐ White-throated Kingfisher (can be seen almost anywhere on campus)
- ☐ Straw-headed Bulbul (a melodious songster found in shrubs near water - quite common in the botanical gardens)
- ☐ Yellow-bellied Prinia
- ☐ Grey Wagtail m (stream beds and wide drains)

Scrub, gardens, secondary forest:
- ☐ Crested Goshawk (probably resident in the area)
- ☐ Pink-necked Pigeon
- ☐ Common Koel (often heard in spr-sum)
- ☐ Greater Coucal
- ☐ Collared Scops-Owl
- ☐ Rufous Woodpecker
- ☐ Banded Woodpecker
- ☐ Common Goldenback
- ☐ Pied Triller
- ☐ Common Iora
- ☐ Yellow-vented Bulbul
- ☐ Olive-winged Bulbul (often near water)
- ☐ Greater Racket-tailed Drongo (look in taller scrub and regrowth; most likely in the botanical gardens)
- ☐ Black-naped Oriole
- ☐ Flyeater
- ☐ Arctic Warbler m
- ☐ Common Tailorbird
- ☐ Asian Brown Flycatcher m
- ☐ Philippine Glossy Starling
- ☐ Purple-backed Starling m (often in large flocks; favours fruiting figs; try the botanical gardens)
- ☐ Brown-throated Sunbird (look in hibiscus shrubs)
- ☐ Scarlet-backed Flowerpecker

Difficult-to-find or rare species:
- ☐ Schrenck's Bittern m (has been seen at dusk along the eastern stream)
- ☐ Grey-faced Buzzard m

- [ ] Changeable Hawk-Eagle
- [ ] Red Junglefowl (may come on to lawns; true wild specimens are hard to find here)
- [ ] Little Ringed Plover m (in fields)
- [ ] Green-winged (Emerald Dove) Pigeon (try the botanical gardens)
- [ ] Blue-crowned Hanging Parrot
- [ ] Fork-tailed Swift m
- [ ] Common Kingfisher (especially win)
- [ ] Black-capped Kingfisher m
- [ ] Dollarbird
- [ ] Coppersmith Barbet
- [ ] Laced Woodpecker
- [ ] Crimson-winged Woodpecker
- [ ] Blue-winged Pitta (especially win; one record only)
- [ ] Red-whiskered Bulbul (Rimba Ilmu)
- [ ] Spectacled Bulbul
- [ ] Abbott's Babbler (in thickets)
- [ ] Hwamei (introduced; birds in scrub near the eastern stream are escapees)
- [ ] Siberian Blue Robin m (in secondary forest)
- [ ] Dark-necked Tailorbird
- [ ] Yellow-rumped Flycatcher m (especially Oct)
- [ ] Pied Fantail
- [ ] Yellow Wagtail m (on fields)
- [ ] Tiger Shrike m
- [ ] White-vented Myna
- [ ] Little Spiderhunter
- [ ] Spectacled Spiderhunter (Rimba Ilmu)

Access and accommodation

Take minibus number 12 from the Globe Silk Store or Jalan Raja in downtown KL, and get off at Jalan Pantai Baru or Jalan Universiti. Alternatively, take bus number 22, 35 or 39 from the Klang bus station in KL to Jalan Pantai Baru, or take a taxi. At either university entrance (KL or PJ - see map) explain that you are going to Rimba Ilmu (the gardens are open only during normal university hours, including 8.30 a.m. to 12.00 noon Saturdays) and ask the security guards for directions (once in the university grounds you'll find Rimba Ilmu is well signposted).

The YMCA nearby at Brickfields provides budget accommodation; otherwise the closest hotels are in downtown KL and Petaling Jaya. There are a few eating places on campus, some of them close to the entrance of Rimba Ilmu.

When to visit

October, November and March are usually the best months for migrants, particularly raptors (raptor movements can be spectacular during October). June-July is probably the worst time for species diversity.

Other attractions

Long-tailed Macaques live in the university grounds - look for them on the way to Rimba Ilmu in the scrub just beyond the IPT building. The botanical gardens contain collections of medicinal plants, orchids, palms, tropical fruit trees, gingers and aquatic plants, and are inhabited by squirrels and other animals. The university has a very good bookshop (it has many of the titles listed under Further Reading at the front of this book), a well-stocked library, and frequent film shows - check at the entrances for details.

4 Templer Park   Selangor

Although a popular recreation area, where multiple waterfalls, a golf course, swimming, fishing and horse-riding attract large numbers of visitors, Templer Park has some remnant lowland forest that offers the birdwatcher quiet, shady walking in pleasant surroundings within easy reach of Kuala Lumpur. About 100 species have been recorded in the area, including many colourful and sought-after birds - trogons, forest kingfishers and broadbills for example.

Covering about 1200 ha, Templer Park lies at the base of the Main Range foothills and was established in 1954. Much of the park consists of scrub and open country (the open areas, the result of years of tin mining, have been partly developed for recreation), but some relatively undisturbed lowland forest remains, the most accessible being that at the park's north-western end. Other natural features include a small river, which flows through the area alongside the main KL to Rawang road, and a spectacular limestone hill - Bukit Takun - which towers some 400 metres above the golf course.

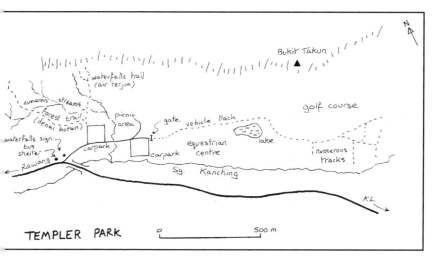

Good birdwatching areas

Many of the more interesting species listed inhabit the lowland forest near the waterfalls carpark, where access is via a walking track marked 'denai hutan'. This track branches off the waterfalls trail ('air terjun') less than 20 metres from the carpark at the Rawang end of Templer Park. Some of the tallest, most impressive trees are within the first 300 metres of the start of the forest trail, around a small stream, and this is generally the best spot for trogons, broadbills and kingfishers. Different birds may be found further on, at or beyond the highest part of the trail (about 800-1000 metres from its start) where the forest is more open. Fortunately, few people use the forest trail whereas hundreds go to the waterfalls.

Access to the open parts of the park can be gained via the vehicle track that runs eastwards from the gate beyond the waterfalls picnic area (see map). After passing the equestrian centre and a small lake, the track veers to the right past the golf course and leads to the scrub and open country south of Bukit Takun. Here, a maze of smaller tracks and old roads enables you to explore the area thoroughly, and birds are easier to see than in the dense lowland forest.

Birds

Open areas, overhead:
☐ Black Baza m (mainly Oct-Nov)
☐ Eurasian (Crested) Honey-Buzzard (especially Oct-Nov)
☐ Crested Serpent-Eagle
☐ Large-tailed Nightjar
☐ White-bellied (Glossy) Swiftlet
☐ Silver-rumped Swift
☐ House Swift
☐ Grey-rumped Treeswift
☐ White-throated Kingfisher (around the golf course)
☐ Blue-tailed Bee-eater (absent in sum; try near the golf course)
☐ Blue-throated Bee-eater (absent in win)
☐ Barn Swallow m
☐ Pacific Swallow
☐ Large-billed Crow

Ground, lower storey:
☐ Peaceful Dove (in scrub near the golf course)
☐ Green-winged (Emerald Dove) Pigeon (along the forest trail)
☐ Straw-headed Bulbul (stream edges, where open)
☐ Olive-winged Bulbul
☐ Grey-cheeked Bulbul (also middle storey)
☐ Yellow-bellied Bulbul (also middle storey)
☐ Grey-headed Babbler
☐ Striped Tit-Babbler (noisy and busy)
☐ Fluffy-backed Tit-Babbler
☐ Siberian Blue Robin m
☐ Magpie Robin (at edges)
☐ White-rumped Shama (often near the start of the forest trail)
☐ Common Tailorbird
☐ Dark-necked Tailorbird
☐ Tiger Shrike m
☐ Ruby-cheeked Sunbird (also middle storey; sometimes in bird waves)
☐ Purple-naped Sunbird
☐ Little Spiderhunter
☐ Scaly-breasted Munia (in scrub near the golf course)

Middle storey, canopy:
- ☐ Pink-necked Pigeon (around the golf course)
- ☐ Blue-crowned Hanging Parrot
- ☐ Indian Cuckoo (more often heard than seen)
- ☐ Banded Bay Cuckoo
- ☐ Brush (Rusty-breasted) Cuckoo
- ☐ Drongo Cuckoo
- ☐ Chestnut-bellied Malkoha
- ☐ Raffles' Malkoha
- ☐ Chestnut-breasted Malkoha
- ☐ Whiskered Treeswift (may be on the powerlines near the start of the forest trail)
- ☐ Scarlet-rumped Trogon (also lower storey)
- ☐ Banded Kingfisher
- ☐ Rufous-collared Kingfisher (also lower storey)
- ☐ Gold-whiskered Barbet
- ☐ Blue-eared Barbet
- ☐ Brown Barbet
- ☐ Crimson-winged Woodpecker
- ☐ Checker-throated Woodpecker
- ☐ Buff-necked Woodpecker (also lower storey)
- ☐ Grey-and-Buff Woodpecker
- ☐ Black-and-Red Broadbill (also in lower storey; try along the middle section of the forest trail)
- ☐ Banded Broadbill
- ☐ Black-and-Yellow Broadbill
- ☐ Black-winged Flycatcher-shrike (often in bird waves)
- ☐ Scarlet Minivet (often in bird waves)
- ☐ Blue-winged Leafbird (especially at trees bearing tiny fruits)
- ☐ Grey-bellied Bulbul
- ☐ Yellow-vented Bulbul (in scrub near the golf course)
- ☐ Cream-vented Bulbul
- ☐ Red-eyed Bulbul (often around the carpark)
- ☐ Spectacled Bulbul (also lower storey)
- ☐ Hairy-backed Bulbul (low in middle storey)
- ☐ Buff-vented Bulbul (also lower storey)
- ☐ Greater Racket-tailed Drongo
- ☐ Dark-throated Oriole (especially along higher parts of the forest trail)
- ☐ Black-naped Oriole (around the golf course)
- ☐ Asian Fairy-Bluebird
- ☐ Rufous-fronted Babbler (at the highest part of the forest trail)
- ☐ White-bellied Yuhina
- ☐ Flyeater
- ☐ Eastern Crowned Warbler m
- ☐ Grey-headed Flycatcher (also in lower storey)
- ☐ Black-naped Monarch
- ☐ Rufous-winged Flycatcher (also in lower storey)

- [ ] Asian Paradise-Flycatcher
- [ ] Brown-throated Sunbird
- [ ] Yellow-breasted Flowerpecker (also lower storey)
- [ ] Orange-bellied Flowerpecker (scrub near the golf course)
- [ ] Scarlet-backed Flowerpecker (at edges)
- [ ] Everett's White-eye

Difficult-to-find or rare species:
- [ ] Crested Goshawk
- [ ] Peregrine Falcon (may breed on Bukit Takun)
- [ ] Red Junglefowl
- [ ] Thick-billed Pigeon
- [ ] Moustached Hawk-Cuckoo
- [ ] Brown Hawk-Owl
- [ ] Brown Needletail
- [ ] Fork-tailed Swift m
- [ ] Red-naped Trogon
- [ ] Diard's Trogon
- [ ] Blue-eared Kingfisher
- [ ] Oriental Dwarf Kingfisher
- [ ] White-crowned Hornbill (one report only, but may be worth watching for)
- [ ] Oriental Pied Hornbill
- [ ] Red-crowned Barbet
- [ ] Maroon Woodpecker
- [ ] Orange-backed Woodpecker
- [ ] Green Broadbill
- [ ] Blue-winged Pitta (especially win)
- [ ] Red-rumped Swallow (try the golf course)
- [ ] Large Wood-shrike
- [ ] Green Iora
- [ ] Lesser Green Leafbird
- [ ] Ashy Bulbul
- [ ] Crow-billed Drongo m
- [ ] Velvet-fronted Nuthatch
- [ ] Black-capped Babbler (feeds on the ground)
- [ ] Short-tailed Babbler
- [ ] Moustached Babbler
- [ ] Rufous-crowned Babbler
- [ ] Black-throated Babbler (on or near the ground)
- [ ] Arctic Warbler m
- [ ] Ferruginous Flycatcher m
- [ ] Malaysian Blue Flycatcher (at edges)
- [ ] Forest Wagtail m
- [ ] Plain Sunbird
- [ ] Crimson-breasted Flowerpecker (look for it around the carpark)
- [ ] White-bellied Munia (at edges)

Access and accommodation

To reach Templer Park, take the main road from KL northwards towards Ipoh for about 25 km; the park is on the right, some 5 km before Rawang. To get to the best of the forest, continue past the golf course and turn sharp right immediately after crossing the small river (there's a large waterfalls sign at the entrance to the turn-off). Buses run at regular intervals along the Ipoh road; the trip from KL takes about 30 minutes and you can catch the bus at the Pudu Raya terminal - take number 66 from platform 20 (there's a bus stop with a shelter near the turn-off to the waterfalls). The nearest accommodation is in KL.

When to visit

Most of the best birds here are residents so that a visit at any time of the year should prove rewarding. February and March are usually the driest months; if you can, avoid weekends and public holidays when the waterfalls and recreation areas are very crowded.

Other attractions

You could see monkeys such as Pig-tailed and Long-tailed Macaques - look for the latter in the scrub south of the golf course - as well as a variety of squirrels. The waterfalls, while worth a quick look, are not particularly spectacular, and the forest in the vicinity of the falls is somewhat degraded. You can get food and drinks at the small restaurant near the waterfalls carpark; on busy days temporary food, drink and icecream stalls spring up everywhere.

5 Gombak Valley
(Ulu Gombak)

Selangor

Located within the Main Range, about a thirty-minute drive north of downtown Kuala Lumpur, the scenic Gombak Valley provides you with the opportunity to birdwatch at different altitudes (though mainly submontane) - and to see the birds you need hardly step off the bitumen. It is an ideal place for an excursion of a few hours or even a full day. More than 150 species have been recorded in the area, and you have a chance of seeing no fewer than 17 species of bulbul (including the handsome Scaly-breasted Bulbul) as well as some 16 species of flycatcher - Pale Blue Flycatcher for example. Other highlights include hornbills, Rufous-bellied Eagle, Orange-breasted Trogon and Sultan Tit. Add Chestnut-naped Forktail - there are several places where this most attractive species is regularly seen - and you have all the ingredients for excellent birding within easy reach of KL.

The generally steep-sided mountain valley, rising in altitude from a hundred or so to about 800 m (300-2500 feet), has a floor that on average is less than a kilometre wide and which is cut by numerous small streams. Although the forests have been extensively logged in places, some lightly disturbed areas remain in both the upper and lower parts of the valley, while along its floor and on the adjacent slopes there are patches of secondary forest and scrub, some groves of giant bamboos, and areas of open grass (lalang).

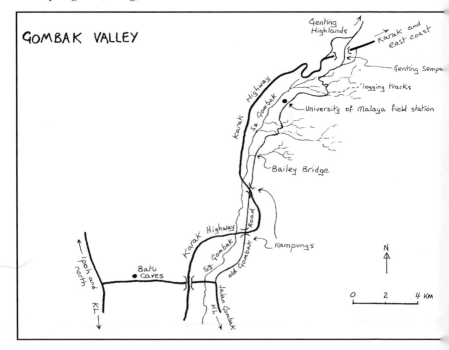

GOMBAK VALLEY

Genting Highlands

Karak and east coast

Genting Sempa

logging tracks

University of Malaya field station

Karak Highway

Sg Gombak

Bailey Bridge

Karak Highway

Road

Kampungs

Ipoh and north

Batu Caves

Sg Gombak

old Gombak

Jalan Gombak

KL

KL

N

0   2   4 KM

Good birdwatching areas

Once beyond the low-valley settlements, you should find a fair variety of species - including plenty of bulbuls and flycatchers - along virtually any stretch of the old Gombak Road (there are many places where you can safely park off the narrow bitumen). Pay particular attention to small streams within tall forest, especially above where they cross the road; for example, the stream at the second bend past Bailey Bridge is a haunt of the Chestnut-naped Forktail.

Ask at the University of Malaya field station (mid valley) for permission to enter the remnant undisturbed forest and bamboo thickets beside the river. This is another site for the forktail, as well as for Great Iora and Black-and-Red Broadbill. Some patches of relatively intact tall forest occur above and below the road for a couple of kilometres downhill from the field station; also, the two-kilometre walk uphill from the station to the deep bend in the road is popular with birders. From the bend, and elsewhere in the vicinity, logging tracks climb steeply up the slopes, providing access to a few areas of undisturbed forest where hornbills are a distinct possibility.

Birds

Open areas, overhead:
- [ ] Crested Serpent-Eagle
- [ ] Rufous-bellied Eagle
- [ ] Changeable Hawk-Eagle
- [ ] Malaysian Eared Nightjar
- [ ] White-bellied (Glossy) Swiftlet
- [ ] Brown Needletail
- [ ] Silver-rumped Swift
- [ ] Fork-tailed Swift m
- [ ] House Swift
- [ ] Grey-rumped Treeswift
- [ ] Blue-throated Bee-eater (scarce in win)
- [ ] Barn Swallow m
- [ ] Pacific Swallow
- [ ] Large-billed Crow
- [ ] Magpie Robin
- [ ] Grey Wagtail m
- [ ] Brown Shrike m

Ground, lower storey:
- [ ] Green-winged (Emerald Dove) Pigeon
- [ ] Oriental Dwarf Kingfisher (along the smallest streams)
- [ ] Black-and-Red Broadbill (in forest over streams; also middle storey)
- [ ] Straw-headed Bulbul (this and the other bulbuls listed range through the lower parts of the forest to the middle storey)
- [ ] Stripe-throated Bulbul
- [ ] Olive-winged Bulbul
- [ ] Grey-cheeked Bulbul

☐ Yellow-bellied Bulbul
☐ Hairy-backed Bulbul
☐ Short-tailed Babbler
☐ Horsfield's Babbler
☐ Moustached Babbler (also middle storey)
☐ Scaly-crowned Babbler (also middle storey)
☐ Rufous-crowned Babbler (also middle storey)
☐ Grey-headed Babbler
☐ Striped Tit-Babbler (look for it in roadside
  shrubbery)
☐ Siberian Blue Robin m
☐ White-rumped Shama
☐ Chestnut-naped Forktail (look along streams and listen
  for the bird's short, piercing whistle; it can be
  rather flighty - follow up glimpses quickly)
☐ Common Tailorbird
☐ Dark-necked Tailorbird
☐ Rufescent Prinia (often in fernery on low cuttings and
  banks)
☐ Yellow-rumped Flycatcher m
☐ Rufous-chested Flycatcher
☐ Rufous-winged Flycatcher
☐ Tiger Shrike m
☐ Purple-naped Sunbird
☐ Little Spiderhunter
☐ Grey-breasted Spiderhunter (also middle storey)
☐ Orange-bellied Flowerpecker (often in roadside shrubs;
  also middle storey)
☐ White-rumped Munia

Middle storey, canopy:
☐ Black-thighed Falconet
☐ Jambu Fruit-Dove
☐ Blue-crowned Hanging Parrot
☐ Indian Cuckoo
☐ Brush (Rusty-breasted) Cuckoo
☐ Drongo Cuckoo
☐ Chestnut-bellied Malkoha
☐ Raffles' Malkoha
☐ Red-billed Malkoha
☐ Chestnut-breasted Malkoha
☐ Whiskered Treeswift (makes short flights from
  treetops)
☐ Scarlet-rumped Trogon (also lower storey)
☐ Bushy-crested Hornbill (all hornbills also overhead)
☐ Rhinoceros Hornbill
☐ Gold-whiskered Barbet
☐ Red-crowned Barbet
☐ Yellow-crowned Barbet
☐ Blue-eared Barbet

- [ ] Brown Barbet
- [ ] Crimson-winged Woodpecker
- [ ] Checker-throated Woodpecker
- [ ] Buff-necked Woodpecker (also lower storey)
- [ ] Grey-and-Buff Woodpecker
- [ ] Banded Broadbill
- [ ] Black-and-Yellow Broadbill
- [ ] Green Broadbill (also lower storey)
- [ ] Scarlet Minivet
- [ ] Green Iora
- [ ] Great Iora
- [ ] Lesser Green Leafbird
- [ ] Blue-winged Leafbird (often in the canopy feeding on small fruits)
- [ ] Black-headed Bulbul
- [ ] Black-crested Bulbul
- [ ] Scaly-breasted Bulbul
- [ ] Grey-bellied Bulbul
- [ ] Cream-vented Bulbul
- [ ] Red-eyed Bulbul
- [ ] Spectacled Bulbul (also lower storey)
- [ ] Buff-vented Bulbul (also lower storey)
- [ ] Streaked Bulbul
- [ ] Ashy Bulbul
- [ ] Greater Racket-tailed Drongo
- [ ] Asian Fairy-Bluebird
- [ ] Sultan Tit
- [ ] Velvet-fronted Nuthatch (look for it on high, exposed limbs)
- [ ] Brown Fulvetta
- [ ] White-bellied Yuhina
- [ ] Flyeater
- [ ] Yellow-bellied Warbler
- [ ] Arctic Warbler m
- [ ] Eastern Crowned Warbler m
- [ ] Dark-sided Flycatcher m (also lower storey; often in clearings)
- [ ] Asian Brown Flycatcher m
- [ ] Verditer Flycatcher (often on high, exposed perches)
- [ ] Pale Blue Flycatcher (mainly middle storey)
- [ ] Grey-headed Flycatcher (also lower storey)
- [ ] Spotted Fantail
- [ ] Black-naped Monarch (also lower storey)
- [ ] Asian Paradise-Flycatcher
- [ ] Plain Sunbird
- [ ] Ruby-cheeked Sunbird (also lower storey)
- [ ] Long-billed Spiderhunter
- [ ] Yellow-eared Spiderhunter
- [ ] Yellow-breasted Flowerpecker (also lower storey)
- [ ] Crimson-breasted Flowerpecker (also in roadside

shrubs)
- [ ] Everett's White-eye

Difficult-to-find or rare species:
- [ ] Eurasian (Crested) Honey-Buzzard (especially Oct-Nov)
- [ ] Japanese Sparrowhawk m
- [ ] Blyth's Hawk-Eagle (upper valley)
- [ ] Ferruginous (Wood) Partridge
- [ ] Crested Wood-Partridge
- [ ] Red Junglefowl
- [ ] Thick-billed Pigeon
- [ ] Violet Cuckoo
- [ ] Collared Scops-Owl
- [ ] Barred Eagle-Owl
- [ ] Red-naped Trogon
- [ ] Orange-breasted Trogon
- [ ] Blue-banded Kingfisher (along streams in forest)
- [ ] Ruddy Kingfisher (mainly win)
- [ ] Red-bearded Bee-eater
- [ ] Wreathed Hornbill
- [ ] Helmeted Hornbill
- [ ] Rufous Piculet
- [ ] Bamboo Woodpecker
- [ ] Buff-rumped Woodpecker
- [ ] Maroon Woodpecker
- [ ] Dusky Broadbill
- [ ] Hooded Pitta m
- [ ] Bar-winged Flycatcher-shrike
- [ ] Large Wood-shrike
- [ ] Lesser Cuckoo-shrike
- [ ] Greater Green Leafbird
- [ ] Finsch's Bulbul
- [ ] Bronzed Drongo (especially edges)
- [ ] Dark-throated Oriole
- [ ] Black Magpie
- [ ] Chestnut-backed Scimitar-Babbler
- [ ] Rufous-fronted Babbler
- [ ] Eye-browed Thrush m (mainly Oct-Dec)
- [ ] Blue-and-White Flycatcher m (upper valley)
- [ ] White-tailed Flycatcher (upper valley)
- [ ] Hill Blue Flycatcher
- [ ] Tickell's Blue Flycatcher
- [ ] Maroon-breasted Flycatcher
- [ ] Scarlet Sunbird
- [ ] Yellow-vented Flowerpecker
- [ ] Pin-tailed Parrotfinch (look for it in the tops of
  bamboo)

Access and accommodation

The University of Malaya field station is approximately 25 km from central KL. To get there, take Jalan Ipoh for about 10 km until you reach the turn-off to Batu Caves (a well-known tourist spot), then go right and continue past the caves and under the Karak Highway until you meet Jalan Gombak at a T-junction. Turn left on to the old Gombak Road and soon you are in the broad, settled part of the valley. Drive on past various kampungs until the one-lane Bailey Bridge that marks the end of the settlements (once through the valley you can, if you wish, return to KL via the Karak Highway).

There is no public transport to the middle or upper valley; if you don't have a car, take a long-distance taxi from KL (you may find others willing to share, at least as far as Batu Caves). Alternatively, you could catch a bus to Batu Caves from the Bangkok Bank bus stand in KL, then either walk or hitch a ride from there. Food and drink can be obtained at the kampungs in the lower valley, or at Genting Sempah at the top; the nearest accommodation, however, is in KL.

When to visit

Most of the special birds here are residents and a visit at any time of the year should prove rewarding. When it rains in the valley it really pours, however, thus you may want to avoid the wettest periods of late October to December, and mid March to mid May. As with many other sites near KL, don't go at weekends (especially Sundays) or during public holidays when the traffic is heaviest.

Other attractions

The lower-valley kampungs are probably the closest old rural settlements to KL, and there is always something of interest as you drive along, including fine views of forests and mountains in the higher parts of the valley. Although monkeys are scarce, some mammals do occur - flying squirrels for example. The road through the valley leads to the Genting Highlands, the next site in this book.

6 Genting Highlands
Pahang/Selangor

If you are staying in Kuala Lumpur, the Genting Highlands to the north-east of the city provide the nearest opportunity to see montane birds, many of which reach their southern limit there. Situated within an hour or so of the capital, the highlands are in fact well worth the drive even if you don't do a lot of birdwatching. The mountain scenery is spectacular and, despite the tourist developments, there are extensive areas of forest where, if you're lucky, you could see both of West Malaysia's endemic bird species - Mountain Peacock-Pheasant and Malayan Whistling Thrush. Other highlights include Black Eagle, Blyth's Hawk-Eagle, Bar-backed (Hill) Partridge, Red-headed Trogon, Great Hornbill, Fire-tufted and Golden-throated Barbet, Silver-breasted Broadbill, Rusty-naped Pitta, Lesser Racket-tailed Drongo, Black-and-Crimson Oriole, Green Magpie, Blue Nuthatch, Pygmy Wren-Babbler, Chestnut-crowned Laughingthrush, Cutia, Black-eared Shrike-Babbler, Chestnut-tailed Minla, Lesser Shortwing, and Slaty-backed Forktail.

Forming part of the Main Range, the highlands consist of a series of peaks clustered around G. Ulu Kali (about 1770 m [5800 feet]), the region's highest point. The peaks drop steeply toward the coastal plain to the west and the interior to the east, and there are many deep gullies and razor-back ridges. From the Main Range pass at Genting Sempah, on the Karak Highway, the access road rises via a winding route westward toward the G. Bunga Buah arm, skirting a minor plateau at about 915 m (3000 feet) before the final, exceedingly steep ascent of G. Ulu Kali. A casino and hotel complex, together with associated fun-parks, occupies an increasing proportion of the summit area, while new developments are springing up around the middle-level plateau.

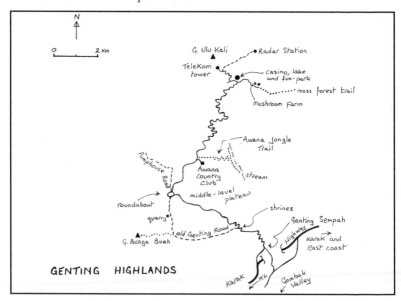

GENTING HIGHLANDS

Good birdwatching areas

There are good birds to be seen almost everywhere - as you go up the mountain simply stop and explore along roads and tracks, but respect private property, especially where there are signs indicating that you'll be shot on sight! Provided the developers haven't got there first - a real possibility here - visits to the following spots should prove particularly rewarding.

Old Genting Road: Lies to the left of the access road, between the Genting Sempah police post and the large roundabout at the middle level. Now closed to vehicles, the old bitumen road is best reached at a point where there are a number of small shrines on the right-hand side of the access road (see map). You can either follow the old road west then north to the middle-level roundabout (along the way you'll pass a quarry that is said to be good for Chestnut-naped Forktail), or you can keep heading west and take the forest trail to G. Bunga Buah.

Pumphouse Road: Is also closed to vehicles and leaves from the middle-level roundabout, taking you in a north-westerly direction towards the upper slopes of the mountain. This was once an area much favoured by birders (a good place to look for hornbills for example), but in recent years construction work has lessened its appeal.

Awana Jungle Trail: Starts from near the Awana Country Club and is reached from a signposted entrance on the main access road, just beyond the entrance to the club's golf course. For the first few hundred metres the track crosses bare, open terraces, zig-zagging toward a deep forested gully. After descending via a narrow, steep path (be careful at the start) you pass through tall forest, then follow close to a stream-course before coming to a long, high cascade where the forest has been partly cleared. The last part of the trail is a haunt of the Slaty-backed Forktail, as well as the Red-headed Trogon (try the slopes above the stream), Streaked Wren-Babbler (often in ginger thickets), Rufous-browed Flycatcher and Pygmy Wren-Babbler (in the shadowy valley bottom). There are some tall fig trees in the valley bottom that may be worth checking for barbets, hornbills and pigeons.

Upper moss forest: To get to an area of superb upper-level forest - probably the most accessible place in the highlands for secretive, rare and ground-dwelling species - drive to the top of the access road, follow around the ornamental lake, then go past the carparks to the Mushroom Farm. Walk from there to the southern (Kuala Lumpur) side of the ridge and look for an indistinct foot track that continues along the ridge. (Recent building work may have obscured the start of the trail, but basically you keep walking along the ridge until you come to the best of the moss forest.) Birds to look for here include the Chestnut-tailed Minla.

Radar Station Road: Is also at the top, but instead of entering the casino area turn left toward some apartments, then right and follow the bitumen toward the Telekom tower. Go past this and continue on the (deteriorating) road until you can go no further. Walk anywhere here looking for canopy birds, raptors and other species.

Birds

Note that in the bird list lower levels refers to the area below the middle-level plateau, while upper levels refers to the area above it.

Open areas, overhead:
- [ ] Crested Serpent-Eagle
- [ ] Blyth's Hawk-Eagle
- [ ] White-bellied (Glossy) Swiftlet
- [ ] Silver-rumped Swift (mainly lower levels)
- [ ] Fork-tailed Swift m
- [ ] House Swift
- [ ] Grey-rumped Treeswift (mainly lower levels)
- [ ] Blue-throated Bee-eater
- [ ] Barn Swallow m
- [ ] Pacific Swallow
- [ ] Asian House-Martin m
- [ ] Yellow-vented Bulbul (mainly lower levels)
- [ ] Large-billed Crow
- [ ] Magpie Robin
- [ ] Grey Wagtail m (often on roads)
- [ ] Richard's Pipit
- [ ] Brown Shrike m
- [ ] White-rumped Munia

Ground, lower storey:
- [ ] Mountain Scops-Owl (upper levels)
- [ ] Stripe-throated Bulbul (mainly lower levels)
- [ ] Streaked Wren-Babbler (look in gullies and around the upper levels)
- [ ] Grey-throated Babbler (often in bird waves)
- [ ] Striped Tit-Babbler (mainly lower levels)
- [ ] Chestnut-crowned Laughingthrush (upper levels)
- [ ] Chestnut-naped Forktail (lower levels)
- [ ] Slaty-backed Forktail (mainly upper levels)
- [ ] Common Tailorbird
- [ ] Dark-necked Tailorbird
- [ ] Mugimaki Flycatcher m
- [ ] Rufous-browed Flycatcher (upper levels)
- [ ] Large Niltava (upper levels; also middle storey)
- [ ] Tiger Shrike m
- [ ] Black-throated Sunbird (mainly upper levels; often in gardens; also middle storey)
- [ ] Little Spiderhunter (mainly lower levels)
- [ ] Orange-bellied Flowerpecker (mainly lower levels; also middle storey)

Middle storey, canopy:
- [ ] Mountain Imperial Pigeon (most often seen in flight, especially early morning and evening)
- [ ] Little Cuckoo-Dove
- [ ] Blue-crowned Hanging Parrot (mainly lower levels)

☐ Red-headed Trogon (mainly upper levels)
☐ Bushy-crested Hornbill (usually in small flocks; all
  hornbills also overhead)
☐ Wreathed Hornbill
☐ Rhinoceros Hornbill
☐ Great Hornbill
☐ Fire-tufted Barbet (upper levels)
☐ Gold-whiskered Barbet (mainly lower levels)
☐ Golden-throated Barbet (only above 1220 m [4000 feet])
☐ Black-browed Barbet
☐ Blue-eared Barbet (lower levels)
☐ Brown Barbet (mainly lower levels)
☐ Crimson-winged Woodpecker (lower levels)
☐ Buff-rumped Woodpecker (lower levels)
☐ Bar-winged Flycatcher-shrike (often in bird waves)
☐ Large (Black-faced) Cuckoo-shrike (upper levels)
☐ Grey-chinned Minivet (upper levels)
☐ Blue-winged Leafbird (mainly lower levels)
☐ Orange-bellied Leafbird (upper levels)
☐ Black-crested Bulbul
☐ Ochraceous Bulbul (also lower storey)
☐ Mountain Bulbul (upper levels)
☐ Ashy Bulbul
☐ Lesser Racket-tailed Drongo (often in bird waves)
☐ Asian Fairy-Bluebird
☐ Green Magpie (upper levels)
☐ Golden Babbler (mainly upper levels; also lower
  storey; often in bird waves)
☐ Chestnut-capped Laughingthrush (upper levels)
☐ Silver-eared Mesia (upper levels; also lower storey)
☐ White-browed Shrike-Babbler (mainly upper levels)
☐ Black-eared Shrike-Babbler (only above 1220 m [4000
  feet])
☐ Blue-winged Minla (upper levels)
☐ Chestnut-tailed Minla (only above 1525 m [5000 feet])
☐ Rufous-winged Fulvetta (upper levels; often in bird
  waves)
☐ Mountain Fulvetta (also lower storey; often in bird
  waves)
☐ Long-tailed Sibia (upper levels)
☐ Yellow-bellied Warbler (favours bamboo)
☐ Arctic Warbler m
☐ Mountain Leaf-Warbler (upper levels)
☐ Mountain Tailorbird (upper levels; also lower storey)
☐ Asian Brown Flycatcher m
☐ Verditer Flycatcher
☐ Little Pied Flycatcher (upper levels; also lower
  storey)
☐ Hill Blue Flycatcher
☐ White-throated Fantail

☐ Streaked Spiderhunter (upper levels; also lower storey)
☐ Yellow-breasted Flowerpecker (mainly lower levels; also lower storey)
☐ Yellow-vented Flowerpecker (lower levels)
☐ Buff-bellied Flowerpecker (mainly upper levels)
☐ Everett's White-eye

Difficult-to-find or rare species:
☐ Chinese Goshawk m
☐ Black Eagle (hunts low over the canopy)
☐ Rufous-bellied Eagle
☐ Peregrine Falcon (possibly resident here)
☐ Long-billed Partridge
☐ Bar-backed (Hill) Partridge (upper levels)
☐ Mountain Peacock-Pheasant* (upper levels)
☐ Wedge-tailed Pigeon
☐ Barred Cuckoo-Dove (upper levels)
☐ Large Hawk-Cuckoo
☐ Oriental Cuckoo
☐ Green-billed Malkoha
☐ Barred Eagle-Owl (lower levels)
☐ Collared Owlet (often active during the day)
☐ Giant Swiftlet (has been mist-netted at Genting Sempah)
☐ Himalayan Swiftlet m
☐ White-vented Needletail m
☐ Orange-breasted Trogon
☐ Red-bearded Bee-eater
☐ Helmeted Hornbill
☐ Greater Yellownape (upper levels)
☐ Lesser Yellownape (upper levels)
☐ Bamboo Woodpecker
☐ Bay Woodpecker (upper levels)
☐ Silver-breasted Broadbill (especially near bamboo)
☐ Long-tailed Broadbill
☐ Rusty-naped Pitta
☐ Bronzed Drongo (forest edge and clearings)
☐ Black-and-Crimson Oriole (mainly upper levels)
☐ Velvet-fronted Nuthatch (mainly lower levels)
☐ Blue Nuthatch (upper levels; often in bird waves)
☐ Buff-breasted Babbler
☐ Large Scimitar-Babbler (upper levels)
☐ Chestnut-backed Scimitar-Babbler
☐ Marbled Wren-Babbler
☐ Eye-browed Wren-Babbler
☐ Pygmy Wren-Babbler (in gullies and around the upper levels)
☐ Black Laughingthrush
☐ Cutia (above 1220 m [4000 feet])

☐ Lesser Shortwing (upper levels)
☐ Malayan Whistling Thrush*
☐ Siberian Thrush m (mainly Oct-Dec)
☐ Eye-browed Thrush m (mainly Oct-Dec)
☐ Chestnut-crowned Warbler (mainly upper levels)
☐ Yellow-breasted Warbler (upper levels)
☐ Snowy-browed Flycatcher (above 1430 m [4700 feet])
☐ Olive Tree-Pipit m
☐ Pin-tailed Parrotfinch
☐ Brown Bullfinch (try looking in native conifers at
  upper levels)

Access and accommodation

The highlands are about an hour from KL via the Karak Highway. Turn off at the Main Range pass just before the tunnel (if you miss, turn right after the tunnel and come back over the top) and from there simply follow the signs. Remember that the road from the middle-level plateau to the top is very steep. Buses run regularly from the Pudu Raya terminal in KL (catch them at platform 13 - the first bus leaves at 8.00 a.m.), and should you need one, taxis are usually easy to find once you reach Genting Sempah. Those travelling on a shoestring will have difficulty getting budget accommodation in the highlands; the cheapest rooms at the Awana Country Club may be affordable, but it would be wise to inquire (and book - 'phone 03-2113015) before leaving KL.

When to visit

February is probably the best month for birds and for weather. At higher levels you could encounter rain and mist at any time of the year, especially during the north-east monsoon from about October to December, and in April. As usual, avoid Sundays and public and school holidays if you can.

Other attractions

The fantastic black gibbon - Siamang - inhabits the middle-level forests; listen for its excited whooping yelps and look for parties in the forest canopy (the Awana Jungle Trail is a good place to search). Floral attractions include pitcher plants; these are quite numerous along Radar Station Road where they grow on the bare rock faces.

   Needless to say most people visit the casino and fun-park, or play golf or go horse-riding. There is a cable car that runs from near the Awana Country Club to the summit; and don't miss the colourful Chinese pagoda-temple beside the road leading up to the casino.

7 Bukit Gasing and Petaling Jaya

Selangor

While not luxuriant forest, Bukit Gasing's green belt and the nearby urban gardens and parks of Petaling Jaya support a surprising number of birds - about 140 species have been recorded, of which about 30 are migrants. Highlights here include a variety of raptors, among them resident Black-thighed Falconets and migrant Black Bazas; many cuckoos, including resident Greater Coucal; up to seven woodpeckers - resident Grey-capped Woodpecker for example; regular migrants such as Yellow-rumped Flycatcher and Tiger Shrike; and colourful residents like Coppersmith Barbet, White-rumped Shama, Crimson-breasted Flowerpecker and Blue-crowned Hanging Parrot. Interestingly, the first and second Chestnut-cheeked (Violet-backed) Starlings recorded in West Malaysia were seen in Petaling Jaya gardens near Bukit Gasing.

The site comprises a long-established urban area that slopes gently to a low ridge and hill - Bukit Gasing - approximately 90 m (300 feet) high. The hill's green belt consists mainly of a mixture of scrub, abandoned rubber plantation (with a well-developed lower storey of gingers, tree seedlings and herbs), secondary forest, and bare or grassy open areas. A small stream runs roughly east-west through the ridge, north of the peak. Gardens in the vicinity vary, some having a few rambutans, star-fruits, mangoes, bananas or coconuts, and others containing sizable collections of quite large spreading trees. The parks are dotted with many mature trees, as well as tall decorative palms and acacias. (Note that the ornamental lake in Taman Jaya is of no value to birds.)

Good birdwatching areas

At the time of writing there are not many entry points to the Bukit Gasing green belt, but access may eventually be improved by the Petaling Jaya city council. There is, however, a popular walking trail (not difficult, though slippery in places) starting at the junction of Jalan 5/4 and Jalan Telok (shown as Jalan Telor on some maps). The trail, which is usually reliable for Tiger Shrike and Crimson-breasted Flowerpecker in the first 100 m or so (Petaling Jaya end), leads to a very pleasant streamside walk that takes you to the Kuala Lumpur side of the ridge. There is some good secondary forest in the middle section of the trail.

A slow walk along Jalan 5/4 in section 5 should also prove rewarding; look in trees overhanging the road, and spend time at the southern end where houses are fewer and tall trees more plentiful. Close to Jalan 5/4, where the road bends westward to eventually join busy Jalan Gasing (see map), there is a grove of giant trees that is home to the delightful, diminutive Black-thighed Falconet and to breeding woodpeckers. Between mid September and mid November, and in March, raptor buffs should go to the small park (with playground swings) off the southern part of Jalan 5/4 and scan the ridge, the Telekom tower area, and the sky to the north. It would be best to go between mid morning and early afternoon, ideally around 11.00 a.m., since the birds get higher as the day wears on.

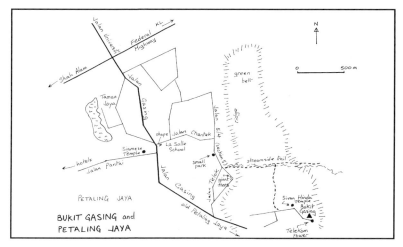

BUKIT GASING and
PETALING JAYA

Birds

Open areas, overhead:
- [ ] Black Baza m (flocks pass through in Oct-Nov)
- [ ] Eurasian (Crested) Honey-Buzzard (especially Sept-Oct)
- [ ] Crested Serpent-Eagle
- [ ] Japanese Sparrowhawk m (especially Sept-Oct)
- [ ] Crested Goshawk
- [ ] White-breasted Waterhen (in drains, crossing roads, and in gardens)
- [ ] Rock Dove (introduced)
- [ ] Long-tailed Parakeet
- [ ] Large-tailed Nightjar (often perches on powerlines after sunset)
- [ ] White-bellied (Glossy) Swiftlet
- [ ] Brown Needletail
- [ ] Fork-tailed Swift m
- [ ] House Swift
- [ ] Grey-rumped Treeswift
- [ ] White-throated Kingfisher
- [ ] Barn Swallow m
- [ ] Pacific Swallow
- [ ] House Crow
- [ ] Large-billed Crow
- [ ] Yellow-bellied Prinia
- [ ] Grey Wagtail m (often in drains)
- [ ] Richard's Pipit (bare ground)
- [ ] Scaly-breasted Munia (also in gardens)
- [ ] White-headed Munia

Gardens, parks:
- [ ] Black-thighed Falconet (localised, but has regular perching sites)

- [ ] Pink-necked Pigeon
- [ ] Spotted Dove
- [ ] Peaceful Dove
- [ ] Blue-crowned Hanging Parrot (around fruiting rambutans and ornamental palms)
- [ ] Plaintive Cuckoo
- [ ] Common Koel
- [ ] Collared Scops-Owl
- [ ] Asian Palm-Swift (roosts at dusk in palms)
- [ ] Black-capped Kingfisher m
- [ ] Blue-tailed Bee-eater (absent in sum)
- [ ] Blue-throated Bee-eater (absent in win)
- [ ] Coppersmith Barbet (look in fruiting figs)
- [ ] Rufous Woodpecker
- [ ] Laced Woodpecker
- [ ] Common Goldenback
- [ ] Grey-capped Woodpecker (small and easy to miss)
- [ ] Pied Triller
- [ ] Common Iora
- [ ] Yellow-vented Bulbul
- [ ] Black-naped Oriole
- [ ] Magpie Robin
- [ ] Flyeater
- [ ] Arctic Warbler m
- [ ] Common Tailorbird
- [ ] Ashy Tailorbird
- [ ] Asian Brown Flycatcher m
- [ ] Yellow-rumped Flycatcher m
- [ ] Brown Shrike m
- [ ] Philippine Glossy Starling
- [ ] Purple-backed Starling m
- [ ] Common Myna
- [ ] Jungle Myna
- [ ] Brown-throated Sunbird (in hibiscus and coconut flowers)
- [ ] Scarlet-backed Flowerpecker (treetops)
- [ ] Eurasian Tree-Sparrow

Scrub, plantation, secondary growth:
- [ ] Malayan (Little) Bronze-Cuckoo
- [ ] Greater Coucal (edges)
- [ ] Dollarbird
- [ ] Banded Woodpecker
- [ ] Olive-winged Bulbul (shrubs along streams)
- [ ] Greater Racket-tailed Drongo
- [ ] Abbott's Babbler (lower storey)
- [ ] Striped Tit-Babbler
- [ ] White-rumped Shama (lower storey)
- [ ] Eastern Crowned Warbler m
- [ ] Dark-necked Tailorbird

☐ Pied Fantail
☐ Tiger Shrike m
☐ Little Spiderhunter (lower storey)
☐ Crimson-breasted Flowerpecker (middle storey)

Difficult-to-find or rare species:
☐ Osprey m
☐ Brahminy Kite
☐ White-bellied Sea-Eagle (look for the larger raptors
   soaring near the Telekom tower)
☐ Chinese Goshawk m
☐ Grey-faced Buzzard m
☐ Changeable Hawk-Eagle (formerly resident, but now
   rarely seen)
☐ Peregrine Falcon m
☐ Red Junglefowl (beware of domestic types)
☐ Barred Buttonquail
☐ Slaty-breasted Rail (drains, gullies)
☐ Thick-billed Pigeon (look in fruiting fig trees)
☐ Green-winged (Emerald Dove) Pigeon
☐ Blue-rumped Parrot
☐ Indian Cuckoo
☐ Banded Bay Cuckoo
☐ Brush (Rusty-breasted) Cuckoo
☐ Violet Cuckoo
☐ Drongo Cuckoo
☐ Green-billed Malkoha
☐ Lesser Coucal
☐ Bay Owl
☐ Oriental (Common) Scops-Owl m
☐ Barred Eagle-Owl
☐ Brown Hawk-Owl
☐ Edible-nest Swiftlet
☐ Oriental Dwarf Kingfisher
☐ Collared Kingfisher (a coastal species increasingly
   found inland)
☐ Red-bearded Bee-eater (one record)
☐ Crimson-winged Woodpecker
☐ Buff-necked Woodpecker
☐ Blue-winged Pitta (especially win)
☐ Red-rumped Swallow
☐ Asian House-Martin m
☐ Large Wood-shrike
☐ Ashy Minivet m
☐ Straw-headed Bulbul (streamsides with shrubs)
☐ Black-headed Bulbul
☐ Red-whiskered Bulbul
☐ Ashy Drongo
☐ Crow-billed Drongo m
☐ Black Magpie

- [ ] Siberian Blue Robin m
- [ ] Eye-browed Thrush m
- [ ] Inornate Warbler m
- [ ] Rufescent Prinia (low shrubs and grass)
- [ ] Brown-streaked Flycatcher (this is one of the few localities in Malaysia where this poorly known species has been recorded)
- [ ] Japanese Paradise-Flycatcher m
- [ ] Asian Paradise-Flycatcher
- [ ] Forest Wagtail m
- [ ] Chestnut-cheeked (Violet-backed) Starling m (not unusual in East Malaysia, but few records from the West)
- [ ] Hill Myna
- [ ] Spectacled Spiderhunter (look in the tops of flowering trees)
- [ ] Orange-bellied Flowerpecker (likes the small fruits of Japanese Cherry trees)
- [ ] Oriental White-eye
- [ ] Baya Weaver

Access and accommodation

Bukit Gasing is about 15 km south-west of Kuala Lumpur. To get there from downtown KL, follow the Federal Highway towards Petaling Jaya, exiting left at Jalan Gasing. Continue for about a couple of kilometres, then turn left again up Jalan Chantek past a row of shops and La Salle School until reaching Jalan 5/4. Follow Jalan 5/4 to the right (south) for best birding - the Telekom tower on Bukit Gasing is a useful landmark. Minibuses 22 and 35 come from KL on to Jalan Gasing, as do a number of larger buses (inquire at the Klang or Jalan Sultan Mohamed bus stations in KL). The buses make frequent stops and the trip takes about 20 minutes. If you come by taxi, head for La Salle School or the nearby Siamese Temple (see map) and walk from there. There are hotels nearby in Petaling Jaya and in downtown KL.

When to visit

October is a good time for migrants, including raptors; so too are late September, early November, and March for return (northward) migration. Spring and early summer (e.g. April-June) can be rewarding for breeding activity. Even in the wetter months, such as October, mornings are often clear and dry with most rain falling in the afternoons (October is the one month when rain does sometimes occur in the morning however). More so than in forest habitats, evenings can be quite good for bird activity in the gardens and parks.

Other attractions

The road to the top of Bukit Gasing provides access to a small but interesting Sivan Hindu Temple, and from the summit there is a splendid panorama over Petaling Jaya and the Klang Valley. There's a more spectacular Siamese (Thai Buddhist) Temple off Jalan Gasing near where you turn into Jalan Chantek.

8 Taman Pertanian, Shah Alam   Selangor

Taman Pertanian - 'Park Agricultural'- has been intensively developed for recreation, and to provide education on Malaysian agriculture, horticulture, forestry, and traditional lifestyles. It's an easy place to explore, and the diverse habitats support a wide variety of birds (more than 130 species have been recorded), including a number that are highly sought after. On the park's list are eight raptors; five forest pigeons, among them the gorgeous Little Green Pigeon (a mixture of maroon, orange, green and grey) and the equally attractive Jambu Fruit-Dove; five malkohas; three trogons; seven kingfishers, including Banded Kingfisher; nine woodpeckers - the magnificent Great Slaty Woodpecker for example; sought-after residents like Whiskered Treeswift, Black Hornbill, Red-crowned Barbet and Fluffy-backed Tit-Babbler; and rarer migrants such as Black Bittern, Masked Finfoot, Chestnut-winged Cuckoo and Narcissus Flycatcher.

Situated on the west coastal plain, on the outskirts of Shah Alam, the new capital city of Selangor, Taman Pertanian covers about 1300 ha. The vegetation is mainly lowland rainforest, but extensive logging has resulted in the removal of all mature trees, except in a few places such as gullies and ridge tops. Nonetheless, some good bird habitat remains; of particular interest are the patches of swamp forest that occur along some of the streams. An arboretum, orchid and mushroom gardens, fruit tree orchards, ricefields and picnic areas add to the range of habitats, while two long-established small reservoirs and three recently built artificial lakes attract a few waterbirds. Some of the wetlands have shrubby or grassy edges, and the northernmost - Sg. Baru Dam - has narrow waterways that extend into overhanging forest.

Good birdwatching areas

Just follow any road or path (get a map from the administration office near the park entrance) and sooner or later you should find cuckoos, malkohas, woodpeckers, and other bird-wave species. Even areas where the undergrowth has been cleared can be productive, especially for woodpeckers and canopy dwellers. The two reservoirs (Air Kuning Dam and Sg. Baru Dam) have paths around them, and are connected by a trail that passes through quite dense forest. Though the dams' deeper waters are not very attractive to waterbirds, the shallower backwaters may hold a few surprises.

Patches of swamp forest are well worth investigation since they approximate the original, heavier lowland forest and hold some species not found elsewhere (there is a boardwalk through the narrow strip of swamp forest below the Sg. Baru Dam spillway). Walking along ridge-top roads or paths offers best prospects for seeing raptors; alternatively, stand in a place where you have an uninterrupted view of a nearby ridge-line.

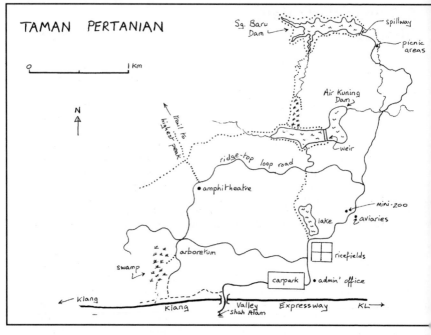

TAMAN PERTANIAN

0 |_____| 1 Km

N ↑

Sg. Baru Dam
spillway
picnic areas
Air Kuning Dam
trail to higher peak
weir
ridge-top loop road
• amphitheatre
mini-zoo
lake
aviaries
arboretum
ricefields
swamp
carpark
• admin' office
← Klang
Klang
Valley Shah Alam
Expressway
KL →

Birds

Open areas, overhead:
- ☐ Black Baza m (especially Oct-Dec)
- ☐ Eurasian (Crested) Honey-Buzzard (during migration [Oct-Nov] groups drift over the taller forest looking for roosting sites, arriving close to sunset)
- ☐ Crested Serpent-Eagle
- ☐ Japanese Sparrowhawk m (especially Oct-Nov)
- ☐ Long-tailed Parakeet
- ☐ Malaysian Eared Nightjar
- ☐ Edible-nest Swiftlet
- ☐ White-bellied (Glossy) Swiftlet
- ☐ Brown Needletail
- ☐ Silver-rumped Swift (especially over reservoirs)
- ☐ Fork-tailed Swift m
- ☐ House Swift
- ☐ Common Kingfisher (especially win)
- ☐ White-throated Kingfisher
- ☐ Black-capped Kingfisher m
- ☐ Blue-tailed Bee-eater (not sum)
- ☐ Blue-throated Bee-eater (not win)
- ☐ Dollarbird
- ☐ Barn Swallow m
- ☐ Pacific Swallow

- [ ] Large-billed Crow
- [ ] Magpie Robin
- [ ] Rufescent Prinia (low shrubs in clearings)
- [ ] Brown Shrike m
- [ ] Philippine Glossy Starling
- [ ] Common Myna
- [ ] Eurasian Tree-Sparrow
- [ ] White-headed Munia (in rice crops)

Ground, lower storey:
- [ ] Large-tailed Nightjar
- [ ] Rufous Woodpecker (also middle storey)
- [ ] Buff-necked Woodpecker (also middle storey)
- [ ] Yellow-vented Bulbul (forest edge and shrubs)
- [ ] Olive-winged Bulbul (especially waterside shrubs)
- [ ] Hairy-backed Bulbul (also middle storey)
- [ ] Striped Tit-Babbler
- [ ] Siberian Blue Robin m (especially Oct-Nov)
- [ ] Common Tailorbird
- [ ] Dark-necked Tailorbird
- [ ] Yellow-rumped Flycatcher m
- [ ] Rufous-winged Flycatcher
- [ ] Tiger Shrike m
- [ ] Purple-naped Sunbird (especially stream edges)
- [ ] Little Spiderhunter
- [ ] White-rumped Munia (edges)

Middle storey, canopy:
- [ ] Crested Goshawk
- [ ] Changeable Hawk-Eagle (breeds locally)
- [ ] Little Green Pigeon
- [ ] Pink-necked Pigeon
- [ ] Jambu Fruit-Dove
- [ ] Blue-crowned Hanging Parrot (one of the most common birds here)
- [ ] Indian Cuckoo
- [ ] Banded Bay Cuckoo
- [ ] Chestnut-bellied Malkoha
- [ ] Raffles' Malkoha
- [ ] Red-billed Malkoha
- [ ] Chestnut-breasted Malkoha
- [ ] Collared Scops-Owl (also lower storey)
- [ ] Grey-rumped Treeswift (also open areas and overhead)
- [ ] Whiskered Treeswift (often at high, exposed perches overlooking dams)
- [ ] Scarlet-rumped Trogon (also lower storey)
- [ ] Banded Kingfisher (especially forested gullies)
- [ ] Black Hornbill
- [ ] Gold-whiskered Barbet
- [ ] Red-crowned Barbet
- [ ] Blue-eared Barbet

☐ Brown Barbet
☐ Crimson-winged Woodpecker
☐ Checker-throated Woodpecker
☐ Great Slaty Woodpecker (try near the Sg. Baru Dam)
☐ Orange-backed Woodpecker
☐ Banded Broadbill
☐ Black-and-Yellow Broadbill
☐ Black-winged Flycatcher-shrike
☐ Large Wood-shrike
☐ Ashy Minivet m
☐ Scarlet Minivet
☐ Green Iora
☐ Blue-winged Leafbird
☐ Cream-vented Bulbul
☐ Red-eyed Bulbul
☐ Spectacled Bulbul (also lower storey)
☐ Buff-vented Bulbul (also lower storey)
☐ Crow-billed Drongo m (especially Oct-Nov)
☐ Greater Racket-tailed Drongo
☐ Arctic Warbler m
☐ Eastern Crowned Warbler m (often in bird waves)
☐ Dark-sided Flycatcher m (also lower storey; favours
   forest clearings)
☐ Asian Brown Flycatcher m
☐ Asian Paradise-Flycatcher
☐ Hill Myna
☐ Ruby-cheeked Sunbird (also lower storey)
☐ Spectacled Spiderhunter
☐ Crimson-breasted Flowerpecker

Difficult-to-find or rare species:
☐ Malayan Night-Heron m (one record, in swamp forest)
☐ Black Bittern m (reservoir backwaters with
   overhanging trees)
☐ Brahminy Kite
☐ Black-thighed Falconet
☐ Red Junglefowl
☐ Masked Finfoot m (mainly Feb-June; look in backwaters
   and along water edges with cover - Air Kuning Dam may
   be worth a try)
☐ Thick-billed Pigeon (in fruiting trees)
☐ Green-winged (Emerald Dove) Pigeon
☐ Chestnut-winged Cuckoo m
☐ Brush (Rusty-breasted) Cuckoo
☐ Violet Cuckoo
☐ Drongo Cuckoo
☐ Black-bellied Malkoha
☐ Barred Eagle-Owl
☐ Buffy Fish-Owl
☐ Red-naped Trogon

- [ ] Diard's Trogon
- [ ] Blue-eared Kingfisher (swamp forest)
- [ ] Oriental Dwarf Kingfisher (swamp forest)
- [ ] Ruddy Kingfisher (try around Sg. Baru Dam)
- [ ] Oriental Pied Hornbill
- [ ] Coppersmith Barbet
- [ ] Common Goldenback
- [ ] Buff-rumped Woodpecker
- [ ] Grey-and-Buff Woodpecker
- [ ] Blue-winged Pitta (especially win)
- [ ] Red-rumped Swallow
- [ ] Lesser Green Leafbird
- [ ] Greater Green Leafbird
- [ ] Straw-headed Bulbul (along streams)
- [ ] Grey-bellied Bulbul
- [ ] Ashy Drongo
- [ ] Bronzed Drongo (forest edge)
- [ ] Black Magpie
- [ ] Black-capped Babbler
- [ ] Short-tailed Babbler
- [ ] Black-throated Babbler (swamp forest)
- [ ] Fluffy-backed Tit-Babbler
- [ ] White-rumped Shama
- [ ] Narcissus Flycatcher m
- [ ] Black-naped Monarch
- [ ] Forest Wagtail m
- [ ] Orange-bellied Flowerpecker

Access and accommodation

The park is located about 30 km west of Kuala Lumpur. To get there from KL, take the Federal Highway (not the new Klang Valley Expressway) towards Klang and look for signs marked 'Bukit Cahaya Sri Alam' or 'Taman Pertanian' as you approach Shah Alam. Take the signposted ramp off to the left, then cross over the highway going north. Continue straight ahead for four or five kilometres, keeping to the right of the enormous blue State Mosque, and near the end of the road, in 'Seksyen 8', follow signs to the right and left, pass through an archway, then over the new expressway and into the park. (Note that there is no access to Taman Pertanian from the new freeway skirting the park's southern boundary.)

Once inside the park, you can either take the first left towards the arboretum, or continue straight on in a northerly direction keeping to the left of the ricefields and the first lake. The latter route climbs steeply to join the ridge-top loop road; from here, you can continue to Air Kuning Dam, then take the trail to Sg. Baru Dam. Unless you can persuade the person at the security post to allow you in with a car, you will have to explore the park on foot - or hire a cycle.

Shah Alam has several good hotels - the Holiday Inn for instance - but if you are staying in KL or Petaling Jaya you can easily reach Shah Alam city centre by bus (in KL, catch the bus at the Klang Bus Station on Jalan Sultan Mohamed) then take a taxi or minibus from there to the park.

When to visit

Since there are quite a number of migrant species to be seen here, a visit between September and December will provide the greatest variety of birds. The park is very popular - perhaps more than at any other site in the vicinity of KL, you should avoid weekends and public and school holidays.

Other attractions

Some interesting mammals occur at Taman Pertanian, including White-handed Gibbon in thicker forest near Sg. Baru Dam, Prevost's Squirrel, and the amazing Colugo or Flying Lemur, which you could see in the evening on the ridge section of the inner loop road. Pig-tailed Macaques roam the ground and trees in packs; look for them near the park entrance and to the west of there.

Visitor attractions include a fishing lake, a fish collection in Sg. Baru Dam, demonstration ricefields, reconstructed traditional houses, a mini-zoo, aviaries, an orchid garden, a fruit orchard, a mushroom farm, a flower garden, an arboretum, and an amphitheatre where cultural shows are performed. Food and drink can be readily obtained from stalls near the entrance, and at times from vendors within the park.

9 Pulau Tengah, Klang   Selangor

If you're a shorebird aficionado a visit to P. Tengah, one of a small group of islands off the historic port city of Klang, should prove a highlight of your stay in Peninsular Malaysia. The southern tip of the island is one of the most important shorebird sites in the region, with more than 10 000 migrants regularly roosting there at high tide between August and May (the largest count was 14 000 plus). About 30 species of shorebird have been recorded, including rarities such as Nordmann's Greenshank and Crab Plover; in addition, the site supports the largest West Malaysian concentrations of Bar-tailed Godwit and Greater Sand-Plover. Among the other avian attractions are Chinese Egret (up to 28 have been seen during a single visit), Lesser Adjutant, Brown-headed Gull, and impressive numbers of curlews and terns. Though only accessible by charter boat from Port Klang, this excellent waterbird spot is well worth reaching - the boat journey through mangrove channels, and past an isolated island fishing village, is a memorable experience in itself.

A feature of P. Tengah is its extensive mudflats spreading south and west from the highest, tree-clad ground. The island, which is mostly covered in mangrove forest, is separated from adjacent islands by narrow channels. At the time of writing there is about 2000 ha of mangroves, and roughly the same area of tidal flats, but both habitats are increasing naturally. While the mangroves have forest reserve status, the mudflats are not protected; this may change, however, since there have been proposals to afford the island better protection - as a bird sanctuary for example.

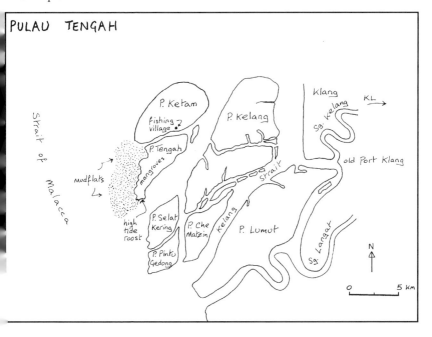

Good birdwatching areas

The principal roost site is within 50 to 100 m of the southernmost mangroves (see map). Since the roost is on one of the highest parts of the island it is seldom flooded, except when the bigger tides of four to five metres occur in spring and autumn. Nevertheless, beware on days when there's a westerly blowing; the water may rise more than usual, leaving you stranded with no retreat! In any case, before going to the island you should get a tide chart for the Port Klang area - anticipate high tide being about 30 minutes earlier at P. Tengah, and try to be on the island an hour or two before a normal high tide of three to four metres. At this stage the mudflats to the west and north-west of the roost will still be extensive, and it should be firm enough underfoot to allow you to walk about and view birds from a distance. In the last 30 to 40 minutes before high tide, move to a position near the southernmost mangroves; with luck, you'll soon be surrounded by birds as the water rises over the lower-lying flats.

Birds

Mangroves:
- [ ] Little Heron (in creeks and at edges; also mudflats)
- [ ] Lesser Adjutant (also mudflats and overhead - look for
  soaring birds on the trip out from Port Klang)
- [ ] Brahminy Kite (also overhead)
- [ ] White-bellied Sea-Eagle (also overhead)
- [ ] Crested Serpent-Eagle
- [ ] Common Sandpiper (also mudflats)
- [ ] Common Kingfisher (especially win)
- [ ] White-throated Kingfisher
- [ ] Black-capped Kingfisher m
- [ ] Collared Kingfisher
- [ ] Laced Woodpecker
- [ ] Ashy Drongo
- [ ] Mangrove Whistler
- [ ] Olive-backed Sunbird

Mudflats:
- [ ] Pacific Reef-Egret
- [ ] Little Egret m
- [ ] Grey Plover m (up to 1200 have been recorded)
- [ ] Asian (Lesser) Golden Plover m
- [ ] Kentish Plover m
- [ ] Mongolian Plover m (up to 700)
- [ ] Greater Sand-Plover m (up to 4000)
- [ ] Eurasian Curlew m (up to 450)
- [ ] Whimbrel m (up to 900)
- [ ] Black-tailed Godwit m (usually in small numbers)
- [ ] Bar-tailed Godwit m (up to 1000)
- [ ] Common Redshank m (up to 600)
- [ ] Marsh Sandpiper m
- [ ] Common Greenshank m
- [ ] Terek Sandpiper m (up to 2300)
- [ ] Great Knot m (up to 300)

☐ Rufous-necked Stint m (up to 300)
☐ Curlew Sandpiper m (up to 4000)
☐ White-winged Tern m
☐ Gull-billed Tern m (up to 2000)
☐ Common Tern m (up to 1000)
☐ Little Tern (up to 750)
☐ Great Crested Tern m (up to 125)
☐ Lesser Crested Tern m (up to 100)

Difficult-to-find or rare species:
☐ Grey Heron
☐ Chinese Egret m
☐ Great Egret
☐ Milky Stork
☐ Malaysian Plover
☐ Eastern Curlew m
☐ Nordmann's Greenshank m
☐ Asian Dowitcher m
☐ Red Knot m
☐ Broad-billed Sandpiper m (up to 15 on occasion)
☐ Red-necked Phalarope m (a vagrant in West Malaysia,
   but 14 were present on one occasion)
☐ Crab Plover m (a vagrant worth watching for - one
   seen in late Jan 1990 was the first recorded in
   Malaysia since Sept 1912)
☐ Common Black-headed Gull m (vagrant, recorded once)
☐ Brown-headed Gull m (a single record)
☐ Caspian Tern m (up to six on occasion)

Access and accommodation

You will need to charter a boat from the P. Ketam (Crab Island) jetty at old Port Klang. Sometimes, charter operators such as Patrick Ong can be found lingering near the end of the jetty; if not, ask any official-looking person for help. The main boat will cost at least $M250-300 (you can haggle of course), plus another $M50 or so for a sampan to ferry you from deep water to the mud edge (and rescue you at high tide!). If possible, get a boat with life-jackets or rafts (smaller operators may never have heard of such things), and allow about an hour and a half to get to P. Tengah, five to six hours for the whole trip. The journey from Kuala Lumpur to Port Klang will take about sixty minutes, if you avoid the rush hour.

   Another option is to take the regular ferry to P. Ketam, then try at the island's fishing village for a boat to transport you the rest of the way. Although this could cost a lot less, you'll be restricted by ferry times and by the availability of boats at the fishing village. On the other hand, the old fishing village - built on stilts - on Ketam is worth a trip in itself, and there's a chance you will see at least a few good birds en route. Whatever you decide be sure to carry your identity card or passport; there is an immigration post at the Port Klang jetty, and on your return officials there may think you've just arrived from Indonesia. There is no accommodation for visitors on either P. Tengah or P. Ketam - plan on staying in Port Klang, or make a day trip from KL.

When to visit

There is more likelihood of rain upsetting your plans if you go between October and December than there is between January and March; April may also be wet. Although the highest counts have been obtained in October, large numbers of shorebirds are usually present early in the year (e.g. January-February). While it probably doesn't matter much whether you go in the morning or afternoon, there is a theory that a mid-afternoon tide is best since birds are more likely to stay at the roost for the night than to move away and resume feeding (as is the case with morning high tides). Arriving at the right time - that is, about an hour or two before high tide - is crucial, however, be it morning or afternoon.

Other attractions

Apart from the fishing village on P. Ketam, there are Long-tailed Macaques to be seen in the mangrove forests, as well as a variety of reptiles like the Mangrove Snake.

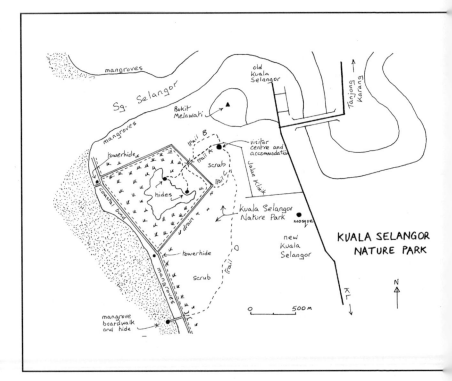

10 Kuala Selangor Nature Park   Selangor

Developed jointly by the Selangor State Government and the Malayan Nature Society, and opened in 1987, Kuala Selangor Nature Park covers approximately 260 ha and is situated at the mouth of the Sg. Selangor, about 70 km north-west of Kuala Lumpur. Each year the park attracts tens of thousands of visitors, including many from overseas (it is the site of an international bird race that draws teams from all over the world). Just inside the park entrance there is a small visitor centre housing educational displays; the park also has inexpensive on-site accommodation, as well as a good network of walking trails (including a mangrove boardwalk) and five bird observation hides, two of which overlook a man-made wetland.

The reserve and surrounding area is especially rich in water and mangrove birds, including herons, egrets, bitterns, rails, shorebirds, terns and kingfishers. Among the species you could see here are Yellow and Cinnamon Bittern, Slaty-breasted Rail, Ruddy-breasted Crake, Black-tailed Godwit, Terek Sandpiper, Asian Dowitcher, Buffy Fish-Owl, Stork-billed and Black-capped Kingfisher, Mangrove Pitta, Mangrove Blue Flycatcher and Mangrove Whistler. In addition, the area supports a wide range of other birds - in total, almost 100 resident species and 50 migrants have been recorded (a bird list can be obtained from the visitor centre, together with a map of the park).

The main habitats here are mangrove forest, the best of which is on the seaward side of a coastal bund that runs along the park's western edge; a man-made brackish wetland, in the centre of the park, which is largely overgrown with low, dense vegetation, as are several wide drains that flow through the park; the low scrub south of the visitor centre and accommodation area; and the mudflats adjacent to the mangroves, which at times are more than a kilometre wide. Outside the reserve, but within easy walking distance, there is a small granite hill - Bukit Melawati - dotted with numerous old spreading trees.

Good birdwatching areas

This excellent birding spot warrants a stay of two or three days, which will enable you to fully explore the six kilometres or so of walking tracks, plus some of the area around the park (notably Bukit Melawati, the place to look for the Buffy Fish-Owl).

There are trails leading around the wetland to the coastal bund, along the bund to the mangrove boardwalk, and through the scrub near the visitor centre (most of the trails are signposted and well maintained). From the two bird observation hides overlooking the main wetland, about 500 m from the park entrance, you can get good views - and photographs perhaps - of herons, kingfishers and other waterbirds; there are two more hides, built on towers, along the coastal bund, and another looking out over the mudflats at the end of the mangrove boardwalk. The boardwalk is about 300 m long and passes through an extensive patch of mangroves; good stands of mangrove forest can also be seen from the coastal bund. Trail D, which starts close to the accommodation area, takes you through low mixed scrub and is the most direct route to the mangrove boardwalk.

Birds

Mangroves, wetlands, scrub:
- [ ] Grey Heron (one of the most common birds in the park)
- [ ] Purple Heron
- [ ] Little Heron (also on mudflats)
- [ ] Chinese Pond-Heron m
- [ ] Intermediate (Plumed) Egret m
- [ ] Little Egret m (also on mudflats)
- [ ] Yellow Bittern (look for it at dusk around the western [seaward] end of the wetland)
- [ ] Cinnamon Bittern (also most often seen at dusk - look in densely vegetated drains)
- [ ] Brahminy Kite (also overhead)
- [ ] Crested Serpent-Eagle (should be easy to find)
- [ ] Red Junglefowl (quite common; look for it on the walking tracks in the early morning)
- [ ] White-breasted Waterhen (common around the wetland and in drains)
- [ ] Asian (Lesser) Golden Plover m (also on mudflats and in open damp areas)
- [ ] Little Ringed Plover m (also mudflats and open areas)
- [ ] Marsh Sandpiper m (also mudflats)
- [ ] Common Greenshank m (also mudflats)
- [ ] Wood Sandpiper m
- [ ] Common Sandpiper m (also mudflats)
- [ ] Pintail Snipe m
- [ ] Pink-necked Pigeon
- [ ] Plaintive Cuckoo (scrub; also open areas)
- [ ] Brush (Rusty-breasted) Cuckoo
- [ ] Malayan (Little) Bronze-Cuckoo
- [ ] Common Koel
- [ ] Chestnut-breasted Malkoha (scrub)
- [ ] Greater Coucal
- [ ] Lesser Coucal (favours marshy areas)
- [ ] Barn Owl (also open areas)
- [ ] Collared Scops-Owl (often heard calling at night from the scrub near the accommodation area; breeds in nest-boxes near the visitor centre)
- [ ] Buffy Fish-Owl (may be found roosting or, at night, seen in action among the large trees on Bukit Melawati)
- [ ] Common Kingfisher (especially win; look along drains and at the wetland)
- [ ] Stork-billed Kingfisher
- [ ] White-throated Kingfisher (also open areas)
- [ ] Black-capped Kingfisher m
- [ ] Collared Kingfisher (especially mangroves)
- [ ] Dollarbird (plentiful at times - often on high exposed perches)

- [ ] Coppersmith Barbet
- [ ] Laced Woodpecker (this and the next species are easily the two most common woodpeckers in the park)
- [ ] Common Goldenback
- [ ] Pied Triller
- [ ] Common Iora
- [ ] Yellow-vented Bulbul
- [ ] Olive-winged Bulbul
- [ ] Ashy Drongo
- [ ] Black-naped Oriole
- [ ] Great Tit (a mangrove denizen in this part of the world)
- [ ] Abbott's Babbler (low down in scrub)
- [ ] Striped Tit-Babbler (another bird of the understorey)
- [ ] Flyeater
- [ ] Arctic Warbler m
- [ ] Great (Oriental) Reed-Warbler m
- [ ] Common Tailorbird
- [ ] Dark-necked Tailorbird
- [ ] Ashy Tailorbird
- [ ] Yellow-bellied Prinia
- [ ] Zitting Cisticola
- [ ] Asian Brown Flycatcher m
- [ ] Mangrove Blue Flycatcher
- [ ] Pied Fantail
- [ ] Mangrove Whistler
- [ ] Tiger Shrike m
- [ ] Brown-throated Sunbird
- [ ] Ruby-cheeked Sunbird
- [ ] Olive-backed Sunbird
- [ ] Little Spiderhunter
- [ ] Scarlet-backed Flowerpecker
- [ ] Oriental White-eye

Mudflats:
- [ ] Great Egret (also on the wetland)
- [ ] Grey Plover m
- [ ] Mongolian Plover m
- [ ] Greater Sand-Plover m
- [ ] Eurasian Curlew m
- [ ] Whimbrel m
- [ ] Black-tailed Godwit m
- [ ] Common Redshank m (also on the wetland)
- [ ] Terek Sandpiper m
- [ ] Rufous-necked Stint m
- [ ] Curlew Sandpiper m
- [ ] White-winged Tern m (also over the wetland)
- [ ] Gull-billed Tern m
- [ ] Common Tern m
- [ ] Little Tern (also over the wetland)

Open (dry) areas, overhead:
- ☐ Black Baza m (mainly Oct-Nov)
- ☐ Eurasian (Crested) Honey-Buzzard (in Oct and Nov, look for birds spiralling over Bukit Melawati during mid morning)
- ☐ Black-shouldered Kite
- ☐ Black Kite m (mainly Oct-Nov)
- ☐ White-bellied Sea-Eagle
- ☐ Japanese Sparrowhawk m (mainly Oct-Nov)
- ☐ Spotted Dove
- ☐ Peaceful Dove (also mangroves)
- ☐ Long-tailed Parakeet
- ☐ Large-tailed Nightjar
- ☐ White-bellied (Glossy) Swiftlet
- ☐ House Swift
- ☐ Asian Palm-Swift
- ☐ Blue-tailed Bee-eater (absent in sum; sometimes in large numbers over the wetland)
- ☐ Blue-throated Bee-eater (absent in win; look for it in sandy areas)
- ☐ Barn Swallow m
- ☐ Pacific Swallow
- ☐ House Crow
- ☐ Magpie Robin
- ☐ Yellow Wagtail m (in flocks during migration)
- ☐ Richard's Pipit
- ☐ Brown Shrike m
- ☐ Philippine Glossy Starling
- ☐ Purple-backed Starling m
- ☐ Common Myna
- ☐ Jungle Myna
- ☐ Eurasian Tree-Sparrow
- ☐ Baya Weaver
- ☐ Scaly-breasted Munia
- ☐ Chestnut Munia (also wetlands)
- ☐ White-headed Munia

Difficult-to-find or rare species:
- ☐ Lesser Adjutant (small numbers can be seen on the mudflats on occasion)
- ☐ Jerdon's Baza m
- ☐ Eastern Marsh-Harrier m
- ☐ Changeable Hawk-Eagle
- ☐ Peregrine Falcon m
- ☐ Slaty-breasted Rail
- ☐ Ruddy-breasted Crake
- ☐ Watercock (mostly win)
- ☐ Greater Paintedsnipe
- ☐ Kentish Plover m
- ☐ Eastern Curlew m

- [ ] Bar-tailed Godwit m
- [ ] Nordmann's Greenshank m
- [ ] Ruddy Turnstone m
- [ ] Asian Dowitcher m
- [ ] Common Snipe m
- [ ] Red Knot m
- [ ] Sanderling m
- [ ] Little Stint m (vagrant)
- [ ] Long-toed Stint m
- [ ] Spoon-billed Sandpiper m (vagrant; this is one of the few places in Malaysia where this sought-after species has been recorded)
- [ ] Black-naped Tern
- [ ] Great Crested Tern m
- [ ] Cinnamon-headed Pigeon (especially mangroves)
- [ ] Chestnut-winged Cuckoo m
- [ ] Chestnut-bellied Malkoha (look in the scrub around the accommodation area)
- [ ] Fork-tailed Swift m
- [ ] Brown-capped Woodpecker (very small and easily overlooked)
- [ ] Greater Goldenback
- [ ] Mangrove Pitta (breeds in the mangroves; look for it alongside the coastal bund)
- [ ] Dusky Warbler m (in the lowest storey of the mangroves; few records from Malaysia)
- [ ] Forest Wagtail m
- [ ] White-breasted Woodswallow
- [ ] Copper-throated Sunbird
- [ ] Plain-backed Sparrow (try the old part of Kuala Selangor town)
- [ ] White-rumped Munia

Access and accommodation

To get to the park by car from KL, you can either head north to Rawang then west to the coast via Bukit Rotan, or you can take the new highway to Klang and then follow the coast road via Kapar. On reaching Kuala Selangor, continue past the mosque and look for a sign marked 'Taman Alam Kuala Selangor' on the left. From here, follow Jalan Klinik for a kilometre or so to the park entrance (if you get as far as the bridge over the Sg. Selangor, turn back and try again - or ask locally for directions). Buses run regularly from KL to this part of the coast; inquire at the Pudu Raya terminal.

Accommodation within the park consists of some simple yet adequate A-frame huts with fans and mosquito nets, but no bathrooms (there's a communal shower and toilet block nearby). There are also some larger chalets with attached bathrooms, fans and fly-screen windows. The huts house two people and cost $M16 per night, while the chalets accommodate four people and are $M40 per night. Since the park is very popular and there is little alternative accommodation close by, you should book in advance by 'phoning 03-8892294 or by writing to Taman Alam Kuala Selangor Nature Park, Jalan Klinik, 45000, Kuala Selangor, Selangor.

When to visit

There is something of interest here all year round - and since it's almost always hot and humid there is no such thing as an ideal month to visit weather-wise. September, October, November and, perhaps, March are the best months for migrant species, while spring is the best time for breeding activity. The park is much used for educational excursions, and you can expect to encounter groups of children throughout the school year - get out on the tracks early or late in the day!

Other attractions

The visitor centre has a few displays featuring the mangrove environment and its flora and fauna. In addition to birds, animals to be seen in the vicinity include the Long-tailed Macaque (these monkeys hunt for crabs in the mangroves, hence the local name 'crab-eating macaque'; they also raid the accommodation area and will carry off anything that looks remotely edible), Hairy-nosed and Smooth Otter, Short-tailed Mongoose, Water Monitor, Dog-faced Water-Snake, and some of the largest mudskippers you'll ever see. Among the most attractive mammals here are the Silvered Leaf Monkeys that roam the slopes of Bukit Melawati, the bright orange youngsters contrasting vividly with their silver-grey parents.

Away from the park, at nearby Kampung Kuantan on the Selangor River, you can take a night-time boat trip to view fireflies flashing from the banks of the river; some people say it's fantastic, others come away disappointed. Bookings can be made at the nature park office - the spectacle is best seen on a moonless night.

11 PBLS Ricefields, Sekinchan

Selangor

Situated about 30 km north of Kuala Selangor, the Projek Barat Laut Selangor ricefields at Sekinchan are the nearest of their type to Kuala Lumpur. At the right time of year the ricefields offer birdwatchers the chance to see many migrant species (about 40 in fact), among them Greater Spotted, Steppe, Imperial and Booted Eagle, as well as a number of other raptor species that are seldom seen elsewhere in Malaysia. In addition, the area generally provides good opportunities for wetland and open-country birding. From about September to February or March there is usually a variety of shorebirds present - Long-toed Stint and Pintail Snipe for example - while other ornithological attractions include White-winged Tern (often in large flocks in winter), migrant Black Drongo, resident White-breasted Woodswallow, Yellow Bittern and Cinnamon Bittern (both bitterns breed here in spring), and rare visitors like Ruff and Yellow-breasted Bunting.

Most of the area consists of large- and small-scale ricefields that extend for about 40 km parallel to the coast, and which have been established on land that once supported freshwater swamp forest and peat swamp forest. Up to 8 km wide, the ricefields are traversed by a network of roads, drains and elevated water channels; a wide, swampy edged canal separates the ricefields from the remaining peat swamp forest that lies a little to the east, while the Sg. Tengi flows from the forest across the fields to the coast at Tanjong Karang. As might be expected, the vegetation consists mainly of rice crops, but mango and other trees are commonly found along the bunds and roadsides, as are coconuts around the houses. Some parts of the fields, near the peat swamp forest for example, are used to grow vegetables, fruit and other crops.

Good birdwatching areas

Depending on the time of year, at least some shorebirds can usually be found in the ricefields near the main road between Tanjong Karang and Sekinchan - the best time to look is during high tide on the adjacent coast. The large-scale, treeless fields just inland from Sekinchan are often good for raptors; birds may be attracted to areas that are being burnt, or they may be seen on the ground or perched on the few posts. Sawah Sempadan, where there are many small-scale ricefields, generally supports a wide variety of species (nesting bitterns for example), although for Black Drongos it might be better to try the fields to the north of the Sg. Tengi.

Birds

Open (dry) areas, overhead:
- [ ] Black-shouldered Kite
- [ ] Black Kite m
- [ ] Brahminy Kite
- [ ] Asian (Lesser) Golden Plover m (also open damp areas and rice crops)
- [ ] Little Ringed Plover m (also damp areas and rice crops)

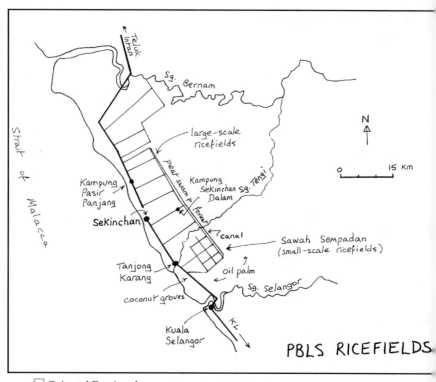

PBLS RICEFIELDS

- [ ] Oriental Pratincole m
- [ ] White-winged Tern m (also rice crops; sometimes in flocks of hundreds)
- [ ] Long-tailed Parakeet
- [ ] House Swift
- [ ] White-throated Kingfisher
- [ ] Blue-tailed Bee-eater (absent in sum)
- [ ] Blue-throated Bee-eater (absent in win)
- [ ] Barn Swallow m (watch for Red-rumped Swallows as well)
- [ ] Pacific Swallow
- [ ] Black Drongo m (perches conspicuously; up to 70 may be present in the area, but birds are usually seen singly)
- [ ] Large-billed Crow
- [ ] Stonechat m (on ground or low perch)
- [ ] Yellow Wagtail m
- [ ] Richard's Pipit (Red-throated Pipit could also occur in win)
- [ ] White-breasted Woodswallow (this is one of the best places in Malaysia for the species - look for it on overhead wires)

- [ ] Brown Shrike m
- [ ] Common Myna
- [ ] Jungle Myna (possibly the more abundant myna here)
- [ ] White-bellied Munia
- [ ] Scaly-breasted Munia

Wetlands, rice crops:
- [ ] Little Heron (breeds in mango trees, sometimes in clusters)
- [ ] Chinese Pond-Heron m
- [ ] Yellow Bittern (breeds in mango trees)
- [ ] Cinnamon Bittern (breeds in rice crops)
- [ ] White-breasted Waterhen
- [ ] Watercock (mostly win)
- [ ] Marsh Sandpiper m
- [ ] Common Greenshank m
- [ ] Wood Sandpiper m (sometimes in hundreds on fields without crops; look out for Green Sandpiper as well)
- [ ] Common Sandpiper m (especially drains)
- [ ] Pintail Snipe m (the most abundant snipe, but easily overlooked - walk along the bunds to flush them, and keep an eye out for Swinhoe's Snipe)
- [ ] Long-toed Stint m (in flocks of 50 plus in some places; look out for vagrant Temminck's Stint)
- [ ] Curlew Sandpiper m
- [ ] Whiskered Tern m
- [ ] Lesser Coucal (in crops and stubble)
- [ ] Great (Oriental) Reed-Warbler m (most easily found in patches of unharvested rice)
- [ ] Black-browed Reed-Warbler m (look in unharvested rice)
- [ ] Yellow-bellied Prinia
- [ ] Zitting Cisticola

Scrub, gardens, plantation edge:
- [ ] Spotted Dove
- [ ] Peaceful Dove
- [ ] Barn Owl (birds are kept in special boxes on tall poles in Sawah Sempadan, for the control of rats)
- [ ] Large-tailed Nightjar
- [ ] Stork-billed Kingfisher (also open areas and rice crops)
- [ ] Oriental Pied Hornbill (raids fruit trees near the swamp forest)
- [ ] Pied Triller
- [ ] Yellow-vented Bulbul
- [ ] Black-naped Oriole
- [ ] Magpie Robin
- [ ] Philippine Glossy Starling
- [ ] Brown-throated Sunbird
- [ ] Eurasian Tree-Sparrow

☐ Baya Weaver

Difficult-to-find or rare species:
☐ Purple Heron
☐ Cattle Egret m (look out for other species of egret)
☐ Lesser (Treeduck) Whistling-Duck (especially when the crops are fully flooded)
☐ Garganey m (one record only, in Jan)
☐ Eurasian (Crested) Honey-Buzzard (high overhead; especially Oct-Nov)
☐ Eastern Marsh-Harrier m (Pied Harrier may also occur; look at dawn and dusk)
☐ Greater Spotted Eagle m (10 or more have been seen on occasion)
☐ Steppe Eagle m (five or more on occasion)
☐ Imperial Eagle m (in ones and twos)
☐ Booted Eagle m (one or two)
☐ Baillon's Crake m (other species of crake may occur; look for birds flying low over crops towards dusk)
☐ Greater Paintedsnipe
☐ Red-wattled Lapwing
☐ Kentish Plover m
☐ Oriental Plover m
☐ Black-tailed Godwit m (bare muddy fields)
☐ Common Snipe m
☐ Rufous-necked Stint m
☐ Ruff m (a vagrant in Malaysia, but up to nine birds have been recorded here on occasion)
☐ Himalayan Swiftlet m
☐ Pallas's (Grasshopper) Warbler m (dense, low cover; try walking through tall stubble to flush the bird)
☐ Lanceolated Warbler m (dense, low cover)
☐ Red Avadavat (introduced)
☐ Yellow-breasted Bunting m (irregular, but up to 100 have been seen foraging in freshly harvested stubble in late Jan; look out for Chestnut-eared Bunting as well)

Access and accommodation

If you are starting out from KL, you should be able to get to Sekinchan in about two and a half hours via Kuala Selangor. Buses run regularly from the Pudu Raya terminal in KL to this part of the coast; however, unless you're prepared to do a lot of walking you will need your own transport to cover this large site thoroughly. There is little chance you'll be questioned while walking along bunds or across bare fields - but you'll attract a lot of curiosity! Needless to say, stay off the rice crops and, if you are driving, be sure to park so that other vehicles can get past (most roads in the area are narrow). Since accommodation in the immediate vicinity is rather limited, it would be best to stay at Kuala Selangor (or KL) and make a day trip from there.

When to visit

January, February and March are probably the best times for shorebirds and other migrants, including raptors. Keep in mind that during these months (and at other times) it could be very hot and there's not much shade out in the fields. The heaviest rainfalls occur from about September to December and during April, although usually the mornings are clear. Migrants are generally totally absent in June and July.

Other attractions

If you're looking for some wide open spaces, and wish to see something of Malaysia's rural lifestyle, a trip to this area will make a pleasant diversion from the crowded streets of the larger towns and cities. Although now highly mechanised, the rice-growing industry is interesting in itself, while other local agricultural activities include the harvesting of atap (nipah palm for thatched roofing) beside the road near the Sg. Tengi, and cocoa and coconut cropping around Tanjong Karang.

12 Tanjong Karang and Pantai Rasa Sayang

Selangor

If you have limited time in Malaysia and shorebirds are your priority, you should try the mudflats and mangroves on the north Selangor coast in the vicinity of Tanjong Karang and Pantai Rasa Sayang. Relatively convenient to get to, in winter the mudflats support a wide variety of shorebird species - more than 20 have been recorded - and although the birds may be scattered at low tide, towards high tide they congregate on or near the shelly beaches, sometimes in dense flocks of more than 2000. The area is perhaps most notable for its concentrations of Grey Plover, Mongolian Plover, Black-tailed Godwit (more than 2300 at times), Common Redshank, Terek Sandpiper (regularly in their hundreds), Rufous-necked Stint and Curlew Sandpiper, while other species of interest recorded on occasion include Garganey, Northern Shoveler, Malaysian Plover, Nordmann's Greenshank, Grey-tailed Tattler, Asian Dowitcher, Broad-billed Sandpiper, Ruff and Brown-headed Gull. As well, an assortment of typical mangrove and scrub species can be found in the narrow zone of vegetation behind the beaches - for example the exotic-looking Copper-throated Sunbird, and the Mangrove Whistler.

The coast in the vicinity of Tanjong Karang and Pantai Rasa Sayang is essentially the same as elsewhere in north Selangor, with soft tidal mudflats - several hundred metres wide at low tide - ending at a shell beach-ridge. Behind the beaches there are stands of mangrove, and at Pantai Rasa Sayang shrubs and grass occur on the older sand and shell deposits. The natural areas end abruptly at the sea-bund, behind which lies a freshwater canal and plantations of coconut, cocoa, oil palm and other crops.

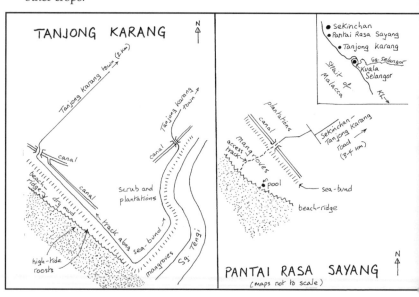

Good birdwatching areas

At Tanjong Karang, simply drive to the end of the beach access road and go over the canal bridge (see map). From there, you can either walk or drive along the track on the sea-bund. When there's no disturbance, and there's a high tide of about 3.5 to 4.5 m, shorebirds can usually be found roosting on the open dry mud between the shelly beach and the sea-bund. At other times you can watch the birds on an incoming tide from near the canal bridge; be careful if you decide to walk out to the mudflats - mud may be firm in places, but very soft elsewhere. Pantai Rasa Sayang is the better of the two localities for mangrove species.

At Pantai Rasa Sayang, you'll probably get best results in the area to the left of the access track (again, see map) - just sit anywhere on the shell beach and watch for shorebirds as the tide comes in. For mangrove birds, the access road west of the sea-bund is as good a place as any (note that there is no track on the sea-bund here); for roosting herons, try the pool in the mangroves about 50 m left of the access track (you can reach it by walking along the beach).

Birds

Mudflats and high-tide roosts:
- [ ] Little Egret m (watch for Chinese Egret also)
- [ ] Grey Plover m (up to 100 or more may be present)
- [ ] Asian (Lesser) Golden Plover m (small groups)
- [ ] Kentish Plover m
- [ ] Mongolian Plover m (up to 400 on occasion)
- [ ] Greater Sand-Plover m (up to 20 or so)
- [ ] Eurasian Curlew m
- [ ] Whimbrel m (small numbers)
- [ ] Black-tailed Godwit m (occasionally in very large numbers - 2300 plus for example)
- [ ] Common Redshank m (up to 300)
- [ ] Marsh Sandpiper m
- [ ] Common Greenshank m
- [ ] Terek Sandpiper m (up to 400)
- [ ] Ruddy Turnstone m (up to 60)
- [ ] Rufous-necked Stint m (up to 200 or more)
- [ ] Curlew Sandpiper m (up to 300)
- [ ] Whiskered Tern m (up to 70)
- [ ] White-winged Tern m (usually more abundant than Whiskered)
- [ ] Gull-billed Tern m
- [ ] Common Tern m
- [ ] Little Tern

Mangroves, scrub:
- [ ] Little Heron (also mudflats)
- [ ] Chinese Pond-Heron m (roosts near the mangrove pool at Pantai Rasa Sayang)
- [ ] Crested Serpent-Eagle (also overhead)
- [ ] White-breasted Waterhen (in canal area)

- [ ] Common Sandpiper m (also mudflats)
- [ ] Spotted Dove (also plantation edge)
- [ ] Common Kingfisher (especially win)
- [ ] White-throated Kingfisher (also open areas)
- [ ] Black-capped Kingfisher m
- [ ] Collared Kingfisher
- [ ] Blue-tailed Bee-eater (absent in sum)
- [ ] Dollarbird
- [ ] Brown-capped Woodpecker
- [ ] Yellow-vented Bulbul
- [ ] Black-naped Oriole (also plantation edge)
- [ ] Flyeater
- [ ] Arctic Warbler m
- [ ] Ashy Tailorbird
- [ ] Pied Fantail
- [ ] Brown-throated Sunbird (favours coconuts)
- [ ] Copper-throated Sunbird
- [ ] Olive-backed Sunbird

Open (dry) areas, overhead:
- [ ] Brahminy Kite
- [ ] White-bellied Sea-Eagle
- [ ] Barn Swallow m

Difficult-to-find or rare species:
- [ ] Black-crowned Night-Heron
- [ ] Garganey m (several records of between 10 and 80 birds in the Nov-Mar period)
- [ ] Northern Shoveler m (this is one of the few places in Peninsular Malaysia where the species has been recorded)
- [ ] Black Baza m (mainly Oct-Nov)
- [ ] Black Kite m
- [ ] Eastern Marsh-Harrier m
- [ ] Japanese Sparrowhawk m (mainly Oct-Nov)
- [ ] Malaysian Plover (look for it at Tanjong Karang, on the dry mud between the beach and the sea-bund)
- [ ] Nordmann's Greenshank m (has been recorded at the Tanjong Karang roosting site)
- [ ] Grey-tailed Tattler m (recorded once)
- [ ] Asian Dowitcher m (up to five may be present)
- [ ] Broad-billed Sandpiper m (up to three)
- [ ] Ruff m (vagrant)
- [ ] Brown-headed Gull m (one record)
- [ ] Lesser Crested Tern m
- [ ] Chestnut-winged Cuckoo m
- [ ] Fork-tailed Swift m
- [ ] Ashy Drongo
- [ ] Great (Oriental) Reed-Warbler m (shrubs)
- [ ] Pallas's (Grasshopper) Warbler m (try the shrubs at Pantai Rasa Sayang)

☐ Yellow-bellied Prinia
☐ Mangrove Whistler

Access and accommodation

For directions to Tanjong Karang, which is situated about 15 km south of Sekinchan, see the previous site (PBLS Ricefields) in this book. On reaching the town, look for a mosque on the left-hand side of the main street soon after crossing the Sg. Tengi, and take the bitumen road leading straight to the sea-bund (a distance of two kilometres or so). The bitumen gives way to gravel, and after crossing a canal the track runs southwards along the sea-bund, then turns inland and back to Tanjong Karang via the mouth of the Sg. Tengi. To get to the shell beach, go over the canal bridge and travel south for approximately 500 m - you'll see where the beach meets the bund.

For Pantai Rasa Sayang, continue beyond Tanjong Karang almost as far as Sekinchan and look for a sign marked 'Pantai Rasa Sayang' low on the left-hand side. Turn left on to the gravel road and follow it for several kilometres through coconuts and palms until you reach a canal (there's a dog-leg to the right shortly before the canal). Park at the canal and walk over the bridge to the narrow track that leads to the mangroves and shell beach.

As mentioned previously, you can catch a bus from Kuala Lumpur to towns along this part of the Selangor coast; however, you'll either have to walk or hitch a ride from the main road to the shore. And you will probably have to stay at Kuala Selangor - in the nature park for example - some 15 km to the south.

When to visit

At least some shorebirds are usually present at any time between August and May, but concentrations of some species reach a peak in September and in April. If you can, try to arrange a visit during an incoming tide; the ranger at Kuala Selangor Nature Park may be able to help you with tide times.

Other attractions

Long-tailed Macaques - the so-called 'crab-eating macaque' - occur in the mangroves along the Sg. Tengi (look for them from the sea-bund track between the beachfront and Tanjong Karang), and mudskippers are abundant on the mudflats, as are various crabs including 'fiddler' types.

13 The Gap
(Semangkok Pass) Selangor/Pahang

The Gap, only 90 km or so to the north of Kuala Lumpur, is truly a splendid birdwatching destination. Indeed, this locality and nearby Fraser's Hill - the next site in this book - make an almost unbeatable combination for birding in Malaysia. It is a place where many lowland species meet or overlap with those of the highlands, a convenient location for often excellent viewing of classic Malaysian tall-forest birds such as hornbills (four or more species), pigeons (up to seven species) and barbets (about five species). As well, The Gap boasts quite a number of birds that either do not occur higher up at Fraser's Hill, or are less likely to be seen there.

Although you'll be mostly restricted to birdwatching along roads, this should not stop you from finding many of the birds on The Gap's list, including at least some of the site's more sought-after species - for example Blyth's Hawk-Eagle, Orange-breasted and Red-headed Trogon, Red-bearded Bee-eater, Bushy-crested, Wreathed, Rhinoceros and Helmeted Hornbill, Crested Jay, Sultan Tit, Velvet-fronted Nuthatch, Black Laughingthrush, White-hooded Babbler, Chestnut-naped Forktail, and Verditer Flycatcher.

For the purposes of this account, The Gap can be broadly defined as the area around the gate at the start of the road up to Fraser's Hill. The site includes the first 3 to 4 km of the Fraser's Hill road, and extends for a similar distance along the road to Kuala Kubu Bharu (south-west of The Gap) and for a kilometre or two along the road to Raub (north-east of The Gap). It is inconceivable, of course, that anyone would visit The Gap but not Fraser's Hill; however, because of the differences in the birds and habitats of the two places, it makes sense to treat the sites separately. In any case, if these two important sites were treated as one the bird list would be very long and unwieldy.

At first, the roads to Kuala Kubu Bharu and Raub drop away fairly gradually from The Gap, which lies about 825 m (2700 feet) above sea level, but the one to Fraser's Hill climbs to over 915 m (3000 feet) within the first kilometre or so. Once above 1000 m, your chances of finding montane birds will increase - to have the best prospect of seeing submontane and lowland species you should walk downhill from The Gap towards Kuala Kubu Bharu. The forests that once covered the steep slopes in the vicinity of The Gap have been partly cleared, but much of the original vegetation remains, albeit patchy. Scrub, regrowth and low ferny vegetation have taken hold where the forest has been lost, and bamboo is widespread, especially in gullies.

Good birdwatching areas

The narrow, winding road from The Gap to Fraser's Hill is one-way - traffic goes up during odd hours (i.e. 9.00, 11.00 a.m. etc.) and down during even hours (i.e. 8.00, 10.00 a.m. etc.) - and as a result it is relatively quiet, except at weekends and during holidays. An early morning walk here should prove rewarding; pay particular attention to fruiting trees

▲ Mangrove boardwalk, Kuala Selangor Nature Park *(photo: J. Bransbury)*

▼ Silvered Leaf Monkeys *(photo: M. Sacchi)*

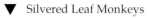

Lake Gardens, Kuala Lumpur - a good place to look for some of Malaysia's more common birds
(photo: J. Bransbury)

► Pitcher plant, Fraser's Hill
(photo: J. Bransbury)

Birding in the grounds of High Pines, Fraser's Hill - one of the best spots in Malaysia for Cutia
(photo: J. Bransbury)

▲ Tea plantations and forested peaks, Cameron Highlands *(photo: J. Bransbury)*

▲ Orang Asli settlement, Cameron Highlands *(photo: J. Bransbury)*

▲ Atlas Moth, Bukit Larut
(photo: M. Sacchi)

▲ Rajah Brooke's Birdwing
(photo: M. Sacchi)

▼ Looking west over Bukit Larut's forested slopes towards Taiping *(photo: J. Bransbury)*

(there's one on the left - the downslope side of the road - just beyond the second or third bend after the gate) as well as to the tall bamboo thickets just uphill from The Gap. Also, spend time at places where you can see into the middle and upper storeys of the forest on the downslope (there are plenty of spots where you can do this), and watch for mixed flocks roving the forest canopy. A kilometre or so above The Gap there is a ridge on the left where the road to Fraser's Hill bends sharply right (look for a sign marked 'Petak Finoloji'). A path leads on to the ridge (it is one of the few places where you can get off the bitumen) and if you walk slowly along it, watching and listening patiently, you could see some good birds - Ferruginous (Wood) Partridge for example.

Although most birders head straight for the Fraser's Hill road, don't overlook the area around the Gap Rest House (which is where you should stay - see Access and accommodation). There is usually a good deal of bird activity here, especially from early to mid morning and in the late afternoon (if you're feeling lazy, you can birdwatch without leaving the grounds of the Rest House). The downhill walk towards Kuala Kubu Bharu is easy going, and while the road is wider than the one to Fraser's Hill the traffic is generally light, especially first thing in the morning. An hour or two spent here should prove productive; to the right of the road, as you walk towards Kuala Kubu Bharu, there is a steep-sided valley that is easy to look into - watch for hornbills here in the early morning, they are often in trees quite close to the bitumen. Also, three or four hundred metres downhill from the Rest House, on the right-hand side of the road, there is a small clearing beyond which an old logging track leads down into the valley. It is worth spending some time along this track, and along the stream in the valley bottom.

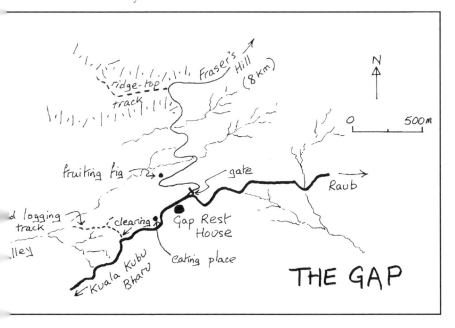

Birds

Open areas, overhead:
- [ ] Crested Serpent-Eagle
- [ ] Blyth's Hawk-Eagle (breeds regularly in the vicinity of The Gap - look in the tall trees on the right-hand side of the Kuala Kubu Bharu road, about a kilometre downhill from the Rest House)
- [ ] Mountain Imperial Pigeon (a long-distance flyer, usually seen early and late in the day)
- [ ] Malaysian Eared Nightjar (at dusk near the Rest House)
- [ ] Edible-nest Swiftlet
- [ ] Himalayan Swiftlet m
- [ ] White-bellied (Glossy) Swiftlet
- [ ] Brown Needletail
- [ ] Fork-tailed Swift m
- [ ] House Swift
- [ ] Grey-rumped Treeswift
- [ ] Blue-throated Bee-eater
- [ ] Barn Swallow m
- [ ] Pacific Swallow
- [ ] Red-rumped Swallow
- [ ] Stripe-throated Bulbul
- [ ] Bronzed Drongo (in small parties near roadsides)
- [ ] Large-billed Crow
- [ ] Magpie Robin
- [ ] Grey Wagtail m (often on roads)
- [ ] Brown Shrike m

Ground, lower storey:
- [ ] Mountain Scops-Owl
- [ ] Grey-throated Babbler
- [ ] Striped Tit-Babbler (busy and vocal)
- [ ] Black Laughingthrush
- [ ] White-hooded Babbler (also middle storey; look along the Fraser's Hill road; often in small parties, and has a loud, harsh chatter)
- [ ] Dark-necked Tailorbird
- [ ] Rufescent Prinia (along the road to Kuala Kubu Bharu)
- [ ] Tiger Shrike m
- [ ] Little Spiderhunter

Middle storey, canopy:
- [ ] Yellow-vented Pigeon (at fruits; try along the Fraser's Hill road)
- [ ] Wedge-tailed Pigeon (also at fruits)
- [ ] Jambu Fruit-Dove
- [ ] Little Cuckoo-Dove (often seen close to sunset coming up mountain sides)
- [ ] Blue-crowned Hanging Parrot
- [ ] Green-billed Malkoha

- [ ] Red-bearded Bee-eater (look for it along the Fraser's Hill road, one or two kilometres above The Gap)
- [ ] Bushy-crested Hornbill (keep a watch for this and other species of hornbill flying over roads and clearings, and listen for their far-carrying calls)
- [ ] Wreathed Hornbill (flies with loud wingbeats)
- [ ] Rhinoceros Hornbill
- [ ] Helmeted Hornbill
- [ ] Gold-whiskered Barbet (common at The Gap)
- [ ] Yellow-crowned Barbet (at its upper limit)
- [ ] Blue-eared Barbet
- [ ] Rufous Piculet (also lower storey)
- [ ] Crimson-winged Woodpecker
- [ ] Maroon Woodpecker
- [ ] Silver-breasted Broadbill (often near bamboo)
- [ ] Bar-winged Flycatcher-shrike (near the Rest House or along the road to Kuala Kubu Bharu)
- [ ] Ashy Minivet m
- [ ] Scarlet Minivet
- [ ] Blue-winged Leafbird
- [ ] Black-headed Bulbul
- [ ] Black-crested Bulbul
- [ ] Grey-bellied Bulbul
- [ ] Ochraceous Bulbul (also in lower storey and open)
- [ ] Ashy Bulbul
- [ ] Greater Racket-tailed Drongo (watch for Lesser Racket -tailed Drongo above The Gap)
- [ ] Asian Fairy-Bluebird
- [ ] Sultan Tit
- [ ] Rufous-fronted Babbler (try along the Kuala Kubu Bharu road)
- [ ] White-bellied Yuhina
- [ ] Yellow-bellied Warbler (favours bamboo)
- [ ] Arctic Warbler m
- [ ] Asian Brown Flycatcher m
- [ ] Verditer Flycatcher (quite common at times along the Kuala Kubu Bharu road)
- [ ] Hill Blue Flycatcher
- [ ] Grey-headed Flycatcher (also lower storey)
- [ ] Asian Paradise-Flycatcher
- [ ] Long-billed Spiderhunter
- [ ] Streaked Spiderhunter (also lower storey; look along the Fraser's Hill road)
- [ ] Yellow-vented Flowerpecker
- [ ] Everett's White-eye

Difficult-to-find or rare species:
- [ ] Eurasian (Crested) Honey-Buzzard (especially Oct-Nov)
- [ ] Rufous-bellied Eagle
- [ ] Changeable Hawk-Eagle

- [ ] Long-billed Partridge
- [ ] Ferruginous (Wood) Partridge (a reliable area for this species; wait patiently on valley slopes, and listen for its distinctive call - a rising trill ending abruptly in two double notes)
- [ ] Thick-billed Pigeon (at fruits)
- [ ] Green-winged (Emerald Dove) Pigeon
- [ ] Oriental Cuckoo
- [ ] Red-billed Malkoha
- [ ] Chestnut-breasted Malkoha (at its upper limit)
- [ ] Collared Scops-Owl (unusual in the highlands, but recorded here)
- [ ] Brown Hawk-Owl
- [ ] Brown Wood-Owl
- [ ] Grey Nightjar m
- [ ] Giant Swiftlet
- [ ] White-throated Needletail m
- [ ] White-vented Needletail m
- [ ] Orange-breasted Trogon
- [ ] Red-headed Trogon (along the Fraser's Hill road)
- [ ] Banded Kingfisher (at its upper limit)
- [ ] White-crowned Hornbill
- [ ] Great Hornbill
- [ ] Red-throated Barbet
- [ ] Brown Barbet (at its upper limit)
- [ ] Rufous Woodpecker
- [ ] Bamboo Woodpecker (follow up wood-tapping noises coming from bamboo)
- [ ] Buff-rumped Woodpecker (not so much rare as small and hard to spot)
- [ ] Grey-and-Buff Woodpecker (rarer and smaller than Buff -rumped)
- [ ] Dusky Broadbill (has been recorded above The Gap)
- [ ] Banded Broadbill (below The Gap)
- [ ] Green Broadbill
- [ ] Asian House-Martin m (look among swifts and swallows passing through The Gap at dawn and dusk)
- [ ] Large Wood-shrike
- [ ] Greater Green Leafbird
- [ ] Scaly-breasted Bulbul (most likely to be found below The Gap)
- [ ] Crested Jay
- [ ] Green Magpie (at its lower limit)
- [ ] Velvet-fronted Nuthatch
- [ ] Moustached Babbler
- [ ] Chestnut-backed Scimitar-Babbler
- [ ] Marbled Wren-Babbler (try the Fraser's Hill road)
- [ ] Eye-browed Wren-Babbler (along the Fraser's Hill road)
- [ ] Chestnut-naped Forktail (at its upper limit; look along streams and at road culverts)

- [ ] Siberian Thrush m (especially Oct-Nov)
- [ ] Inornate Warbler m
- [ ] Eastern Crowned Warbler m
- [ ] Dark-sided Flycatcher m
- [ ] Ferruginous Flycatcher m
- [ ] Mugimaki Flycatcher m
- [ ] Blue-and-White Flycatcher m
- [ ] Pale Blue Flycatcher
- [ ] Maroon-breasted Flycatcher
- [ ] Grey-breasted Spiderhunter
- [ ] Yellow-breasted Flowerpecker
- [ ] Pin-tailed Parrotfinch (look for flocks in bamboo)

Access and accommodation

To get to The Gap by car from KL, take the main road to Rawang and Kuala Kubu Bharu, a distance of about 60 km, then head north-east for 30 km or so towards Raub. (Take extra care when driving along the steep mountain road between Kuala Kubu Bharu and The Gap - on-coming traffic may be on the wrong side of the road!) Buses run fairly regularly from KL to Kuala Kubu Bharu; catch number 66 at platform 20 in the Pudu Raya terminal, then take the bus from Kuala Kubu Bharu to Raub and get off at The Gap. (Note that the last bus leaves Kuala Kubu Bharu for Raub at 2.30 p.m., and if you miss it you'll have to hitch a ride or take a taxi at a cost of $M25-30.)

There is only one place to stay at The Gap - the famous Gap Rest House, a well-maintained, old-fashioned hotel much loved by birders from all over the world. There are eight or nine rooms on two levels, each with fine old furniture and wonderful, deep, old-style baths where you can soak in hot water at the end of the day. The kitchen serves a range of meals, including nasi goreng and mee hoon, or you can go to a small eating place near the hotel for cheaper - and more limited - fare. Since the Rest House is very popular it would be wise to book a room in advance; 'phone the office in Kuala Kubu Bharu on 03-8041026 (the hotel's direct number is 09-382227). At the time of writing rooms cost $M21 a double, but they will soon cost twice that amount because TV sets are to be put in every room (the hotel is government-run and someone has decided the facilities need 'upgrading').

When to visit

You could encounter heavy rain and mist at virtually any time of the year (but especially during November and December); however, it is never cold and the mountains have a special beauty when enveloped in swirling clouds. In any case, October-November is a good time for bird variety, and during these months there are usually fewer people about than in July and August for example. February is probably the most reliable month for weather - and there will still be some migrant species to be seen. If possible, avoid weekends (including Friday afternoons) and public holidays when the one-way road to Fraser's Hill will be busier than usual.

Other attractions

The spectacular, entirely black highland gibbon Siamang inhabits the forests in the vicinity of The Gap, and even if you don't see this magnificent ape you'll almost certainly hear it. Among the other forest dwellers in the area are the Siamang's close relative, the White-handed Gibbon, as well as leaf monkeys, squirrels, numerous butterflies, and a wide variety of reptiles.

14 Fraser's Hill
(Bukit Fraser)

Selangor/Pahang

Situated about 1300 m (4250 feet) above sea level, Fraser's Hill is a cool mountain retreat that has changed little since the days when the British established a hill station there in the early 1900s. But it may not remain a quiet and relatively isolated haven for much longer, for already there are new apartments being built overlooking the quaint, English-style town centre and, to the dismay of those who are campaigning to save the area's forests, there is talk of a highway linking Fraser's Hill with the Cameron Highlands to the north and the Genting Highlands to the south. Ironically, should the highway be built the unique charm of the place will be lost, and the reasons many people go there - to enjoy the superb forest scenery, to breathe the clean mountain air, and for peace and solitude, to name a few - will largely disappear. (And isn't it depressing that this happens time and time again, the world over, but we never seem to learn from our mistakes?)

There is some good news however. For the time being, the only way you can reach Fraser's Hill is via the eight-kilometre one-way road from The Gap, and except at weekends and during holidays you can still enjoy fairly peaceful birding even on roads close to the main centre. Almost 250 species have been recorded in the area, making this one of Malaysia's top birdwatching sites (Fraser's Hill is the venue for an annual international bird race, but foreign teams have boycotted the event in recent years in protest at the development plans). Provided you stay at least a couple of days, and walk the Bishop's Trail where you should come across one or two really good bird waves, you will have little difficulty finding many of the site's most attractive species - for example, Fire-tufted and Black-browed Barbet, Grey-chinned Minivet, Orange-bellied Leafbird, Lesser Racket-tailed Drongo, Green Magpie, Blue Nuthatch, Chestnut-capped and Chestnut-crowned Laughingthrush, Silver-eared Mesia, Little Pied Flycatcher, Large Niltava, Black-throated Sunbird and Buff-bellied Flowerpecker.

As considered here, Fraser's Hill includes all of the area around the town centre, which is readily accessible via a network of roads and walking tracks, as well as 3 to 4 km of the road leading down to The Gap. Habitats vary from open areas (like the golf course) and public and private gardens, to scrub, regrowth and forest (the last is mostly in near-original condition and in places very extensive).

Good birdwatching areas

As mentioned, the network of roads generally provides good birding (you should, of course, avoid the main centre and places where building construction is in full swing), but the following roads in particular are recommended: Semantan Road (leading to the waterfall) and Sg. Hijau Road; Lady Maxwell Road, including the side road to Muar Cottage; Valley Road west of Quarry Road; Mager Road and Richmond Road; and Girdle Road, which runs around the Telekom tower. Most of the walking tracks in the area are in quite good repair, but some have steep, slippery

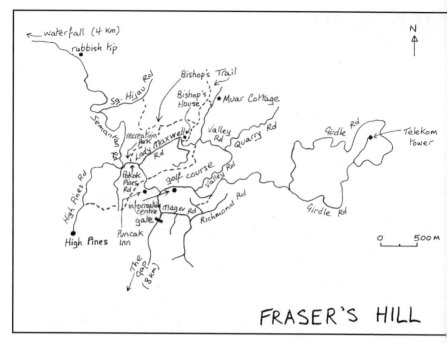

FRASER'S HILL

sections and almost all are poorly signposted. (You can get a map showing the roads and trails from the information centre near the Merlin Hotel.)

The Bishop's Trail is probably the best of the walks, especially the section between Bishop's House and the recreation park. On occasion, however, even this area can be seemingly devoid of bird life - don't give up, one large bird wave can bring 15 or more species flooding through the forest. The trail can be reached from the recreation park near the junction of Pokok Pines Road and Lady Maxwell Road, from behind Bishop's House, or from near Muar Cottage (none of the entrances to the trail is clearly marked - if in doubt, ask locally for directions). As always, it is well worth seeking out local birders for up-to-date information on the whereabouts of particular species: Fraser's Hill has several resident birdwatchers, inquire at the Puncak Inn in the town centre.

Birds

Open areas, overhead:
- [ ] Crested Serpent-Eagle
- [ ] Blyth's Hawk-Eagle
- [ ] White-bellied (Glossy) Swiftlet
- [ ] Brown Needletail
- [ ] Silver-rumped Swift
- [ ] Fork-tailed Swift m
- [ ] House Swift
- [ ] Blue-throated Bee-eater
- [ ] Grey Wagtail m (often along roads)

Ground, lower storey:
☐ Mountain Scops-Owl
☐ Stripe-throated Bulbul (look near the mini zoo)
☐ Ochraceous Bulbul (also middle storey)
☐ Buff-breasted Babbler (try around the rubbish tip)
☐ Marbled Wren-Babbler
☐ Streaked Wren-Babbler (likes rocky outcrops and, at Fraser's Hill, garden walls)
☐ Eye-browed Wren-Babbler
☐ Pygmy Wren-Babbler (quite common along the Bishop's Trail)
☐ Rufous-fronted Babbler (along the road to The Gap; also middle storey)
☐ Grey-throated Babbler
☐ Black Laughingthrush
☐ White-hooded Babbler (also middle storey)
☐ Malayan Whistling Thrush* (favours moist, shady gullies; usually solitary)
☐ Mountain Tailorbird (also middle storey)
☐ Ferruginous Flycatcher m (try near the rubbish tip)
☐ Rufous-browed Flycatcher (common along the Bishop's Trail)
☐ Black-throated Sunbird (common in gardens; also occurs in forest where it ranges into the middle and upper storeys)

Middle storey, canopy:
☐ Black-thighed Falconet (also in open areas)
☐ Thick-billed Pigeon (at fruits)
☐ Mountain Imperial Pigeon (also overhead)
☐ Barred Cuckoo-Dove (at the highest levels)
☐ Little Cuckoo-Dove (also in the open - flying along quiet roads for example)
☐ Large Hawk-Cuckoo
☐ Oriental Cuckoo (try the Bishop's Trail)
☐ Green-billed Malkoha
☐ Collared Owlet (also lower storey; often active during the day)
☐ Orange-breasted Trogon (along the road to The Gap)
☐ Red-headed Trogon
☐ Wreathed Hornbill (all hornbills also overhead)
☐ Rhinoceros Hornbill
☐ Great Hornbill
☐ Fire-tufted Barbet (one of the most common birds at Fraser's Hill; can be seen - and heard - close to the town centre)
☐ Black-browed Barbet (common, but not so easy to find as the Fire-tufted)
☐ Speckled Piculet (often in bird waves)
☐ Greater Yellownape

- [ ] Lesser Yellownape
- [ ] Bay Woodpecker (occurs quite close to the town centre; look for it along quieter roads in the highest areas)
- [ ] Silver-breasted Broadbill (along the road to The Gap)
- [ ] Long-tailed Broadbill
- [ ] Large (Black-faced) Cuckoo-shrike
- [ ] Grey-chinned Minivet (often in bird waves)
- [ ] Scarlet Minivet (along the road to The Gap)
- [ ] Orange-bellied Leafbird
- [ ] Black-crested Bulbul (also lower storey)
- [ ] Mountain Bulbul (also lower storey)
- [ ] Ashy Bulbul (along The Gap road)
- [ ] Lesser Racket-tailed Drongo (often in bird waves)
- [ ] Black-and-Crimson Oriole (often in bird waves - try along the Bishop's Trail)
- [ ] Green Magpie (common; occurs along roads quite close to the town centre)
- [ ] Sultan Tit
- [ ] Blue Nuthatch (almost a certainty; a bird-wave species, regularly seen along the Bishop's Trail)
- [ ] Golden Babbler (also lower storey; often in bird waves)
- [ ] Chestnut-capped Laughingthrush (common and widespread)
- [ ] Chestnut-crowned Laughingthrush (also lower storey; in smaller parties than the Chestnut-capped, and often in bird waves)
- [ ] Silver-eared Mesia (also lower storey; a most attractive bird, common and widespread)
- [ ] White-browed Shrike-Babbler
- [ ] Black-eared Shrike-Babbler (only at the highest levels)
- [ ] Blue-winged Minla
- [ ] Rufous-winged Fulvetta (often in bird waves)
- [ ] Mountain Fulvetta (also lower storey; very common and widespread)
- [ ] Long-tailed Sibia (often in small parties)
- [ ] Chestnut-crowned Warbler
- [ ] Mountain Leaf-Warbler (at the highest levels)
- [ ] Little Pied Flycatcher (common; look for it along roads)
- [ ] Large Niltava (common and widespread at the highest levels)
- [ ] Hill Blue Flycatcher
- [ ] Grey-headed Flycatcher (also lower storey)
- [ ] White-throated Fantail (common; also in lower storey)
- [ ] Streaked Spiderhunter (also lower storey; often seen in gardens)
- [ ] Buff-bellied Flowerpecker

Difficult-to-find or rare species:

- [ ] Eurasian (Crested) Honey-Buzzard (especially Oct-Nov and Mar-Apr)
- [ ] Black Eagle (hunts low over forest canopy)
- [ ] Rufous-bellied Eagle
- [ ] Bar-backed (Hill) Partridge (not rare, just hard to find)
- [ ] Mountain Peacock-Pheasant*
- [ ] Yellow-vented Pigeon (at fruits)
- [ ] Wedge-tailed Pigeon (at fruits)
- [ ] Grey Nightjar m
- [ ] White-crowned Hornbill
- [ ] Helmeted Hornbill
- [ ] Golden-throated Barbet (restricted to the highest areas)
- [ ] Rusty-naped Pitta (at one time this much sought-after species could be found close to the town centre - behind the golf course for example - but the disturbance caused by construction work has made it harder to find. A recent sighting, however, was made on The Gap road, 2 km below the Fraser's Hill gate; also, try along the road to the waterfall, especially in the vicinity of the rubbish tip)
- [ ] Blue-winged Pitta (mainly Oct-Nov)
- [ ] Hooded Pitta m (mainly Oct-Nov)
- [ ] Large Scimitar-Babbler
- [ ] Cutia (only at the highest levels; try looking in the grounds of High Pines - see map)
- [ ] Lesser Shortwing (quite common but can be elusive; try the Bishop's Trail)
- [ ] White-tailed Robin (at the highest levels; try around the Bishop's Trail)
- [ ] Slaty-backed Forktail (along streams and at road culverts)
- [ ] Orange-headed Thrush m
- [ ] Siberian Thrush m (especially Oct-Nov and Feb-Mar)
- [ ] Eye-browed Thrush m (especially Oct-Nov and Feb-Mar)
- [ ] Mugimaki Flycatcher m
- [ ] Pygmy Blue Flycatcher (try the Bishop's Trail)
- [ ] Brown Bullfinch (restricted to the highest areas; try the grounds of High Pines for this somewhat elusive species)

Access and accommodation

You can drive to Fraser's Hill from Kuala Lumpur via The Gap or, if you don't have your own transport, you can catch a bus from the Pudu Raya terminal in KL to Kuala Kubu Bharu, then take the Fraser's Hill bus from there. Note, however, that there are only two buses a day from Kuala Kubu Bharu to Fraser's Hill - one leaves at 8.00 a.m. and the other at 12.00 noon. (The buses reach Fraser's Hill at about 9.30 a.m. and 1.30 p.m., stay for half an hour or so, then return to Kuala Kubu Bharu.) If you miss the noon connection you can get the Kuala Kubu Bharu to Raub bus at 2.30 p.m., then get off at The Gap and hitch a lift up the hill (lifts should be easy to find). A taxi from Kuala Kubu Bharu to Fraser's Hill will cost you around $M30-40. Keep in mind that vehicles are allowed to go up the one-way road between The Gap and Fraser's Hill only during odd hours, and down during even hours.

Accommodation includes chalets, bungalows, apartments and hotels (the 109-room Merlin Resort and the smaller Puncak Inn, for example), and prices range from about $M40 to $M100 plus per night. At weekends and during holidays rooms may be hard to find; in any case, it would be wise to inquire about vacancies by telephoning the Fraser's Hill Development Corporation on 09-382044, 382248 or 382201 (the FHDC owns a number of chalets and bungalows which it rents), the Merlin Resort on 09-382300, or the Puncak Inn on 09-382055.

For real old-style charm, with the bonus of (usually) excellent birding right at your doorstep, try the High Pines bungalow where rooms cost about $M70 a double. Situated at the end of a no-through road, and offering magnificent views over forest-clad mountains, High Pines is some distance from most of the new construction sites - it is also several kilometres from the town centre, which makes it rather difficult to get to. Rooms at High Pines can be booked by 'phoning the owners, Boh Plantations Sdn Bhd, on Ampang (Selangor) 4910422.

As an alternative to staying at Fraser's Hill, you could use the Gap Rest House as a base, then take the Kuala Kubu Bharu bus up the hill (it passes through The Gap at about 9.15 a.m.), spend the morning birdwatching at the top, and either catch the bus down again at about 2.00 p.m. or, better still, walk the eight kilometres back to The Gap and enjoy the birds and scenery along the way.

When to visit

The daytime temperature at Fraser's Hill seldom gets above 24 degrees C, and the nights are very comfortable for sleeping - you'll even need a blanket or two. As a result, it is the ideal place to go when you want a break from the heat and humidity of the lowlands. As with The Gap, rain is always a possibility, but it's never really cold and the wet is more of an inconvenience than anything else (more often than not it only rains in the afternoon anyway). A visit during October-November, when migrants start to arrive, would probably be best for bird variety. Since Fraser's Hill is becoming increasingly popular as a weekend retreat, try to arrange a visit between Monday and Friday, and avoid holiday periods if you can.

Other attractions

The Siamang, largest of the gibbons, is quite common in the area and its far-carrying wild whoopings and deep boomings can be heard throughout the day. It is a difficult animal to see, however, as is the attractive White-handed Gibbon, which also occurs locally. Easier to find are the leaf monkeys, squirrels, reptiles, butterflies, orchids and pitcher plants - look for the last mentioned on steep, bare roadside embankments such as those along High Pines Road, and along the top section of the road down to The Gap.

15 Kuala Gula   Perak

Kuala Gula is a small fishing village on the Perak coast, about 40 km north-west of Taiping. Though not the most attractive birding spot in Malaysia, the village is a handy place to stay for a few nights while you explore the adjacent coastal areas, in particular Kuala Gula Bird Sanctuary and the Matang Mangrove Forest Reserve (the bird sanctuary forms part of the forest reserve and is situated towards its northern end).

Consisting of a vast expanse of tidal mudflats, mangrove forests and islands, and extending some 40 km from about Kuala Kurau in the north to beyond Kuala Sepetang (Port Weld) in the south, the area is perhaps best known as the place to see Milky Storks. A number of other sought-after species can also be found here, among them Black-crowned Night-Heron, Lesser Adjutant, Masked Finfoot, rare migrant shorebirds, Brown-headed Gull, rare terns, and Ruddy Kingfisher. In all, about 140 bird species have been recorded, and the experienced observer could probably add a further 20 or 30 to the list.

At the time of writing, the sanctuary at Kuala Gula has few visitor facilities - there's just a park office (where you can get a bird list and a map of the area) and accommodation for up to nine people. There is also a resident ranger who will guide you around the local area (if he is available); in addition, the ranger can organise for you to be taken out in a boat by one of the local fishermen. Facilities at Kuala Gula may soon be improved, however, since there are plans to make the sanctuary more attractive to ecotourists by building chalets to accommodate a larger number of visitors.

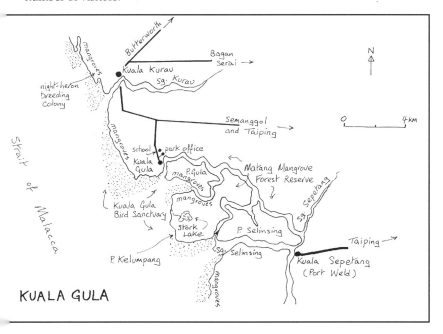

KUALA GULA

Good birdwatching areas

A boat is almost essential to get the best out of this site, for access to Perak's northern coast is somewhat limited (apart from Kuala Gula, the only convenient points of entry are Kuala Kurau and Kuala Sepetang). If you have time, be sure to take a boat trip from Kuala Gula; you will of course have to pay for fuel and for the boatman (it could cost $M50 to 100, depending on how long you stay out), and you will need to arrange the trip in advance - 'phone the park office on 04-557207 (Azman Said is currently in charge of the sanctuary and he is very helpful). The ranger at Kuala Gula may be able to accompany you in the boat and he will know where the best birds are to be found - for example, he will probably suggest you go to the lake on P. Kelumpang, about 2 km south of the park office. Known locally as Stork Lake, the area is usually reliable for Milky Storks, Lesser Adjutants and a variety of waders.

If you don't manage to get out in a boat, you can still enjoy quite good birding around Kuala Gula fishing village, where tracks provide access to areas of mangrove, and to the drains, canals, scrub and plantations along this part of the coast. (If you can't arrange a boat trip, you will probably be better off going to Kuala Selangor Nature Park - site 10 - where you'll find a greater variety of birds in a smaller, more accessible area.)

Birds

Mangroves, wetlands, scrub:
- [ ] Grey Heron
- [ ] Little Heron (also on mudflats)
- [ ] Chinese Pond-Heron m
- [ ] Intermediate (Plumed) Egret m
- [ ] Little Egret m (also on mudflats)
- [ ] Yellow Bittern
- [ ] Cinnamon Bittern
- [ ] Brahminy Kite (also overhead)
- [ ] Crested Serpent-Eagle
- [ ] White-breasted Waterhen
- [ ] Asian (Lesser) Golden Plover m (also on mudflats and in open damp areas)
- [ ] Little Ringed Plover m (also mudflats and open areas)
- [ ] Marsh Sandpiper m (also mudflats)
- [ ] Common Greenshank m (also mudflats)
- [ ] Common Sandpiper m (also mudflats)
- [ ] Pink-necked Pigeon
- [ ] Peaceful Dove (also open areas)
- [ ] Common Koel
- [ ] Chestnut-bellied Malkoha
- [ ] Greater Coucal
- [ ] Lesser Coucal (favours marshy areas)
- [ ] Common Kingfisher (especially win)
- [ ] Stork-billed Kingfisher
- [ ] White-throated Kingfisher (also open areas)
- [ ] Black-capped Kingfisher m

- [ ] Collared Kingfisher (especially mangroves)
- [ ] Dollarbird
- [ ] Laced Woodpecker
- [ ] Common Goldenback
- [ ] Brown-capped Woodpecker (sparrow-sized and often overlooked)
- [ ] Pied Triller
- [ ] Common Iora
- [ ] Yellow-vented Bulbul
- [ ] Olive-winged Bulbul
- [ ] Ashy Drongo
- [ ] Black-naped Oriole
- [ ] Great Tit (mangroves)
- [ ] Flyeater
- [ ] Arctic Warbler m
- [ ] Great (Oriental) Reed-Warbler m
- [ ] Common Tailorbird
- [ ] Dark-necked Tailorbird
- [ ] Ashy Tailorbird
- [ ] Yellow-bellied Prinia
- [ ] Zitting Cisticola
- [ ] Mangrove Blue Flycatcher (occurs in mangroves close to Kuala Gula fishing village)
- [ ] Pied Fantail
- [ ] Mangrove Whistler (like the flycatcher, can be found close to the fishing village)
- [ ] Brown-throated Sunbird
- [ ] Copper-throated Sunbird
- [ ] Olive-backed Sunbird
- [ ] Oriental White-eye
- [ ] White-rumped Munia

Mudflats:
- [ ] Great Egret (also wetlands)
- [ ] Grey Plover m
- [ ] Mongolian Plover m
- [ ] Greater Sand-Plover m
- [ ] Eurasian Curlew m
- [ ] Whimbrel m
- [ ] Black-tailed Godwit m
- [ ] Common Redshank m (also wetlands)
- [ ] Terek Sandpiper m
- [ ] Rufous-necked Stint m
- [ ] Curlew Sandpiper m
- [ ] Whiskered Tern m (also wetlands)
- [ ] White-winged Tern m (also wetlands)
- [ ] Gull-billed Tern m
- [ ] Common Tern m
- [ ] Little Tern (also wetlands)

Open (dry) areas, overhead:
- [ ] Osprey m
- [ ] Black-shouldered Kite
- [ ] White-bellied Sea-Eagle
- [ ] Barred Buttonquail
- [ ] Spotted Dove
- [ ] Long-tailed Parakeet
- [ ] Large-tailed Nightjar
- [ ] House Swift
- [ ] Blue-tailed Bee-eater (absent in sum; look for them perched on roadside wires as you approach Kuala Gula)
- [ ] Blue-throated Bee-eater (absent in win)
- [ ] Barn Swallow m
- [ ] Pacific Swallow
- [ ] Large-billed Crow
- [ ] Magpie Robin
- [ ] Brown Shrike m
- [ ] Philippine Glossy Starling
- [ ] Common Myna
- [ ] Jungle Myna
- [ ] Eurasian Tree-Sparrow

Difficult-to-find or rare species:
- [ ] Javan Pond-Heron m (vagrant; virtually inseparable from Chinese Pond-Heron in winter and immature plumages)
- [ ] Pacific Reef-Egret
- [ ] Chinese Egret m
- [ ] Black-crowned Night-Heron (breeds near Kuala Kurau, a little to the north of Kuala Gula)
- [ ] Schrenck's Bittern m
- [ ] Black Bittern m
- [ ] Milky Stork (often at the lake just south of Kuala Gula - see earlier comments)
- [ ] Lesser Adjutant (at the lake and on mudflats)
- [ ] Eastern Marsh-Harrier m
- [ ] Red-legged Crake m
- [ ] Ruddy-breasted Crake
- [ ] Masked Finfoot m (mainly Feb-June; on sluggish rivers such as the Sg. Selinsing)
- [ ] Bar-tailed Godwit m
- [ ] Wood Sandpiper m
- [ ] Grey-tailed Tattler m
- [ ] Ruddy Turnstone m
- [ ] Asian Dowitcher m
- [ ] Red Knot m
- [ ] Great Knot m
- [ ] Little Stint m (vagrant)
- [ ] Long-toed Stint m
- [ ] Broad-billed Sandpiper m

Rainforest bloom, Pulau Langkawi
(photo: J. Bransbury)

▲ Great Hornbill, one of Malaysia's nine
hornbill species *(photo: J. Bransbury)*

◄ The view from
G. Raya, Pulau
Langkawi
(photo: J. Bransbury)

▼ A backwater on the Sg. Tahan, Taman
Negara *(photo: J. Bransbury)*

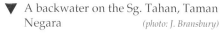

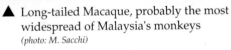

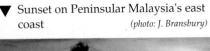

- [ ] Ruff m (vagrant)
- [ ] Brown-headed Gull m
- [ ] Black-naped Tern
- [ ] Great Crested Tern m
- [ ] Lesser Crested Tern m
- [ ] Cinnamon-headed Pigeon
- [ ] Little Green Pigeon
- [ ] Bay Owl
- [ ] Buffy Fish-Owl
- [ ] Oriental Dwarf Kingfisher
- [ ] Ruddy Kingfisher
- [ ] Mangrove Pitta
- [ ] Large Wood-shrike
- [ ] Crow-billed Drongo m
- [ ] Siberian Thrush m (in mangroves on passage - mainly Oct-Nov and Mar)
- [ ] Eye-browed Thrush m (in mangroves on passage - mainly Oct-Nov and Mar)
- [ ] Dusky Warbler m (in the lowest storey of the mangroves)
- [ ] Pallas's (Grasshopper) Warbler m
- [ ] Lanceolated Warbler m
- [ ] Yellow-rumped Flycatcher m
- [ ] Forest Wagtail m
- [ ] Hill Myna

Access and accommodation

Kuala Gula lies to the west of the main Ipoh to Butterworth road. To get there from Taiping, head north towards Butterworth until you reach Semanggol, then turn west on the road to Kuala Kurau. (At present there are a lot of roadworks between Taiping and Butterworth, and there are detours everywhere. Should you become lost, ask for directions to the Balai Polis Simpang Empat Semanggol - the road to Kuala Kurau passes right by the police station.) About 18 km along the Kuala Kurau road there's a turn-off to the left leading to Kuala Gula; follow this road for about 4 km and look for a school on the left. Immediately beyond the school there's a sign marked 'Projek Konservasi Burung-Burung Laut', and a single-lane road leading to the park office behind the school. There are no regular buses to Kuala Gula - a long-distance taxi from Taiping will cost you around $M40.

Accommodation is available close to the park office, but since it is used by visiting government officials and research workers you should book a room in advance by writing to the Director General, Department of Wildlife and National Parks, Km 10 Jalan Cheras, Kuala Lumpur 56100, or by 'phoning 03-9052872 (ask for Mr Jasmi). Given that there are plans to upgrade the accommodation it would pay to check with the office at Kuala Gula (tel. 04-557207) before you book; for meals, you can either take along your own food or go to one of the several small eating places in Kuala Gula village.

When to visit

Milky Storks, Lesser Adjutants, Black-crowned Night-Herons and at least some of the site's other sought-after species are present throughout the year, but the Milky Stork population (and probably those of some of the other waterbirds) fluctuates from season to season. Up to a hundred or so Milky Storks may be in the area at any one time; July is said to be the best month for them - for example, about 50 were present in July 1992. If you are mainly interested in looking for migrant shorebirds, you should visit from about September to January or February.

Other attractions

There is little to see at Kuala Gula other than birds (the fishing village can hardly be described as picturesque), but you could find Long-tailed (crab-eating) Macaques in the mangroves and, if you're lucky, you may see Plumbeous Dolphins from the boat. Other animals to look for include the Spectacled Leaf Monkey (distinguished by its conspicuous white eye rings) and the Smooth Otter.

16 Penang Island

Pulau Pinang

The site of the first British trading outpost in the Far East, Penang has changed a great deal since 1786 when Captain Francis Light acquired possession of the island on behalf of the East India Company. Some two hundred years ago Penang was covered in virgin rainforest; today, with less than a quarter of the original vegetation remaining, almost all of the island's lowland areas have been cleared, and only the north-central and north-western uplands - the water catchment areas - have escaped deforestation.

Given the island's recent history, it is hardly surprising that Penang is not one of Malaysia's premier birding spots. Nor is the island quite the tropical paradise portrayed in the glossy tourist brochures; its 'sun-kissed, palm-fringed beaches', for example, are mostly very ordinary - and most are overlooked by gigantic hotel complexes. All the same, it is well worth taking the trouble to visit the island's thriving capital, Georgetown, where you'll find - just as the tourist literature says - a fascinating mix of cultures, narrow, bustling streets packed with batik, silverware, jewellery and antique shops, and a seemingly endless array of eating places.

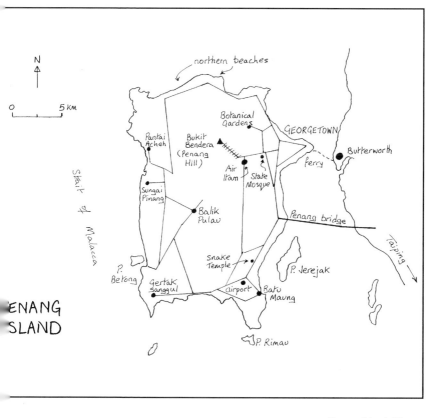

Good birdwatching areas

When the noise and confusion of Georgetown wears a bit thin - more than half of Penang's one million inhabitants live in the city - it's nice to know that the relatively peaceful summit of Penang Hill is just a short bus and train ride away. (Penang Hill is in fact a collective term referring to the hill resort that comprises a group of peaks; the summit or top station is Bukit Bendera [735 m], the most developed and heavily visited part of the range.) Access to the summit is gained via a funicular railway; trains leave from the lower station at Air Itam every half an hour from 6.30 a.m. until 9.30 p.m., the trip takes 30 minutes and costs $M3 return.

If you have only half a day or so to spare, the best plan is to take the first train up Bukit Bendera in the morning, birdwatch around the top, then walk down the hill by way of the roads and tracks that lead to Moon Gate, some 300 m from the main entrance to the Botanical Gardens (the downhill walk will take you around three hours). You can then birdwatch in the 30 ha gardens for a short while (the gardens hold nothing special bird-wise), have lunch at one of the nearby food stalls, and return to Georgetown centre by bus (buses stop regularly outside the entrance to the Botanical Gardens).

If you have a day or more to fill, there are plenty of other routes up and down Penang Hill, as well as a number of walking trails elsewhere on Penang Island. A useful book to have is *Nature Trails of Penang Island,* published by the Malayan Nature Society (you can get a copy from any of the larger bookstores in Georgetown or from the MNS office in Petaling Jaya - see Useful Addresses at the front of this book).

Birds

Open areas, overhead:
- ☐ Little Heron
- ☐ Brahminy Kite
- ☐ White-bellied Sea-Eagle
- ☐ Common Sandpiper m
- ☐ Plaintive Cuckoo
- ☐ Large-tailed Nightjar
- ☐ Edible-nest Swiftlet
- ☐ Silver-rumped Swift
- ☐ House Swift
- ☐ Asian Palm-Swift (look in the Botanical Gardens)
- ☐ Grey-rumped Treeswift
- ☐ Stork-billed Kingfisher
- ☐ White-throated Kingfisher
- ☐ Collared Kingfisher
- ☐ Chestnut-headed Bee-eater (look for them from the funicular railway on the way up Penang Hill)
- ☐ Blue-tailed Bee-eater
- ☐ Blue-throated Bee-eater (not win)
- ☐ Common Goldenback
- ☐ Barn Swallow m
- ☐ Pacific Swallow

- [ ] Red-whiskered Bulbul
- [ ] Yellow-vented Bulbul
- [ ] Black-naped Oriole
- [ ] House Crow
- [ ] Large-billed Crow
- [ ] Magpie Robin
- [ ] Grey Wagtail m
- [ ] Richard's Pipit
- [ ] Brown Shrike m
- [ ] Philippine Glossy Starling
- [ ] Common Myna
- [ ] White-vented Myna (introduced)
- [ ] Crested Myna (introduced)
- [ ] Brown-throated Sunbird
- [ ] Eurasian Tree-Sparrow
- [ ] Baya Weaver
- [ ] Scaly-breasted Munia
- [ ] Chestnut Munia
- [ ] White-headed Munia

Ground, lower storey:
- [ ] White-breasted Waterhen
- [ ] Spotted Dove
- [ ] Peaceful Dove
- [ ] Greater Coucal
- [ ] Common Iora (also middle storey)
- [ ] Olive-winged Bulbul
- [ ] Abbott's Babbler
- [ ] Grey-throated Babbler
- [ ] Striped Tit-Babbler
- [ ] White-rumped Shama
- [ ] Common Tailorbird
- [ ] Dark-necked Tailorbird
- [ ] Yellow-bellied Prinia
- [ ] Pied Fantail
- [ ] Tiger Shrike m
- [ ] Olive-backed Sunbird
- [ ] Little Spiderhunter
- [ ] Orange-bellied Flowerpecker (also middle storey)
- [ ] White-rumped Munia

Middle storey, canopy:
- [ ] Crested Serpent-Eagle (also overhead)
- [ ] Pink-necked Pigeon (also open areas)
- [ ] Chestnut-breasted Malkoha
- [ ] Coppersmith Barbet
- [ ] Rufous Woodpecker (also lower storey)
- [ ] Grey-capped Woodpecker
- [ ] Pied Triller
- [ ] Black-headed Bulbul
- [ ] Red-eyed Bulbul

- [ ] Greater Racket-tailed Drongo
- [ ] Asian Fairy-Bluebird
- [ ] Flyeater
- [ ] Arctic Warbler m
- [ ] Asian Brown Flycatcher m
- [ ] Asian Paradise-Flycatcher
- [ ] Crimson-breasted Flowerpecker
- [ ] Scarlet-backed Flowerpecker

Difficult-to-find or rare species:
- [ ] Black-shouldered Kite
- [ ] Grey-faced Buzzard m
- [ ] Changeable Hawk-Eagle
- [ ] Blue-breasted Quail
- [ ] Barred Buttonquail
- [ ] Pintail Snipe m
- [ ] Brown-headed Gull m
- [ ] Thick-billed Pigeon
- [ ] Little Green Pigeon
- [ ] Pied Imperial Pigeon
- [ ] Green-winged (Emerald Dove) Pigeon
- [ ] Malayan (Little) Bronze-Cuckoo
- [ ] Drongo Cuckoo
- [ ] Raffles' Malkoha
- [ ] Lesser Coucal
- [ ] Barn Owl
- [ ] Collared Scops-Owl
- [ ] Spotted Wood-Owl
- [ ] Malaysian Eared Nightjar
- [ ] Brown Needletail
- [ ] Common Kingfisher (especially win)
- [ ] Black-capped Kingfisher m
- [ ] Buff-necked Woodpecker
- [ ] Ashy Minivet m
- [ ] Straw-headed Bulbul
- [ ] Grey-bellied Bulbul
- [ ] Crow-billed Drongo m
- [ ] Short-tailed Babbler
- [ ] Inornate Warbler m
- [ ] Ashy Tailorbird
- [ ] Forest Wagtail m
- [ ] Purple-backed Starling m
- [ ] Hill Myna
- [ ] Ruby-cheeked Sunbird
- [ ] Purple-throated Sunbird
- [ ] Copper-throated Sunbird
- [ ] Crimson Sunbird
- [ ] Yellow-eared Spiderhunter
- [ ] Grey-breasted Spiderhunter
- [ ] Plain Flowerpecker

☐ Oriental White-eye
☐ Plain-backed Sparrow
☐ Java Sparrow (introduced)

Access and accommodation

You can get to Penang by road (via a most impressive bridge - the longest in Asia), by ferry (there's a 24-hour vehicle and passenger service between Butterworth and Georgetown), or by air (Malaysia Airlines fly there daily from most major centres in the region).

There is of course plenty of accommodation on the island, including international-standard hotels in Georgetown and along the northern beach strip. You can get a room at one of the cheaper hotels in Georgetown for around $M25 a night; the YMCA is at 211 Jalan Macalister, and the YWCA is off Jalan Air Itam (near the State Mosque).

When to visit

Penang is a hot and sticky place at any time of the year, but the top of Penang Hill, where it is usually about 5 degrees C cooler than in the lowlands, provides some relief from the heat - and crowds - of Georgetown. At weekends and during holiday times, when all of Penang seems to head for the hills, the summit area is packed with people and you may have to wait an hour or more for a train.

Other attractions

The tourist brochures claim that Penang 'is a gourmet's paradise' - it is, and it's worth going there for the food alone. As well, Georgetown has many interesting historic buildings (most of them are in the vicinity of Fort Cornwallis, where Captain Francis Light first landed on the island) and there are a number of temples worth seeing - for example, Wat Chayamangkalaram (a Thai Buddhist temple housing what's said to be the world's third largest reclining Buddha), Snake Temple (with venomous pit vipers coiled around the altars - in a dazed state!) and Kuan Yin Teng Temple (the oldest temple in Penang, built around 1800).

17 Cameron Highlands Pahang

A region famous for its tea plantations, hill resorts and colourful gardens, the Cameron Highlands is a good place to go walking and birdwatching, not least because of its relatively cool climate (the daytime temperature seldom exceeds 25 degrees C). Although not as well known among birders as Fraser's Hill, the Cameron Highlands supports most of the montane birds found in West Malaysia, including Mountain Peacock-Pheasant, Barred Cuckoo-Dove, Golden-throated Barbet (almost a certainty on G. Brinchang), Grey-headed Woodpecker (this site and G. Tahan in Taman Negara are the only places in Malaysia where you'll find the species), Bay Woodpecker, Orange-bellied Leafbird, Green Magpie, Blue Nuthatch, Chestnut-crowned Laughingthrush, Cutia, Black-eared Shrike-Babbler, Chestnut-tailed Minla (above 1525 m [5000 feet]; G. Brinchang is one of the best places in Malaysia for this beautiful bird), White-tailed Robin, Slaty-backed Forktail (there are several places where this bird is usually easy to find), Malayan Whistling Thrush, Snowy-browed Flycatcher, Rufous-vented Niltava (above 1525 m; G. Brinchang is probably the best place in Malaysia for the species), Pygmy Blue Flycatcher, Tawny-breasted Parrotfinch and Brown Bullfinch.

The Cameron Highlands can be broadly defined as the area stretching from Ringlet in the south to G. Brinchang in the north (see map). Forming part of the Main Range, the highlands consist of a series of steep-sided mountains that are mostly over 1525 m (5000 feet); G. Brinchang, the region's highest point, rises to over 2000 m (about 6600 feet). A winding mountain road runs through the area, connecting the villages of Ringlet, Tanah Rata and Brinchang, and providing access to a lake, a golf course, numerous forest walks, and other points of interest.

Much of the southern part of the highlands, around Ringlet, is given over to tea plantations; tea is also grown extensively beyond Brinchang village, as are vegetables and flowers. Despite widespread clearing for agriculture, extensive tracts of forest remain, particularly on the higher slopes away from the main road. At the highest elevations - such as the summit of G. Brinchang - the forest gives way to ericaceous (stunted) scrub, which in West Malaysia occurs only on the most lofty peaks.

Good birdwatching areas

The Cameron Highlands is an easy place to explore, both by car and on foot. In general, the roads are busy and therefore not very good for birdwatching; however, there is an extensive network of walking trails, centred on the village of Tanah Rata, and although some tracks are rather steep in places, others are fairly level and most are productive for birds. (You can get a map showing the walking trails from shops and hotels in Tanah Rata.)

There are walks of about an hour or so to waterfalls such as Parit Falls (path 4) and Robinson Falls (path 9), as well as longer treks of three hours or more to mountain peaks such as G. Beremban (1840 m [6041 feet]), G. Jasar (1636 m [5365 feet]) and G. Perdah (1576 m [5170 feet]). You should, however, take care not to get lost - many of the signposts are in urgent need of repair! For Slaty-backed Forktail and Malayan Whistling Thrush

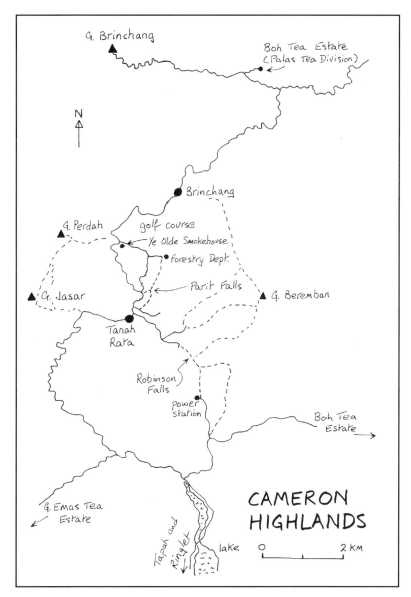

try the walk to Robinson Falls, especially the first section (Tanah Rata end). If you miss out on the forktail here, take the path to Parit Falls where your chances of seeing the bird are probably even better (get out early in the morning though, before too many people are about). Along the Parit Falls track the best spot for the forktail is within the first 500 or 600 m, beyond the buildings at the edge of Tanah Rata. At this point you look down on a fast-flowing stream with numerous rocks and boulders; watch for sudden movements below, and listen for the forktail's sharp, metallic whistle. If you haven't found the bird by the time you reach the falls, turn back and try again - the forktail is easy to overlook.

You shouldn't even think of leaving the Cameron Highlands until you have made at least one trip to the summit of G. Brinchang. Being off the beaten track it is not the easiest place to get to, but that of course means that you'll have the place virtually to yourself. And as you go higher up the mountain the vegetation becomes more stunted, enabling you to get eyeball-to-eyeball views of some of Malaysia's most attractive birds - Golden-throated Barbet, Chestnut-capped Laughingthrush, Silver-eared Mesia, Chestnut-tailed Minla and Rufous-vented Niltava to name a few. If you don't have your own transport, the best way to get to G. Brinchang is by taxi; ask the driver to keep going up Jalan G. Brinchang for a kilometre or so beyond the turn-off to the Boh Tea Estate (Palas Tea Division - see map), then get out and walk the remaining two or three kilometres to the summit. Don't forget to arrange for the taxi to come back and collect you; alternatively, you can walk all the way down to the main road and get a lift or a taxi from there.

Birds

Open areas, overhead:
☐ Eurasian (Crested) Honey-Buzzard (especially Oct-Nov)
☐ Crested Serpent-Eagle
☐ Japanese Sparrowhawk m (especially Oct-Nov)
☐ Blyth's Hawk-Eagle
☐ Mountain Imperial Pigeon (also forest canopy)
☐ Spotted Dove
☐ White-bellied (Glossy) Swiftlet
☐ Brown Needletail
☐ Fork-tailed Swift m
☐ House Swift
☐ Barn Swallow m
☐ Pacific Swallow
☐ Stripe-throated Bulbul (lower levels - e.g. below
  Ringlet)
☐ Yellow-vented Bulbul
☐ Large-billed Crow
☐ Magpie Robin
☐ Yellow-bellied Prinia
☐ Grey Wagtail m
☐ Richard's Pipit
☐ Brown Shrike m
☐ Common Myna
☐ Eurasian Tree-Sparrow
☐ Scaly-breasted Munia

Ground, lower storey:
☐ Mountain Scops-Owl
☐ Collared Owlet (often active during the day)

☐ Ochraceous Bulbul (also middle storey)
☐ Streaked Wren-Babbler
☐ Golden Babbler (also middle storey; often in bird waves)
☐ Grey-throated Babbler (often in bird waves)
☐ Mountain Fulvetta (also middle storey)
☐ White-tailed Robin (try the road to G. Brinchang)
☐ Slaty-backed Forktail
☐ Malayan Whistling Thrush*
☐ Blue Whistling Thrush
☐ Siberian Thrush m (mainly Oct-Dec and Mar-Apr)
☐ Eye-browed Thrush m (mainly Oct-Dec and Mar-Apr)
☐ Dark-necked Tailorbird (lower levels)
☐ Mugimaki Flycatcher m
☐ Large Niltava (also middle storey)
☐ Black-throated Sunbird (also middle storey; often seen in gardens)
☐ Little Spiderhunter (lower levels)

Middle storey, canopy:
☐ Black-thighed Falconet
☐ Little Cuckoo-Dove
☐ Large Hawk-Cuckoo
☐ Fire-tufted Barbet (one of the most common birds in the highlands)
☐ Golden-throated Barbet
☐ Black-browed Barbet
☐ Speckled Piculet (often in bird waves)
☐ Greater Yellownape
☐ Lesser Yellownape
☐ Bay Woodpecker (look along the road to G. Brinchang)
☐ Bar-winged Flycatcher-shrike
☐ Large (Black-faced) Cuckoo-shrike
☐ Lesser Cuckoo-shrike (lower levels)
☐ Grey-chinned Minivet
☐ Orange-bellied Leafbird
☐ Black-crested Bulbul
☐ Mountain Bulbul
☐ Ashy Bulbul
☐ Lesser Racket-tailed Drongo (a bird-wave species)
☐ Black-and-Crimson Oriole (a bird-wave species)
☐ Green Magpie
☐ Chestnut-capped Laughingthrush
☐ Silver-eared Mesia (also lower storey)
☐ White-browed Shrike-Babbler
☐ Black-eared Shrike-Babbler
☐ Blue-winged Minla
☐ Chestnut-tailed Minla
☐ Rufous-winged Fulvetta
☐ Long-tailed Sibia

- [ ] Chestnut-crowned Warbler
- [ ] Yellow-breasted Warbler (also lower storey)
- [ ] Mountain Leaf-Warbler
- [ ] Mountain Tailorbird (also lower storey)
- [ ] Asian Brown Flycatcher m (lower levels)
- [ ] Little Pied Flycatcher
- [ ] White-throated Fantail (also lower storey)
- [ ] Streaked Spiderhunter (also lower storey; often in gardens)
- [ ] Buff-bellied Flowerpecker
- [ ] Everett's White-eye

Difficult-to-find or rare species:
- [ ] Chinese Goshawk m
- [ ] Black Eagle (hunts low over the canopy)
- [ ] Rufous-bellied Eagle
- [ ] Changeable Hawk-Eagle
- [ ] Bar-backed (Hill) Partridge
- [ ] Mountain Peacock-Pheasant*
- [ ] White-breasted Waterhen (grass beside streams)
- [ ] Yellow-vented Pigeon
- [ ] Wedge-tailed Pigeon
- [ ] Barred Cuckoo-Dove
- [ ] Oriental Cuckoo
- [ ] Green-billed Malkoha
- [ ] Giant Swiftlet
- [ ] Himalayan Swiftlet m
- [ ] White-vented Needletail m
- [ ] Orange-breasted Trogon
- [ ] Red-headed Trogon
- [ ] Grey-headed Woodpecker (above 1380 m [4500 feet]; in Malaysia, known only from this locality and G. Tahan in Taman Negara)
- [ ] Silver-breasted Broadbill
- [ ] Long-tailed Broadbill
- [ ] Asian House-Martin m
- [ ] Sultan Tit
- [ ] Blue Nuthatch
- [ ] Pygmy Wren-Babbler
- [ ] Chestnut-crowned Laughingthrush
- [ ] Cutia
- [ ] Lesser Shortwing
- [ ] Rufous-headed Robin m (one record only - in March 1963 one was mist-netted at 2000 m [6600 feet] on G. Brinchang)
- [ ] Inornate Warbler m
- [ ] Pallas's (Grasshopper) Warbler m
- [ ] Lanceolated Warbler m
- [ ] Common Tailorbird (listen for it in tea plantations)
- [ ] Ferruginous Flycatcher m
- [ ] Rufous-browed Flycatcher

☐ Snowy-browed Flycatcher (above 1430 m [4700 feet])
☐ Rufous-vented Niltava
☐ Hill Blue Flycatcher
☐ Pygmy Blue Flycatcher
☐ Olive Tree-Pipit m (try around the edge of the golf
  course)
☐ Scarlet Sunbird
☐ Tawny-breasted Parrotfinch (favours bamboo)
☐ Brown Bullfinch

Access and accommodation

Tanah Rata is about 60 km from the town of Tapah, which is on the Kuala Lumpur to Ipoh road about 160 km north of KL. Those starting out from KL can catch a bus to the highlands from the Pudu Raya terminal; buses leave daily at 8.30 a.m. and the fare is about $M20. You can also get to Tanah Rata by bus from Tapah for about $M8, and from Ipoh for about $M15. Taxis are easy to find in Tanah Rata, Brinchang and Ringlet.

There is of course no shortage of accommodation in the highlands, including hotels, resthouses, chalets and bungalows. Prices range from $M20 to $M50 for a double room at some of the cheaper hotels, but you can pay as much as $M100 or more at places like the Lakehouse Hotel and Ye Olde Smokehouse. At certain times of the year, particularly during school holidays (international as well as local), it would be wise to book a room in advance - for more information 'phone Malaysia Tourism in KL on 03-2935188, or the Cameron Highlands Tourist Office on 05-901266.

When to visit

As is usual in the Malaysian highlands, low cloud, mist and rain could disrupt outdoor activities at any time of the year, although this is less likely in February-March and July-August. Most of the more sought-after birds are residents, but for migratory species such as raptors a visit during autumn (Sept-Nov) or spring (Feb-Apr) would be best.

Other attractions

Despite there being a number of shops selling mounted butterflies to souvenir-hungry tourists, there are still many beautiful specimens to be seen in the wild - Rajah Brooke's Birdwing is perhaps the most striking and handsome of all; look for it around waterfalls, including the big cascade half way up the main road from Tapah. Large animals are generally scarce in the Cameron Highlands, possibly because so much of the area is used for agriculture (this may account for the scarcity of birds like hornbills too).

Scenic attractions are certainly not hard to find: forested slopes rising above manicured tea estates and terraced vegetable gardens, crystal-clear waterfalls plunging to natural swimming pools, and stately bungalows set in grounds brilliant with all sorts of garden flowers are just some of the sights the tourists come to see. Another is Ye Olde Smokehouse at Brinchang - try the tea and cakes even if you can't afford to stay there. At the other end of the cultural scale are the traditional Orang Asli ('original people') settlements that you'll see beside the main road as you travel up from Tapah.

18 Bukit Larut (Maxwell Hill) Perak

Bukit Larut, or Maxwell Hill as it used to be called, is Malaysia's oldest and least known hill station. Consisting of nothing more than a handful of bungalows and resthouses, the area has so far escaped the attentions of developers who no doubt have been put off by the remoteness of the place. At one time you could only get to Bukit Larut on foot or on horseback - today the horses have been replaced by Land Rovers, and the exciting ten-kilometre journey from Taiping to the hill station takes about 30 minutes, along a narrow, one-way road with more than 70 hair-pin bends.

In stark contrast to the hot and humid plains below, the hill station is set a delightful 1100 m (3600 feet) above sea level where dense, swirling clouds provide welcome relief from the midday sun. And unlike nearby Taiping, with its seemingly endless hustle and bustle, Bukit Larut is marvellously tranquil with hardly a human or vehicle in sight. Needless to say it makes an excellent birdwatching destination, and although there are only a few walking tracks in the area, the road to the top provides plenty of opportunities for birding. More than 200 species have been recorded, including such highlights as Great Argus, Orange-breasted and Red-headed Trogon, Red-bearded Bee-eater, White-crowned and six other hornbills, Fire-tufted and Black-browed Barbet, Silver-breasted and Long-tailed Broadbill, Lesser Racket-tailed Drongo, Black-and-Crimson Oriole, Green Magpie, Large and Chestnut-backed Scimitar-Babbler, Streaked and Pygmy Wren-Babbler, Chestnut-naped and Slaty-backed Forktail, Verditer Flycatcher, Black-throated and Scarlet Sunbird, Streaked Spiderhunter and Buff-bellied Flowerpecker.

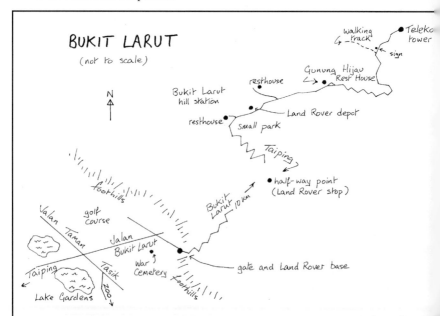

Good birdwatching areas

The road from the foot of the hill climbs steeply to the small collection of buildings that make up Bukit Larut, then continues for a further two or three kilometres to a Telekom tower at the summit of G. Hijau, almost 1450 m (4750 feet) above sea level. If you spend two or three days in the area, you'll have time to explore not only the hill station itself, but also at least part of the road up from Taiping. You could for example walk the first four or five kilometres down to the half-way point, where the Land Rovers stop for a short time, then get a ride back up. Better still, walk all the way to the bottom, then catch the Land Rover from there.

By spending time at different altitudes you will, of course, increase your chances of seeing the greatest variety of birds, and to get the most out of this site you should also allow time for birding around Taiping's Lake Gardens, which lie at the base of the hill. Near the top, there are a couple of walking tracks leading into the dense rainforest - one leaves the bitumen about 1.5 km uphill from the Gunung Hijau Rest House, near a sign marked 'Gunung Hijau 4751 feet'. If you're not fond of leeches, however, it would be best to stay on the road!

Birds

As used here, the term 'lower levels' indicates that the bird is most likely to be found from the bottom of the hill to just beyond the half-way point along the Bukit Larut road, while 'upper levels' indicates that you should look for the species around the hill station, or between the hill station and the Telekom tower. If neither term is used, the bird could occur anywhere.

Open areas, overhead:
- ☐ Crested Serpent-Eagle
- ☐ Black Eagle (upper levels; hunts low over forest canopy)
- ☐ Rufous-bellied Eagle (upper levels)
- ☐ Changeable Hawk-Eagle
- ☐ Blyth's Hawk-Eagle (upper levels)
- ☐ Mountain Imperial Pigeon (upper levels; often seen flying past early in the day)
- ☐ White-bellied (Glossy) Swiftlet
- ☐ Brown Needletail
- ☐ House Swift
- ☐ Blue-throated Bee-eater
- ☐ Red-rumped Swallow
- ☐ Grey Wagtail m (often along roads)

Ground, lower storey:
- ☐ Mountain Scops-Owl (upper levels)
- ☐ Ochraceous Bulbul (upper levels; also middle storey)
- ☐ Streaked Wren-Babbler (upper levels)
- ☐ Pygmy Wren-Babbler (upper levels; quite common, but can be hard to see - try just uphill from the Gunung Hijau Rest House)
- ☐ Grey-throated Babbler (upper levels; often in bird waves)

- [ ] Grey-headed Babbler (lower levels)
- [ ] Striped Tit-Babbler
- [ ] Chestnut-crowned Laughingthrush (upper levels; also middle storey)
- [ ] White-rumped Shama (lower levels)
- [ ] Chestnut-naped Forktail (lower levels; often along streams close to the road up from Taiping - look for it flying ahead of the Land Rover, especially early in the day)
- [ ] Slaty-backed Forktail (upper levels)
- [ ] Dark-necked Tailorbird
- [ ] Mountain Tailorbird (upper levels; also middle storey)
- [ ] Yellow-rumped Flycatcher m (lower levels)
- [ ] Rufous-browed Flycatcher (upper levels)
- [ ] Grey-headed Flycatcher (also middle storey)
- [ ] Rufous-winged Flycatcher (lower levels; also middle storey)
- [ ] Scarlet Sunbird (lower levels; look for it in the flowering shrubs around the buildings at the half-way stop)
- [ ] Little Spiderhunter (lower levels)

Middle storey, canopy:
- [ ] Wedge-tailed Pigeon (upper levels; at fruits)
- [ ] Thick-billed Pigeon (at fruits)
- [ ] Little Cuckoo-Dove (upper levels; often seen flying along the road)
- [ ] Blue-crowned Hanging Parrot
- [ ] Oriental Cuckoo (upper levels)
- [ ] Banded Bay Cuckoo (lower levels)
- [ ] Drongo Cuckoo (lower levels)
- [ ] Green-billed Malkoha (upper levels)
- [ ] Red-billed Malkoha (lower levels)
- [ ] Chestnut-breasted Malkoha (lower levels)
- [ ] Collared Owlet (upper levels; also lower storey; often active during the day)
- [ ] Orange-breasted Trogon (upper levels, although not as high as the next species)
- [ ] Red-headed Trogon (upper levels)
- [ ] Banded Kingfisher
- [ ] Red-bearded Bee-eater
- [ ] White-crowned Hornbill (upper levels; all hornbills also overhead)
- [ ] Bushy-crested Hornbill
- [ ] Wreathed Hornbill
- [ ] Rhinoceros Hornbill
- [ ] Great Hornbill
- [ ] Helmeted Hornbill
- [ ] Fire-tufted Barbet (upper levels)
- [ ] Gold-whiskered Barbet (lower levels)

☐ Golden-throated Barbet (only at the highest levels)
☐ Black-browed Barbet (upper levels)
☐ Blue-eared Barbet (lower levels)
☐ Brown Barbet (lower levels)
☐ Speckled Piculet (upper levels; a bird-wave species)
☐ Crimson-winged Woodpecker (lower levels)
☐ Banded Woodpecker (lower levels)
☐ Buff-rumped Woodpecker (lower levels)
☐ Maroon Woodpecker (lower levels)
☐ Black-and-Yellow Broadbill (lower levels)
☐ Silver-breasted Broadbill (upper levels)
☐ Long-tailed Broadbill (upper levels)
☐ Bar-winged Flycatcher-shrike
☐ Grey-chinned Minivet (upper levels)
☐ Blue-winged Leafbird
☐ Orange-bellied Leafbird (upper levels)
☐ Black-headed Bulbul (lower levels)
☐ Black-crested Bulbul (upper levels)
☐ Red-eyed Bulbul (lower levels)
☐ Mountain Bulbul (upper levels)
☐ Ashy Bulbul (upper levels)
☐ Bronzed Drongo (edges; also open areas)
☐ Lesser Racket-tailed Drongo (upper levels)
☐ Greater Racket-tailed Drongo (lower levels)
☐ Black-and-Crimson Oriole (upper levels)
☐ Asian Fairy-Bluebird
☐ Green Magpie (upper levels; try around the Gunung Hijau Rest House)
☐ Sultan Tit (upper levels)
☐ Velvet-fronted Nuthatch
☐ Chestnut-backed Scimitar-Babbler (upper levels; try along the road just downhill from the Gunung Hijau Rest House)
☐ Golden Babbler (upper levels; also lower storey; a bird-wave species)
☐ Chestnut-capped Laughingthrush (upper levels)
☐ Silver-eared Mesia (upper levels; also lower storey)
☐ White-browed Shrike-Babbler (upper levels)
☐ Blue-winged Minla (upper levels)
☐ Rufous-winged Fulvetta (upper levels)
☐ Mountain Fulvetta (upper levels; also lower storey)
☐ Long-tailed Sibia (upper levels)
☐ White-bellied Yuhina
☐ Chestnut-crowned Warbler (upper levels)
☐ Inornate Warbler m
☐ Eastern Crowned Warbler m (lower levels)
☐ Mountain Leaf-Warbler (upper levels)
☐ Asian Brown Flycatcher m
☐ Verditer Flycatcher (upper levels)
☐ Little Pied Flycatcher (upper levels; often along

roadsides)
- [ ] Large Niltava (upper levels; also lower storey)
- [ ] Hill Blue Flycatcher (upper levels)
- [ ] White-throated Fantail (upper levels; also lower storey)
- [ ] Asian Paradise-Flycatcher
- [ ] Black-throated Sunbird (upper levels; also lower storey and in gardens)
- [ ] Long-billed Spiderhunter (lower levels)
- [ ] Streaked Spiderhunter (upper levels; also in garden shrubs - look for it around the bungalows)
- [ ] Crimson-breasted Flowerpecker (lower levels)
- [ ] Buff-bellied Flowerpecker (upper levels)
- [ ] Everett's White-eye

Difficult-to-find or rare species:
- [ ] Black Baza m (mainly Sept-Nov)
- [ ] Eurasian (Crested) Honey-Buzzard (mainly Sept-Nov)
- [ ] Japanese Sparrowhawk m (mainly Sept-Nov)
- [ ] Bar-backed (Hill) Partridge (upper levels)
- [ ] Crested Wood-Partridge (lower levels; look along the road from Taiping early in the morning)
- [ ] Red Junglefowl
- [ ] Great Argus (lower levels; quite often heard, but seldom seen)
- [ ] Jambu Fruit-Dove
- [ ] Green Imperial Pigeon (lower levels)
- [ ] Barred Cuckoo-Dove (upper levels)
- [ ] Large Hawk-Cuckoo (upper levels)
- [ ] Hodgson's Hawk-Cuckoo (lower levels)
- [ ] Reddish Scops-Owl
- [ ] Collared Scops-Owl (lower levels)
- [ ] Barred Eagle-Owl (lower levels)
- [ ] Grey Nightjar m
- [ ] Wrinkled Hornbill (lower levels)
- [ ] Red-throated Barbet (lower levels)
- [ ] Yellow-crowned Barbet (lower levels)
- [ ] Lesser Yellownape (upper levels)
- [ ] Dusky Broadbill (lower levels)
- [ ] Rusty-naped Pitta (upper levels)
- [ ] Blue-winged Pitta (mainly Sept-Nov)
- [ ] Hooded Pitta m (mainly Sept-Nov)
- [ ] Asian House-Martin m (upper levels)
- [ ] Large (Black-faced) Cuckoo-shrike (upper levels)
- [ ] Lesser Cuckoo-shrike (lower levels)
- [ ] Crow-billed Drongo m (lower levels)
- [ ] Blue Nuthatch (upper levels)
- [ ] Large Scimitar-Babbler (upper levels)
- [ ] Marbled Wren-Babbler (upper levels)
- [ ] Cutia (at the highest levels; one record only)

- [ ] Lesser Shortwing (upper levels)
- [ ] White-tailed Robin (upper levels)
- [ ] White-throated Rock-Thrush m (vagrant; a male was seen in Dec 1983 in a roadside fruiting tree, together with the next two species)
- [ ] Orange-headed Thrush m (mainly Oct-Dec)
- [ ] Siberian Thrush m (mainly Oct-Dec)
- [ ] Eye-browed Thrush m (mainly Oct-Dec)
- [ ] Ferruginous Flycatcher m
- [ ] Mugimaki Flycatcher m (chiefly upper levels)
- [ ] Blue-and-White Flycatcher m (chiefly upper levels)
- [ ] Tickell's Blue Flycatcher (lower levels)
- [ ] Pygmy Blue Flycatcher (upper levels)
- [ ] Spotted Fantail (mostly lower levels)
- [ ] Forest Wagtail m
- [ ] Olive Tree-Pipit m (upper levels)
- [ ] Tawny-breasted Parrotfinch (upper levels; recorded only once, in 1989)

Additional species for Taiping (Lake Gardens and vicinity):
- [ ] Black-thighed Falconet
- [ ] White-breasted Waterhen
- [ ] Pink-necked Pigeon
- [ ] Common Koel
- [ ] Greater Coucal
- [ ] Large-tailed Nightjar
- [ ] Asian Palm-Swift
- [ ] Common Kingfisher (especially win)
- [ ] Stork-billed Kingfisher
- [ ] White-throated Kingfisher
- [ ] Blue-tailed Bee-eater (absent in sum)
- [ ] Dollarbird
- [ ] Coppersmith Barbet
- [ ] Rufous Woodpecker
- [ ] Common Goldenback
- [ ] Grey-capped Woodpecker
- [ ] Barn Swallow m
- [ ] Pacific Swallow
- [ ] Common Iora
- [ ] Yellow-vented Bulbul
- [ ] Olive-winged Bulbul
- [ ] Black-naped Oriole
- [ ] Large-billed Crow
- [ ] Magpie Robin
- [ ] Common Tailorbird
- [ ] Pied Fantail
- [ ] Brown Shrike m
- [ ] Tiger Shrike m
- [ ] Philippine Glossy Starling
- [ ] Common Myna

- [ ] Jungle Myna
- [ ] Brown-throated Sunbird
- [ ] Scarlet-backed Flowerpecker
- [ ] Eurasian Tree-Sparrow
- [ ] Scaly-breasted Munia

Access and accommodation

Once you reach Taiping, which is approximately 300 km north of Kuala Lumpur via Ipoh, make for the Lake Gardens and get on to Jalan Taman Tasik. Near the zoo, turn into Jalan Bukit Larut and keep going for a kilometre or so past the War Cemetery until you reach the gate at the start of the road up to the hill station. (Any taxi driver in Taiping will know how to get there.) Land Rovers leave for the top every half an hour or so between 8.00 a.m. and 6.00 p.m., and at weekends and during holiday periods you should book your ride in advance - 'phone 05-827243. At other times a place in a Land Rover should be easy to get, but you will need to prove to the official at the gatehouse that you have booked accommodation, otherwise you will not be allowed to go up. (It may seem bureaucratic, but you wouldn't want to be stuck at the top with nowhere to stay overnight!) The Land Rover trip is an experience in itself, and it's worth every cent of the two or three dollars you'll be charged.

Accommodation at Bukit Larut consists of three bungalows and two resthouses, with prices ranging from $M15 to $M100 a night for a double room (the bungalows and resthouses accommodate between six and 10 people each). By far the best place to stay is the Gunung Hijau Rest House; not only is it comfortable, cheap ($M15 a double at present) and clean, it is situated well away from the other bungalows in a truly superb forest setting where the views are magnificent, and where the only sound you'll hear at night is that of the wind in the trees. What's more, the present manager - Guna - has spent almost all his life at Bukit Larut and he knows the area intimately, including the haunts of many of the birds and other animals. To reserve accommodation at the hill station 'phone 05-827241, or write to the Officer-in-Charge, Bukit Larut Hill Resort, Taiping, Perak 34020. Guna at the Gunung Hijau Rest House can be contacted direct on 05-827240, or by writing to Rumah Rehat Gunung Hijau, Bukit Larut, Taiping, Perak 34020.

When to visit

With daytime temperatures averaging little more than 20 degrees C, Bukit Larut is a pleasant place to go walking and birdwatching all year round, although since this is West Malaysia's wettest spot you may want to avoid the height of the north-east monsoon season (usually November-January). For migrant birds, a visit between late September and late November would probably be most productive. While the place is nowhere near as popular as Malaysia's other hill stations (Fraser's Hill for example), more and more people are going there during school and public holidays, and at weekends - if possible, don't go at these times.

Other attractions

Among the other animals you could see here are the White-handed Gibbon, Siamang (Black Gibbon), Spectacled Leaf Monkey, Pig-tailed Macaque (lower levels), Colugo (Flying Lemur), Brush-tailed Porcupine (a semi-tame one visits the Gunung Hijau Rest House most nights), Clouded Leopard (ask Guna where to look for this beautiful but elusive cat), Barking Deer, Malay Tapir, and a wide variety of squirrels. There are also numerous butterflies and moths (including the Atlas Moth, the world's largest), as well as countless plants, among them many delicate orchids and fascinating pitcher plants.

19 Pulau Langkawi   Kedah

Langkawi is one of a group of more than a hundred islands off the north-western coast of Peninsular Malaysia, just south of the Thai border. Measuring some 30 km (east to west) by 20 km, it is the largest island in the group and, with an airport and a good road system, it is the easiest to get to and the most convenient to explore. Needless to say, any island that can be promoted as a 'true tropical paradise' is fair game for developers, and since Langkawi fits that description quite readily it has its share of beach resorts and the other paraphernalia that sun-seeking tourists demand. All the same, so far at least, this large island has not been devastated by development - the resorts have in fact been designed with some sensitivity - and thus it is still possible to find areas of relatively undisturbed habitat, as well as villagers living more or less the same rural lifestyle they have for decades.

Although Langkawi is not exactly teeming with bird life, the island does have some special attractions - for example, Red-wattled Lapwing and Brown-winged Kingfisher are probably easier to find here than anywhere else in Malaysia, and there are some splendid forests where you have a good chance of seeing Great Slaty Woodpecker and Great Hornbill. Added to that, the area's bird list includes 10 species of pigeon (among them Green and Pied Imperial Pigeon and, on the smaller islands, Nicobar Pigeon) as well as six species of sunbird. In all, some 150 species have been recorded on the Langkawi group of islands.

PULAU LANGKAWI

Good birdwatching areas

You can see most of what Langkawi has to offer in two or three days - but you will need a car to get around the main island, and you'll need more time if you want to visit smaller islands such as Pulau Singa Besar, where there are walking tracks and shelter huts, and Pulau Dayang Bunting, which has a large freshwater lake and a 90-metre high limestone cave.

On Langkawi, the best of the forests are those on the slopes of G. Raya, which rises about 900 m (3000 feet) above sea level, and those at the western end of the island where there are several forest reserves, including G. Machinchang Forest Reserve which contains Langkawi's most famous waterfall - Telaga Tujuh. There's a bitumen road leading to the summit of G. Raya, which is situated roughly in the centre of the island, and the forests here are usually good for Great Hornbill, Great Slaty Woodpecker and a number of other species. For G. Machinchang Forest Reserve, drive to Pantai Kok, west of the airport, then continue on to Tanjung Burau and take the gravel road to the Telaga Tujuh waterfall where there are a number of forest trails.

Some good ricefield habitat can be found in the central and southern parts of Langkawi, for example along the roads between Kuah town and the airport, while mudflats and mangroves occur mainly along the island's eastern and northern shores. There are some well-established gardens - good for a variety of species, including sunbirds - in the vicinity of the Langkawi Island Resort, at the south-eastern end of the island.

Birds

Open (dry) areas, overhead:
- [ ] Black-shouldered Kite (also ricefields)
- [ ] Barred Buttonquail
- [ ] Spotted Dove (also gardens, scrub, plantations)
- [ ] Greater Coucal
- [ ] Large-tailed Nightjar
- [ ] Brown Needletail
- [ ] Fork-tailed Swift m
- [ ] House Swift
- [ ] Asian Palm-Swift
- [ ] White-throated Kingfisher (also ricefields)
- [ ] Blue-tailed Bee-eater (scarce in sum)
- [ ] Blue-throated Bee-eater (absent in win)
- [ ] Barn Swallow m
- [ ] Pacific Swallow
- [ ] Red-rumped Swallow (try the grounds of the Langkawi Island Resort)
- [ ] Large-billed Crow
- [ ] Grey Wagtail m (often on roads and in drains)
- [ ] Forest Wagtail m (look in areas of short, cut grass close to the forest edge; also gardens and mangroves)
- [ ] Richard's Pipit (also ricefields)
- [ ] Brown Shrike m (often seen perched along roadsides)
- [ ] Philippine Glossy Starling

☐ Common Myna
☐ Eurasian Tree-Sparrow

Mudflats, mangroves:
☐ Brahminy Kite (could occur almost anywhere on the island)
☐ White-bellied Sea-Eagle (also over coastal forests)
☐ Greater Sand-Plover m
☐ Common Redshank m
☐ Common Tern m
☐ Chestnut-breasted Malkoha (mangroves)
☐ Common Kingfisher (especially win; also ricefields)
☐ Black-capped Kingfisher m (also ricefields)
☐ Collared Kingfisher
☐ Green Iora (mangroves; also forest edge)
☐ Ashy Drongo (mangroves; also coastal scrub)
☐ Abbott's Babbler (mangroves; also coastal scrub and forests)
☐ Ashy Tailorbird (mangroves; also coastal scrub)
☐ Mangrove Whistler
☐ Copper-throated Sunbird (mangroves; also coastal scrub)

Ricefields:
☐ Little Heron (common; sometimes in groups of 20 or more; also mudflats and mangroves)
☐ Cattle Egret m (associates with water buffalo)
☐ White-breasted Waterhen
☐ Asian (Lesser) Golden Plover m (also mudflats)
☐ Little Ringed Plover m (also mudflats)
☐ Mongolian Plover m (also mudflats)
☐ Wood Sandpiper m
☐ Common Sandpiper m (also mudflats)
☐ Pintail Snipe m
☐ Lesser Coucal
☐ Zitting Cisticola

Gardens, scrub, plantations:
☐ Pink-necked Pigeon (also forests)
☐ Peaceful Dove
☐ Plaintive Cuckoo
☐ Common Koel
☐ Chestnut-headed Bee-eater
☐ Dollarbird (also forests; often in high bare branches)
☐ Oriental Pied Hornbill (common in places - frequents large fruiting trees near the Langkawi Island Resort, for example; also forests)
☐ Stripe-throated Bulbul (also forest edge)
☐ Yellow-vented Bulbul
☐ Olive-winged Bulbul
☐ Black-naped Oriole
☐ Magpie Robin

☐ Flyeater (also mangroves)
☐ Common Tailorbird
☐ Dark-necked Tailorbird
☐ Yellow-bellied Prinia (also ricefield edge and forest edge)
☐ Pied Fantail (also mangroves)
☐ Tiger Shrike m (also mangroves and forest edge)
☐ Brown-throated Sunbird (also mangroves and forest edge)
☐ Olive-backed Sunbird (also mangroves)
☐ Orange-bellied Flowerpecker (also forest edge)
☐ Scarlet-backed Flowerpecker (also forest edge)
☐ Baya Weaver
☐ White-rumped Munia (breeds in the grounds of the Langkawi Island Resort)
☐ Scaly-breasted Munia

Forests:
☐ Crested Serpent-Eagle (also overhead)
☐ Crested Goshawk
☐ Thick-billed Pigeon (at fruits; also visits well -established gardens such as those around Langkawi Island Resort)
☐ Green-winged (Emerald Dove) Pigeon
☐ Indian Cuckoo
☐ Drongo Cuckoo
☐ Collared Scops-Owl
☐ Wreathed Hornbill
☐ Great Hornbill
☐ Laced Woodpecker (also coastal scrub and mangroves)
☐ Great Slaty Woodpecker
☐ Ashy Minivet m (also coastal scrub and mangroves)
☐ Black-headed Bulbul
☐ Scaly-breasted Bulbul
☐ Red-eyed Bulbul
☐ Ochraceous Bulbul
☐ Greater Racket-tailed Drongo
☐ Asian Fairy-Bluebird
☐ Short-tailed Babbler
☐ Moustached Babbler
☐ Rufous-crowned Babbler
☐ Chestnut-winged Babbler
☐ Striped Tit-Babbler (also mangroves and scrub)
☐ White-bellied Yuhina
☐ White-rumped Shama
☐ Arctic Warbler m (also mangroves and scrub)
☐ Eastern Crowned Warbler m
☐ Asian Brown Flycatcher m
☐ Black-naped Monarch
☐ Hill Myna

- [ ] Ruby-cheeked Sunbird
- [ ] Crimson Sunbird (also mangroves and coastal scrub)
- [ ] Little Spiderhunter (also gardens and plantations)

Difficult-to-find or rare species:
- [ ] Chinese Pond-Heron m (ricefields)
- [ ] Pacific Reef-Egret (rocky shores and mudflats)
- [ ] Intermediate (Plumed) Egret m
- [ ] Black-crowned Night-Heron (mangroves and ricefields)
- [ ] Malayan Night-Heron m
- [ ] Lesser (Treeduck) Whistling-Duck (ricefields,
      especially when fully flooded)
- [ ] Black Baza m (mainly Oct-Nov)
- [ ] Bat Hawk
- [ ] Grey-headed Fish-Eagle
- [ ] Eastern Marsh-Harrier m
- [ ] Chinese Goshawk m (mainly Oct-Nov)
- [ ] Grey-faced Buzzard m
- [ ] Changeable Hawk-Eagle
- [ ] Eurasian Kestrel m (vagrant)
- [ ] Peregrine Falcon m
- [ ] Slaty-legged Crake m
- [ ] Red-wattled Lapwing (Langkawi is probably the best
      place in Malaysia for this species - try looking in
      the more extensive ricefields, well away from roads)
- [ ] Kentish Plover m
- [ ] Malaysian Plover
- [ ] Bridled Tern
- [ ] Little Green Pigeon
- [ ] Large Green Pigeon
- [ ] Green Imperial Pigeon
- [ ] Pied Imperial Pigeon
- [ ] Nicobar Pigeon (try the more remote, least disturbed
      islands in the group)
- [ ] Chestnut-winged Cuckoo m
- [ ] Hodgson's Hawk-Cuckoo
- [ ] Bay Owl
- [ ] Oriental (Common) Scops-Owl m
- [ ] Brown Hawk-Owl
- [ ] Short-eared Owl m (vagrant)
- [ ] Grey Nightjar m
- [ ] Himalayan Swiftlet m
- [ ] White-vented Needletail m
- [ ] Orange-breasted Trogon
- [ ] Blue-eared Kingfisher
- [ ] Oriental Dwarf Kingfisher
- [ ] Brown-winged Kingfisher (try all areas of mangrove,
      including small patches like those in the vicinity
      of the Langkawi Island Resort)
- [ ] Banded Kingfisher

- [ ] Ruddy Kingfisher
- [ ] Greater Goldenback
- [ ] Blue-winged Pitta (has been recorded breeding here)
- [ ] Mangrove Pitta
- [ ] Crow-billed Drongo m
- [ ] Black-hooded Oriole
- [ ] Puff-throated Babbler
- [ ] Siberian Blue Robin m
- [ ] Blue Rock-Thrush
- [ ] Blue Whistling Thrush
- [ ] Orange-headed Thrush m
- [ ] Eye-browed Thrush m
- [ ] Inornate Warbler m
- [ ] Pale-legged Leaf-Warbler m (vagrant)
- [ ] Pallas's (Grasshopper) Warbler m
- [ ] Yellow-rumped Flycatcher m
- [ ] Mugimaki Flycatcher m
- [ ] Red-throated Flycatcher m
- [ ] Tickell's Blue Flycatcher
- [ ] Purple-throated Sunbird
- [ ] Plain-backed Sparrow

Access and accommodation

Malaysia Airlines (MAS) offers a daily service to Langkawi from Kuala Lumpur; you can also get there by air from some other cities in Malaysia if you go via Penang (for MAS addresses see the front of this book). In addition, there are express ferry services to Kuah (the main town on Langkawi) from Kuala Kedah and Kuala Perlis on the mainland - the trip takes about one hour and the one-way fare is about $M15. Once on the island, you can get around by taxi, minibus or hire car - inquire at the Langkawi Tourist Information Centre, Kompleks Jeti Kuah, Kuah, or 'phone 04-789789. The information centre will also tell you how to get to some of the smaller islands in the group.

There is a range of accommodation on Langkawi. At the top end of the scale you can choose from a number of international-class resorts, including the Pelangi Beach Resort and the Langkawi Island Resort, where double rooms cost $M200 or more. (For sheer unabashed luxury, fabulous views over island-studded waters, and often excellent birding in the surrounding park-like gardens, treat yourself to a stay at the Langkawi Island Resort.) For those with less money to spare, there are hotels in Kuah - not the most picturesque of towns - with rooms from about $M20, or smaller, more modest resorts where you can get a chalet on the beach for around $M30 per night (try the Delta Motel and Restaurant at Kampung Tanjung Mali). Only a few of the other islands in the group have accommodation - ask at the information centre in Kuah.

When to visit

It is hot and humid on Langkawi all year round, although the sea breezes help make conditions a little more bearable than they are on the adjacent mainland. You should of course avoid the main summer holiday period

(June to September); in any case, migrant birds are on the island during winter (September to March). During the south-west monsoon season - July to mid September - seas may be too rough for boat trips to some of the smaller islands.

Other attractions

Unfortunately, turtles do not breed on the Langkawi group, but the snorkelling is said to be good in the waters around Pulau Singa Besar, Pulau Payar and some of the other islands to the south of Langkawi. Other than birds, animals you can expect to see here include Island Flying Fox, Long-tailed Macaque, the beautiful chestnut, black and white Prevost's Squirrel, Mouse-Deer, Water Monitor, geckos and mudskippers.

20 Kenyir Dam
(Tasik Kenyir)   Terengganu

From a birdwatcher's point of view, there are few places on Peninsular Malaysia's east coast that are worth visiting. For instance, nowhere in the east are there hill stations like Fraser's Hill and Bukit Larut, and throughout much of the area oil palm plantations - not the most productive of bird habitats - dominate the landscape. The Kota Bharu to Kuala Terengganu stretch of the coast does have some attractions, however, including long sandy beaches and picturesque fishing villages (both are harder to find further south, despite what the tourist brochures say).

If you do go to Kuala Terengganu, you should consider making a detour to Kenyir Dam, approximately 55 km to the south-west. Covering some 370 square kilometres (two and a half times the size of Singapore), the generally steep-sided dam is not all that attractive to birds; even so, you could spend quite an eventful few days taking a boat trip across the lake, then jungle trekking in the dense forest that grows right to the water's edge.

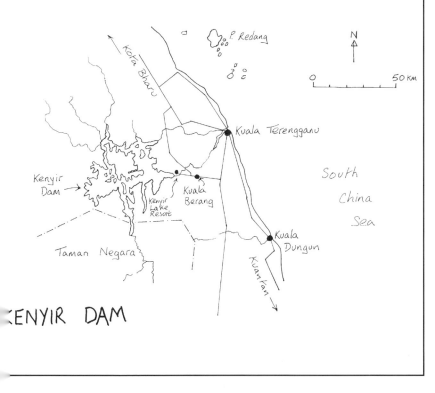

Good birdwatching areas

As mentioned, the dam itself is not particularly good for birds - even in suitable habitat, waterbirds such as pelicans, cormorants, ibis, spoonbills and ducks are scarce in Malaysia - but the forested slopes surrounding the lake support a fair variety of species, and since the area has not been greatly explored by birders you could turn up a few surprises.

The best approach is to organise a boat to take you to one of the more remote parts of the lake and jungle trek from there. To arrange this in advance contact Khairul Annuar of Khairul Adventures, Jalan Sultan Zainal Abidin, Kuala Terengganu, Malaysia 20000, telephone 09-633529. Khairul is a cheerful, very knowledgeable ex-army man who knows this part of the country well and who specialises in jungle trekking and camping holidays. By Malaysian standards his trips are not cheap - $M550 per person for four days, three nights for example - but he arranges everything from the boat to camping equipment, food and a guide. (By the way, he is the person to contact if you want to go to any of the small islands north of Kuala Terengganu, including Pulau Redang, the next site in this book.)

Birds

Open areas (including the lake), overhead:
- [ ] White-bellied Sea-Eagle (breeds locally)
- [ ] Crested Serpent-Eagle
- [ ] Changeable Hawk-Eagle
- [ ] Malaysian Eared Nightjar
- [ ] White-bellied (Glossy) Swiftlet
- [ ] Brown Needletail
- [ ] Silver-rumped Swift
- [ ] Grey-rumped Treeswift
- [ ] Common Kingfisher (especially win)
- [ ] Blue-throated Bee-eater
- [ ] Barn Swallow m
- [ ] Pacific Swallow
- [ ] Red-rumped Swallow (try below the dam wall)
- [ ] Yellow-vented Bulbul
- [ ] Magpie Robin
- [ ] Grey Wagtail m
- [ ] Common Myna
- [ ] Brown-throated Sunbird
- [ ] Eurasian Tree-Sparrow

Ground, lower storey:
- [ ] Red Junglefowl
- [ ] Green-winged (Emerald Dove) Pigeon
- [ ] Maroon Woodpecker (also middle storey)
- [ ] Stripe-throated Bulbul
- [ ] Spectacled Bulbul (also middle storey)
- [ ] Grey-cheeked Bulbul (also middle storey)
- [ ] Yellow-bellied Bulbul
- [ ] Hairy-backed Bulbul

- [ ] Short-tailed Babbler
- [ ] Abbott's Babbler (forest edge)
- [ ] Moustached Babbler (also middle storey)
- [ ] Rufous-crowned Babbler (also middle storey)
- [ ] Grey-headed Babbler
- [ ] Striped Tit-Babbler
- [ ] White-rumped Shama
- [ ] Chestnut-naped Forktail
- [ ] Dark-necked Tailorbird
- [ ] Rufescent Prinia
- [ ] Scarlet Sunbird (also middle storey)
- [ ] Little Spiderhunter
- [ ] Grey-breasted Spiderhunter (also middle storey)
- [ ] Orange-bellied Flowerpecker (also middle storey)
- [ ] White-rumped Munia

Middle storey, canopy:
- [ ] Crested Goshawk
- [ ] Blue-crowned Hanging Parrot
- [ ] Indian Cuckoo
- [ ] Brush (Rusty-breasted) Cuckoo
- [ ] Drongo Cuckoo
- [ ] Raffles' Malkoha
- [ ] Chestnut-breasted Malkoha
- [ ] Whiskered Treeswift (watch for them in dead trees around the lake edge)
- [ ] Scarlet-rumped Trogon (also lower storey)
- [ ] Dollarbird
- [ ] Oriental Pied Hornbill
- [ ] Rhinoceros Hornbill
- [ ] Red-throated Barbet
- [ ] Blue-eared Barbet
- [ ] Brown Barbet
- [ ] Crimson-winged Woodpecker
- [ ] Buff-rumped Woodpecker
- [ ] Great Slaty Woodpecker
- [ ] Black-and-Yellow Broadbill
- [ ] Green Broadbill (also lower storey)
- [ ] Scarlet Minivet
- [ ] Green Iora
- [ ] Blue-winged Leafbird
- [ ] Black-headed Bulbul
- [ ] Grey-bellied Bulbul
- [ ] Cream-vented Bulbul
- [ ] Red-eyed Bulbul
- [ ] Bronzed Drongo (forest edge; also open areas)
- [ ] Greater Racket-tailed Drongo
- [ ] Asian Fairy-Bluebird
- [ ] Black Magpie
- [ ] Brown Fulvetta (also lower storey)

- [ ] White-bellied Yuhina
- [ ] Black-naped Monarch (also lower storey)
- [ ] Rufous-winged Flycatcher (also lower storey)
- [ ] Asian Paradise-Flycatcher
- [ ] Hill Myna
- [ ] Plain Sunbird
- [ ] Ruby-cheeked Sunbird
- [ ] Yellow-eared Spiderhunter
- [ ] Yellow-breasted Flowerpecker (also lower storey)
- [ ] Crimson-breasted Flowerpecker
- [ ] Scarlet-backed Flowerpecker
- [ ] Everett's White-eye

Difficult-to-find or rare species:
- [ ] Little Cormorant m
- [ ] Black Bittern m
- [ ] Osprey m
- [ ] Grey-headed Fish-Eagle
- [ ] Peregrine Falcon m
- [ ] Long-billed Partridge
- [ ] Crested Wood-Partridge
- [ ] Great Argus (probably not rare, but heard more often than seen)
- [ ] Large Green Pigeon
- [ ] Jambu Fruit-Dove
- [ ] Chestnut-bellied Malkoha
- [ ] Red-billed Malkoha
- [ ] Collared Scops-Owl
- [ ] Fork-tailed Swift m
- [ ] Asian Palm-Swift
- [ ] Bushy-crested Hornbill
- [ ] Wreathed Hornbill
- [ ] Buff-necked Woodpecker
- [ ] White-bellied Woodpecker
- [ ] Bar-bellied Cuckoo-shrike
- [ ] Lesser Cuckoo-shrike
- [ ] Black-capped Babbler
- [ ] Scaly-crowned Babbler

Access and accommodation

The dam is about an hour's drive from Kuala Terengganu via Kuala Berang, and is open daily from 8.00 a.m. until 6.00 p.m. If you haven't arranged your trip through Khairul Adventures (or some other tour operator), you can stay overnight in one of the floating chalets at the Kenyir Lake Resort. A chalet will cost you around $M100 per night; be sure to book in advance by 'phoning the resort on 01-950609 or 09-523687. There is a restaurant at the resort.

When to visit

The monsoon season on the east coast is from about November to January, at which time you may have difficulty getting around because of floods. Other than that there is no particular time when you should visit - just avoid peak periods (public holidays and so on) when accommodation will be hard to find.

Other attractions

Most people go to Kenyir for the fishing - it is one of the best places in the country for this - and boats and canoes are readily available for hire. Those going on a jungle trek could see some exciting animals (the dam lies close to the north-eastern boundary of Taman Negara) such as Tiger, Barking Deer, Asian Elephant, Wild Pig, Sun Bear, Malay Tapir and, if you are extremely fortunate, Sumatran Rhinoceros. If jungle trekking isn't your style, head for the nearby coast where, from May to September, you can see giant leatherback turtles coming ashore to lay their eggs.

21 Pulau Redang

Terengganu

The many small islands clustered off Peninsular Malaysia's north-east coast certainly look inviting, but they are not particularly good for birds (you'd be better off heading south to P. Tioman, site 24, which is large enough to support quite a variety of species). Even so, if you are looking for somewhere to go snorkelling or scuba diving, with the chance of at least a few interesting birds (Green and Pied Imperial Pigeons for example), then you should consider visiting P. Redang.

Good birdwatching areas

Redang is two or three hours by boat from Kuala Terengganu, and during the trip you'll have plenty of opportunities for seabirding. There are a number of walking tracks on the island and, since it is less than 10 km from north to south, and on average only a few kilometres wide, you can explore virtually the whole of Redang in a couple of days.

You can also get to Redang from Kuala Besut, a small fishing village to the south-east of Kota Bharu. Kuala Besut is the place to make for if you want to go to the Perhentian islands, which lie some 30 km north-west of Redang. As far as birds are concerned, there's not much to choose between the Perhentians and Redang; however, the coastal scrub in the vicinity of Kuala Besut may hold something of interest - Indian Roller and Lineated Barbet are two species to watch for.

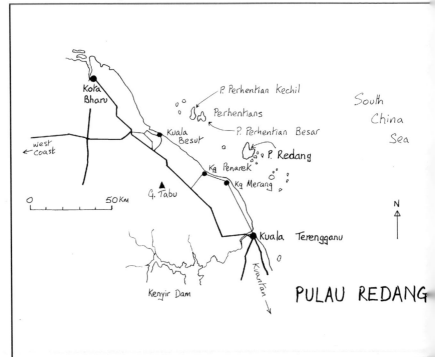

Birds

Seabirds and shorebirds:
- ☐ Red-footed Booby m (vagrant)
- ☐ Lesser Frigatebird m
- ☐ Great-billed Heron (probably extinct, but may still occur)
- ☐ Little Heron
- ☐ Pacific Reef-Egret
- ☐ Common Sandpiper m
- ☐ Roseate Tern
- ☐ Black-naped Tern
- ☐ Bridled Tern
- ☐ Great Crested Tern m
- ☐ Collared Kingfisher

Landbirds:
- ☐ Brahminy Kite
- ☐ White-bellied Sea-Eagle
- ☐ Grey-headed Fish-Eagle
- ☐ White-breasted Waterhen
- ☐ Pink-necked Pigeon
- ☐ Green Imperial Pigeon
- ☐ Pied Imperial Pigeon
- ☐ Green-winged (Emerald Dove) Pigeon
- ☐ Nicobar Pigeon
- ☐ Hodgson's Hawk-Cuckoo (especially Sept)
- ☐ Common Koel (especially win)
- ☐ Black-nest Swiftlet
- ☐ Fork-tailed Swift m (especially Sept-Oct)
- ☐ Common Kingfisher (especially win)
- ☐ Oriental Dwarf Kingfisher (especially Sept)
- ☐ Pacific Swallow
- ☐ White-rumped Shama
- ☐ Arctic Warbler m
- ☐ Dark-necked Tailorbird
- ☐ Mangrove Whistler
- ☐ Brown Shrike m
- ☐ Philippine Glossy Starling
- ☐ Purple-backed Starling m
- ☐ Copper-throated Sunbird
- ☐ White-rumped Munia

Access and accommodation

Because Redang is not as developed as some of the other islands off Peninsular Malaysia's east coast, there are no regular ferry services like those to Tioman for example, and accommodation on the island is limited. One way to get there is to contact Khairul Adventures in Kuala Terengganu; for around $M550 per person Khairul will provide transport to and from Redang, as well as food, a guide, and camping equipment. While the cost is a little high, for your money you'll get an all-inclusive four-day camping trip - and importantly, if you wish you can vary the itinerary so as to combine a visit to Redang with some camping and jungle trekking on the adjacent mainland, either at Kenyir Dam or Gunung Tabu (the latter rises to over a thousand metres and looks a very promising area for birds). Khairul Adventures can be contacted by 'phone on 09-633529 - ask for Khairul Annuar (see site 20 for his address).

If camping out doesn't appeal to you, you can stay at the Redang Bay Resort; to arrange this contact the resort's office at 139 Jalan Bandar, Kuala Terengganu, 'phone 09-636048. A four-day package (including transport, dormitory accommodation at the resort, meals and snorkelling equipment) will cost you around $M350, or $M500 if you want scuba diving equipment as well. (These prices are for groups of 10 or more - you'll have to pay an extra $M50 or so per person per day if there are only three or four of you.)

When to visit

The monsoon season here is from about November to January, and during these months rough seas could prevent boats reaching Redang. For birdwatching, the best time to go is just before the monsoon - September or October - when there could be some interesting migrants about.

Other attractions

The seas around Redang, and the five or six tiny islands that lie nearby, are a marine park where fish, coral and shells are protected. Most people go there for water sports such as snorkelling, diving, sailing and windsurfing.

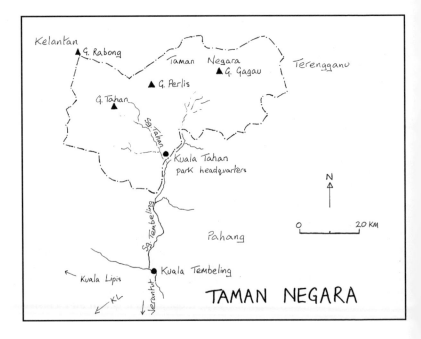

22 Taman Negara
Pahang/Kelantan/Terengganu

Having looked at the bird list for this site (which is impressive by any standards) you will probably feel the urge to catch the next flight to Malaysia and to rush straight from Kuala Lumpur airport to Taman Negara. Restrain yourself, however, for the park is not quite the birdwatchers' mecca that it appears to be. In fact, many first-time visitors to Taman Negara express disappointment at the number of species they have seen even after three or four days of intensive birding.

There are a number of reasons why Taman Negara doesn't always live up to peoples' expectations. For one, the park is heavily promoted as a wildlife paradise, which indeed it is, yet it covers such a large area (more than 4300 square kilometres) that to see even a small part of what it has to offer you need weeks, not days. As well, the habitat around the park headquarters and resort at Kuala Tahan - which at the time of writing is where the majority of visitors stay - consists mainly of dense lowland rainforest, a particularly difficult environment for birdwatching, especially if you are accustomed to more open situations.

Despite this, Taman Negara is a destination not to be missed: almost two-thirds of the 550 or so bird species (excluding vagrants) that occur in West Malaysia have been recorded in the park, with about 250 species occurring in the lowlands and a further 75 or so in the highlands. Special birds in the lowlands - at least some of which you've a fair chance of seeing in the vicinity of Kuala Tahan - include Bat Hawk (not easy to find, but harder to get elsewhere in the peninsula), Lesser Fish-Eagle, Crestless and Crested Fireback (the latter should be easy to find), Malaysian Peacock-Pheasant, Great Argus, Masked Finfoot (at the right time of year), Large Green Pigeon, Reddish Scops-Owl, Gould's Frogmouth, Cinnamon-rumped Trogon, Blue-banded, Banded and Rufous-collared Kingfisher, Wrinkled Hornbill, Malaysian Honeyguide, White-bellied Woodpecker, Dusky Broadbill, Giant, Garnet and Banded Pitta, Bar-bellied Cuckoo-shrike, Black-and-White, Puff-backed and Finsch's Bulbul, Crested Jay, White-chested, Grey-breasted and White-necked Babbler, Malaysian Rail-Babbler, Rufous-tailed Shama, White-crowned Forktail, Rufous-chested and Malaysian Blue Flycatcher, Thick-billed Spiderhunter and Yellow-vented Flowerpecker.

Birds of Taman Negara's highlands include Hill Prinia (in Malaysia, found only on G. Tahan above 1500 m [4900 feet]), Grey-headed Woodpecker (at between 915 and 1830 m [3000 to 6000 feet] on G. Tahan; the only other site in Malaysia where you'll get this species is the Cameron Highlands) and Crested Argus (up to around 915 m [3000 feet] on G. Tahan). Among the other mountain highlights are Black Eagle, Mountain Peacock-Pheasant (above 975 m [3200 feet]), Golden-throated Barbet (above 1220 m [4000 feet]), Long-tailed Broadbill, Blue Nuthatch (above 1070 m [3500 feet]), Large Scimitar-Babbler (above 1070 m), Black-eared Shrike-Babbler (above 1220 m), Chestnut-tailed Minla (above 1525 m [5000 feet]), Lesser Shortwing (above 975 m), Slaty-backed Forktail, Mountain Leaf-Warbler (above 1220 m), Snowy-browed Flycatcher (above 1430 m

[4700 feet]), Pygmy Blue Flycatcher, Pin-tailed Parrotfinch, and Brown Bullfinch (above 1280 m [4200 feet]).

Good birdwatching areas

On average, the boat journey from Kuala Tembeling to the park hq at Kuala Tahan takes three hours (see Access and accommodation), and along the way you should see some interesting species - scan the river edge and the sandy islands for birds such as fish-eagles and kingfishers.

At the park hq, you'll find plenty of open areas and edge habitat where birds are easier to see than in the surrounding forest. For example, if you cross over the Sg. Tahan - a boatman will take you over for a small fee - you'll almost certainly find Black-thighed Falconets perching on TV antennas in the village on the other side. There are also a number of forest trails in the vicinity of park hq; some, like the Swamp Loop trail and the track to Bumbun Tahan, will take you only an hour or two to complete, while others will take a full day. For birdwatching, the better trails include the Bukit Teresek-Bumbun Tabing circuit (see map), a good walk for Crested Fireback (look for them along the first part of the track, between park hq and the turn-off to Bukit Teresek), Great Argus (try the area around Jenut Muda), pittas, and Malaysian Rail-Babbler. About a kilometre beyond Bukit Teresek you can either turn right (again, see map) and go to Bumbun Tabing, or left and return to park hq along the banks of the Sg. Tahan (usually an especially good place for birds). Another walk worth doing is that to Gua Telinga (Telinga Cave); as you approach the cave keep a watch for White-crowned Forktail.

For the sheer joy of it - and for birds too of course - you should take at least one boat trip during your stay in Taman Negara. The one-hour trip up the Sg. Tahan to the rapids at Lata Berkoh is highly recommended for Lesser Fish-Eagle, Black-and-Red Broadbill and Masked Finfoot (the last between February and June). If you wish, you can get off the boat during the return journey and walk back to park hq via the Bumbun Tabing trail. Also, try to get on the first trip in the morning to Lata Berkoh because birds like the fish-eagle will be disturbed by the sound of the boats' engines (there's quite a din when three or four boats head up the river in convoy).

For the best of the highland birds you will need to trek to the summit of G. Tahan, which at 2187 m (7174 feet) is the highest mountain in Peninsular Malaysia. You must be fit, however, for the 130-kilometre return trek (from Kuala Tahan) takes about nine days, and since there are no huts along the route you'll have to carry camping equipment, food and water. You must also be accompanied by a guide - for more details see Other attractions.

Birds

Open areas, overhead:
☐ Crested Serpent-Eagle
☐ Japanese Sparrowhawk m (especially Oct-Nov)
☐ Black-thighed Falconet (fair numbers - six to 10 birds
  - can usually be found perched on TV antennas in the
  small kampung on the west bank of the Sg. Tahan, at
  the start of the Gua Telinga trail)

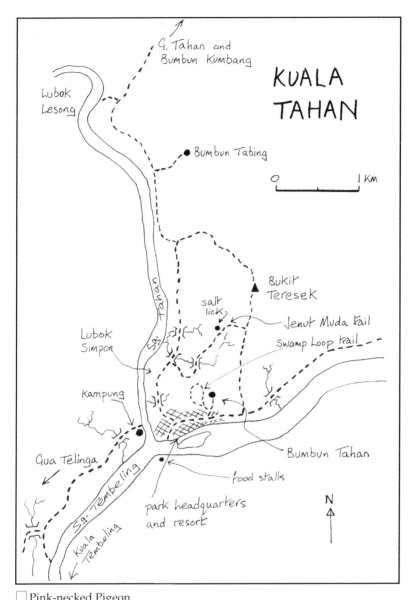

Pink-necked Pigeon
Lesser Coucal
Malaysian Eared Nightjar
Large-tailed Nightjar (clearings near Kuala Tahan
  Resort)
White-bellied (Glossy) Swiftlet
Brown Needletail
Silver-rumped Swift

- [ ] Fork-tailed Swift m
- [ ] House Swift
- [ ] Asian Palm-Swift
- [ ] Blue-throated Bee-eater
- [ ] Dollarbird
- [ ] Common Goldenback
- [ ] Barn Swallow m
- [ ] Pacific Swallow
- [ ] Common Iora
- [ ] Yellow-vented Bulbul
- [ ] Black-naped Oriole
- [ ] Large-billed Crow
- [ ] Magpie Robin
- [ ] Common Tailorbird
- [ ] Ashy Tailorbird
- [ ] Grey Wagtail m
- [ ] Common Myna
- [ ] Brown-throated Sunbird
- [ ] Eurasian Tree-Sparrow

Rivers:
- [ ] Little Heron
- [ ] Lesser Fish-Eagle (along the Sg. Tahan; watch for the bird in trees overhanging the water)
- [ ] White-breasted Waterhen
- [ ] Masked Finfoot m (mainly Feb-June; take an early morning boat trip and look along the quiet stretches of the Sg. Tahan, especially where vegetation overhangs the water)
- [ ] Common Sandpiper m
- [ ] Buffy Fish-Owl (riverside forest - try near Lubok Simpon)
- [ ] Common Kingfisher (especially win)
- [ ] Stork-billed Kingfisher
- [ ] White-throated Kingfisher (also open areas)
- [ ] Black-capped Kingfisher m
- [ ] Straw-headed Bulbul (stream and river edges)
- [ ] White-chested Babbler (riverside shrubs)
- [ ] Yellow-bellied Prinia (river edge)

Ground, lower storey:
- [ ] Crested Fireback (occurs close to Kuala Tahan Resort, often in groups of 10 or more; look for them in the early morning, before too many people are about)
- [ ] Red Junglefowl
- [ ] Malaysian Peacock-Pheasant (like the fireback, can be found close to the resort; try the Swamp Loop trail or in the vicinity of Jenut Muda)
- [ ] Great Argus (heard more often than seen; try the Bukit Teresek-Bumbun Tabing circuit, especially the area around Jenut Muda)

☐ Green-winged (Emerald Dove) Pigeon
☐ Greater Coucal
☐ Diard's Trogon (also middle storey)
☐ Rufous Piculet (also middle storey)
☐ Buff-rumped Woodpecker (also middle storey)
☐ Black-and-Red Broadbill (also middle storey; look for
nests in vines overhanging the Sg. Tahan)
☐ Garnet Pitta (try the Bukit Teresek-Bumbun Tabing
circuit in the vicinity of Jenut Muda)
☐ Hooded Pitta m (try the Sg. Tahan section of the
Bukit Teresek-Bumbun Tabing circuit)
☐ Banded Pitta (look around Bumbun Tabing)
☐ Stripe-throated Bulbul
☐ Olive-winged Bulbul
☐ Grey-cheeked Bulbul
☐ Yellow-bellied Bulbul
☐ Black-capped Babbler
☐ Short-tailed Babbler
☐ Ferruginous Babbler (also middle storey)
☐ Abbott's Babbler
☐ Moustached Babbler (also middle storey)
☐ Scaly-crowned Babbler (also middle storey)
☐ Rufous-crowned Babbler (also middle storey)
☐ Large Wren-Babbler (try the Swamp Loop trail)
☐ Grey-headed Babbler
☐ Chestnut-rumped Babbler
☐ White-necked Babbler (along the Bukit Teresek-Bumbun
Tabing circuit)
☐ Black-throated Babbler
☐ Chestnut-winged Babbler
☐ Striped Tit-Babbler
☐ Fluffy-backed Tit-Babbler
☐ Siberian Blue Robin m
☐ White-rumped Shama
☐ Chestnut-naped Forktail (try the Bukit Teresek-Bumbun
Tabing circuit)
☐ White-crowned Forktail (along the Gua Telinga trail,
especially the area close to the limestone cave)
☐ Dark-necked Tailorbird
☐ Rufous-tailed Tailorbird
☐ Rufous-chested Flycatcher (look in shady gullies)
☐ Tickell's Blue Flycatcher (also middle storey)
☐ Grey-headed Flycatcher (also middle storey)
☐ Rufous-winged Flycatcher (also middle storey)
☐ Tiger Shrike m
☐ Ruby-cheeked Sunbird (also middle storey)
☐ Purple-naped Sunbird (especially river edges)
☐ Little Spiderhunter
☐ Grey-breasted Spiderhunter (also middle storey)
☐ Orange-bellied Flowerpecker (also middle storey)

- [ ] White-rumped Munia
- [ ] White-bellied Munia

Middle storey, canopy:
- [ ] Changeable Hawk-Eagle
- [ ] Thick-billed Pigeon
- [ ] Little Green Pigeon
- [ ] Large Green Pigeon
- [ ] Jambu Fruit-Dove
- [ ] Blue-rumped Parrot (visits fruiting trees in the grounds of Kuala Tahan Resort, as does the next species)
- [ ] Blue-crowned Hanging Parrot
- [ ] Indian Cuckoo
- [ ] Brush (Rusty-breasted) Cuckoo
- [ ] Drongo Cuckoo
- [ ] Chestnut-bellied Malkoha
- [ ] Raffles' Malkoha
- [ ] Chestnut-breasted Malkoha
- [ ] Reddish Scops-Owl (also lower storey; try the Swamp Loop trail)
- [ ] Collared Scops-Owl (also lower storey)
- [ ] Brown Hawk-Owl
- [ ] Gould's Frogmouth (also lower storey; can be heard - if not seen - along the Swamp Loop trail)
- [ ] Grey-rumped Treeswift
- [ ] Whiskered Treeswift (look along the Sg. Tahan)
- [ ] Red-naped Trogon
- [ ] Scarlet-rumped Trogon (also lower storey)
- [ ] Banded Kingfisher
- [ ] Rufous-collared Kingfisher (also lower storey; try the Bukit Teresek-Bumbun Tabing circuit)
- [ ] Red-bearded Bee-eater
- [ ] Wreathed Hornbill (all hornbills also overhead)
- [ ] Black Hornbill
- [ ] Oriental Pied Hornbill
- [ ] Rhinoceros Hornbill
- [ ] Helmeted Hornbill
- [ ] Gold-whiskered Barbet
- [ ] Red-throated Barbet
- [ ] Yellow-crowned Barbet
- [ ] Blue-eared Barbet
- [ ] Brown Barbet
- [ ] Rufous Woodpecker
- [ ] Crimson-winged Woodpecker
- [ ] Checker-throated Woodpecker
- [ ] Banded Woodpecker
- [ ] Great Slaty Woodpecker (look in tall, mature trees)
- [ ] Grey-and-Buff Woodpecker
- [ ] Maroon Woodpecker

- [ ] Banded Broadbill
- [ ] Black-and-Yellow Broadbill
- [ ] Green Broadbill (also lower storey)
- [ ] Black-winged Flycatcher-shrike
- [ ] Large Wood-shrike
- [ ] Bar-bellied Cuckoo-shrike
- [ ] Scarlet Minivet
- [ ] Green Iora (clearings along the Sg. Tahan)
- [ ] Lesser Green Leafbird
- [ ] Greater Green Leafbird
- [ ] Blue-winged Leafbird
- [ ] Black-headed Bulbul
- [ ] Grey-bellied Bulbul
- [ ] Cream-vented Bulbul
- [ ] Red-eyed Bulbul
- [ ] Spectacled Bulbul (also lower storey)
- [ ] Hairy-backed Bulbul (also lower storey)
- [ ] Buff-vented Bulbul
- [ ] Bronzed Drongo (clearings and edges)
- [ ] Greater Racket-tailed Drongo
- [ ] Dark-throated Oriole (especially along the Sg. Tahan)
- [ ] Asian Fairy-Bluebird
- [ ] Black Magpie
- [ ] Slender-billed Crow
- [ ] Sooty-capped Babbler (also lower storey)
- [ ] Brown Fulvetta (also lower storey)
- [ ] White-bellied Yuhina
- [ ] Flyeater
- [ ] Arctic Warbler m
- [ ] Eastern Crowned Warbler m
- [ ] Asian Brown Flycatcher m
- [ ] Black-naped Monarch (also lower storey)
- [ ] Asian Paradise-Flycatcher
- [ ] Hill Myna
- [ ] Plain Sunbird
- [ ] Long-billed Spiderhunter
- [ ] Spectacled Spiderhunter
- [ ] Yellow-eared Spiderhunter
- [ ] Yellow-breasted Flowerpecker (also lower storey)
- [ ] Crimson-breasted Flowerpecker (often in clearings)
- [ ] Yellow-vented Flowerpecker
- [ ] Scarlet-backed Flowerpecker

Difficult-to-find or rare species:
- [ ] Malayan Night-Heron m
- [ ] Storm's Stork
- [ ] Osprey m
- [ ] Black Baza m (mainly Oct-Nov)
- [ ] Eurasian (Crested) Honey-Buzzard (mainly Oct-Nov)
- [ ] Bat Hawk (best prospect is to go to the eating places on the south bank of the Sg. Tembeling, opposite Kuala

Tahan Resort, and watch the river closely just before nightfall - a bird often appears here and makes swoops low over the water, probably hunting bats that use the river as a flyway)

- [ ] Grey-headed Fish-Eagle (try around the jetty at Kuala Tembeling)
- [ ] Crested Goshawk
- [ ] Wallace's Hawk-Eagle
- [ ] Long-billed Partridge
- [ ] Black Wood-Partridge
- [ ] Ferruginous (Wood) Partridge (try the Bukit Teresek area)
- [ ] Crested Wood-Partridge (try around Jenut Muda)
- [ ] Crestless Fireback (look around Jenut Muda or in the Bumbun Kumbang area)
- [ ] Red-legged Crake m
- [ ] Band-bellied Crake m
- [ ] Green Imperial Pigeon
- [ ] Moustached Hawk-Cuckoo
- [ ] Hodgson's Hawk-Cuckoo
- [ ] Oriental Cuckoo
- [ ] Violet Cuckoo
- [ ] Black-bellied Malkoha
- [ ] Red-billed Malkoha
- [ ] Short-toed Coucal
- [ ] Bay Owl
- [ ] White-fronted Scops-Owl
- [ ] Oriental (Common) Scops-Owl m
- [ ] Barred Eagle-Owl (has been seen in the Kuala Tahan Resort grounds, feeding on insects attracted to the lights)
- [ ] Brown Wood-Owl
- [ ] Large Frogmouth
- [ ] Javan Frogmouth (try the Swamp Loop trail)
- [ ] White-vented Needletail m
- [ ] Cinnamon-rumped Trogon
- [ ] Blue-eared Kingfisher
- [ ] Blue-banded Kingfisher (look along the Sg. Tahan)
- [ ] Oriental Dwarf Kingfisher
- [ ] Indian Roller (look for it along the Sg. Tembeling en route to the park hq)
- [ ] Bushy-crested Hornbill
- [ ] Wrinkled Hornbill
- [ ] Red-crowned Barbet
- [ ] Malaysian Honeyguide
- [ ] Olive-backed Woodpecker
- [ ] Buff-necked Woodpecker
- [ ] White-bellied Woodpecker
- [ ] Orange-backed Woodpecker
- [ ] Dusky Broadbill

- [ ] Giant Pitta
- [ ] Blue-winged Pitta (especially win)
- [ ] Lesser Cuckoo-shrike
- [ ] Ashy Minivet m
- [ ] Fiery Minivet
- [ ] Black-and-White Bulbul
- [ ] Puff-backed Bulbul
- [ ] Finsch's Bulbul
- [ ] Streaked Bulbul
- [ ] Crow-billed Drongo m
- [ ] Crested Jay
- [ ] Velvet-fronted Nuthatch
- [ ] Grey-breasted Babbler
- [ ] Chestnut-backed Scimitar-Babbler
- [ ] Striped Wren-Babbler (look around Bukit Teresek or near Bumbun Kumbang)
- [ ] Rufous-fronted Babbler
- [ ] Malaysian Rail-Babbler (try the Bukit Teresek-Bumbun Tabing circuit - around Jenut Muda for example)
- [ ] Rufous-tailed Shama
- [ ] Blue Whistling Thrush
- [ ] Chestnut-capped Thrush
- [ ] Orange-headed Thrush m
- [ ] Eye-browed Thrush m
- [ ] Pale-legged Leaf-Warbler m (one in secondary growth at Kuala Tahan in March 1987; keeps low to the ground)
- [ ] Grey-chested Flycatcher (try the Jenut Muda area)
- [ ] Ferruginous Flycatcher m
- [ ] Blue-and-White Flycatcher m
- [ ] Blue-throated Flycatcher m
- [ ] Malaysian Blue Flycatcher
- [ ] Spotted Fantail
- [ ] Maroon-breasted Flycatcher
- [ ] Forest Wagtail m
- [ ] Red-throated Sunbird (favours clearings)
- [ ] Scarlet Sunbird
- [ ] Thick-billed Spiderhunter
- [ ] Scarlet-breasted Flowerpecker
- [ ] Thick-billed Flowerpecker
- [ ] Plain Flowerpecker

Additional species for those able to explore the more remote parts of Taman Negara, particularly highland areas such as G. Tahan. Most of the birds listed do not occur in the vicinity of Kuala Tahan.

Open areas, overhead:
- [ ] Chinese Goshawk m
- [ ] Black Eagle (hunts low over forest canopy)
- [ ] Rufous-bellied Eagle
- [ ] Blyth's Hawk-Eagle
- [ ] Mountain Imperial Pigeon

Ground, lower storey:
- ☐ Mountain Peacock-Pheasant*
- ☐ Crested Argus (look for it at around 915 m [3000 feet]; Taman Negara is the only place in Malaysia where this species occurs)
- ☐ Mountain Scops-Owl
- ☐ Collared Owlet (also middle storey)
- ☐ Bamboo Woodpecker
- ☐ Ochraceous Bulbul
- ☐ Horsfield's Babbler
- ☐ Large Scimitar-Babbler
- ☐ Streaked Wren-Babbler
- ☐ Eye-browed Wren-Babbler
- ☐ Pygmy Wren-Babbler
- ☐ Grey-throated Babbler
- ☐ Chestnut-crowned Laughingthrush (also middle storey)
- ☐ Lesser Shortwing
- ☐ Slaty-backed Forktail
- ☐ Hill Prinia (found only in low vegetation on G. Tahan, above 1500 m [4900 feet])
- ☐ Dark-sided Flycatcher m (also middle storey)
- ☐ Mugimaki Flycatcher m
- ☐ Rufous-browed Flycatcher
- ☐ Snowy-browed Flycatcher
- ☐ Pygmy Blue Flycatcher
- ☐ Black-throated Sunbird (also middle storey)

Middle storey, canopy:
- ☐ Wedge-tailed Pigeon
- ☐ Little Cuckoo-Dove
- ☐ Large Hawk-Cuckoo
- ☐ Orange-breasted Trogon
- ☐ White-crowned Hornbill
- ☐ Great Hornbill
- ☐ Golden-throated Barbet
- ☐ Black-browed Barbet
- ☐ Speckled Piculet
- ☐ Grey-headed Woodpecker (at between 915 and 1830 m [3000 to 6000 feet] on G. Tahan; this locality and the Cameron Highlands are the only places in Malaysia where you'll find the species)
- ☐ Long-tailed Broadbill
- ☐ Bar-winged Flycatcher-shrike
- ☐ Large (Black-faced) Cuckoo-shrike
- ☐ Grey-chinned Minivet
- ☐ Black-crested Bulbul
- ☐ Scaly-breasted Bulbul
- ☐ Mountain Bulbul
- ☐ Ashy Bulbul
- ☐ Lesser Racket-tailed Drongo

- [ ] Green Magpie
- [ ] Sultan Tit
- [ ] Blue Nuthatch
- [ ] Golden Babbler (also lower storey)
- [ ] Chestnut-capped Laughingthrush
- [ ] Silver-eared Mesia
- [ ] White-browed Shrike-Babbler
- [ ] Black-eared Shrike-Babbler
- [ ] Chestnut-tailed Minla (above 1525 m [5000 feet])
- [ ] Rufous-winged Fulvetta
- [ ] Mountain Fulvetta (also lower storey)
- [ ] Long-tailed Sibia
- [ ] Siberian Thrush m (also lower storey)
- [ ] Yellow-breasted Warbler
- [ ] Yellow-bellied Warbler
- [ ] Mountain Leaf-Warbler
- [ ] Mountain Tailorbird (also lower storey)
- [ ] Verditer Flycatcher
- [ ] Little Pied Flycatcher
- [ ] Large Niltava
- [ ] Pale Blue Flycatcher
- [ ] Hill Blue Flycatcher
- [ ] White-throated Fantail (also lower storey)
- [ ] Buff-bellied Flowerpecker
- [ ] Everett's White-eye
- [ ] Pin-tailed Parrotfinch
- [ ] Brown Bullfinch

Access and accommodation

Getting to Taman Negara is half the fun - the park hq at Kuala Tahan can only be reached by boat from Kuala Tembeling, a small town about 220 km north-east of Kuala Lumpur via the Karak Highway, Temerloh and Jerantut. Boats to Taman Negara leave the Kuala Tembeling jetty at 9.00 a.m. and 2.00 p.m.; you must book a place in advance - this is usually done at the same time as booking your accommodation. (If you don't have your own transport, you can also book a seat on a minibus to take you from KL to Kuala Tembeling.) The boat trip to park hq and return costs around $M30 per person; the minibus from KL to Kuala Tembeling and return will cost you about $M50.

At the time of writing the only place you can get accommodation in the park is at the Kuala Tahan Resort, a privately operated complex that looks somewhat out of place in an area of near-pristine rainforest. Unfortunately, the resort's new owners - it has only recently changed hands - have taken full advantage of their monopoly and have done away with the mid-range accommodation (at one time you could get a comfortable chalet for around $M30 a night). Those on a tight budget now have only two choices - to camp (not recommended given the climate), or to stay in the hostel where a bunk bed (there are eight to a room) will cost you $M11 a night. If you want more comfort and privacy, you'll have to pay $M120 a night for an air-conditioned chalet.

There are plans to establish four more visitor centres in Taman Negara; until they are built, however, you must book through Pernas International, suite 1901, 19th floor Pernas International Building, Jalan Sultan Ismail, Kuala Lumpur 50250. The telephone number is 03-2610393. You have the choice of two eating places within the resort; there's the Tahan Restaurant, where the prices are in keeping with those charged for the chalets, and the Teresek Cafeteria with its curiously clinical atmosphere. More authentic Malaysian fare can be obtained - at considerably cheaper prices - from one of the open-air food stalls on the south bank of the Sg. Tembeling, opposite the resort.

When to visit

The park is open 10 months of the year; between mid November and mid January it is closed because of the heavy flooding that occurs in the monsoon season. February and March are the driest months so that a visit during this time would probably be best; alternatively, go in May or June.

Other attractions

As you might expect, Taman Negara supports a wide range of wildlife but, like many of the sought-after birds, the park's mammals are often difficult to see. Around the park hq the animals you are most likely to encounter include Long-tailed Macaque, Smooth Otter, bats and squirrels, while along nearby trails you could see Wild Pig, Banded and Dusky (Spectacled) Leaf Monkey, White-handed Gibbon, and Giant, Prevost's, Black-banded and Grey-bellied Squirrel.

To see animals like the Slow Loris and the Colugo (Flying Lemur) you should go out at night with a spotlight; for Barking and Sambar Deer, Malay Tapir, Malay Civet and Gaur (wild cattle) you should spend a night in a hide (book at the park hq). There are five or six hides in the park, each overlooking a salt lick where plant-eating animals come to supplement their mineral intake. Opinions differ as to the value of staying overnight in a hide; some people thoroughly enjoy the experience, others say that the only animals you can be sure of seeing are the rats that come looking for food scraps! If you decide to give a hide a try, go to Bumbun Kumbang; situated some 11 km - a comfortable day's walk - north-east of Kuala Tahan, Kumbang is not only good for mammals but for birds too.

To have any real hope of sighting Taman Negara's more celebrated inhabitants - Asian Elephant, Tiger, Leopard, Sun Bear, and the highly endangered Sumatran Rhinoceros - you will need to go on a long-distance jungle trek. Some treks are relatively easy and take just two or three days, but others are quite demanding - the nine-day return trip to the summit of G. Tahan for example. Before setting off on a long trek you must be properly equipped, of course, and on most of the walks you must take along a guide. Guides must be booked in advance through the Department of Wildlife and National Parks, Km 10 Jalan Cheras, Kuala Lumpur 56100, telephone 03-9052872 or 9052873. (Note that you cannot book guides through Pernas International.)

23 Tasik Chini   Pahang

Tasik Chini lies approximately 90 km south-west of Kuantan, on Peninsular Malaysia's east coast. It is the second-largest natural lake in the country, and is joined to the Sg. Pahang by a five-kilometre stretch of fast-flowing water - the Sg. Cini. Although Tasik Chini is almost surrounded by oil palm plantations, there are some extensive stands of lowland rainforest close to the lake, particularly to the west, between the Lake Chini Resort and the Sg. Pahang. The lake itself is fringed by dense reedbeds, and there are large areas of lotus; for several months of the year, between July and January, thousands of lotus flowers transform the lake's blue waters into a collage of pink and white.

   Needless to say, Tasik Chini is a very pleasant place to spend a few days - the ideal spot to head for when you need a break from the monotony of the east coast's oil palm estates. From the resort on the lake's edge you can take a boat trip - better still, hire a canoe - that will give you a chance of seeing birds like Black Bittern, Lesser and Grey-headed Fish-Eagle, White-browed Crake, Masked Finfoot and Pheasant-tailed Jacana. As well, there are many kilometres of forest trails (you can walk right around the lake) that provide plenty of scope for birding.

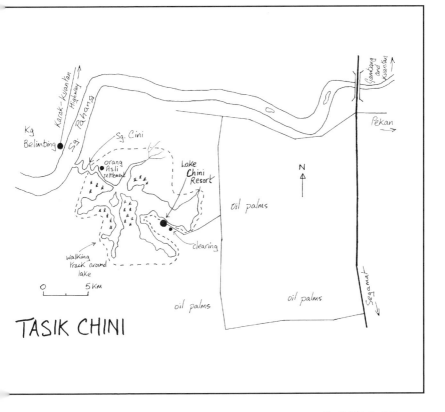

TASIK CHINI

Good birdwatching areas

The best way to explore the lake is, of course, by boat or canoe. For about $M40, a boatman will take you around Tasik Chini; if you ask, he'll also take you along the narrow Sg. Cini and across the wide Sg. Pahang to the small village (Kampung Belimbing) on the other side. (It is worth spending some time at Kg Belimbing since the birding in the vicinity of the village is usually quite good.) If you do go out in a boat, be sure to get away first thing in the morning; as a rule, by 9.00 a.m. or so the noise made by the resort's fleet of motor boats is enough to scare off even the most confiding of birds. A more appropriate way to see the lake would be to hire a canoe for the day - inquire at the resort.

For forest birds, try any of the marked tracks near the resort, but if you go on one of the long treks seek advice beforehand from the resort's resident ranger. If you just want an early morning stroll, walk from the resort out along the entrance road; after about two or three hundred metres you'll see a large clearing on the right, just beyond the resort's generator, and some time spent here should prove productive.

Birds

Open areas (including wetlands), overhead:
☐ Little Grebe
☐ Purple Heron (lake edge)
☐ Black-shouldered Kite
☐ Crested Serpent-Eagle
☐ Changeable Hawk-Eagle
☐ Masked Finfoot m (mainly Feb-June; on the quieter backwaters of the lake and along the slower-moving parts of the Sg. Cini)
☐ Pink-necked Pigeon (common around the resort)
☐ Long-tailed Parakeet (especially oil palm plantations)
☐ Blue-rumped Parrot (oil palms)
☐ Plaintive Cuckoo
☐ Lesser Coucal
☐ Malaysian Eared Nightjar
☐ Large-tailed Nightjar
☐ White-bellied (Glossy) Swiftlet
☐ Brown Needletail
☐ Silver-rumped Swift
☐ Fork-tailed Swift m
☐ House Swift
☐ Asian Palm-Swift
☐ Grey-rumped Treeswift
☐ Stork-billed Kingfisher (look along the Sg. Cini)
☐ White-throated Kingfisher
☐ Black-capped Kingfisher m
☐ Blue-tailed Bee-eater (absent in sum)
☐ Blue-throated Bee-eater (absent in win)
☐ Common Goldenback (look for it around Kg Belimbing)
☐ Barn Swallow m

- [ ] Pacific Swallow
- [ ] Yellow-vented Bulbul
- [ ] Large-billed Crow
- [ ] Magpie Robin
- [ ] Common Tailorbird
- [ ] Brown Shrike m
- [ ] Long-tailed Shrike
- [ ] Philippine Glossy Starling (Kg Belimbing)
- [ ] Common Myna
- [ ] Eurasian Tree-Sparrow
- [ ] Scaly-breasted Munia

Ground, lower storey:
- [ ] Red Junglefowl
- [ ] Barred Buttonquail (best looked for early and late in the day; try the road in to the resort, especially where it passes through open grassy areas)
- [ ] White-breasted Waterhen
- [ ] Green-winged (Emerald Dove) Pigeon (look along the road in to the resort first thing in the morning)
- [ ] Greater Coucal
- [ ] Diard's Trogon (also middle storey)
- [ ] Buff-necked Woodpecker (also middle storey)
- [ ] Maroon Woodpecker (also middle storey)
- [ ] Black-and-Red Broadbill (also middle storey; quite common around Kg Belimbing)
- [ ] Stripe-throated Bulbul (along the river edge at Kg Belimbing)
- [ ] Olive-winged Bulbul
- [ ] Grey-cheeked Bulbul
- [ ] Yellow-bellied Bulbul
- [ ] Black-capped Babbler
- [ ] Short-tailed Babbler
- [ ] Ferruginous Babbler (also middle storey)
- [ ] Abbott's Babbler (chiefly forest edge and scrub)
- [ ] Rufous-crowned Babbler (also middle storey)
- [ ] Striped Tit-Babbler
- [ ] Siberian Blue Robin m
- [ ] White-rumped Shama
- [ ] Dark-necked Tailorbird
- [ ] Ashy Tailorbird (around Kg Belimbing)
- [ ] Yellow-bellied Prinia
- [ ] Pied Fantail
- [ ] Ruby-cheeked Sunbird (also middle storey)
- [ ] Purple-naped Sunbird
- [ ] Little Spiderhunter
- [ ] Grey-breasted Spiderhunter (also middle storey)
- [ ] Orange-bellied Flowerpecker (also middle storey)
- [ ] Plain Flowerpecker (also middle storey and mainly forest edge)

☐ White-rumped Munia (around Kg Belimbing)

Middle storey, canopy:
☐ Lesser Fish-Eagle (Sg. Cini)
☐ Crested Goshawk
☐ Black-thighed Falconet (perches in high, bare branches; look along the road near the resort)
☐ Little Green Pigeon
☐ Jambu Fruit-Dove
☐ Blue-crowned Hanging Parrot
☐ Indian Cuckoo
☐ Banded Bay Cuckoo
☐ Brush (Rusty-breasted) Cuckoo
☐ Drongo Cuckoo
☐ Raffles' Malkoha
☐ Chestnut-breasted Malkoha
☐ Collared Scops-Owl (also lower storey; often heard at night in the resort area)
☐ Whiskered Treeswift (perches high in trees at the edge of forest clearings - try along the road in to the resort)
☐ Red-naped Trogon
☐ Scarlet-rumped Trogon (also lower storey)
☐ Rufous-collared Kingfisher (also lower storey)
☐ Red-bearded Bee-eater
☐ Dollarbird
☐ Oriental Pied Hornbill (occurs in the vicinity of the resort)
☐ Rhinoceros Hornbill (often near the resort)
☐ Red-throated Barbet
☐ Blue-eared Barbet
☐ Brown Barbet
☐ Rufous Woodpecker (also lower storey)
☐ Crimson-winged Woodpecker
☐ Buff-rumped Woodpecker
☐ Grey-and-Buff Woodpecker
☐ Banded Broadbill
☐ Black-and-Yellow Broadbill
☐ Green Broadbill (also lower storey)
☐ Black-winged Flycatcher-shrike
☐ Scarlet Minivet
☐ Green Iora
☐ Blue-winged Leafbird
☐ Cream-vented Bulbul
☐ Red-eyed Bulbul
☐ Spectacled Bulbul (also lower storey)
☐ Hairy-backed Bulbul (also lower storey)
☐ Buff-vented Bulbul
☐ Bronzed Drongo (chiefly forest edge)
☐ Greater Racket-tailed Drongo

- [ ] Dark-throated Oriole
- [ ] Asian Fairy-Bluebird
- [ ] Black Magpie (try along the road in to the resort)
- [ ] Arctic Warbler m
- [ ] Eastern Crowned Warbler m
- [ ] Asian Brown Flycatcher m
- [ ] Black-naped Monarch
- [ ] Rufous-winged Flycatcher (also lower storey)
- [ ] Asian Paradise-Flycatcher
- [ ] Hill Myna (often around the resort)
- [ ] Plain Sunbird
- [ ] Yellow-eared Spiderhunter
- [ ] Crimson-breasted Flowerpecker
- [ ] Yellow-vented Flowerpecker
- [ ] Scarlet-backed Flowerpecker
- [ ] Everett's White-eye

Difficult-to-find or rare species:
- [ ] Little Cormorant m
- [ ] Black Bittern m
- [ ] Cotton Pygmy-Goose
- [ ] Osprey m
- [ ] Grey-headed Fish-Eagle
- [ ] Crested Wood-Partridge
- [ ] Crested Fireback
- [ ] Red-legged Crake m
- [ ] Slaty-legged Crake m
- [ ] White-browed Crake
- [ ] Pheasant-tailed Jacana m
- [ ] Large Green Pigeon
- [ ] Chestnut-winged Cuckoo m
- [ ] Violet Cuckoo
- [ ] Chestnut-bellied Malkoha
- [ ] Red-billed Malkoha
- [ ] Barn Owl
- [ ] Barred Eagle-Owl
- [ ] Gould's Frogmouth
- [ ] Blue-banded Kingfisher
- [ ] Oriental Dwarf Kingfisher
- [ ] Bushy-crested Hornbill
- [ ] Black Hornbill
- [ ] Helmeted Hornbill
- [ ] Red-crowned Barbet
- [ ] Rufous Piculet
- [ ] White-bellied Woodpecker
- [ ] Orange-backed Woodpecker
- [ ] Dusky Broadbill
- [ ] Blue-winged Pitta (especially win)
- [ ] Garnet Pitta
- [ ] Hooded Pitta m

- [ ] Banded Pitta
- [ ] Red-rumped Swallow
- [ ] Large Wood-shrike
- [ ] Lesser Cuckoo-shrike
- [ ] Great Iora
- [ ] Lesser Green Leafbird
- [ ] Greater Green Leafbird
- [ ] Straw-headed Bulbul
- [ ] Grey-bellied Bulbul
- [ ] Crow-billed Drongo m
- [ ] Crested Jay
- [ ] Velvet-fronted Nuthatch
- [ ] White-chested Babbler (river edge)
- [ ] Sooty-capped Babbler
- [ ] Scaly-crowned Babbler
- [ ] Large Wren-Babbler
- [ ] Rufous-chested Flycatcher
- [ ] Spotted Fantail
- [ ] Scarlet Sunbird

Access and accommodation

There are two ways of getting to the Lake Chini Resort, which is, at the time of writing, the only place you can stay at the lake. If you don't have your own transport, make your way by bus or by long-distance taxi to Kg Belimbing, about 25 km south of the Karak to Kuantan road. From Belimbing you travel by boat to the resort; the boat trip will be arranged - at a cost of about $M20 per person - when you book your accommodation.

If you have your own transport, you can either drive to Belimbing and take a boat from there, or you can drive all the way to the resort. To get to the resort by road turn off the Karak to Kuantan highway near Gambang, then travel south until you reach the bridge over the Sg. Pahang. Go across the bridge and take the first road on the right; continue for approximately 19 km then turn left on to a gravel road, follow this for about 8 km, then turn right and after about 5 km you'll come to the resort. For the last 12 or 13 km the route is quite rough (there are lots of potholes), but except after heavy rain you should have no problems. Also, it is not always easy to find the signs to Lake Chini Resort that mark the route; just ask someone for directions if you become lost.

Accommodation at the resort consists of about 10 chalets and five dormitories. A chalet for two costs around $M70 a night; a bunk bed in a dormitory (there are six beds in each) costs $M15. These prices include breakfast; there's a restaurant where you can get other meals. Since the resort is very popular it would be wise to book accommodation in advance: write to Malaysian Overland Adventures, Lot 1. 23, 1st floor, Bangunan Angkasaraya, Jalan Ampang, Kuala Lumpur 50450, or 'phone 03-2413569 or 2414095.

When to visit

To have the best chance of seeing migrant birds, such as Black Bittern and Pheasant-tailed Jacana, you should visit between September and March. Keep in mind that the monsoon season here is from November to January, and at this time the resort may be impossible to reach by car (and on occasion by boat). If you can, avoid weekends and (especially) public and school holidays when accommodation will be difficult to find and there'll be a lot of disturbance on the lake.

Other attractions

The lake is mainly used for boating, canoeing and fishing, and there are several guides at the resort who will take you jungle trekking. There are a number of Orang Asli ('original people') settlements in the area; during your boat tour you can ask to stop at one of the settlements, on the banks of the Sg. Cini, where you'll be given a blowpipe demonstration.

24 Pulau Tioman

Pahang

Some 19 km from north to south, and 12 km from east to west (at its widest point), Tioman is the largest of a group of 60 or so volcanic islands off Peninsular Malaysia's south-east coast. The island is mountainous (G. Kajang, its highest peak, rises to 1039 m [3406 feet]), heavily forested and relatively unspoilt, making it one of the more attractive of Malaysia's major tourist destinations.

Although Tioman's avifauna is somewhat impoverished (less than a hundred species have been recorded on the island, and at least 20 of those are migrants) it does have some interesting birds, a few of which are more difficult to find elsewhere. Among the highlights are Lesser Frigatebird (there's a chance of Christmas Frigatebird too), Black-naped Tern, Cinnamon-headed Pigeon, Green and Pied Imperial Pigeon, Black-nest Swiftlet, Ruddy Kingfisher and Purple-throated Sunbird.

In addition to G. Kajang, Tioman has a number of high mountains - for example, Bukit Seperok at 960 m (3144 feet) - with dense forest extending from their lofty, cloud-covered peaks right down to the water's edge. The largest area of level ground is on the island's west coast, around Kampung Tekek, which is the site of Tioman's airport, golf course, and much of the accommodation.

Good birdwatching areas

If you stay at Kg Tekek or nearby, you can enjoy quite good birding almost anywhere in the vicinity of the village, although at times this part of the island can be very crowded and noisy. If you wish, you can walk from Kg Tekek northwards past the airport to Kg Air Batang; a far better walk, however, is the one southwards past the Tioman Island Resort to the golf course. Try to get to the golf course early in the morning, and pay particular attention to the many small lakes that dot the course, and to the forest around its edge. From the golf course you can continue walking south to Bunot Beach (see map), then take the forest track to Kg Paya. Just before you reach Kg Paya there's a foot bridge over a tidal creek; some time spent in the mangroves here could produce Cinnamon-headed Pigeon, Purple-throated Sunbird and, perhaps, Ruddy Kingfisher.

For the best views of frigatebirds, go to the beach just south of the Tioman Island Resort and position yourself opposite P. Rengis, an islet several hundred metres offshore. Lesser Frigatebirds roost in their hundreds on P. Rengis; from about September to April the birds can be seen circling overhead just before sunset, and on occasion a few Christmas Frigatebirds join the flock.

Longer walks from Kg Tekek include the Juara track, a two- to three-hour trek that takes you across the middle of Tioman to Kg Juara on its eastern side. Many of the more isolated kampungs - for example, Kg Mukut and Kg Asah on Tioman's south coast - can only be reached by boat; there are several places in Kg Tekek where you can charter boats for excursions around Tioman or to nearby islands, but be prepared to pay $M100 or more for the day.

Birds

Open areas, overhead:

☐ Lesser Frigatebird m (P. Rengis; can also be seen
 from the ferry between the mainland and Tioman)
☐ Chinese Pond-Heron m (golf course lakes)
☐ Cattle Egret m (try the resort's riding stables)
☐ Brahminy Kite
☐ White-bellied Sea-Eagle
☐ Japanese Sparrowhawk m
☐ Peregrine Falcon m
☐ White-breasted Waterhen (common around the golf
 course)
☐ Black-naped Tern (look for terns during the ferry
 crossing)
☐ Bridled Tern
☐ Great Crested Tern m
☐ Spotted Dove (mostly around the resort)
☐ Edible-nest Swiftlet
☐ Black-nest Swiftlet
☐ Fork-tailed Swift m
☐ House Swift
☐ Black-capped Kingfisher m (golf course lakes; also
 mangroves)

- ☐ Barn Swallow m
- ☐ Pacific Swallow
- ☐ Large-billed Crow (mostly around the resort)
- ☐ Magpie Robin
- ☐ Grey Wagtail m (usually less common than the Yellow Wagtail here)
- ☐ Yellow Wagtail m (try the golf course in the vicinity of the resort)
- ☐ Brown Shrike m
- ☐ Philippine Glossy Starling
- ☐ Common Myna (mostly around the resort)
- ☐ Eurasian Tree-Sparrow (mostly around the resort)
- ☐ White-rumped Munia (look around the edge of the golf course)

Beaches, mudflats, mangroves:
- ☐ Little Heron
- ☐ Pacific Reef-Egret
- ☐ Little Ringed Plover m
- ☐ Common Greenshank m
- ☐ Common Sandpiper m (also golf course lakes)
- ☐ Common Kingfisher (especially win; also golf course lakes)
- ☐ Collared Kingfisher
- ☐ Purple-throated Sunbird (mangroves; also coastal scrub)
- ☐ Olive-backed Sunbird (mangroves; also coastal scrub)
- ☐ Oriental White-eye (mangroves; also coastal scrub)

Forest and scrub:
- ☐ Crested Serpent-Eagle
- ☐ Cinnamon-headed Pigeon (also mangroves)
- ☐ Pink-necked Pigeon
- ☐ Jambu Fruit-Dove (also mangroves)
- ☐ Green Imperial Pigeon (less numerous than the Pied)
- ☐ Pied Imperial Pigeon (look for birds flying over the forest early and late in the day)
- ☐ Green-winged (Emerald Dove) Pigeon
- ☐ Chestnut-breasted Malkoha
- ☐ Collared Scops-Owl
- ☐ Dollarbird (mainly win; try the forest edge near the golf course)
- ☐ Green Iora
- ☐ Red-eyed Bulbul (possibly an endemic subspecies)
- ☐ Hairy-backed Bulbul
- ☐ Greater Racket-tailed Drongo
- ☐ Black-naped Oriole (try the grounds of the resort)
- ☐ Moustached Babbler
- ☐ Grey-throated Babbler (possibly an endemic subspecies)
- ☐ White-rumped Shama
- ☐ Flyeater (also mangroves)

- ☐ Arctic Warbler m
- ☐ Dark-necked Tailorbird
- ☐ Hill Myna (try the forest at the back of the golf course)
- ☐ Brown-throated Sunbird (common around the resort)
- ☐ Crimson-breasted Flowerpecker
- ☐ Orange-bellied Flowerpecker (try the trees on the golf course)
- ☐ Scarlet-backed Flowerpecker (also mangroves)

Difficult-to-find or rare species:
- ☐ Bulwer's Petrel m
- ☐ Christmas Frigatebird m (recorded on several occasions roosting among Lesser Frigatebirds on P. Rengis)
- ☐ Great-billed Heron (probably extinct, but may still occur)
- ☐ Yellow Bittern (can be reasonably plentiful in win; try the overgrown edges of golf course lakes, particularly early and late in the day)
- ☐ Cinnamon Bittern (use the same approach as for Yellow Bittern)
- ☐ Blyth's Hawk-Eagle
- ☐ Watercock (golf course lakes)
- ☐ Malaysian Plover
- ☐ Grey-tailed Tattler m
- ☐ Roseate Tern
- ☐ Nicobar Pigeon
- ☐ Hodgson's Hawk-Cuckoo
- ☐ Brush (Rusty-breasted) Cuckoo
- ☐ Grey Nightjar m
- ☐ Ruddy Kingfisher (mangroves)
- ☐ Bar-bellied Cuckoo-shrike (try the forest at the rear of the golf course)
- ☐ Olive-winged Bulbul (the status of this species is uncertain)
- ☐ Ashy Drongo (six birds seen near the resort in late Oct 1992 were either of this species or the similar-looking Black Drongo)
- ☐ Streaked Wren-Babbler (the only truly montane species on Tioman)
- ☐ Chestnut-winged Babbler (status uncertain)
- ☐ Forest Wagtail m
- ☐ Red-throated Pipit m (two were seen among wagtails on the golf course in 1990)
- ☐ White-shouldered Starling m (a scarce visitor to Malaysia, but worth keeping a watch for - a pair were seen near the airport in late Oct 1992)

Access and accommodation

There are daily Malaysia Airlines flights to Tioman from Kuala Lumpur and from Singapore - for MAS addresses see the front of this book. There are also daily ferry services to the island from Mersing on the adjacent mainland; the one-way fare is about $M30, and you can get tickets at any of the travel agents in Mersing or from the town jetty. Be sure to take an express boat that will get you to Tioman in about one and a half hours; the crossing can be quite rough, especially in the monsoon season, and some of the slower vessels can take four hours to complete the journey.

Accommodation prices on Tioman vary considerably, not only from place to place but also from season to season. If you go when there are not too many people on the island (which is the best time for birdwatching of course), you can haggle with the owners of the smaller establishments and get a nice place on the beach near Kg Tekek for as little as $M40 a night. Except when the island is really busy, and rooms may be hard to find, you shouldn't take the first vacant place you come to; there's a lot of second-rate accommodation, particularly in the vicinity of the airport, and if you look around you will almost certainly find somewhere suitable at a reasonable price. For this reason it is best not to book accommodation in advance (unless you feel it is really necessary) because you may arrive to find you haven't got good value for your money.

A night at the very smart Tioman Island Resort will cost you at least $M100; in contrast, you can get a chalet on the beach at Kg Paya, a few kilometres south of the resort, for around $M30 a night. Keep in mind, however, that if you stay at Paya, or at Salang on Tioman's north-west coast or Juara on the east coast, you'll have a long walk or boat ride to get to Kg Tekek. If you want to check on the availability of accommodation before you leave for the island, just ask any of the travel agents in Mersing. Alternatively, 'phone the Pahang Tourist Information Centre in Kuantan on 09-505566.

When to visit

For migrant birds the best time to go to Tioman is between early October and late March. During the monsoon season the crossing is often very rough, and boat excursions to the smaller islands are frequently cancelled, therefore plan your visit before mid November or after mid January. The worst time for bird variety - and for tourists - is June to September.

Other attractions

Most people go to Tioman for the beaches, and for the snorkelling and diving. The waters off Kg Salang are said to be especially rich in coral and fish; many of the small islands around Tioman are also good for snorkelling - talk to the charter boat operators at Kg Tekek. From May to September turtles come ashore to lay their eggs; Kg Nipah and P. Tulai are the best places to see them. Other animals are generally scarce, although you've a good chance of seeing Water Monitors (try the golf course), Mouse-Deer, and a variety of bats.

25 Endau-Rompin

Pahang/Johor

For many years conservationists in Malaysia - in particular members of the Malayan Nature Society - have been campaigning for the protection of a large tract of forested country straddling the boundary between Pahang and Johor. Encompassing the watershed of the Endau and Rompin rivers, the area in question covers about 800 square kilometres of rugged terrain, most of which lies below 600 m.

Although the hill and lowland forests that once covered this part of Malaysia have been extensively logged, or cleared to make way for oil palms, Endau-Rompin remains an exceedingly rich botanical reserve containing many rare and endemic plants. In addition, recent expeditions have shown that the area supports no fewer than eight species of hornbill, 13 species of woodpecker, 17 species of bulbul (among them the normally difficult-to-find Black-and-White Bulbul), and 24 species of babbler. Other ornithological highlights include Storm's Stork, Giant Pitta and Malaysian Rail-Babbler, while mammals include Slow Loris, Banded and Dusky (Spectacled) Leaf Monkey, White-handed (Lar) Gibbon, Grey-bellied, Prevost's, Black-banded and Giant Squirrel, Common Porcupine, Common Palm Civet, Sun Bear, Leopard, Asian Elephant, Wild Pig, Lesser and Greater Mouse-Deer, and Sambar Deer.

At the time of writing Endau-Rompin is still only a proposed national park; by the time you read this, however, let's hope that those who have worked so hard to prevent further degradation of the area have been given their reward.

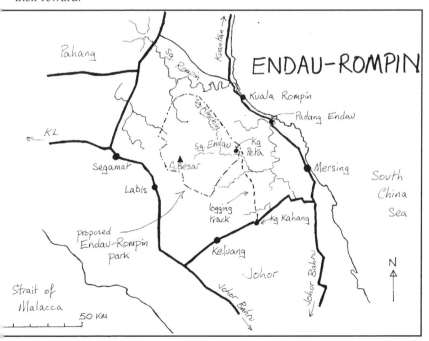

Good birdwatching areas

Two of the richest areas for birds at Endau-Rompin are the Sg. Endau and Sg. Kinchin valleys, near Kampung Peta on the proposed park's eastern boundary. During surveys of the two sites in the mid to late 1980s, close to 200 bird species were found at each place, with tall lowland forest being the most productive habitat.

At present, access to the Endau-Rompin area (including Kampung Peta) is somewhat limited - you'll need a four-wheel-drive vehicle to get along the logging tracks. If Endau-Rompin is made a national park, however, the roads will probably be upgraded; meanwhile, the lack of access does at least keep the tourists out, making the region something of a wilderness. If you want to go there the best plan is to contact the Malayan Nature Society (the address and 'phone number are at the front of this book). The staff at MNS will give you up-to-date information about Endau-Rompin, and will probably put you in touch with someone who knows how you can get there. Alternatively, you could try one of the several tour operators who take special interest groups to the area; MNS may be able to give you some advice, or you could contact Wilderness Experiences, 6B Jalan SS 21/39, Damansara Utama, 47400 Petaling Jaya, Selangor, 'phone 03-7178221.

Birds

Open areas, overhead:
☐ Crested Serpent-Eagle
☐ Japanese Sparrowhawk m
☐ Changeable Hawk-Eagle
☐ Black-thighed Falconet
☐ Long-tailed Parakeet
☐ Blue-rumped Parrot
☐ Malaysian Eared Nightjar
☐ White-bellied (Glossy) Swiftlet
☐ Brown Needletail
☐ Silver-rumped Swift
☐ Fork-tailed Swift m
☐ Asian Palm-Swift
☐ Grey-rumped Treeswift
☐ Blue-throated Bee-eater
☐ Barn Swallow m
☐ Pacific Swallow
☐ Magpie Robin
☐ Common Tailorbird (edges)
☐ Dark-necked Tailorbird (edges)
☐ Richard's Pipit
☐ Eurasian Tree-Sparrow
☐ White-bellied Munia (edges)

Rivers:
☐ Little Heron
☐ Lesser Fish-Eagle
☐ Masked Finfoot m (mainly Feb-June)
☐ Common Sandpiper m

☐ Common Kingfisher (mainly win)
☐ Blue-eared Kingfisher (often along small streams)
☐ White-throated Kingfisher
☐ Black-capped Kingfisher m
☐ Black-and-Red Broadbill
☐ Straw-headed Bulbul
☐ Grey Wagtail m

Ground, lower storey:
☐ Red Junglefowl
☐ Great Argus
☐ Green-winged (Emerald Dove) Pigeon
☐ Plaintive Cuckoo (also middle storey)
☐ Greater Coucal
☐ Gould's Frogmouth (also middle storey)
☐ Scarlet-rumped Trogon (also middle storey)
☐ Oriental Dwarf Kingfisher
☐ Rufous-collared Kingfisher (also middle storey)
☐ Rufous Piculet (also middle storey)
☐ Rufous Woodpecker (also middle storey)
☐ Buff-necked Woodpecker (also middle storey)
☐ Maroon Woodpecker (also middle storey)
☐ Garnet Pitta
☐ Hooded Pitta m
☐ Banded Pitta
☐ Black-and-White Bulbul (also middle storey)
☐ Olive-winged Bulbul (edges)
☐ Spectacled Bulbul (also middle storey)
☐ Grey-cheeked Bulbul (also middle storey)
☐ Yellow-bellied Bulbul
☐ Black-capped Babbler
☐ Short-tailed Babbler
☐ White-chested Babbler (often along streams and rivers)
☐ Abbott's Babbler (edges, including rivers)
☐ Moustached Babbler (also middle storey)
☐ Sooty-capped Babbler (also middle storey)
☐ Scaly-crowned Babbler (also middle storey)
☐ Rufous-crowned Babbler (also middle storey)
☐ Large Wren-Babbler
☐ Grey-headed Babbler
☐ Chestnut-rumped Babbler
☐ Black-throated Babbler
☐ Chestnut-winged Babbler (also middle storey)
☐ Striped Tit-Babbler (also middle storey)
☐ Fluffy-backed Tit-Babbler
☐ Siberian Blue Robin m
☐ White-rumped Shama
☐ Chestnut-naped Forktail (usually near rivers and streams)
☐ Rufous-tailed Tailorbird (edges)

☐ Rufous-chested Flycatcher
☐ Rufous-winged Flycatcher
☐ Tiger Shrike m (edges)
☐ Purple-naped Sunbird
☐ Little Spiderhunter (edges)
☐ Grey-breasted Spiderhunter (also middle storey)
☐ Yellow-breasted Flowerpecker (also middle storey)
☐ Orange-bellied Flowerpecker (also middle storey)
☐ White-rumped Munia (edges)

Middle storey, canopy:
☐ Crested Goshawk
☐ Thick-billed Pigeon
☐ Little Green Pigeon
☐ Jambu Fruit-Dove
☐ Blue-crowned Hanging Parrot (also overhead)
☐ Indian Cuckoo
☐ Banded Bay Cuckoo
☐ Brush (Rusty-breasted) Cuckoo
☐ Violet Cuckoo
☐ Drongo Cuckoo
☐ Chestnut-bellied Malkoha
☐ Raffles' Malkoha
☐ Chestnut-breasted Malkoha
☐ Collared Scops-Owl (also lower storey)
☐ Whiskered Treeswift
☐ Red-naped Trogon
☐ Diard's Trogon (also lower storey)
☐ Banded Kingfisher (also lower storey)
☐ Red-bearded Bee-eater
☐ Dollarbird
☐ Wreathed Hornbill (all hornbills also overhead)
☐ Black Hornbill
☐ Oriental Pied Hornbill (often along rivers)
☐ Rhinoceros Hornbill
☐ Helmeted Hornbill
☐ Gold-whiskered Barbet
☐ Red-throated Barbet
☐ Yellow-crowned Barbet
☐ Blue-eared Barbet
☐ Brown Barbet
☐ Crimson-winged Woodpecker
☐ Checker-throated Woodpecker (also lower storey)
☐ Banded Woodpecker
☐ Buff-rumped Woodpecker
☐ Great Slaty Woodpecker
☐ White-bellied Woodpecker
☐ Grey-and-Buff Woodpecker
☐ Orange-backed Woodpecker
☐ Banded Broadbill

- [ ] Black-and-Yellow Broadbill
- [ ] Green Broadbill (also lower storey)
- [ ] Bar-winged Flycatcher-shrike
- [ ] Black-winged Flycatcher-shrike
- [ ] Bar-bellied Cuckoo-shrike
- [ ] Lesser Cuckoo-shrike
- [ ] Ashy Minivet m (often along rivers)
- [ ] Scarlet Minivet
- [ ] Green Iora
- [ ] Lesser Green Leafbird
- [ ] Greater Green Leafbird
- [ ] Blue-winged Leafbird
- [ ] Black-headed Bulbul
- [ ] Scaly-breasted Bulbul
- [ ] Grey-bellied Bulbul
- [ ] Cream-vented Bulbul
- [ ] Red-eyed Bulbul
- [ ] Hairy-backed Bulbul (also lower storey)
- [ ] Buff-vented Bulbul (also lower storey)
- [ ] Bronzed Drongo (edges)
- [ ] Greater Racket-tailed Drongo
- [ ] Dark-throated Oriole
- [ ] Asian Fairy-Bluebird
- [ ] Black Magpie
- [ ] Velvet-fronted Nuthatch
- [ ] Brown Fulvetta (also lower storey)
- [ ] Flyeater
- [ ] Arctic Warbler m
- [ ] Eastern Crowned Warbler m
- [ ] Pale Blue Flycatcher
- [ ] Grey-headed Flycatcher (also lower storey)
- [ ] Spotted Fantail (also lower storey)
- [ ] Black-naped Monarch (also lower storey)
- [ ] Asian Paradise-Flycatcher (also lower storey)
- [ ] Hill Myna
- [ ] Ruby-cheeked Sunbird (also lower storey)
- [ ] Long-billed Spiderhunter
- [ ] Spectacled Spiderhunter
- [ ] Scarlet-breasted Flowerpecker
- [ ] Crimson-breasted Flowerpecker
- [ ] Yellow-vented Flowerpecker
- [ ] Everett's White-eye

Difficult-to-find or rare species:
- [ ] Storm's Stork
- [ ] Osprey m
- [ ] Eurasian (Crested) Honey-Buzzard
- [ ] Bat Hawk
- [ ] Rufous-bellied Eagle
- [ ] Wallace's Hawk-Eagle

- [ ] Long-billed Partridge
- [ ] Crested Wood-Partridge
- [ ] Crestless Fireback
- [ ] Crested Fireback
- [ ] Pheasant-tailed Jacana m
- [ ] Swinhoe's Snipe m
- [ ] Green Imperial Pigeon
- [ ] Hodgson's Hawk-Cuckoo
- [ ] Black-bellied Malkoha
- [ ] Red-billed Malkoha
- [ ] Short-toed Coucal
- [ ] Bay Owl
- [ ] Reddish Scops-Owl
- [ ] Oriental (Common) Scops-Owl m
- [ ] Barred Eagle-Owl
- [ ] Brown Hawk-Owl
- [ ] Javan Frogmouth
- [ ] White-vented Needletail m
- [ ] Cinnamon-rumped Trogon
- [ ] Orange-breasted Trogon
- [ ] Blue-banded Kingfisher
- [ ] Ruddy Kingfisher (especially win)
- [ ] White-crowned Hornbill
- [ ] Bushy-crested Hornbill
- [ ] Wrinkled Hornbill
- [ ] Red-crowned Barbet
- [ ] Olive-backed Woodpecker
- [ ] Dusky Broadbill
- [ ] Giant Pitta
- [ ] Blue-winged Pitta (mainly win)
- [ ] Large Wood-shrike
- [ ] Fiery Minivet
- [ ] Great Iora
- [ ] Puff-backed Bulbul
- [ ] Finsch's Bulbul
- [ ] Streaked Bulbul
- [ ] Ashy Bulbul
- [ ] Crested Jay
- [ ] Slender-billed Crow
- [ ] Sultan Tit
- [ ] Ferruginous Babbler
- [ ] Horsfield's Babbler
- [ ] Grey-breasted Babbler
- [ ] Chestnut-backed Scimitar-Babbler
- [ ] Striped Wren-Babbler
- [ ] Eye-browed Wren-Babbler
- [ ] Rufous-fronted Babbler
- [ ] Grey-throated Babbler
- [ ] White-necked Babbler
- [ ] White-bellied Yuhina

- [ ] Malaysian Rail-Babbler
- [ ] Rufous-tailed Shama
- [ ] Inornate Warbler m
- [ ] Grey-chested Flycatcher
- [ ] Verditer Flycatcher
- [ ] White-tailed Flycatcher
- [ ] Forest Wagtail m
- [ ] Red-throated Sunbird
- [ ] Purple-throated Sunbird
- [ ] Scarlet Sunbird
- [ ] Thick-billed Spiderhunter
- [ ] Plain Flowerpecker

Access and accommodation

The proposed park lies roughly midway between Segamat, a town on the Kuala Lumpur to Johor Bahru road, and Mersing on the peninsula's east coast. As mentioned, getting into the area is difficult, though with a four-wheel-drive vehicle you can get to Kampung Peta along a logging track that leaves the Keluang to Mersing road at Kampung Kahang (the journey takes around two hours). There are no facilities for visitors of course - you'll have to camp.

When to visit

It would be wise to avoid the height of the monsoon season (late November to mid January) when many of the region's rivers will be swollen, making access even more difficult. Otherwise a visit at any time of the year should prove fruitful, especially the October-November and February-March periods when there could be some interesting migrants about.

Other attractions

Apart from its wealth of flora and fauna, Endau-Rompin offers you the chance to explore along rivers seldom seen by Europeans, and to visit falls and cascades where you can swim in crystal-clear waters. There's a real possibility you'll see at least some of the mammals mentioned earlier, especially the primates, and the area is said to be a stronghold of the endangered Sumatran Rhinoceros.

26 Pasoh Forest Reserve

Negeri Sembilan

Pasoh Forest Reserve consists of a small area (about 600 ha) of primary lowland forest situated within about 1400 ha of selectively logged forest. The site of a forestry research centre, the reserve is almost surrounded by oil palm plantations; however, although isolated from other tracts of lowland forest Pasoh supports a good variety of birds, including at least 11 species of bulbul, 13 species of babbler, three species of pitta, and no fewer than 14 species of woodpecker. As well, it's a site where you have a fair chance of seeing sought-after birds like Long-billed Partridge, Malaysian Peacock-Pheasant, Short-toed Coucal, Banded Kingfisher, Malaysian Rail-Babbler, Rufous-tailed Shama and Grey-chested Flycatcher.

Not surprisingly, Pasoh attracts a steady stream of visiting birders, and the reserve is well known as a good place for owls, frogmouths and nightjars with Bay Owl, Reddish Scops-Owl, Spotted Wood-Owl, and Large and Javan Frogmouth being among the highlights.

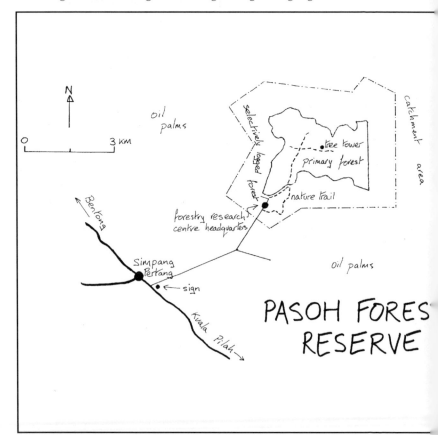

Good birdwatching areas

From the forestry research centre headquarters, just inside the reserve's south-western boundary, there is a short, circular nature trail that takes you through an area of logged forest. To get to the primary forest (usually the better area for birds), keep walking for about a kilometre beyond the hq and take the track that runs northwards to an old tree tower (see map). As is often the case in lowland forest the birding can be very slow at times, but if you spend three or four days at Pasoh you should find at least some of the special birds. Species to look for between the reserve hq and the tree tower include Long-billed Partridge, Short-toed Coucal, Diard's Trogon, Oriental Dwarf Kingfisher, Rufous-collared Kingfisher, Olive-backed Woodpecker, Garnet and Banded Pitta, Grey-breasted Babbler, Large Wren-Babbler, Fluffy-backed Tit-Babbler, Malaysian Rail-Babbler, Rufous-tailed Shama and Grey-chested Flycatcher.

While the primary forest is the main attraction here, don't neglect clearings and the forest edge. Indeed, for owls and other nocturnal birds you should walk from the hq out along the access road; dusk to midnight is probably the best time to go - and, of course, you'll need a good torch or spotlight (and a tape recorder if you have one).

Birds

Open areas, overhead:
- [ ] Black Baza m
- [ ] Crested Serpent-Eagle
- [ ] Pink-necked Pigeon (edges)
- [ ] Long-tailed Parakeet (common; favours oil palms)
- [ ] Blue-rumped Parrot (oil palms)
- [ ] Malaysian Eared Nightjar (especially at dusk)
- [ ] Large-tailed Nightjar
- [ ] Silver-rumped Swift
- [ ] Dollarbird (edges)
- [ ] Common Goldenback
- [ ] Barn Swallow m
- [ ] Pacific Swallow
- [ ] Common Iora (edges)
- [ ] Stripe-throated Bulbul (edges)
- [ ] Yellow-vented Bulbul (edges)
- [ ] Olive-winged Bulbul (edges)
- [ ] Bronzed Drongo (edges)
- [ ] Philippine Glossy Starling

Ground, lower storey:
- [ ] Malaysian Peacock-Pheasant
- [ ] Green-winged (Emerald Dove) Pigeon
- [ ] Gould's Frogmouth (also middle storey)
- [ ] Oriental Dwarf Kingfisher
- [ ] Banded Kingfisher (also middle storey)
- [ ] Rufous Piculet (also middle storey)
- [ ] Rufous Woodpecker (also middle storey)
- [ ] Buff-necked Woodpecker (also middle storey)

- ☐ Garnet Pitta (usually the easiest pitta to find)
- ☐ Hooded Pitta m
- ☐ Banded Pitta
- ☐ Yellow-bellied Bulbul
- ☐ Hairy-backed Bulbul (also middle storey)
- ☐ Black-capped Babbler
- ☐ Short-tailed Babbler
- ☐ Moustached Babbler (also middle storey)
- ☐ Sooty-capped Babbler (edges; also middle storey)
- ☐ Scaly-crowned Babbler (also middle storey)
- ☐ Rufous-crowned Babbler (also middle storey)
- ☐ Large Wren-Babbler
- ☐ Chestnut-rumped Babbler
- ☐ Black-throated Babbler
- ☐ Chestnut-winged Babbler (also middle storey)
- ☐ Fluffy-backed Tit-Babbler
- ☐ Siberian Blue Robin m
- ☐ White-rumped Shama
- ☐ Dark-necked Tailorbird (edges)
- ☐ Yellow-rumped Flycatcher m
- ☐ Rufous-winged Flycatcher (also middle storey)
- ☐ Purple-naped Sunbird
- ☐ Little Spiderhunter (also open areas)
- ☐ Yellow-breasted Flowerpecker (also middle storey)

Middle storey, canopy:
- ☐ Blue-crowned Hanging Parrot (also overhead)
- ☐ Indian Cuckoo
- ☐ Brush (Rusty-breasted) Cuckoo
- ☐ Drongo Cuckoo
- ☐ Chestnut-bellied Malkoha
- ☐ Raffles' Malkoha
- ☐ Chestnut-breasted Malkoha
- ☐ Brown Hawk-Owl
- ☐ Red-naped Trogon
- ☐ Diard's Trogon
- ☐ Scarlet-rumped Trogon (also lower storey)
- ☐ Black Hornbill (also overhead)
- ☐ Gold-whiskered Barbet
- ☐ Blue-eared Barbet
- ☐ Brown Barbet
- ☐ Crimson-winged Woodpecker
- ☐ Checker-throated Woodpecker (also lower storey)
- ☐ Banded Woodpecker
- ☐ Buff-rumped Woodpecker
- ☐ Great Slaty Woodpecker
- ☐ Grey-and-Buff Woodpecker (small and easily overlooked)
- ☐ Maroon Woodpecker (also lower storey)
- ☐ Banded Broadbill
- ☐ Black-and-Yellow Broadbill

- ☐ Green Broadbill (also lower storey)
- ☐ Lesser Cuckoo-shrike
- ☐ Ashy Minivet m
- ☐ Scarlet Minivet
- ☐ Blue-winged Leafbird
- ☐ Black-headed Bulbul
- ☐ Cream-vented Bulbul
- ☐ Spectacled Bulbul (also lower storey)
- ☐ Greater Racket-tailed Drongo
- ☐ Dark-throated Oriole
- ☐ Black Magpie
- ☐ Brown Fulvetta (also lower storey)
- ☐ Flyeater
- ☐ Eastern Crowned Warbler m
- ☐ Grey-headed Flycatcher (also lower storey)
- ☐ Black-naped Monarch (also lower storey)
- ☐ Asian Paradise-Flycatcher (also lower storey)
- ☐ Plain Sunbird
- ☐ Ruby-cheeked Sunbird (also lower storey)
- ☐ Spectacled Spiderhunter
- ☐ Grey-breasted Spiderhunter (also lower storey)
- ☐ Crimson-breasted Flowerpecker (especially edges and clearings)

Difficult-to-find or rare species:
- ☐ Crested Goshawk
- ☐ Changeable Hawk-Eagle
- ☐ Wallace's Hawk-Eagle
- ☐ Long-billed Partridge
- ☐ Black Wood-Partridge
- ☐ Crested Wood-Partridge
- ☐ Crestless Fireback
- ☐ Great Argus (often heard, seldom seen)
- ☐ Little Green Pigeon
- ☐ Large Green Pigeon
- ☐ Jambu Fruit-Dove
- ☐ Violet Cuckoo
- ☐ Red-billed Malkoha
- ☐ Short-toed Coucal
- ☐ Bay Owl
- ☐ White-fronted Scops-Owl
- ☐ Reddish Scops-Owl
- ☐ Barred Eagle-Owl
- ☐ Spotted Wood-Owl (not so much rare as difficult to see)
- ☐ Brown Wood-Owl
- ☐ Large Frogmouth
- ☐ Javan Frogmouth
- ☐ Cinnamon-rumped Trogon
- ☐ Blue-eared Kingfisher (usually near streams and pools)
- ☐ Rufous-collared Kingfisher

☐ Red-crowned Barbet
☐ Malaysian Honeyguide
☐ Olive-backed Woodpecker
☐ White-bellied Woodpecker
☐ Grey-capped Woodpecker
☐ Orange-backed Woodpecker
☐ Lesser Green Leafbird
☐ Black-and-White Bulbul (irregular)
☐ Grey-bellied Bulbul
☐ Puff-backed Bulbul
☐ Crested Jay
☐ Slender-billed Crow
☐ Grey-breasted Babbler
☐ White-necked Babbler
☐ Malaysian Rail-Babbler (very furtive, but responds to
   imitations of its call)
☐ Rufous-tailed Shama
☐ Grey-chested Flycatcher
☐ Narcissus Flycatcher m
☐ Blue-throated Flycatcher m
☐ Japanese Paradise-Flycatcher m

Access and accommodation

Pasoh Forest Reserve is located about 150 km south-east of Kuala Lumpur. To get there from KL, take the bus to Seremban from the Pudu Raya terminal, then catch the bus to Kuala Pilah. From Kuala Pilah you can either try hitching a ride almost into Simpang Pertang, or you can take the bus. About 500 m before Simpang Pertang there's a sign on the right marked 'Felda Pasoh Dua'; from here you may be able to hitch the 5 km to the reserve hq, otherwise you'll have to walk. Allow half a day or more to reach Pasoh from KL.

You can get a bed in the hostel at Pasoh for around $M5 a night; the hostel has cooking facilities, but you'll need to bring your own food. Before visiting the reserve you must get permission by 'phoning the Forest Research Institute of Malaysia on 03-6342633 (FRIM's address is 52109 Kepong, Selangor), and you should book your accommodation at the same time.

When to visit

While almost all of the good birds at Pasoh are residents, there are some interesting migrants on the list (flycatchers for example) thus a visit between September and April would probably be best.

Other attractions

Being small, Pasoh does not support a large variety of mammals, but there are some species to be seen - Banded and Dusky (Spectacled) Leaf Monkey, White-handed (Lar) Gibbon, and Plantain Squirrel are some to look out for.

27 Bako National Park   Sarawak

Situated on a sandstone headland about 40 km north-east of Kuching, the capital of Sarawak, Bako is one of the most accessible parks in Borneo. It is also one of the easiest of the region's parks to explore, for within the 2742 ha reserve there are 16 well-marked walking tracks with a total length of more than 30 kilometres. Although small, the park contains a wide range of habitats, including mudflats, mangroves, peat swamp forest, mixed dipterocarp forest, kerangas forest and padang scrub (the last occurs on top of a sandstone plateau where the desert-like terrain resembles that found in parts of Australia).

While Bako's bird life is not especially rich - about 150 species have been recorded in the area - the park is a convenient place to see shorebirds and forest species almost side by side. And since it is located at the end of a north-facing peninsula, the park attracts fair numbers of migrants, especially from September to November. Among the 50 or so migrant species you could see here are Lesser Frigatebird, Chinese Egret, Mongolian Plover, Greater Sand-Plover, Eastern Curlew, Nordmann's Greenshank, Terek Sandpiper, Grey-tailed Tattler, Asian Dowitcher, and Mugimaki Flycatcher.

Bako is perhaps best known as the place to see animals such as Long-tailed Macaques, Silvered Leaf Monkeys, Plantain Squirrels, Bearded Pigs and giant monitor lizards, all of which occur around the park headquarters at Telok Assam. The rare Proboscis Monkey, an odd-looking, long-nosed animal confined to the larger rivers and coastal swamps of Borneo, is quite common in the park and can be found in mangroves close to Telok Assam.

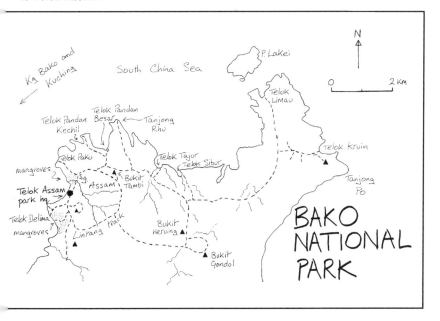

Good birdwatching areas

Depending on the time of year, a variety of shorebirds can usually be seen around Telok Assam, where the mud and sand flats are several hundred metres wide at low tide, and at the five or six bays that lie to the north and east of Telok Assam (see map). You should also keep a watch for shorebirds during the 30-minute boat trip from Kg Bako to the park hq - see Access and accommodation. Mangrove species can be found quite readily near the park hq; try the mangroves a little to the north, at the mouth of the Sg. Assam, where there's an elevated boardwalk that allows you to look into the forest canopy. There is another, more extensive area of mangrove forest at Telok Delima, about a 45-minute walk to the south of park hq (Telok Delima is the best spot in Bako for Proboscis Monkeys).

The park's walking tracks are well maintained, and there are several easy walks of less than a kilometre, as well as a number of quite strenuous treks of six kilometres or longer (a park information leaflet, with a map showing the walking trails, can be obtained from the hq at Telok Assam). One of the most popular walks is the Lintang track, a 5.25 km circular trail that starts at park hq and passes through many of the vegetation types found at Bako, including mangrove forest, kerangas forest and padang scrub.

Birds

Open areas (including beaches and mudflats), overhead:
☐ Little Heron
☐ Pacific Reef-Egret
☐ Chinese Egret m
☐ Little Egret m
☐ Brahminy Kite
☐ White-bellied Sea-Eagle
☐ Japanese Sparrowhawk m (especially Oct-Nov)
☐ Mongolian Plover m
☐ Greater Sand-Plover m
☐ Whimbrel m
☐ Common Redshank m
☐ Terek Sandpiper m
☐ Common Sandpiper m
☐ Grey-tailed Tattler m
☐ Ruddy Turnstone m
☐ Asian Dowitcher m
☐ Rufous-necked Stint m
☐ Curlew Sandpiper m
☐ Black-naped Tern
☐ Little Tern
☐ Great Crested Tern m
☐ Lesser Crested Tern m
☐ Malaysian Eared Nightjar
☐ Large-tailed Nightjar (try around the park hq)
☐ Edible-nest Swiftlet

☐ White-bellied (Glossy) Swiftlet
☐ Silver-rumped Swift
☐ House Swift
☐ Grey-rumped Treeswift
☐ Stork-billed Kingfisher
☐ Black-capped Kingfisher m
☐ Collared Kingfisher
☐ Blue-throated Bee-eater (scarce in win)
☐ Barn Swallow m
☐ Pacific Swallow
☐ Magpie Robin
☐ Yellow Wagtail m
☐ Richard's Pipit
☐ White-breasted Woodswallow (try the mangroves just
  north of the park hq)
☐ Brown Shrike m
☐ Philippine Glossy Starling
☐ Eurasian Tree-Sparrow

Ground, lower storey:
☐ Green-winged (Emerald Dove) Pigeon
☐ Plaintive Cuckoo (favours kerangas forest)
☐ Greater Coucal (look around the park hq)
☐ Scarlet-rumped Trogon (also middle storey)
☐ Blue-eared Kingfisher (especially streams)
☐ Oriental Dwarf Kingfisher
☐ Straw-headed Bulbul (along small streams)
☐ Olive-winged Bulbul (chiefly forest edge)
☐ White-chested Babbler (stream edges)
☐ Horsfield's Babbler (also middle storey)
☐ Abbott's Babbler (edges)
☐ Scaly-crowned Babbler (also middle storey)
☐ Chestnut-winged Babbler
☐ Striped Tit-Babbler
☐ White-rumped Shama
☐ Ashy Tailorbird (mangroves north of park hq)
☐ Rufous-tailed Tailorbird
☐ Grey-chested Flycatcher
☐ Mugimaki Flycatcher m
☐ Malaysian Blue Flycatcher (along forest streams)
☐ Mangrove Blue Flycatcher (also middle storey)
☐ Pied Fantail
☐ Tiger Shrike m
☐ Little Spiderhunter
☐ Yellow-breasted Flowerpecker
☐ Oriental White-eye (chiefly mangroves)
☐ Dusky Munia*

Middle storey, canopy:
☐ Crested Serpent-Eagle (also overhead)
☐ Crested Goshawk

☐ Pink-necked Pigeon (chiefly forest edge)
☐ Drongo Cuckoo
☐ Chestnut-bellied Malkoha
☐ Chestnut-breasted Malkoha
☐ Collared Scops-Owl (also lower storey)
☐ Buffy Fish-Owl (also lower storey; can be active
   during the day)
☐ Dollarbird
☐ Oriental Pied Hornbill (also overhead)
☐ Red-crowned Barbet (try the mangroves just north of park hq)
☐ Blue-eared Barbet
☐ Brown Barbet
☐ Common Goldenback (also open areas)
☐ Grey-capped Woodpecker (favours kerangas forest; also
   mangroves)
☐ Brown-capped Woodpecker (mangroves and coastal scrub)
☐ Black-winged Flycatcher-shrike (look along the beach
   front near park hq)
☐ Bar-bellied Cuckoo-shrike
☐ Lesser Cuckoo-shrike (often in mangroves, as is the next species)
☐ Pied Triller
☐ Fiery Minivet
☐ Scarlet Minivet
☐ Green Iora
☐ Common Iora (also lower storey; favours mangroves)
☐ Greater Green Leafbird
☐ Yellow-vented Bulbul (also lower storey)
☐ Cream-vented Bulbul
☐ Red-eyed Bulbul
☐ Streaked Bulbul
☐ Crow-billed Drongo m (favours mangroves)
☐ Bronzed Drongo (edges)
☐ Greater Racket-tailed Drongo
☐ Asian Fairy-Bluebird
☐ Velvet-fronted Nuthatch (often in the mangroves north of park hq)
☐ Arctic Warbler m
☐ Large-billed Blue Flycatcher
☐ Black-naped Monarch (also lower storey)
☐ Asian Paradise-Flycatcher
☐ Mangrove Whistler (also lower storey)
☐ Hill Myna
☐ Brown-throated Sunbird
☐ Ruby-cheeked Sunbird (also lower storey; try the beach
   front near park hq)
☐ Copper-throated Sunbird (favours mangroves)
☐ Scarlet-breasted Flowerpecker (favours kerangas forest)
☐ Orange-bellied Flowerpecker (around park hq)
☐ Scarlet-backed Flowerpecker

Difficult-to-find or rare species:
- [ ] Bulwer's Petrel m
- [ ] Lesser Frigatebird m
- [ ] Great-billed Heron
- [ ] Great Egret m
- [ ] Intermediate (Plumed) Egret m
- [ ] Lesser Adjutant
- [ ] Osprey m
- [ ] Grey-headed Fish-Eagle
- [ ] Peregrine Falcon m
- [ ] Malaysian Plover
- [ ] Eurasian Curlew m
- [ ] Eastern Curlew m
- [ ] Black-tailed Godwit m
- [ ] Bar-tailed Godwit m
- [ ] Spotted Redshank m
- [ ] Marsh Sandpiper m
- [ ] Common Greenshank m
- [ ] Nordmann's Greenshank m
- [ ] Red Knot m
- [ ] Great Knot m
- [ ] Broad-billed Sandpiper m
- [ ] Ruff m
- [ ] Red-necked Phalarope m (chiefly Sept-Nov)
- [ ] Red (Grey) Phalarope m (chiefly Sept-Nov)
- [ ] Great (Beach) Thick-knee
- [ ] Whiskered Tern m
- [ ] White-winged Tern m
- [ ] Gull-billed Tern m
- [ ] Roseate Tern
- [ ] Bridled Tern
- [ ] Sooty Tern m
- [ ] Cinnamon-headed Pigeon (mainly mangroves)
- [ ] Green Imperial Pigeon
- [ ] Pied Imperial Pigeon
- [ ] Violet Cuckoo
- [ ] Bay Owl
- [ ] Sunda Frogmouth
- [ ] White-throated Needletail m (mainly Oct-Dec)
- [ ] Fork-tailed Swift m (mainly Sept-Oct)
- [ ] Black Hornbill
- [ ] Malaysian Honeyguide (though somewhat rare, this species has been recorded a number of times in the Kuching area and has been seen in Bako National Park)
- [ ] White-bellied Woodpecker
- [ ] Ashy Minivet m
- [ ] Great Tit (rarely reported, but one to watch out for in mangroves)
- [ ] White Wagtail m
- [ ] Plain Sunbird

☐ Red-throated Sunbird
☐ Olive-backed Sunbird
☐ Crimson Sunbird

Access and accommodation

To reach Bako National Park you must first travel by road to Kg Bako, which is about a 45-minute drive from Kuching, then you take a boat to the park hq at Telok Assam. The Petra Jaya Transport Company in Kuching operates a bus service to Kg Bako (catch bus number 6); alternatively you can take a taxi, but it'll cost you about $M50. For the journey from Kg Bako to Telok Assam you can either hire a private boat or go in the official park boat. The average price of the boat trip is $M20 per person; however, if there are only two or three of you the fare could be quite a bit more.

Accommodation at park hq consists mainly of two-roomed bungalows where a room will cost you around $M30 per night (you can book the whole bungalow - each one houses up to 10 people - for about $M60 a night). There is also a hostel where a bunk bed costs about $M3 per night (if you want a room to yourself in the hostel you'll pay about $M13 a night). The bungalows and the hostel have bedding, cooking facilities and fans, but no air-conditioners. All accommodation must be booked in advance through the Sarawak National Parks Booking Office, Tourist Information Centre, Main Bazaar, Kuching 93000, 'phone 082-248088 or 410944. There is a canteen at park hq where you can get cheap meals, as well as a shop that sells basic items.

If you don't want to go to the trouble of arranging your own visit to Bako, there are a number of tour operators in Kuching who will take you there (at a price!) - inquire at the Tourist Information Centre.

When to visit

Since about a third of the birds on Bako's list are migrants, a visit between early September and late November will be best. Remember that the monsoon season here is from November to February or March, and during this time there may be occasions when seas are too rough for boats to get to the park. If you can, avoid June, July and August when the park may be crowded and accommodation difficult to find.

Other attractions

In addition to animals like the Proboscis Monkey, Bako supports a rich assemblage of plants - in the kerangas forest and padang scrub on the plateau you will find three types of pitcher plant, as well as four species of the equally fascinating ant plant. For more details about the park's natural history, call at the information centre at park hq where there are displays, exhibits and audio-visual programmes. Those interested in snorkelling should try the Telok Limau-Pulau Lakei area, north-east of Telok Assam.

28 Niah National Park   Sarawak

Covering an area of 3140 ha, Niah National Park lies about 110 km south-west of Miri via the road to Bintulu. For most visitors the main attraction at Niah is the limestone cave complex, a system that includes the Great Cave, which is one of the largest caves in the world, the Painted Cave, with its prehistoric haematite rock paintings, and the Traders Cave. The last is so named because until 1975, when Niah was made a national park, it contained a village that was home to the hundreds of local people who collect guano and swiftlet nests from the caves. This practice has now been curtailed to some extent for conservation reasons; however, nests are still harvested in their thousands for making the famous birds' nest soup - you can see people at work collecting swiftlet nests in the Great Cave.

For birdwatchers, the cave system at Niah is of considerable interest because of the vast numbers of Black-nest Swiftlets that breed there; as well, Mossy-nest Swiftlets breed in the Great Cave and, if you're fortunate, you could find Bat Hawk and Barred Eagle-Owl near the main cave entrance. In addition to caves, Niah contains extensive stands of peat swamp forest and mixed dipterocarp forest, and since the park has several good walking tracks - including a four-kilometre boardwalk - it is an excellent place to look for birds such as malkohas, trogons (Red-naped, Diard's and Scarlet-rumped), forest kingfishers (especially Oriental Dwarf and Rufous-collared), barbets (including Red-crowned and Red-throated), woodpeckers, broadbills (including Banded and Black-and-Yellow), Garnet Pitta, leafbirds, bulbuls, Dark-throated Oriole, babblers and flycatchers.

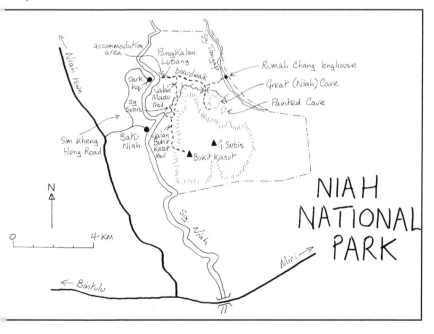

Good birdwatching areas

Much of what Niah has to offer can be seen from the boardwalk that starts at Pangkalan Lubang, on the east bank of the Sg. Niah opposite the park headquarters (see map). The boardwalk leads to the main cave complex, and it's an easy trek with no steep sections.

Before you set off to the caves it is worth spending some time birding along the forest edge in the vicinity of the accommodation area; birds are often easier to see here than they are in the dense forest along parts of the boardwalk. Likewise, en route to the caves you should stop for a while shortly after passing the Jalan Madu trail (this track leaves the main boardwalk about 600 m beyond the accommodation area); some 50 m after the Madu trail there's a section where the boardwalk is raised, allowing you to look into forest that at this point is relatively open. Another good spot along the boardwalk is near the bridge over the stream close to the turn-off to the Rumah Chang longhouse.

For the more intrepid birder there are two other trails in the park - the Jalan Madu track, which takes you through peat swamp forest along the edge of the Sg. Subis, and the Jalan Bukit Kasut trail, which runs through alluvial and riparian forest, then through kerangas forest to the 300 m summit of Bukit Kasut. Both walks will take you about an hour to complete (each way), and both tracks can be muddy and slippery, especially after heavy rain.

Birds

Open areas, overhead:
- [ ] Bat Hawk (look around the cave entrances, especially at dusk)
- [ ] Brahminy Kite (Sg. Niah)
- [ ] Malaysian Eared Nightjar
- [ ] Black-nest Swiftlet
- [ ] Mossy-nest (Uniform) Swiftlet
- [ ] White-bellied (Glossy) Swiftlet
- [ ] Silver-rumped Swift
- [ ] Pacific Swallow

Ground, lower storey:
- [ ] Crested Wood-Partridge (favours bamboo groves and forest clearings)
- [ ] Crested Fireback
- [ ] Green-winged (Emerald Dove) Pigeon
- [ ] Collared Scops-Owl (also middle storey)
- [ ] Gould's Frogmouth (also middle storey)
- [ ] Diard's Trogon (also middle storey)
- [ ] Blue-eared Kingfisher (streams)
- [ ] Oriental Dwarf Kingfisher (probably the most common kingfisher here)
- [ ] Rufous-collared Kingfisher (also middle storey)
- [ ] Black-and-Red Broadbill (especially the Sg. Niah; also middle storey)
- [ ] Garnet Pitta (probably the most common pitta here)
- [ ] Hooded Pitta (especially win)

☐ Straw-headed Bulbul (stream and river edges)
☐ Olive-winged Bulbul (forest edge)
☐ Spectacled Bulbul (also middle storey)
☐ Grey-cheeked Bulbul (also middle storey)
☐ Yellow-bellied Bulbul
☐ Black-capped Babbler
☐ Short-tailed Babbler
☐ White-chested Babbler (along streams)
☐ Sooty-capped Babbler (forest edge; also middle storey)
☐ Scaly-crowned Babbler (also middle storey)
☐ Rufous-crowned Babbler (also middle storey)
☐ Grey-headed Babbler
☐ Chestnut-rumped Babbler
☐ Black-throated Babbler
☐ Chestnut-winged Babbler
☐ Siberian Blue Robin m
☐ White-rumped Shama
☐ Dark-necked Tailorbird
☐ Ashy Tailorbird (edges)
☐ Grey-chested Flycatcher
☐ Malaysian Blue Flycatcher (along rivers and streams)
☐ Pied Fantail (edges)
☐ Maroon-breasted Flycatcher (along streams)
☐ Rufous-winged Flycatcher
☐ Purple-naped Sunbird (stream and river edges)
☐ Little Spiderhunter
☐ Orange-bellied Flowerpecker (also middle storey)
☐ Dusky Munia* (look around the park hq)

Middle storey, canopy:
☐ Crested Serpent-Eagle (also overhead)
☐ Crested Goshawk
☐ Black-thighed Falconet (edges; also open areas)
☐ Pink-necked Pigeon (edges; also open areas)
☐ Blue-crowned Hanging Parrot (try around the park hq)
☐ Banded Bay Cuckoo
☐ Brush (Rusty-breasted) Cuckoo
☐ Violet Cuckoo
☐ Drongo Cuckoo
☐ Black-bellied Malkoha
☐ Chestnut-bellied Malkoha
☐ Raffles' Malkoha
☐ Chestnut-breasted Malkoha
☐ Barred Eagle-Owl (try the main cave entrance just before nightfall)
☐ Brown Hawk-Owl
☐ Grey-rumped Treeswift (forest edge; also overhead)
☐ Whiskered Treeswift (edges; also overhead)
☐ Red-naped Trogon
☐ Scarlet-rumped Trogon (also lower storey)
☐ Red-bearded Bee-eater

- [ ] Bushy-crested Hornbill
- [ ] Red-crowned Barbet
- [ ] Red-throated Barbet
- [ ] Blue-eared Barbet
- [ ] Brown Barbet
- [ ] Rufous Woodpecker (also lower storey)
- [ ] Crimson-winged Woodpecker
- [ ] Buff-rumped Woodpecker
- [ ] Buff-necked Woodpecker (also lower storey)
- [ ] Maroon Woodpecker
- [ ] Orange-backed Woodpecker
- [ ] Banded Broadbill
- [ ] Black-and-Yellow Broadbill
- [ ] Green Broadbill
- [ ] Black-winged Flycatcher-shrike
- [ ] Green Iora
- [ ] Common Iora (edges; also lower storey)
- [ ] Lesser Green Leafbird
- [ ] Greater Green Leafbird
- [ ] Black-headed Bulbul
- [ ] Cream-vented Bulbul
- [ ] Red-eyed Bulbul
- [ ] Hairy-backed Bulbul (also lower storey)
- [ ] Crow-billed Drongo m
- [ ] Bronzed Drongo (favours clearings)
- [ ] Greater Racket-tailed Drongo
- [ ] Dark-throated Oriole
- [ ] Crested Jay (also lower storey)
- [ ] Black Magpie
- [ ] Flyeater
- [ ] Large-billed Blue Flycatcher
- [ ] Spotted Fantail (also lower storey)
- [ ] Black-naped Monarch (also lower storey)
- [ ] Asian Paradise-Flycatcher
- [ ] Hill Myna
- [ ] Brown-throated Sunbird (edges; also open areas)
- [ ] Ruby-cheeked Sunbird
- [ ] Grey-breasted Spiderhunter (also lower storey)
- [ ] Scarlet-breasted Flowerpecker
- [ ] Yellow-breasted Flowerpecker (also lower storey)

Difficult-to-find or rare species:
- [ ] Jerdon's Baza
- [ ] Wallace's Hawk-Eagle
- [ ] Peregrine Falcon m
- [ ] Crestless Fireback
- [ ] Red-billed Malkoha
- [ ] Reddish Scops-Owl
- [ ] Large Frogmouth
- [ ] White-throated Needletail m (especially Oct-Dec)

- [ ] Blue-banded Kingfisher
- [ ] Banded Kingfisher
- [ ] White-crowned Hornbill
- [ ] Black Hornbill
- [ ] Dusky Broadbill
- [ ] Fairy Pitta m
- [ ] Blue-headed Pitta*
- [ ] Grey-bellied Bulbul
- [ ] Ashy Bulbul
- [ ] Chestnut-backed Scimitar-Babbler
- [ ] Striped Wren-Babbler
- [ ] Fluffy-backed Tit-Babbler
- [ ] Malaysian Rail-Babbler
- [ ] Rufous-tailed Shama
- [ ] Chestnut-naped Forktail
- [ ] White-crowned Forktail
- [ ] Chestnut-capped Thrush
- [ ] Crimson Sunbird
- [ ] Long-billed Spiderhunter
- [ ] Yellow-eared Spiderhunter

Access and accommodation

You can get to Niah National Park by bus or by taxi from either Miri or Bintulu. From Miri the bus fare is about $M10 (the journey takes about two and a half hours - catch the bus at the Malay Street terminal) while a taxi will cost around $M80 (you can of course share the cost if there are several of you). From Bintulu the bus fare is about $M12; a taxi will cost you about $M100. If you travel by bus you'll either be dropped off at Batu Niah or in Niah town. You will then have to take a taxi to the park hq at the end of Sim Kheng Hong Road, at a cost of about $M10 (or you can walk, but it'll take you about an hour to get there on foot).

At the park hq you can stay in a chalet for around $M30 per night (or $M60 if you want a chalet to yourself); alternatively, a bunk bed in the hostel will cost you about $M3 a night (or $M18 if you want a room to yourself). You must book accommodation in advance - write to the National Parks and Wildlife Office, Forest Department, Miri 98000, Sarawak, or 'phone 085-36637 (the NP&W Office is located off Jalan Kingsway in Miri). There is a shop at park hq where you can buy basic items, as well as a canteen where you can get simple meals.

When to visit

Almost all of the birds at Niah are residents, therefore a visit at any time of the year should prove productive. It is always hot and humid in this part of Borneo, with November, December and January being among the worst months for rain and humidity.

Other attractions

You can explore the Great Cave on your own, but you'll need a permit and a park guide if you wish to enter the Painted Cave (inquire about permits and guides at the NP&W Office in Miri). Not only do the caves hold tens of thousands of breeding swiftlets, they are also inhabited by huge numbers of bats - Bornean Horseshoe Bat, Cave Nectar Bat, Lesser Bent-winged Bat and Black-bearded Tomb Bat are just some of the species found at Niah.

Among the other animals to be seen in the park are Long-tailed Macaque, squirrels, Malay Weasel, flying lizards, Water Monitor and Mouse-Deer; you can find out more about the park's natural history at the information centre at park hq. As well, it is worth taking a trip to the Iban longhouse at Rumah Chang, which is about 45 minutes from park hq via the cave boardwalk.

29 Lambir Hills
National Park   Sarawak

Lambir Hills National Park is located some 24 km south of Miri, along the
road to Bintulu. With an area of 6952 ha, the park protects the central
portion of the Lambir Hills, a rugged east-west sandstone escarpment
rising to 465 m (about 1500 feet) at Bukit Lambir. Mixed dipterocarp forest,
dominated by meranti, kapur and keruing with an understorey of palms,
gingers and ferns, covers about half the reserve; as well, there are
extensive stands of kerangas forest characterised by pole-like trees with
small sclerophyllous (hard) leaves. Although much of the vegetation in the
park is undisturbed, the dipterocarp forest has been heavily logged in
places, while other areas have been cleared for cultivation and to make
room for visitor facilities.

From the park headquarters, which is situated just off the Miri to Bintulu
road, in the western part of the reserve, there are walking tracks leading to
eight small waterfalls, and to the summits of Bukit Pantu and Bukit
Lambir. All of the trails are well marked and some, like the 30-minute
walk to the Third (Latak) Waterfall, take you through superb forest and
along crystal-clear streams. Needless to say, you could spend a very
enjoyable day or so in the park - just some of the birds to look forward to
here are Oriental Dwarf and Rufous-collared Kingfisher, Red-crowned
Barbet, Black-and-Yellow Broadbill, Green Broadbill, Lesser Green
Leafbird, Black-and-White Bulbul, Dark-throated Oriole, Asian Fairy-
Bluebird, White-chested Babbler, Ruby-cheeked Sunbird and Yellow-
rumped Flowerpecker.

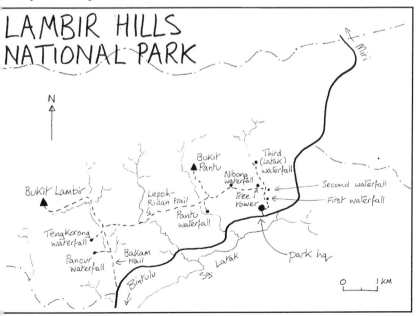

Good birdwatching areas

All of the park's trails offer good birding. However, the main walk to the First, Second and Third waterfalls can be very busy at weekends and during holiday periods when large numbers of people go to the park to swim. At these times it would be best to get out first thing in the morning, before the crowds arrive; otherwise, if you're not an early riser try the Lepoh-Ridan and Bakam trails, west of the park hq, which will take you into the more remote parts of the reserve and away from the most popular swimming spots.

Birds

Open areas, overhead:
- [ ] Crested Serpent-Eagle
- [ ] Japanese Sparrowhawk m (especially Oct-Nov)
- [ ] White-bellied (Glossy) Swiftlet
- [ ] Pacific Swallow
- [ ] Magpie Robin
- [ ] Grey Wagtail m
- [ ] Eurasian Tree-Sparrow

Ground, lower storey:
- [ ] Crested Wood-Partridge (especially bamboo groves and forest clearings)
- [ ] Crested Fireback
- [ ] Green-winged (Emerald Dove) Pigeon
- [ ] Collared Scops-Owl (also middle storey)
- [ ] Gould's Frogmouth (also middle storey)
- [ ] Diard's Trogon (also middle storey)
- [ ] Blue-eared Kingfisher (along streams)
- [ ] Oriental Dwarf Kingfisher (not uncommon, but easily overlooked)
- [ ] Rufous-collared Kingfisher (again, not uncommon but can be hard to pick up)
- [ ] Black-and-Red Broadbill (along the larger streams; also middle storey)
- [ ] Garnet Pitta
- [ ] Straw-headed Bulbul (along streams)
- [ ] Black-and-White Bulbul (also middle storey)
- [ ] Olive-winged Bulbul (forest edge)
- [ ] Grey-cheeked Bulbul (also middle storey)
- [ ] Yellow-bellied Bulbul
- [ ] Black-capped Babbler
- [ ] Short-tailed Babbler
- [ ] White-chested Babbler (along streams)
- [ ] Sooty-capped Babbler (forest edge; also middle storey)
- [ ] Rufous-crowned Babbler (also middle storey)
- [ ] Grey-headed Babbler
- [ ] Chestnut-rumped Babbler
- [ ] Black-throated Babbler
- [ ] Chestnut-winged Babbler (also middle storey)
- [ ] Siberian Blue Robin m (especially along streams)
- [ ] White-rumped Shama

- ☐ Dark-necked Tailorbird
- ☐ Malaysian Blue Flycatcher (along streams)
- ☐ Spotted Fantail (also middle storey)
- ☐ Maroon-breasted Flycatcher (often close to streams)
- ☐ Rufous-winged Flycatcher
- ☐ Ruby-cheeked Sunbird (also middle storey)
- ☐ Purple-naped Sunbird (stream edges)
- ☐ Little Spiderhunter
- ☐ Yellow-breasted Flowerpecker
- ☐ Orange-bellied Flowerpecker
- ☐ Dusky Munia*

Middle storey, canopy:
- ☐ Crested Goshawk
- ☐ Black-thighed Falconet (forest edge)
- ☐ Little Green Pigeon
- ☐ Pink-necked Pigeon (also open areas)
- ☐ Blue-crowned Hanging Parrot
- ☐ Hodgson's Hawk-Cuckoo (especially win; also lower storey)
- ☐ Indian Cuckoo
- ☐ Plaintive Cuckoo (favours kerangas forest)
- ☐ Drongo Cuckoo
- ☐ Black-bellied Malkoha
- ☐ Chestnut-bellied Malkoha
- ☐ Raffles' Malkoha
- ☐ Chestnut-breasted Malkoha
- ☐ Grey-rumped Treeswift (forest edge; also open areas)
- ☐ Whiskered Treeswift (forest edge)
- ☐ Red-naped Trogon
- ☐ Scarlet-rumped Trogon (also lower storey)
- ☐ Red-bearded Bee-eater
- ☐ Dollarbird (edges; also open areas)
- ☐ Bushy-crested Hornbill
- ☐ Red-crowned Barbet
- ☐ Red-throated Barbet
- ☐ Blue-eared Barbet
- ☐ Brown Barbet
- ☐ Rufous Woodpecker (also lower storey)
- ☐ Crimson-winged Woodpecker
- ☐ Buff-rumped Woodpecker
- ☐ Buff-necked Woodpecker (also lower storey)
- ☐ Maroon Woodpecker (also lower storey)
- ☐ Orange-backed Woodpecker
- ☐ Banded Broadbill
- ☐ Black-and-Yellow Broadbill
- ☐ Green Broadbill (also lower storey)
- ☐ Black-winged Flycatcher-shrike
- ☐ Green Iora
- ☐ Lesser Green Leafbird
- ☐ Greater Green Leafbird

- [ ] Blue-winged Leafbird
- [ ] Black-headed Bulbul
- [ ] Cream-vented Bulbul
- [ ] Red-eyed Bulbul
- [ ] Spectacled Bulbul (also lower storey)
- [ ] Crow-billed Drongo m
- [ ] Bronzed Drongo (forest edge and clearings)
- [ ] Greater Racket-tailed Drongo
- [ ] Dark-throated Oriole
- [ ] Asian Fairy-Bluebird
- [ ] Crested Jay (also lower storey)
- [ ] Black Magpie
- [ ] Velvet-fronted Nuthatch
- [ ] Moustached Babbler (also lower storey)
- [ ] Large-billed Blue Flycatcher
- [ ] Black-naped Monarch (also lower storey)
- [ ] Asian Paradise-Flycatcher
- [ ] Hill Myna
- [ ] Plain Sunbird
- [ ] Grey-breasted Spiderhunter (also lower storey)
- [ ] Scarlet-breasted Flowerpecker
- [ ] Yellow-rumped Flowerpecker* (forest edge)

Difficult-to-find or rare species:
- [ ] Jerdon's Baza
- [ ] Eurasian (Crested) Honey-Buzzard
- [ ] Changeable Hawk-Eagle
- [ ] Crestless Fireback
- [ ] Great Argus
- [ ] Thick-billed Pigeon
- [ ] Large Green Pigeon
- [ ] Jambu Fruit-Dove
- [ ] Violet Cuckoo
- [ ] Red-billed Malkoha
- [ ] Reddish Scops-Owl
- [ ] Brown Wood-Owl
- [ ] Large Frogmouth
- [ ] Blue-banded Kingfisher
- [ ] Banded Kingfisher
- [ ] Black Hornbill
- [ ] Rufous Piculet
- [ ] Fairy Pitta m
- [ ] Blue-headed Pitta*
- [ ] Hooded Pitta (especially win)
- [ ] Large Wood-shrike
- [ ] Bar-bellied Cuckoo-shrike
- [ ] Hairy-backed Bulbul
- [ ] Rufous-tailed Shama
- [ ] Chestnut-naped Forktail
- [ ] White-crowned Forktail

☐ Crimson Sunbird
☐ Long-billed Spiderhunter
☐ Yellow-eared Spiderhunter

Access and accommodation

You can reach Lambir Hills National Park by bus from Miri (take the Batu Niah bus and get off at the park hq), but it's probably better to take a taxi so that you get there early in the morning. A taxi from Miri will cost around $M40 and the trip takes less than thirty minutes.

Accommodation at park hq consists of a number of chalets where a room will cost you about $M30 a night (or $M60 for the whole chalet), and a hostel where a bunk bed costs $M3 (a room to yourself will cost you $M18). Bookings for accommodation must be made in advance through the National Parks and Wildlife Office, Forest Department, Miri 98000, Sarawak, 'phone 085-36637 (the NP&W Office is situated off Jalan Kingsway in Miri). There is a small information centre at park hq, as well as a canteen where you can buy cheap meals and basic necessities.

When to visit

As with Niah National Park, almost all of the birds here are residents thus a visit at any time of the year will be rewarding. It's hot and humid year round, but at the end of your walk you can cool off in one of the park's natural swimming pools.

Other attractions

In addition to about 150 bird species, Lambir Hills National Park supports some 30 species of mammal, about 20 different types of reptile, and more than 20 species of butterfly. Among the mammals to look for are Bornean Gibbon, Slow Loris, Sambar Deer (Rusa), Bearded Pig, Pangolin (Scaly Anteater) and Lesser Sheath-tailed Bat. Butterflies include the magnificent Rajah Brooke's Birdwing - look for it along streams and near waterfalls.

30 Gunung Mulu National Park

Sarawak

Opened to the public as recently as 1985, Gunung Mulu National Park encompasses some 544 square kilometres and is situated in the north of Sarawak, on the Brunei border. Although the park has a great many other interesting features, Mulu is best known for its spectacular caves; during expeditions in the 1970s and 1980s, more than 30 caves and almost 200 km of passages were surveyed - and it's thought that this represents only about a third of the park's cave system. Other statistics are equally impressive: for example, Mulu's Sarawak Chamber - 600 m long, 450 m wide and 100 m high - is the largest cave in the world; the passage in Deer Cave, at about 100 m wide and 120 m high, is said to be the largest on earth; and the 60-kilometre Clearwater Cave is the longest cave system in south-east Asia.

Not all the attractions at Mulu are underground. The park is named after Sarawak's second highest mountain, G. Mulu (2376 m [about 7800 feet]), while another of the reserve's high peaks, G. Api (1710 m [5600 feet]), is famous for the fantastic, dagger-like limestone formations, known as the Pinnacles, that rise 45 m above the trees on the mountain's northern slopes.

For the birdwatcher, it is not so much Mulu's caves and mountains that are of interest, it's the park's rich diversity of plants and animals. All the major inland vegetation types found in Borneo occur within the reserve, including peat swamp forest, mixed dipterocarp forest, kerangas forest and moss forest. Scientific surveys, namely the joint Sarawak Government-Royal Geographical Society expedition in the late 1970s, have shown that Mulu supports at least 1500 species of flowering plants, among them some 170 species of orchid and 10 species of pitcher plant. As well, nearly 70 mammal species (including 12 bats), about 75 frog species, and almost 300 species of butterfly have been recorded.

Mulu is undoubtedly one of the best birding destinations in Malaysia (and in south-east Asia for that matter). More than 300 bird species occur in the park, including no fewer than 25 Bornean endemics. Among the more sought-after species you can expect to see in the lower lying areas are Bat Hawk, Lesser Fish-Eagle, Crested Wood-Partridge, Large Green Pigeon, Blue-headed Pitta, White-crowned Forktail and Sunda Whistling Thrush, while lowland rarities to look for include Storm's Stork, Wallace's Hawk-Eagle, Black Wood-Partridge, Sunda Ground-Cuckoo, Large Frogmouth, Malaysian Honeyguide and Hook-billed Bulbul. The park's slopes and mountain peaks hold a wide variety of submontane and montane birds, including Kinabalu (Mountain) Serpent-Eagle, Blyth's Hawk-Eagle, Red-breasted Partridge, Crimson-headed Partridge, Bulwer's Pheasant, Orange-breasted Trogon, Hose's Broadbill, Whitehead's Broadbill, Black-breasted Triller, Mountain Wren-Babbler, White-browed Shortwing, Everett's Thrush, Mountain (Sunda) Bush-Warbler, Indigo Flycatcher and Whitehead's Spiderhunter.

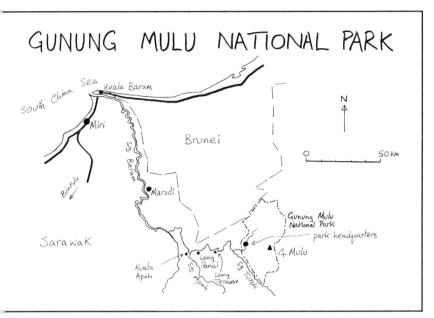

GUNUNG MULU NATIONAL PARK

Map labels: South China Sea, Kuala Baram, South China, Miri, Sg. Baram, Brunei, Bintulu, Marudi, Sarawak, N, 0 50 KM, Gunung Mulu National Park, park headquarters, G. Mulu, Kuala Apoh, Long Panai, Sg. Apoh, Long Terawan, Sg. Tutoh

Good birdwatching areas

At the time of writing the visitor facilities at Mulu are still being developed, and the walking track system is nowhere near as extensive as those in Malaysia's other major parks. Even so, there is plenty of scope for the average birder to spend a week exploring around the park headquarters, while the more adventurous visitor could easily fill two or more weeks with treks to the Pinnacles and to the summit of G. Mulu. From park hq, the trip to the Pinnacles and back takes three to four days (for part of the journey you go by boat up the Sg. Melinau, shooting rapids along the way); the return trek to the top of G. Mulu takes four days.

Around the park hq, there's good birding to be had along the banks of the Sg. Melinau, and along the fringes of the lowland forest bordering the cleared areas. Also rewarding is the three to four kilometre walk to Long Pala and Deer Cave. The walk from park hq to the cave takes around an hour - or considerably longer if the birding is really good - and the well-marked trail (there's a boardwalk most of the way) cuts through a patch of freshwater swamp forest where you've a fair chance of seeing pittas, forktails and other interesting species. Deer Cave is famous because of the millions of bats (mainly Wrinkle-lipped) that roost deep within its dark confines; at dusk, the bats stream out of the cave en masse and head off to their feeding grounds, and in a clearing near the cave entrance an observatory has been built so that visitors can view the spectacle - it's one not to be missed. The bat observatory, which is situated close to a small stream, is usually a good area for birds - keep a watch for Bat Hawk in the early evening.

As well as walking to Deer Cave, it's well worth taking a boat trip up the Sg. Melinau to Clearwater Cave. En route to the cave you'll almost certainly see Black-and-Red Broadbills in the trees overhanging the river, while Lesser Fish-Eagle and Buffy Fish-Owl are distinct possibilities. At the cave there's a picnic area that is often crowded around lunchtime, but if you get there in the early morning you'll have the place virtually to yourself (as a rule, everybody heads straight underground). Though there are no walking tracks at Clearwater, with a bit of scrambling you can get across the river - it's quite narrow - and into the forest opposite the picnic ground. Birds to look for in the area include Hose's Broadbill, White-crowned Forktail and Sunda Whistling Thrush.

Birds

Open areas, overhead:
☐ Eurasian (Crested) Honey-Buzzard
☐ Bat Hawk (can be seen most evenings at or near Deer Cave)
☐ Crested Serpent-Eagle
☐ Black-thighed Falconet (look around the park hq)
☐ Peregrine Falcon (a pair, apparently resident birds,
  inhabit the cliffs above Deer Cave)
☐ Pink-necked Pigeon
☐ Malaysian Eared Nightjar (around park hq)
☐ Black-nest Swiftlet
☐ Mossy-nest (Uniform) Swiftlet
☐ White-bellied (Glossy) Swiftlet
☐ Silver-rumped Swift
☐ Barn Swallow m
☐ Pacific Swallow
☐ Yellow-vented Bulbul (around park hq and Long Pala)
☐ Magpie Robin
☐ Yellow Wagtail m (in short grass)
☐ Philippine Glossy Starling
☐ Eurasian Tree-Sparrow
☐ Dusky Munia* (around park hq and Long Pala)

Rivers:
☐ Little Heron
☐ Brahminy Kite (along the larger rivers)
☐ Lesser Fish-Eagle (try the Sg. Melinau)
☐ White-breasted Waterhen
☐ Common Sandpiper m
☐ Greater Coucal (river edge; has been recorded near park hq)
☐ Buffy Fish-Owl (river edge; look for it en route to Clearwater
  Cave; can be active by day)
☐ Stork-billed Kingfisher
☐ Black-capped Kingfisher m
☐ Black-and-Red Broadbill (riverside vegetation; almost
  a certainty between park hq and Clearwater Cave)

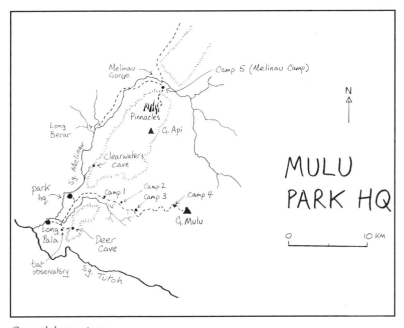

MULU
PARK HQ

Ground, lower storey:
☐ Blue-breasted Quail (in grassland; try around Long Pala)
☐ Crested Wood-Partridge (especially bamboo groves and
   clearings; look along the track to Deer Cave)
☐ Crested Fireback
☐ Spotted Dove (around park hq)
☐ Green-winged (Emerald Dove) Pigeon (look along the
   track to Deer Cave)
☐ Collared Scops-Owl (also middle storey)
☐ Diard's Trogon (also middle storey)
☐ Blue-eared Kingfisher (along small streams)
☐ Oriental Dwarf Kingfisher (try the Deer Cave track)
☐ Rufous-collared Kingfisher (also middle storey)
☐ Rufous Piculet (also middle storey)
☐ Garnet Pitta
☐ Blue-headed Pitta*
☐ Straw-headed Bulbul (river and stream edges)
☐ Black-and-White Bulbul (also middle storey)
☐ Olive-winged Bulbul (forest edge)
☐ Grey-cheeked Bulbul (also middle storey)
☐ Yellow-bellied Bulbul
☐ Black-capped Babbler
☐ Short-tailed Babbler
☐ White-chested Babbler (along streams)
☐ Ferruginous Babbler (also middle storey)
☐ Horsfield's Babbler (also middle storey)

☐ Grey-headed Babbler
☐ Chestnut-rumped Babbler
☐ Black-throated Babbler
☐ Chestnut-winged Babbler (also middle storey)
☐ Striped Tit-Babbler (look around Long Pala)
☐ Siberian Blue Robin m
☐ White-rumped Shama (occurs close to park hq)
☐ Rufous-tailed Shama
☐ Chestnut-naped Forktail
☐ White-crowned Forktail (try in the vicinity of
   Clearwater Cave)
☐ Sunda Whistling Thrush (can usually be found at or
   just inside the entrance to Deer Cave; if you don't
   find it there, try around the picnic area at Clearwater Cave)
☐ Ashy Tailorbird (favours kerangas forest)
☐ Rufous-tailed Tailorbird (around park hq)
☐ Yellow-bellied Prinia (try around Long Pala)
☐ Grey-chested Flycatcher
☐ Dark-sided Flycatcher m (also middle storey; favours
   forest clearings)
☐ Rufous-chested Flycatcher
☐ Malaysian Blue Flycatcher (along streams and rivers;
   also middle storey)
☐ Spotted Fantail (also middle storey)
☐ Pied Fantail (edges and cultivated areas)
☐ Maroon-breasted Flycatcher (often along streams)
☐ Rufous-winged Flycatcher (also middle storey)
☐ Grey Wagtail m (especially mountain streams and paths)
☐ Purple-naped Sunbird (riverside vegetation)
☐ Crimson Sunbird (also middle storey; try around hq and
   Long Pala)
☐ Little Spiderhunter
☐ Grey-breasted Spiderhunter (also middle storey; try
   around Deer Cave)
☐ Yellow-breasted Flowerpecker (also middle storey)
☐ Orange-bellied Flowerpecker (also middle storey)
☐ White-bellied Munia (try around Long Pala)

Middle storey, canopy:
☐ Crested Goshawk
☐ Changeable Hawk-Eagle
☐ Wallace's Hawk-Eagle (has been recorded breeding in
   the vicinity of Clearwater Cave)
☐ Little Green Pigeon (try around Long Pala)
☐ Large Green Pigeon (has been seen at park hq and Long Pala)
☐ Jambu Fruit-Dove
☐ Blue-crowned Hanging Parrot
☐ Hodgson's Hawk-Cuckoo (also lower storey)
☐ Indian Cuckoo
☐ Banded Bay Cuckoo

- [ ] Plaintive Cuckoo (also lower storey; favours kerangas forest)
- [ ] Brush (Rusty-breasted) Cuckoo
- [ ] Violet Cuckoo (try around Long Pala or along the track to Deer Cave)
- [ ] Drongo Cuckoo
- [ ] Black-bellied Malkoha
- [ ] Chestnut-bellied Malkoha
- [ ] Raffles' Malkoha
- [ ] Chestnut-breasted Malkoha
- [ ] Brown Hawk-Owl
- [ ] Brown Wood-Owl
- [ ] Grey-rumped Treeswift (forest edge; also open areas)
- [ ] Whiskered Treeswift (forest edge)
- [ ] Red-naped Trogon
- [ ] Scarlet-rumped Trogon (also lower storey)
- [ ] Red-bearded Bee-eater
- [ ] Dollarbird
- [ ] Bushy-crested Hornbill (all hornbills also overhead)
- [ ] Wreathed Hornbill
- [ ] Black Hornbill
- [ ] Rhinoceros Hornbill
- [ ] Helmeted Hornbill
- [ ] Gold-whiskered Barbet
- [ ] Red-crowned Barbet
- [ ] Red-throated Barbet
- [ ] Yellow-crowned Barbet
- [ ] Blue-eared Barbet
- [ ] Brown Barbet
- [ ] Rufous Woodpecker (also lower storey)
- [ ] Crimson-winged Woodpecker
- [ ] Buff-rumped Woodpecker
- [ ] Buff-necked Woodpecker (also lower storey)
- [ ] Great Slaty Woodpecker
- [ ] Maroon Woodpecker (also lower storey)
- [ ] Orange-backed Woodpecker
- [ ] Banded Broadbill
- [ ] Black-and-Yellow Broadbill
- [ ] Green Broadbill (also lower storey)
- [ ] Black-winged Flycatcher-shrike
- [ ] Bar-bellied Cuckoo-shrike (try along the Sg. Melinau)
- [ ] Lesser Cuckoo-shrike
- [ ] Green Iora (try around Long Pala)
- [ ] Common Iora
- [ ] Lesser Green Leafbird
- [ ] Greater Green Leafbird
- [ ] Blue-winged Leafbird
- [ ] Black-headed Bulbul
- [ ] Cream-vented Bulbul
- [ ] Red-eyed Bulbul (around park hq)
- [ ] Spectacled Bulbul (also lower storey)

- [ ] Hairy-backed Bulbul (also lower storey)
- [ ] Buff-vented Bulbul (also lower storey)
- [ ] Streaked Bulbul
- [ ] Crow-billed Drongo m (try the Deer Cave track)
- [ ] Greater Racket-tailed Drongo
- [ ] Dark-throated Oriole
- [ ] Asian Fairy-Bluebird
- [ ] Crested Jay (also lower storey)
- [ ] Black Magpie (look around park hq)
- [ ] Slender-billed Crow (along rivers and around park hq)
- [ ] Moustached Babbler (also lower storey; favours hillside forest)
- [ ] Sooty-capped Babbler (also lower storey)
- [ ] Scaly-crowned Babbler (also lower storey)
- [ ] Rufous-crowned Babbler (also lower storey)
- [ ] Flyeater
- [ ] Arctic Warbler m
- [ ] Asian Brown Flycatcher m
- [ ] Pale Blue Flycatcher (try around Deer Cave)
- [ ] Large-billed Blue Flycatcher
- [ ] Grey-headed Flycatcher (also lower storey)
- [ ] Black-naped Monarch (also lower storey)
- [ ] Asian Paradise-Flycatcher
- [ ] Hill Myna
- [ ] Plain Sunbird (try around park hq)
- [ ] Brown-throated Sunbird (also lower storey; around park hq and Long Pala)
- [ ] Ruby-cheeked Sunbird (also lower storey)
- [ ] Long-billed Spiderhunter
- [ ] Yellow-eared Spiderhunter (try around park hq and Long Pala)
- [ ] Scarlet-breasted Flowerpecker (favours kerangas forest)
- [ ] Yellow-rumped Flowerpecker* (forest edge and scrub)

Difficult-to-find or rare species:
- [ ] Oriental Darter
- [ ] Malayan Night-Heron m (usually in forest away from rivers)
- [ ] Storm's Stork (look for it flying along rivers or standing on river banks; has been seen in the vicinity of the park hq)
- [ ] Jerdon's Baza
- [ ] Black Wood-Partridge
- [ ] Crestless Fireback
- [ ] Great Argus (often heard, seldom seen)
- [ ] Thick-billed Pigeon
- [ ] Green Imperial Pigeon
- [ ] Ruddy (Red) Cuckoo-Dove (try around Long Pala)
- [ ] Moustached Hawk-Cuckoo
- [ ] Chestnut-winged Cuckoo m
- [ ] Red-billed Malkoha
- [ ] Sunda Ground-Cuckoo (favours dry, level forest)
- [ ] Short-toed Coucal
- [ ] Bay Owl

Kuching, Sarawak - gateway to Bako National Park *(photo: J. Bransbury)*

▲ Tiger butterflies are a common sight at Bako *(photo: J. Bransbury)*

Bako National Park, one of the most accessible reserves in Sarawak *(photo: J. Bransbury)*

Bearded Pig - you'll come face to face with one at Bako *(photo: M. Sacchi)*

▼ Good birding can be had along the boardwalk at Niah National Park, Sarawak *(photo: J. Bransbury)*

▲ Rainbow Tree Snake, Gunung Mulu National Park, Sarawak   *(photo: M. Sacchi)*

▲ Sapsucking Bug - just one of thousa of insects at Mulu   *(photo: M. Sa*

▲ The walk to Deer Cave, Mulu, takes you through luxuriant lowland rainforest
(photo: J. Bransbury)

▼ Lambir Hills National Park, Sarawak, has many stream-side trails
(photo: J. Bransbury)

▲ Mulu's caves are home to millions bats   *(photo: M. Sacchi)*

▼ National Park headquarters, Mulu
(photo: J. Bransbury)

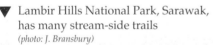

☐ Reddish Scops-Owl
☐ Large Frogmouth
☐ Brown Needletail
☐ Fork-tailed Swift m
☐ Blue-banded Kingfisher (small streams)
☐ Banded Kingfisher
☐ White-crowned Hornbill
☐ Wrinkled Hornbill
☐ Oriental Pied Hornbill
☐ Malaysian Honeyguide
☐ Checker-throated Woodpecker
☐ Banded Woodpecker
☐ Olive-backed Woodpecker
☐ Grey-and-Buff Woodpecker
☐ Dusky Broadbill
☐ Hooded Pitta (especially win)
☐ Large Wood-shrike
☐ Grey-bellied Bulbul
☐ Puff-backed Bulbul
☐ Finsch's Bulbul
☐ Hook-billed Bulbul
☐ Velvet-fronted Nuthatch
☐ Grey-breasted Babbler (lowland peat swamp and kerangas forest)
☐ Chestnut-backed Scimitar-Babbler
☐ Bornean Wren-Babbler* (especially peat swamp forest)
☐ Striped Wren-Babbler
☐ Black-throated Wren-Babbler*
☐ Fluffy-backed Tit-Babbler
☐ Malaysian Rail-Babbler
☐ Fulvous-chested Flycatcher
☐ Verditer Flycatcher
☐ White-tailed Flycatcher (especially hillsides)
☐ Bornean Blue Flycatcher* (near streams)
☐ Red-throated Sunbird
☐ Thick-billed Spiderhunter (try near Deer Cave)
☐ Yellow-vented Flowerpecker

Additional species for those able to explore the more remote parts of the national park, particularly the section of the track to G. Mulu above Camp 3 (about 1200 m [4000 feet]), and the track to the Pinnacles beyond Camp 5 (Melinau Camp). Most of the birds listed do not occur in the vicinity of the park hq.

Open areas, overhead:
☐ Kinabalu (Mountain) Serpent-Eagle*
☐ Besra (favours clearings)
☐ Black Eagle (hunts low over the canopy)
☐ Blyth's Hawk-Eagle (try the track to the Pinnacles)

Ground, lower storey:
☐ Red-breasted Partridge*
☐ Crimson-headed Partridge*

- [ ] Bulwer's Pheasant*
- [ ] Mountain Scops-Owl
- [ ] Rajah Scops-Owl (evidently very rare)
- [ ] Collared Owlet (often active during the day)
- [ ] Blue-banded Pitta* (favours dense bamboo thickets)
- [ ] Flavescent Bulbul (also middle storey)
- [ ] Ochraceous Bulbul (also middle storey)
- [ ] Temminck's Babbler (try the track to the Pinnacles)
- [ ] Mountain Wren-Babbler*
- [ ] Eye-browed Wren-Babbler
- [ ] Rufous-fronted Babbler (also Deer Cave area)
- [ ] Grey-throated Babbler
- [ ] White-necked Babbler (try along the Pinnacles track)
- [ ] Black Laughingthrush (also middle storey)
- [ ] White-browed Shortwing (along the G. Mulu track at or above Camp 4 [about 1800 m - 6000 feet])
- [ ] Everett's Thrush*
- [ ] Mountain Tailorbird (also middle storey)
- [ ] Mountain (Sunda) Bush-Warbler (upper montane moss forest)
- [ ] Short-tailed Bush-Warbler* (upper montane moss forest)
- [ ] White-browed Flycatcher
- [ ] Snowy-browed Flycatcher
- [ ] Blue-and-White Flycatcher m
- [ ] Pygmy Blue Flycatcher (also middle storey)
- [ ] Scarlet Sunbird (also middle storey)
- [ ] Mountain Black-eye* (also middle storey)

Middle storey, canopy:
- [ ] Mountain Imperial Pigeon (also overhead; seen mainly in the highlands but moves to the lowlands to feed)
- [ ] Little Cuckoo-Dove (also overhead and lower storey)
- [ ] Large Hawk-Cuckoo
- [ ] Oriental Cuckoo
- [ ] Whitehead's Trogon*
- [ ] Cinnamon-rumped Trogon (also lower storey)
- [ ] Orange-breasted Trogon
- [ ] Mountain Barbet* (also open areas)
- [ ] Golden-naped Barbet* (also lower storey)
- [ ] Black-throated Barbet*
- [ ] Long-tailed Broadbill
- [ ] Hose's Broadbill* (lower montane; mainly middle storey; try the Clearwater Cave area)
- [ ] Whitehead's Broadbill* (also lower storey)
- [ ] Bar-winged Flycatcher-shrike
- [ ] Sunda (Large) Cuckoo-shrike
- [ ] Black-breasted Triller*
- [ ] Grey-chinned Minivet
- [ ] Scarlet Minivet
- [ ] Scaly-breasted Bulbul
- [ ] Ashy Bulbul

- [ ] Ashy Drongo
- [ ] Spangled Drongo (favours clearings)
- [ ] Black-and-Crimson Oriole
- [ ] Sunda (Malaysian) Treepie
- [ ] Grey-and-Brown (Sunda) Laughingthrush
- [ ] Chestnut-capped Laughingthrush (at or beyond Camp 4 on the G. Mulu track)
- [ ] White-browed Shrike-Babbler
- [ ] Brown Fulvetta (also lower storey)
- [ ] White-bellied Yuhina (also Deer Cave area)
- [ ] Chestnut-crested (Babbler) Yuhina* (also Deer Cave)
- [ ] Yellow-breasted Warbler (also lower storey)
- [ ] Yellow-bellied Warbler (favours bamboo)
- [ ] Mountain Leaf-Warbler
- [ ] Rufous-tailed Flycatcher
- [ ] Indigo Flycatcher
- [ ] Little Pied Flycatcher
- [ ] Hill Blue Flycatcher (also around Deer Cave)
- [ ] White-throated Fantail (also lower storey)
- [ ] Bornean Mountain Whistler* (also lower storey)
- [ ] Whitehead's Spiderhunter*
- [ ] Black-sided Flowerpecker (also lower storey; try the Pinnacles track)
- [ ] Black-capped White-eye (also lower storey)
- [ ] Tawny-breasted Parrotfinch (bamboo forest)

Access and accommodation

A few years ago getting to Mulu was an adventure in itself. First you had to get a taxi to take you from Miri to Kuala Baram, a village about 20 km north of Miri at the mouth of the Sg. Baram, then you had to take a three-hour boat trip up the river to Marudi. At Marudi you changed boats for another three-hour trip up the Baram and Tutoh rivers to Kuala Apoh or Long Panai, then changed again to a smaller boat for the final one- to two-hour leg to Long Terawan or Mulu park hq (at each stage in the boat journey, the destination depended on the level of the river). In all, the trip from Miri to park hq could have taken a day or more.

These days you can fly from Miri direct to Mulu park with Malaysia Airlines; there are several flights a day, the one-way fare is about $M50, and the journey takes around 35 minutes. From the airstrip at Mulu it's only 15 minutes or so by boat to the park hq, thus you can get there from Miri in about an hour.

At the time of writing, the main accommodation at Mulu park hq consists of a resthouse with eight rooms containing six beds each. There are also several guesthouses and two hostels in the vicinity of Long Pala, on the Sg. Melinau about 15 minutes by boat from park hq. Overnight charges range from about $M80 per room at the park hq resthouse, to around $M10 per person at the hostels. For meals, you can either take your own food and do your own cooking - there are kitchens in the resthouse and at the hostels - or you can eat at the inexpensive canteen at park hq (a much better alternative since carrying in all your food is a real chore). Bookings for accommodation should be made in advance through the National Parks and Wildlife Office, Forest Department, Miri 98000, Sarawak, 'phone 085-36637 (the NP&W Office is situated off Jalan Kingsway in Miri).

A visit to Mulu will not come cheap - by the time you've paid for the return air fare (or boat fares if you decide to go by river), a week's accommodation and food, plus various extras such as fees for permits and guides (you'll need a guide to take you into the caves, as well as to the Pinnacles and G. Mulu summit), you'll probably be looking at a total cost of between $M400 and $M600. Given the time and effort required to make your own arrangements for a trip to Mulu, you should consider paying a little more and going through a travel agency in Miri (you'll find some addresses at the front of this book). The agencies handle all the arrangements, including bookings for accommodation and transport.

When to visit

Although Mulu is open all year round, it can be very wet from about October to February. At present, accommodation at the park is somewhat limited; if you can, avoid the main holiday periods (European as well as local) when rooms may be hard to find.

Other attractions

At the time of writing, only three of Mulu's numerous caves are open to the public, but at least a few of the others will no doubt be developed in the near future. In Deer Cave you will probably get close-up views of bats, since the animals have taken to roosting on the handrails along the walkways - be prepared, as soon as you enter the cave you will almost be overcome by the smell of millions of bat droppings! At Clearwater Cave, where there's an underground river, your guide will take you on a tour that involves wading through waist-high, crystal-clear rushing water - a most pleasant experience. The other cave open to visitors is Lang Cave (175 m long), which has many beautiful formations including the usual stalactites and stalagmites.

The park abounds with wildlife but, except for birds, bats, reptiles and butterflies (notably Rajah Brooke's Birdwing at Clearwater Cave and elsewhere), you will be lucky to see many animals, although squirrels are quite plentiful around the park hq - look for the delightful, diminutive Plain Pygmy Squirrel (a Bornean endemic) running along the boardwalk handrails on your way to Deer Cave. Spotlighting at night could produce some of the park's nocturnal inhabitants - Slow Loris and Western Tarsier are two you should watch for.

31 Tunku Abdul Rahman National Park

Sabah

Tunku Abdul Rahman National Park encompasses a group of five islands (Mamutik, Sulug, Manukan, Sapi and Gaya) off Sabah's north-west coast, a few kilometres from the state capital of Kota Kinabalu. Being almost surrounded by coral reefs, and having many superb beaches, the islands are ideal for snorkelling and scuba diving - or you can simply sit around and enjoy the sun and the scenery.

There are birds too of course, including migrant shorebirds, terns (look for them in the waters around the islands), forest species such as pigeons and sunbirds, and the highly sought-after Tabon Scrubfowl or Megapode. With an area of about 1500 ha, Pulau Gaya is by far the largest of the islands; it has many kilometres of walking tracks and, except for the fishing village at its eastern end, the island is almost completely covered with undisturbed lowland dipterocarp forest. As well, Gaya has pockets of mangrove forest and beach flora along its shores.

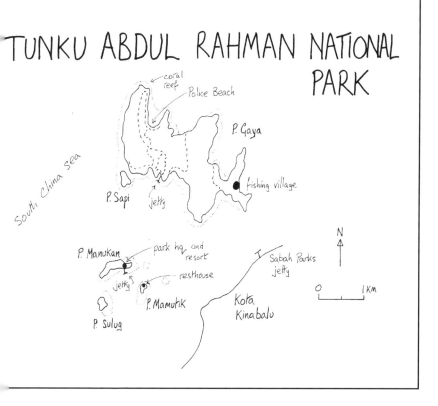

Good birdwatching areas

As you might expect, Gaya is easily the best of the islands for birdwatching. Not only is Gaya relatively quiet (most people go to P. Manukan, the site of the park headquarters and resort) it also supports one of the few unspoilt areas of coastal dipterocarp forest remaining in Sabah. From the jetty, on the island's south coast, you can either walk northwards across the centre of Gaya - it rises to over 300 m (about 1000 feet) - to Police Beach, or you can head west towards P. Sapi, which lies a few hundred metres off Gaya's south-western tip. At times the forest on Gaya can seem totally devoid of bird life; if you persevere, however, you should see some good birds, including Oriental Pied Hornbill, White-chested Babbler, Black-naped Monarch and Purple-throated Sunbird. Although scarce, Tabon Scrubfowls have been recorded breeding on Gaya and on nearby Sapi.

P. Manukan, the second largest island in the group, is the most developed area of the park and has chalets, a restaurant, and sports facilities such as a swimming pool, a football field and tennis courts. While it is often crowded, Manukan is worth a visit for birds like Pied Fantail, White-breasted Woodswallow, Olive-backed Sunbird and Dusky Munia, all of which occur in the grounds of the resort. The island is also an excellent place to go snorkelling - you can hire equipment from the information centre. The park's two most southerly islands - Mamutik and Sulug - are noted for their beaches and coral, but both are too small to be of much value to birds.

Birds

Open areas (including beaches and mudflats), overhead:
- [ ] Little Heron
- [ ] Pacific Reef-Egret
- [ ] Brahminy Kite
- [ ] White-bellied Sea-Eagle
- [ ] Mongolian Plover m
- [ ] Greater Sand-Plover m
- [ ] Whimbrel m
- [ ] Common Redshank m
- [ ] Terek Sandpiper m
- [ ] Common Sandpiper m
- [ ] Ruddy Turnstone m
- [ ] Rufous-necked Stint m
- [ ] Red-necked Phalarope m (especially Sept-Nov; look for them resting at sea between the islands and the mainland)
- [ ] Black-naped Tern
- [ ] Bridled Tern
- [ ] Great Crested Tern m (often seen sitting on driftwood in the sea between the islands and the mainland)
- [ ] Edible-nest Swiftlet
- [ ] Collared Kingfisher
- [ ] Pacific Swallow
- [ ] Yellow-vented Bulbul

- ☐ Magpie Robin
- ☐ Grey Wagtail m
- ☐ White-breasted Woodswallow
- ☐ Philippine Glossy Starling
- ☐ Brown-throated Sunbird
- ☐ Eurasian Tree-Sparrow
- ☐ Dusky Munia* (also forests)

Forests:
- ☐ Tabon (Megapode) Scrubfowl (nests along the forest edge, usually close to beaches)
- ☐ Pink-necked Pigeon
- ☐ Green Imperial Pigeon
- ☐ Green-winged (Emerald Dove) Pigeon
- ☐ Hodgson's Hawk-Cuckoo
- ☐ Brush (Rusty-breasted) Cuckoo
- ☐ Brown Hawk-Owl (especially win)
- ☐ Oriental Dwarf Kingfisher
- ☐ Oriental Pied Hornbill (also overhead; almost a certainty on P. Gaya)
- ☐ Buff-rumped Woodpecker
- ☐ Pied Triller (favours casuarinas and mangroves)
- ☐ Common Iora (edges)
- ☐ Olive-winged Bulbul (edges)
- ☐ Cream-vented Bulbul
- ☐ White-chested Babbler
- ☐ Moustached Babbler
- ☐ Striped Tit-Babbler
- ☐ Ashy Tailorbird (edges and mangroves)
- ☐ Rufous-tailed Tailorbird
- ☐ Grey-chested Flycatcher
- ☐ Mangrove Blue Flycatcher
- ☐ Pied Fantail (also open areas)
- ☐ Black-naped Monarch
- ☐ Mangrove Whistler
- ☐ Hill Myna
- ☐ Purple-throated Sunbird
- ☐ Olive-backed Sunbird (also open areas)
- ☐ Orange-bellied Flowerpecker
- ☐ Scarlet-backed Flowerpecker

Difficult-to-find or rare species:
- ☐ Brown Booby (mainly Dec-May)
- ☐ Osprey m
- ☐ Grey-headed Fish-Eagle
- ☐ Grey-tailed Tattler m
- ☐ Red (Grey) Phalarope m (vagrant, but worth looking for among the Red-necked Phalaropes)
- ☐ Great (Beach) Thick-knee
- ☐ Roseate Tern
- ☐ Little Tern

☐ Lesser Crested Tern m
☐ Cinnamon-headed Pigeon (especially mangroves)
☐ Grey Imperial Pigeon
☐ Pied Imperial Pigeon
☐ Ruddy Kingfisher
☐ White-crowned Hornbill
☐ White-bellied Woodpecker
☐ Grey-streaked Flycatcher m
☐ Tiger Shrike m
☐ Red-throated Sunbird
☐ Copper-throated Sunbird

Access and accommodation

The two main islands - Gaya and Manukan - are readily accessible by boat from Kota Kinabalu; you can either go in the official Sabah Parks boat, which leaves from a jetty opposite the Hyatt International Hotel, or you can use one of the many private operators who will accost you as you approach the Sabah Parks jetty. Sabah Parks charge about $M15 per person for the return trip; private operators usually charge a bit more ($M20-25 per person - be sure to haggle), but they are more flexible than Sabah Parks and will take you more or less any place you want to go and at any time. Don't forget to arrange to be picked up at the end of your stay - as insurance against being left stranded, it's a good idea not to pay the boatman the fare until you get back to Kota Kinabalu. Travel between islands will not be so easy to arrange; your best option is to go to the jetty on P. Manukan and negotiate with the boatmen there.

Most people stay in Kota Kinabalu, where there's a wide range of accommodation, and make day trips to the islands from the city. You can, however, stay overnight on two of the islands - Manukan and Mamutik - but at a price! A night in one of the chalets on Manukan will cost you around $M150 during the week, or $M200 during weekends and public holidays. Each chalet accommodates up to four people, thus you can share the cost if there's a group of you. On Mamutik you can stay in a three-roomed resthouse for about $M120 a night during the week, or $M180 during weekends and public holidays. The resthouse sleeps up to eight people and has cooking facilities, but you will need to take food because there is no canteen on Mamutik. All accommodation must be booked in advance through the Sabah Parks office, which is situated in Block K of the Sinsuran Shopping Complex on Jalan Tun Fuad Stephens ('phone 088-211585, 211881 or 211652; the postal address is PO Box 10626, Kota Kinabalu 88806, Sabah).

When to visit

To have the best chance of seeing migrant birds you should visit between early September and late November. Heavy downpours can occur at almost any time of the year; however, rain and rough seas are more likely to be a problem between about October and February (the monsoon season) than between March and June (the 'dry' season). The waters around the islands are usually calm and clear - and therefore best for snorkelling - from February to May.

Other attractions

The greatest attraction at TAR (other than birds of course) is undoubtedly the marine life. If you've dreamed of snorkelling over coral gardens with multi-coloured fish coming at you from all directions, then this is the place to do just that. What's more, the water is always marvellously warm - no standing around on the shore trying to muster the courage to dive in here.

Some of the best reefs along Sabah's west coast are those around the islands of Manukan, Mamutik and Sulug; patches of excellent coral can also be found between Sapi and Gaya. The reefs are home to myriads of fish - butterfly fish, parrot fish, clown fish, dragon fish, stone fish - as well as giant clams, scorpion shells, starfish, sea cucumbers, sea urchins and cowry shells. Sharks are seldom encountered, but between January and May whales are sometimes seen close to the islands. There are a number of private companies in Kota Kinabalu that hire out scuba diving equipment should you need it.

32 Pulau Tiga Park

Sabah

If you have time, and can afford the boat trip, Pulau Tiga is certainly worth a visit. For one thing the park is off the usual tourist track, for another it offers good birding with frigatebirds, migrant shorebirds, scrubfowls, pigeons and sunbirds among the highlights. And although Tiga has no caves or Orang-utans or turtles, the island's luxuriant plant life is virtually undisturbed, and the readily accessible coral reefs that fringe parts of its shores hold some species of fish not found elsewhere on Sabah's west coast.

Good birdwatching areas

The park consists of three islands but only P. Tiga is easily accessible, and in any case the other two islands - P. Kalampunian Damit and P. Kalampunian Besar - are much too small to be of any real interest to birdwatchers.

The park headquarters is situated in a grassy clearing near a beach on the southern side of Tiga. From the hq there's a network of trails leading to various points of interest (to one of the island's three mud volcanoes for example); as well, the small mangrove lagoon close to the park hq is well worth a look. P. Tiga is not large, less than a thousand hectares, so that in a couple of days or so you should be able to cover most of its area.

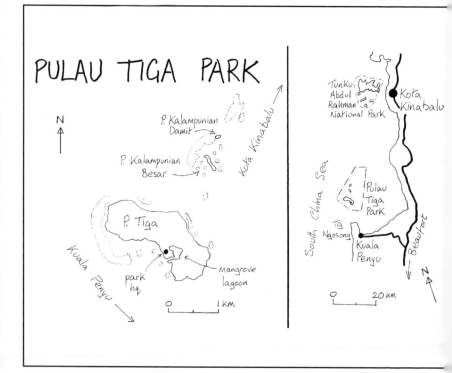

Birds

Seabirds and shorebirds:
- [ ] Brown Booby (mostly Dec-May)
- [ ] Great Cormorant m (only a few records)
- [ ] Lesser Frigatebird m (absent May-June)
- [ ] Little Heron
- [ ] Pacific Reef-Egret
- [ ] Mongolian Plover m
- [ ] Greater Sand-Plover m
- [ ] Whimbrel m
- [ ] Common Redshank m
- [ ] Common Sandpiper m
- [ ] Grey-tailed Tattler m
- [ ] Ruddy Turnstone m
- [ ] Red-necked Phalarope m (especially Sept-Nov)
- [ ] Great (Beach) Thick-knee
- [ ] Roseate Tern
- [ ] Black-naped Tern (breeds locally, as does the Bridled Tern)
- [ ] Bridled Tern
- [ ] Little Tern
- [ ] Great Crested Tern m
- [ ] Lesser Crested Tern m

Landbirds:
- [ ] Brahminy Kite
- [ ] White-bellied Sea-Eagle
- [ ] Tabon (Megapode) Scrubfowl (P. Tiga is a stronghold for this species)
- [ ] Grey Imperial Pigeon
- [ ] Pied Imperial Pigeon
- [ ] Metallic Wood-Pigeon
- [ ] Green-winged (Emerald Dove) Pigeon
- [ ] Nicobar Pigeon
- [ ] Common Koel (especially Sept-Mar)
- [ ] Brown Hawk-Owl (mainly win)
- [ ] Large-tailed Nightjar
- [ ] Collared Kingfisher
- [ ] Dollarbird (chiefly win)
- [ ] Oriental Pied Hornbill
- [ ] Blue-winged Pitta (chiefly Oct-Nov and Mar-Apr)
- [ ] Pacific Swallow
- [ ] Pied Triller
- [ ] Common Iora
- [ ] Yellow-vented Bulbul
- [ ] Striped Tit-Babbler
- [ ] Magpie Robin
- [ ] Dark-sided Flycatcher m (mainly Sept-Oct)
- [ ] Pied Fantail
- [ ] Black-naped Monarch
- [ ] White-breasted Woodswallow

- [ ] Philippine Glossy Starling
- [ ] Brown-throated Sunbird
- [ ] Copper-throated Sunbird
- [ ] Olive-backed Sunbird
- [ ] Orange-bellied Flowerpecker
- [ ] Scarlet-backed Flowerpecker

Access and accommodation

You can get to P. Tiga by charter boat from Kota Kinabalu, but expect to pay around $M150 per person for the return trip. A cheaper alternative is to go by road to Kuala Penyu, a small settlement on the coast about 120 km south-west of Kota Kinabalu. From Kuala Penyu you can hire a boat to take you the 20 km to Tiga.

Since Pulau Tiga Park is visited mainly by scientists and researchers, there are no special facilities for tourists. You are, however, allowed to camp on Tiga; for a permit and further information contact the Sabah Parks office in Kota Kinabalu (see site 31 for the address and 'phone numbers). If you do visit the park remember to take along all your food.

When to visit

As is the case with nearby Tunku Abdul Rahman National Park, you may not be able to reach Tiga during the monsoon season (October to February) when seas may be too rough to make the crossing. Late August to mid October is a good time for migrant birds, while February to May is best for dry weather and calm seas.

Other attractions

There are few large animals on Tiga, although flying foxes often roost around the mangrove lagoon and Long-tailed Macaques frequent the park hq area. Monitor lizards are abundant, as are Golden Skinks, and as previously mentioned the waters around the three islands are rich in marine life.

33 Kota Belud
Bird Sanctuary

Sabah

It is easy to see why the Kota Belud area features so prominently in Borneo's ornithological literature. There are more than 70 migrants on the site's bird list, and over the years a wealth of interesting species have turned up - Black Bittern, Black-headed Ibis, White Spoonbill, Pied Harrier, Temminck's Stint, Petchora Pipit and Little Bunting to name a few. Although the chance of seeing some rare migrants is a big attraction, it is Kota Belud's rich variety of open-country birds that makes this the ideal place to go when you want a break from forest birding.

Despite its name, Kota Belud Bird Sanctuary is not a reserve - birds are protected (that is, they cannot be shot) in an area stretching approximately fifteen kilometres north of Kota Belud town, but the land itself has not been declared a park. The country within and adjoining the sanctuary consists chiefly of rice fields and other cultivated areas, interspersed with small seasonal swamps and reed-fringed lakes. Along the shores to the north and west of Kota Belud there are beaches, mudflats, mangroves and coastal scrub, while the Tempasuk Plain - an area used extensively for grazing - lies just west of the Kota Belud to Kudat road.

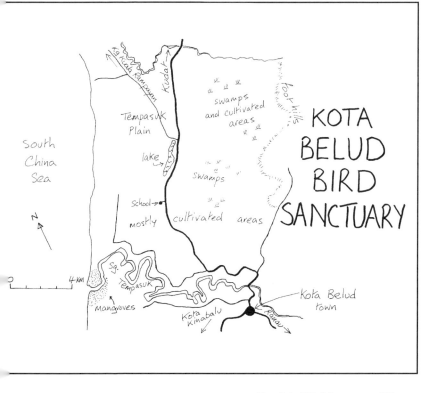

Good birdwatching areas

The entire area shown in the map is worth exploring, but be sure to try the following spots: the long narrow lake beside the Kota Belud to Kudat road (the lake is a good place to look for Black Bittern); the seasonal swamps, rice fields and cultivated plains east of the Kudat road (usually a rewarding area for herons, egrets, bitterns, and waders such as plovers and snipe); and the coastal scrub to the north of the Tempasuk Plain for birds like Pied Triller and White-breasted Woodswallow. The mangroves at the mouth of the Sg. Tempasuk, west of Kota Belud town, hold Cinnamon-headed Pigeon and Brown-capped Woodpecker, as well as other mangrove species.

Birds

Open (dry) areas, overhead:
☐ Brahminy Kite
☐ White-bellied Sea-Eagle
☐ Japanese Sparrowhawk m
☐ Peregrine Falcon m
☐ Blue-breasted Quail (favours dry rice fields)
☐ Little Ringed Plover m (often in dry rice fields)
☐ Kentish Plover m (along the coast and in rice fields)
☐ Mongolian Plover m
☐ Greater Sand-Plover m
☐ Oriental Pratincole m
☐ Large-tailed Nightjar
☐ White-bellied (Glossy) Swiftlet
☐ Brown Needletail
☐ Asian Palm-Swift
☐ Blue-throated Bee-eater
☐ Barn Swallow m
☐ Pacific Swallow
☐ Yellow-vented Bulbul (also scrub and plantations)
☐ Magpie Robin
☐ Grey Wagtail m
☐ Yellow Wagtail m
☐ Richard's Pipit
☐ White-breasted Woodswallow
☐ Brown Shrike m
☐ Philippine Glossy Starling
☐ Eurasian Tree-Sparrow

Wetlands, rice crops:
☐ Grey Heron (not as likely as the next two species)
☐ Purple Heron
☐ Little Heron
☐ Cattle Egret m
☐ Great Egret
☐ Intermediate (Plumed) Egret m
☐ Little Egret m
☐ Yellow Bittern

☐ Cinnamon Bittern
☐ White-browed Crake
☐ White-breasted Waterhen
☐ Asian (Lesser) Golden Plover m
☐ Common Redshank m
☐ Common Greenshank m
☐ Wood Sandpiper m
☐ Common Sandpiper m
☐ Pintail Snipe m
☐ Swinhoe's Snipe m
☐ Long-toed Stint m
☐ Curlew Sandpiper m
☐ Whiskered Tern m
☐ White-winged Tern m
☐ Lesser Coucal
☐ Common Kingfisher (mainly win)
☐ Stork-billed Kingfisher
☐ Collared Kingfisher
☐ Great (Oriental) Reed-Warbler m
☐ Striated Warbler
☐ Yellow-bellied Prinia
☐ Chestnut Munia

Scrub and plantations:
☐ Pink-necked Pigeon
☐ Spotted Dove
☐ Plaintive Cuckoo
☐ Greater Coucal
☐ Dollarbird (chiefly win)
☐ Blue-eared Barbet
☐ Brown-capped Woodpecker (also mangroves)
☐ Pied Triller (also mangroves)
☐ Common Iora (also mangroves)
☐ Straw-headed Bulbul (also secondary growth)
☐ Black-headed Bulbul (also secondary growth)
☐ Olive-winged Bulbul
☐ Red-eyed Bulbul
☐ Striped Tit-Babbler
☐ Arctic Warbler m
☐ Ashy Tailorbird (also mangroves)
☐ Rufous-tailed Tailorbird
☐ Pied Fantail
☐ Brown-throated Sunbird
☐ Olive-backed Sunbird
☐ Dusky Munia*

Difficult-to-find or rare species:
☐ Oriental Darter
☐ Christmas Frigatebird m (an occasional visitor to the
   coastal zone; possible at almost any time of the year)
☐ Lesser Frigatebird m

- [ ] Chinese Pond-Heron m
- [ ] Black-crowned Night-Heron (look out for Rufous and Malayan Night-Herons as well)
- [ ] Black Bittern m (try the lake about 10 km north of Kota Belud - see map)
- [ ] Lesser Adjutant
- [ ] Black-headed Ibis m (vagrant)
- [ ] White Spoonbill m (vagrant)
- [ ] Lesser (Treeduck) Whistling-Duck
- [ ] Mallard m (vagrant)
- [ ] Eurasian Wigeon m (vagrant)
- [ ] Garganey m (easily the most likely migrant duck)
- [ ] Northern Shoveler m (vagrant)
- [ ] Tufted Duck m (vagrant)
- [ ] Black-shouldered Kite
- [ ] Eastern Marsh-Harrier m
- [ ] Hen (Northern) Harrier m
- [ ] Pied Harrier m
- [ ] Eurasian Kestrel m
- [ ] Slaty-breasted Rail
- [ ] Ruddy-breasted Crake m (vagrant)
- [ ] Watercock (mostly win)
- [ ] Common Moorhen
- [ ] Purple Swamphen
- [ ] Eurasian Coot m (vagrant)
- [ ] Greater Paintedsnipe
- [ ] Malaysian Plover
- [ ] Oriental Plover m
- [ ] Whimbrel m
- [ ] Little Curlew m
- [ ] Bar-tailed Godwit m
- [ ] Marsh Sandpiper m
- [ ] Green Sandpiper m
- [ ] Ruddy Turnstone m
- [ ] Common Snipe m
- [ ] Red Knot m
- [ ] Great Knot m
- [ ] Sanderling m
- [ ] Rufous-necked Stint m
- [ ] Temminck's Stint m (vagrant)
- [ ] Black-winged Stilt m
- [ ] Roseate Tern
- [ ] Black-naped Tern
- [ ] Little Tern
- [ ] Great Crested Tern m
- [ ] Lesser Crested Tern m
- [ ] Cinnamon-headed Pigeon (try the mangroves north-west of Kota Belud - see map)
- [ ] Green-winged (Emerald Dove) Pigeon
- [ ] Fork-tailed Swift m

Snorkelling at Tunku Abdul Rahman National Park, Sabah *(photo: J. Bransbury)*

▲ Pulau Manukan, TAR National Park *(photo: J. Bransbury)*

Dragon-lizard, Pulau Gaya, TAR National Park *(photo: M. Sacchi)*

▲ Birding near Kinabalu National Park headquarters, Sabah *(photo: J. Bransbury)*

The view from the summit of Mt Kinabalu, the highest peak in Malaysia
(photo: M. Sacchi)

▲ Orang-utan - ' man of the forest'
(photo: J. Bransbury)

▼ At Sepilok Forest Reserve, Sabah, you
can watch semi-wild Orang-utans at
close range   *(photo: J. Bransbury)*

▲ The canopy walkway at Poring Hot
Springs, Sabah, allows you to look i
the treetops for a change
(photo: J. Bransbury)

▼ Arboreal gecko, Poring Hot Springs
(photo: M. Sacchi)

▼ Green Turtles are the main attractio
Turtle Islands Park, Sabah
(photo: M. Sacchi)

- [ ] Hoopoe m (vagrant)
- [ ] Sand Martin m
- [ ] Crow-billed Drongo m
- [ ] Stonechat m (vagrant)
- [ ] Pallas's (Grasshopper) Warbler m
- [ ] Fulvous-chested Flycatcher
- [ ] White Wagtail m
- [ ] Forest Wagtail m
- [ ] Red-throated Pipit m
- [ ] Petchora Pipit m
- [ ] Little Bunting m

Access and accommodation

There are plenty of minibuses that go from Kota Kinabalu to Kota Belud every day; go to Kota Kinabalu's main bus terminal at the end of Jalan Bandaran (opposite the State Library) and ask at the office. The journey to Kota Belud takes around one and a half hours (it's about a 75 km trip) and the fare is about $M5. You should have little difficulty hitching rides out from Kota Belud along the Kudat road, then you can explore along side tracks on foot. If need be there are usually at least a few taxis cruising up and down Kota Belud's main street, and there is a bus that goes from Kota Belud to Kudat once a day (it leaves about 10.00 a.m.).

Kota Belud has only two hotels - the Tai Seng has rooms for about $M25 and the Hotel Kota Belud (the better of the two) has rooms for around $M30. There's also a government resthouse in the town (for visiting officials) where you may be able to stay, although more often than not there is nobody there to answer the door.

When to visit

Given that migrants are an important component of the area's avifauna, you should try to visit Kota Belud between October and April. Many of the wetlands are seasonal and the smaller swamps especially can be dry for months at a time; this is unlikely to be the case late in the monsoon season (January to April), however, and in any event you should be able to find at least a few flooded rice fields to explore.

Other attractions

Kota Belud town is well known for its tamu or open-air market. Said to be the largest and most colourful tamu in Sabah, it's the place to buy everything from fresh fruit and vegetables to herbal remedies, clothes, watches and jewellery. The market takes place every Sunday - don't forget your camera.

34 Kinabalu National Park Sabah

At 4101 m (13 455 feet) Kinabalu is the highest mountain in Malaysia. It dominates the whole of north-western Sabah, and on a clear day the mountain's forest-clad slopes provide an impressive backdrop to the city of Kota Kinabalu. The climb to Kinabalu's summit, while no Sunday stroll, is relatively easy if you are reasonably fit; every year many thousands of people of all ages go to the top of the mountain from the national park headquarters, a trek that takes two to three days (there and back).

For birdwatchers, the summit trail offers more than just spectacular views. Those who climb the mountain have a fair chance of seeing the Kinabalu Friendly (Bush) Warbler, a Bornean endemic confined to the upper slopes of Kinabalu and those of G. Trus Madi, another mountain some 65 km to the south. As well, climbers will almost certainly find the Island Thrush, or Mountain Blackbird, which in Malaysia is found only on the higher levels of Kinabalu and G. Trus Madi. Other high-altitude birds include White-browed Shortwing, Everett's Thrush, Mountain (Sunda) Bush-Warbler, Short-tailed Bush-Warbler, Black-capped White-eye and Mountain Black-eye.

Even if you don't make it to the top of Kinabalu you'll still see some very good birds around the park hq, which is situated about 1560 m (5120 feet) above sea level. Of the 31 Bornean endemics that occur in East Malaysia, more than 20 can be found in Kinabalu National Park, and about 14 can be seen in the vicinity of the park hq.

Among the more sought-after endemics are Red-breasted and Crimson-headed Partridge, Whitehead's Trogon, Mountain, Golden-naped and Black-throated Barbet, Whitehead's Broadbill, Mountain Wren-Babbler, Bornean Mountain Whistler and Whitehead's Spiderhunter. Kinabalu park hq is easily the best place in Sabah for all of these birds; in addition, a host of other interesting species occur in the area, including Kinabalu (Mountain) Serpent-Eagle, Black Eagle, Large Hawk-Cuckoo, Mountain Scops-Owl, Collared Owlet, Long-tailed Broadbill, Grey-chinned Minivet, Flavescent Bulbul, Spangled Drongo, Black-and-Crimson Oriole, Short-tailed Magpie, Sunda (Malaysian) Treepie, Grey-and-Brown (Sunda) Laughingthrush, Black Laughingthrush, Chestnut-capped Laughingthrush, Chestnut-crested Yuhina (Babbler), Sunda Whistling Thrush, Yellow-breasted Warbler, Mountain Leaf-Warbler, White-browed, Indigo, Snowy-browed and White-tailed Flycatcher, Scarlet Sunbird, Black-sided Flowerpecker and Pygmy White-eye.

Kinabalu's bird list is indeed enough to make your mouth water!

Good birdwatching areas

Although Kinabalu National Park covers a very large area (75 370 ha) there are visitor facilities at only two sites, park hq and Poring Hot Springs, both of which are located just inside the reserve's southern boundary. Of the 520 or so bird species that occur in East Malaysia, some 300 can be found in the national park; to have the greatest chance of seeing a wide variety of birds you should spend time at both the park hq and Poring Hot Springs. Most birders go from Kota Kinabalu to the park hq for montane species, then on to Poring Hot Springs for lowland and

KINABALU NATIONAL PARK

submontane birds (for this reason Poring is treated as a separate site - see the next section of this book).

Around the park hq there are many kilometres of roads and walking tracks that afford plenty of opportunities for birding. While it can be busy at times, the road that runs from the park entrance downhill to the old administration building (see map) is often a very productive area, particularly early in the day. Likewise the road between the old admin' building and the power station is usually good (and much quieter than the entrance road); the power station lies at 1830 m (6000 feet), at the start of the Kinabalu summit trail, and the surrounding area is worth exploring for some of the higher altitude birds mentioned earlier.

There's a maze of walking tracks between the park entrance and the power station. For birdwatching, one of the best walks is the Silau-Silau Trail, which commences from behind the old admin' building and takes you northwards along a stream-course to the power station road. Another good walk is the Kiau View Trail, which starts from the power station road at the first sharp bend after the old admin' building. The Kiau View Trail zigzags southwards to the park entrance, and along the way there are five or six side paths leading to lookouts offering fine views over Kinabalu's lower slopes.

The Silau-Silau and Kiau View trails are both easy walks of less than two kilometres. If you want a longer walk, with the chance of really excellent birding, try the Liwagu Trail, especially the section along the Sg. Liwagu between Liwagu Cave and the power station. You'll need four or five hours to complete this walk, or an hour or two longer if the birds are particularly plentiful.

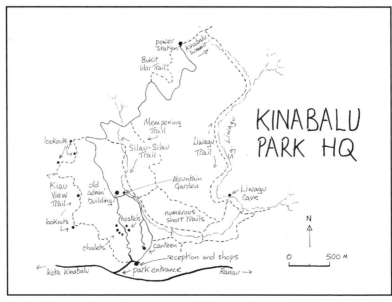

Map showing labels: power station, Kinabalu summit, Bukit Ular Trail, Mempening Trail, Silau-Silau Trail, Liwagu Trail, Liwagu, lookouts, Kiau View Trail, old admin building, Mountain Garden, Liwagu Cave, lookouts, hostels, numerous short trails, chalets, canteen, reception and shops, kota Kinabalu, park entrance, Ranau, KINABALU PARK HQ, N, 0 500 M

Birds

Open areas, overhead:

☐ Crested Serpent-Eagle

☐ Kinabalu (Mountain) Serpent-Eagle* (above 915 m [3000 feet] - try around the power station)

☐ Besra (favours clearings)

☐ Black Eagle (hunts low over the canopy)

☐ Blyth's Hawk-Eagle (look near the power station)

☐ White-bellied (Glossy) Swiftlet

☐ Brown Needletail

☐ Barn Swallow m

☐ Pacific Swallow

☐ Yellow-vented Bulbul

☐ Ashy Drongo (common and confiding; also forest edge)

☐ Grey Wagtail m

Ground, lower storey:

☐ Red-breasted Partridge* (try the Kiau View Trail; the Liwagu Trail is also good)

☐ Crimson-headed Partridge* (look along the Liwagu Trail, especially the power station end)

☐ Green-winged (Emerald Dove) Pigeon

☐ Mountain Scops-Owl

☐ Collared Owlet (also middle storey; often active during the day)

☐ Cinnamon-rumped Trogon (also middle storey)

☐ Mountain Wren-Babbler* (the Liwagu Trail is very good for this species)

- [ ] Grey-throated Babbler
- [ ] Black Laughingthrush (also middle storey)
- [ ] White-browed Shortwing (especially close to and above the treeline)
- [ ] Sunda Whistling Thrush (look along the stream behind the old admin' building)
- [ ] Island (Mountain Blackbird) Thrush (above 2100 m [7000 feet])
- [ ] Mountain Tailorbird (also middle storey)
- [ ] Mountain (Sunda) Bush-Warbler
- [ ] Kinabalu Friendly (Bush) Warbler* (above 2100 m, and especially above 3000 m [10 000 feet])
- [ ] White-browed Flycatcher
- [ ] Snowy-browed Flycatcher
- [ ] White-tailed Flycatcher (try along the entrance road)
- [ ] White-throated Fantail (common; also middle storey)
- [ ] Scarlet Sunbird (often in garden areas; also middle storey)
- [ ] Black-sided Flowerpecker (try the Mountain Garden near the old admin' building; also middle storey)
- [ ] Pygmy White-eye*
- [ ] Mountain Black-eye* (also middle storey)

Middle storey, canopy:
- [ ] Mountain Imperial Pigeon (also overhead; flocks move down the mountain in the early morning, then go up again in the evening)
- [ ] Little Cuckoo-Dove (also lower storey)
- [ ] Large Hawk-Cuckoo
- [ ] Whitehead's Trogon* (favours dark, damp areas in old forest; try the Silau-Silau Trail behind the old admin' building)
- [ ] Orange-breasted Trogon
- [ ] Wreathed Hornbill (all hornbills also overhead)
- [ ] Rhinoceros Hornbill
- [ ] Helmeted Hornbill
- [ ] Gold-whiskered Barbet
- [ ] Mountain Barbet* (also open areas)
- [ ] Golden-naped Barbet* (look along the power station road)
- [ ] Black-throated Barbet*
- [ ] Rufous Woodpecker (also lower storey)
- [ ] Crimson-winged Woodpecker
- [ ] Checker-throated Woodpecker (also lower storey)
- [ ] Maroon Woodpecker (also lower storey)
- [ ] Long-tailed Broadbill
- [ ] Whitehead's Broadbill* (occurs close to the accommodation area - along the entrance road for example; also lower storey)
- [ ] Bar-winged Flycatcher-shrike
- [ ] Sunda (Large) Cuckoo-shrike (look along the power station road)
- [ ] Grey-chinned Minivet (common; try the power station road)
- [ ] Blue-winged Leafbird

- [ ] Black-crested Bulbul
- [ ] Flavescent Bulbul (also lower storey)
- [ ] Ochraceous Bulbul (also lower storey)
- [ ] Ashy Bulbul
- [ ] Spangled Drongo (favours clearings)
- [ ] Black-and-Crimson Oriole
- [ ] Short-tailed Magpie (above 915 m [3000 feet])
- [ ] Sunda (Malaysian) Treepie (common; often seen around the accommodation area)
- [ ] Velvet-fronted Nuthatch
- [ ] Chestnut-backed Scimitar-Babbler
- [ ] Grey-and-Brown (Sunda) Laughingthrush (this and the next species can often be found in the vicinity of the old admin' building)
- [ ] Chestnut-capped Laughingthrush
- [ ] White-browed Shrike-Babbler
- [ ] White-bellied Yuhina
- [ ] Chestnut-crested (Babbler) Yuhina* (can be seen along roadsides)
- [ ] Yellow-breasted Warbler (also lower storey)
- [ ] Mountain Leaf-Warbler
- [ ] Asian Brown Flycatcher m
- [ ] Indigo Flycatcher (try the power station road)
- [ ] Little Pied Flycatcher (roadsides; also lower storey)
- [ ] Grey-headed Flycatcher (also lower storey)
- [ ] Bornean Mountain Whistler* (also lower storey)
- [ ] Whitehead's Spiderhunter* (often in gardens)
- [ ] Black-capped White-eye (also lower storey)

Difficult-to-find or rare species:
- [ ] Rufous-bellied Eagle
- [ ] Changeable Hawk-Eagle
- [ ] Peregrine Falcon
- [ ] Ruddy (Red) Cuckoo-Dove
- [ ] Oriental Cuckoo
- [ ] Lesser Coucal
- [ ] Reddish Scops-Owl
- [ ] Banded Kingfisher
- [ ] White-crowned Hornbill
- [ ] Banded Woodpecker
- [ ] Grey-capped Woodpecker
- [ ] Orange-backed Woodpecker (try the Liwagu Trail)
- [ ] Dusky Broadbill
- [ ] Hose's Broadbill*
- [ ] Blue-winged Pitta (especially Oct-Nov)
- [ ] Banded Pitta
- [ ] Asian House-Martin m
- [ ] Black-breasted Triller* (not always hard to get - has been seen in the accommodation area)
- [ ] Grey-cheeked Bulbul
- [ ] Green Magpie (below 915 m [3000 feet])

- [ ] Temminck's Babbler
- [ ] Eye-browed Wren-Babbler
- [ ] White-crowned Forktail (try the Liwagu Trail)
- [ ] Blue Rock-Thrush m
- [ ] Everett's Thrush* (try near Liwagu Cave)
- [ ] Eye-browed Thrush m
- [ ] Yellow-bellied Warbler (favours bamboo on steep slopes)
- [ ] Short-tailed Bush-Warbler* (look around the power station)
- [ ] Rufous-tailed Flycatcher
- [ ] Dark-sided Flycatcher m
- [ ] Ferruginous Flycatcher m
- [ ] Mugimaki Flycatcher m
- [ ] Rufous-chested Flycatcher
- [ ] Blue-and-White Flycatcher m
- [ ] Hill Blue Flycatcher
- [ ] Bornean Blue Flycatcher* (often near streams)
- [ ] Pygmy Blue Flycatcher (best along the Liwagu Trail)
- [ ] Spotted Fantail
- [ ] Spectacled Spiderhunter
- [ ] Tawny-breasted Parrotfinch (favours bamboo)

Access and accommodation

Kinabalu National Park hq is about 90 km from Kota Kinabalu via the main road to Ranau and Sandakan. The park is readily accessible by bus from the capital; just go to the main bus terminal at the end of Jalan Bandaran (opposite the State Library) and inquire at the office. As a rule, two or three minibuses leave for the park hq at around 8.00 a.m. every day; however, it would pay to get to the terminal shortly after 7.00 a.m. because the buses are usually crowded - if you can't get on one of the early buses, you may have to wait until midday when the next lot depart. The bus fare is about $M10 and the journey takes around two hours. You can also get to the park by taxi, either from the bus terminal or from the airport, but expect to pay $M100 or more for the trip (remember to haggle).

At the park hq there's a wide range of accommodation. For example, you can get a bunk bed in one of the two hostels for about $M10 a night, or you can stay in a twin-bed cabin for around $M60 per cabin per night during the week, or $M90 at weekends and public holidays. There are also some basement rooms in the old admin' building that sleep two and cost about the same as the twin-bed cabins. If you are looking for more luxury, there are chalets and villas ranging in price from $M150 to $M250 a night (most of the chalets accommodate four people or more, thus if there's a group of you the prices aren't too bad).

Every year some 200 000 people visit Kinabalu National Park, and it is essential that you book accommodation well in advance. If you are planning to visit during the park's busiest periods - April, July-August and December - you should book at least six months ahead; at other times three months should be enough, and during the quieter months (October and November for example) you might get away with booking only a few weeks in advance. Bookings must be made through the Sabah Parks office, PO Box 10626, Kota Kinabalu 88806, 'phone 088-211585, 211652 or 211881.

Sabah Parks is located in Block K of the Sinsuran Shopping Complex on Jalan Tun Fuad Stephens, Kota Kinabalu. If you intend climbing Mount Kinabalu, don't forget to book your overnight accommodation at the Laban Rata Resthouse, which is situated at 3350 m (11 000 feet) and costs $M30 per person per night.

At park hq there are shops where you can buy a variety of basic items, as well as two or three canteens where you can get inexpensive meals. There's another canteen in the resthouse on the summit trail.

When to visit

It is always relatively cool at the park hq (the average daytime temperature is 20 degrees C), thus the climate is ideal for walking and birdwatching. On most days of the year the mornings are clear and sunny, but from about midday the clouds gradually build up and by mid to late afternoon it is usually pouring with rain. Prolonged showers and low cloud can be a problem during the monsoon season (October to January), but the damp weather does at least keep the crowds away. The driest part of the year is from February to May, which is the time when many people climb Mount Kinabalu.

Other attractions

Mount Kinabalu's amazingly rich plant life has made the national park one of the most famous in the world. More than half of the world's families of flowering plants are represented in the park, an astonishing array that includes 26 species of rhododendron, 1200 species of orchid, and the world's largest flower - *Rafflesia*. With a bloom that can measure up to a metre across, the *Rafflesia* is found at low altitudes; Poring Hot Springs is the place to look for the plant. Another major attraction for plant enthusiasts is the nine species of pitcher plants that occur on Kinabalu, one of the most spectacular being Rajah Brooke's Pitcher (*Nepenthes rajah*), which can hold up to two litres of water. Pitcher plants grow at high altitudes - look for them around the power station and along the Kinabalu summit trail.

Mammals found in the park include some 30 species of squirrel, ranging in size from the giant Tufted Ground Squirrel to the finger-length Whitehead's Pygmy Squirrel, as well as various rats, treeshrews and bats. These are the animals you are most likely to see around the park hq; to have the best chance of seeing deer, Maroon Langur (Red Leaf Monkey), Bornean Gibbon and, perhaps, Orang-utan, you should go to Poring Hot Springs.

The old administration building has displays on the flora, fauna and geology of the park; as well, slide shows and talks are arranged several times a week. A range of books about Kinabalu National Park is available at the shop near the park entrance.

35 Poring Hot Springs   Sabah

You can't really claim to have 'done' Kinabalu National Park until you've been to Poring Hot Springs. Although the scenery here isn't nearly as spectacular as that around the park hq, the birds at Poring more than make up for the site's lack of dramatic vistas. As is often the case in lowland rainforest, however, the richness of the avifauna may not be immediately apparent - but if you strike it lucky, you could get 10 or 20 new species in as many minutes.

Top of the list of hoped fors at Poring are birds like Besra, White-fronted Falconet, Great Argus, Red-billed Malkoha, Blue-banded Kingfisher, Red-bearded Bee-eater, Helmeted Hornbill, Rufous Piculet, Banded Woodpecker, Hose's Broadbill, Blue-banded Pitta, Black-and-White Bulbul, Scaly-breasted Bulbul, Crested Jay, Velvet-fronted Nuthatch, Chestnut-backed Scimitar-Babbler, Striped Wren-Babbler, Fluffy-backed Tit-Babbler, White-crowned Forktail, Chestnut-capped Thrush, Rufous-chested Flycatcher, Rufous-winged Flycatcher, Crimson Sunbird and Yellow-rumped Flowerpecker. If you can't get at least half a dozen of these species, it's time to hang up your binoculars!

Good birdwatching areas

At Poring there's some good edge habitat along the entrance road, which runs for a kilometre or so beyond the accommodation area. The hot springs (and the tiled baths that visitors use) are a five-minute walk from the park entrance; when there are not too many people about the bathing area can be quite productive for birds, with sunbirds and spiderhunters darting around in the dozens of hibiscus shrubs that grow there.

Beyond the baths there are trails leading to a canopy walkway (the walkway is not especially good for birds, but it allows you to view the rainforest from a totally different perspective) as well as to several caves and two waterfalls, the Kipungit Waterfall and the Langanan Waterfall. The 20-minute walk from the baths to the Kipungit Waterfall is often excellent for birding, particularly early in the day; some of the species to look out for are Green-winged (Emerald Dove) Pigeon, Rufous Piculet, Banded Woodpecker, Black-and-Red Broadbill, Green Broadbill, Greater Green Leafbird, Scaly-breasted Bulbul, Black Magpie, Black-naped Monarch and Long-billed Spiderhunter. As you approach the waterfall keep a close watch for White-crowned Forktail.

Some of Poring's more sought-after species - the Blue-banded Pitta for example - can be rather hard to find, but perseverance should bring results. For the pitta, and for birds such as Great Argus, Blue-banded Kingfisher, Red-bearded Bee-eater, Helmeted Hornbill, Dusky Broadbill, Crested Jay and Bornean Blue Flycatcher, try the 90-minute walk to the Langanan Waterfall; at least a few of the species just mentioned can be found along the first section of the Langanan Trail, in the vicinity of the Kipungit Waterfall, but the Blue-banded Pitta is best looked for towards the end of the walk, where there are areas of bamboo forest. Also, it is worth going out at night with a spotlight - Reddish Scops-Owl is one of the birds you could see.

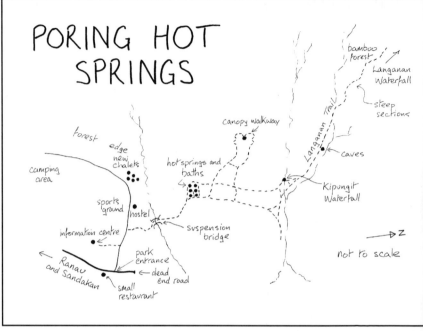

PORING HOT SPRINGS

bamboo forest
Langanan Waterfall
steep sections
Langanan Trail
canopy walkway
forest edge
new chalets
hot springs and baths
caves
camping area
Kipungit Waterfall
sports ground
hostel
information centre
suspension bridge
park entrance
Ranau and Sandakan
dead end road
small restaurant
not to scale

Birds

Open areas, overhead:

☐ Eurasian (Crested) Honey-Buzzard
☐ Crested Serpent-Eagle
☐ Japanese Sparrowhawk m
☐ Mountain Imperial Pigeon
☐ Plaintive Cuckoo
☐ Malaysian Eared Nightjar
☐ Large-tailed Nightjar
☐ White-bellied (Glossy) Swiftlet
☐ Silver-rumped Swift
☐ Yellow-vented Bulbul
☐ Magpie Robin
☐ Yellow-bellied Prinia
☐ Grey Wagtail m
☐ Brown-throated Sunbird
☐ Dusky Munia*
☐ Chestnut Munia

Ground, lower storey:

☐ Blue-breasted Quail (favours lalang on hillsides)
☐ Crested Wood-Partridge (especially bamboo groves and
   forest clearings)
☐ Green-winged (Emerald Dove) Pigeon

- [ ] Greater Coucal
- [ ] Reddish Scops-Owl (also middle storey)
- [ ] Collared Scops-Owl (also middle storey)
- [ ] Blue-banded Kingfisher
- [ ] Oriental Dwarf Kingfisher
- [ ] Black-and-Red Broadbill (also middle storey; usually near water, sometimes close to the baths)
- [ ] Blue-banded Pitta* (favours dense bamboo thickets)
- [ ] Banded Pitta (try the Langanan Waterfall Trail)
- [ ] Common Iora (also middle storey)
- [ ] Straw-headed Bulbul (along streams)
- [ ] Olive-winged Bulbul (forest edge)
- [ ] Grey-cheeked Bulbul (also middle storey)
- [ ] Yellow-bellied Bulbul
- [ ] Black-capped Babbler
- [ ] Short-tailed Babbler
- [ ] White-chested Babbler (along streams)
- [ ] Ferruginous Babbler (also middle storey)
- [ ] Horsfield's Babbler (also middle storey)
- [ ] Scaly-crowned Babbler (also middle storey)
- [ ] Rufous-crowned Babbler (also middle storey)
- [ ] Chestnut-rumped Babbler
- [ ] Black-throated Babbler
- [ ] Chestnut-winged Babbler (also middle storey)
- [ ] Striped Tit-Babbler (also middle storey)
- [ ] Siberian Blue Robin m (especially along streams)
- [ ] White-rumped Shama
- [ ] Chestnut-naped Forktail (especially along streams)
- [ ] White-crowned Forktail (try the Kipungit Waterfall area early in the day)
- [ ] Ashy Tailorbird (edges)
- [ ] Rufous-tailed Tailorbird (edges)
- [ ] Grey-chested Flycatcher
- [ ] Malaysian Blue Flycatcher (along streams)
- [ ] Pied Fantail
- [ ] Black-naped Monarch (also middle storey)
- [ ] Rufous-winged Flycatcher (also middle storey)
- [ ] Purple-naped Sunbird (along streams)
- [ ] Crimson Sunbird (also middle storey; often near the baths)
- [ ] Little Spiderhunter (easy to find around the baths)
- [ ] Grey-breasted Spiderhunter (also middle storey)
- [ ] Yellow-breasted Flowerpecker (also middle storey)

Middle storey, canopy:
- [ ] Crested Goshawk
- [ ] White-fronted Falconet* (look in dead trees; try along the entrance road)
- [ ] Thick-billed Pigeon
- [ ] Pink-necked Pigeon (also open areas)
- [ ] Jambu Fruit-Dove

- [ ] Blue-crowned Hanging Parrot
- [ ] Hodgson's Hawk-Cuckoo (also lower storey)
- [ ] Indian Cuckoo
- [ ] Banded Bay Cuckoo
- [ ] Drongo Cuckoo
- [ ] Black-bellied Malkoha
- [ ] Chestnut-bellied Malkoha
- [ ] Raffles' Malkoha
- [ ] Chestnut-breasted Malkoha
- [ ] Grey-rumped Treeswift (also open areas)
- [ ] Whiskered Treeswift (forest edge)
- [ ] Diard's Trogon (also lower storey)
- [ ] Scarlet-rumped Trogon (also lower storey)
- [ ] Rufous-collared Kingfisher (also lower storey)
- [ ] Red-bearded Bee-eater
- [ ] Bushy-crested Hornbill (all hornbills also overhead)
- [ ] Helmeted Hornbill
- [ ] Gold-whiskered Barbet
- [ ] Red-crowned Barbet
- [ ] Red-throated Barbet
- [ ] Blue-eared Barbet
- [ ] Rufous Piculet (also lower storey)
- [ ] Rufous Woodpecker (also lower storey)
- [ ] Crimson-winged Woodpecker
- [ ] Banded Woodpecker
- [ ] Buff-rumped Woodpecker
- [ ] Buff-necked Woodpecker (also lower storey)
- [ ] Maroon Woodpecker (also lower storey)
- [ ] Black-and-Yellow Broadbill (this and the next species can often be found close to the baths)
- [ ] Green Broadbill (also lower storey)
- [ ] Hose's Broadbill* (mainly middle storey)
- [ ] Black-winged Flycatcher-shrike
- [ ] Green Iora
- [ ] Lesser Green Leafbird
- [ ] Greater Green Leafbird
- [ ] Black-headed Bulbul
- [ ] Scaly-breasted Bulbul
- [ ] Cream-vented Bulbul
- [ ] Red-eyed Bulbul
- [ ] Spectacled Bulbul (also lower storey)
- [ ] Hairy-backed Bulbul (also lower storey)
- [ ] Bronzed Drongo (forest edge)
- [ ] Greater Racket-tailed Drongo
- [ ] Dark-throated Oriole
- [ ] Asian Fairy-Bluebird
- [ ] Crested Jay (also lower storey)
- [ ] Black Magpie
- [ ] Slender-billed Crow
- [ ] Velvet-fronted Nuthatch

☐ Moustached Babbler (also lower storey)
☐ Sooty-capped Babbler (also lower storey; favours forest edge)
☐ Chestnut-crested (Babbler) Yuhina*
☐ Yellow-bellied Warbler (favours dense bamboo)
☐ Arctic Warbler m
☐ Grey-headed Flycatcher (also lower storey)
☐ Spotted Fantail (also lower storey)
☐ Asian Paradise-Flycatcher
☐ Purple-throated Sunbird (also open areas)
☐ Long-billed Spiderhunter
☐ Yellow-eared Spiderhunter
☐ Yellow-rumped Flowerpecker* (forest edge)
☐ Orange-bellied Flowerpecker (also lower storey)
☐ Scarlet-backed Flowerpecker
☐ Everett's White-eye

Difficult-to-find or rare species:
☐ Kinabalu (Mountain) Serpent-Eagle* (look near the Langanan Waterfall)
☐ Besra (favours clearings)
☐ Chinese Goshawk m
☐ Grey-faced Buzzard m
☐ Rufous-bellied Eagle
☐ Changeable Hawk-Eagle
☐ Blyth's Hawk-Eagle
☐ Oriental Hobby m (vagrant)
☐ Crimson-headed Partridge* (try the Langanan Waterfall Trail)
☐ Great Argus (heard more often than seen)
☐ Red-legged Crake
☐ Green Imperial Pigeon
☐ Little Cuckoo-Dove
☐ Ruddy (Red) Cuckoo-Dove
☐ Chestnut-winged Cuckoo m
☐ Brush (Rusty-breasted) Cuckoo
☐ Violet Cuckoo
☐ Malayan (Little) Bronze-Cuckoo
☐ Red-billed Malkoha
☐ Lesser Coucal
☐ Barred Eagle-Owl
☐ Brown Hawk-Owl
☐ Brown Needletail
☐ Asian Palm-Swift
☐ Cinnamon-rumped Trogon
☐ Orange-breasted Trogon
☐ Blue-throated Bee-eater
☐ White-crowned Hornbill
☐ Wreathed Hornbill
☐ Black Hornbill
☐ Rhinoceros Hornbill
☐ Yellow-crowned Barbet

- [ ] Brown Barbet
- [ ] Malaysian Honeyguide
- [ ] Checker-throated Woodpecker
- [ ] Olive-backed Woodpecker
- [ ] Grey-capped Woodpecker
- [ ] Orange-backed Woodpecker
- [ ] Dusky Broadbill
- [ ] Banded Broadbill
- [ ] Large Wood-shrike
- [ ] Bar-bellied Cuckoo-shrike
- [ ] Lesser Cuckoo-shrike
- [ ] Blue-winged Leafbird
- [ ] Black-and-White Bulbul
- [ ] Streaked Bulbul
- [ ] Crow-billed Drongo m
- [ ] Chestnut-backed Scimitar-Babbler
- [ ] Striped Wren-Babbler
- [ ] Rufous-fronted Babbler
- [ ] Grey-throated Babbler
- [ ] Grey-headed Babbler
- [ ] Fluffy-backed Tit-Babbler
- [ ] Brown Fulvetta
- [ ] White-bellied Yuhina
- [ ] Rufous-tailed Shama
- [ ] Sunda Whistling Thrush
- [ ] Chestnut-capped Thrush (this and the next species are shy and elusive; the Chestnut-capped Thrush has, however, been seen near the Kipungit Waterfall)
- [ ] Orange-headed Thrush
- [ ] Flyeater
- [ ] Fulvous-chested Flycatcher
- [ ] Dark-sided Flycatcher m
- [ ] Asian Brown Flycatcher m
- [ ] Ferruginous Flycatcher m
- [ ] Verditer Flycatcher
- [ ] Narcissus Flycatcher m
- [ ] Rufous-chested Flycatcher
- [ ] Blue-and-White Flycatcher m
- [ ] Hill Blue Flycatcher
- [ ] Bornean Blue Flycatcher* (near streams)
- [ ] Maroon-breasted Flycatcher (along streams)
- [ ] Ruby-cheeked Sunbird
- [ ] Olive-backed Sunbird
- [ ] Scarlet Sunbird (try around the baths)
- [ ] Thick-billed Spiderhunter
- [ ] Spectacled Spiderhunter
- [ ] Crimson-breasted Flowerpecker
- [ ] Yellow-vented Flowerpecker
- [ ] Plain Flowerpecker

Access and accommodation

As mentioned earlier, most people go to Poring after they have visited Kinabalu National Park headquarters. By road, Poring is about 45 km from the park hq via the town of Ranau. There is no regular bus service between the two areas of the park; however, if you go to the park hq entrance first thing in the morning, there will almost certainly be one or two minibuses there waiting for passengers to Poring. The fare will cost you between $M10 and $M20, depending on the number of people wanting to go. At least one minibus calls at Poring every morning looking for passengers - you can either go back to the park hq and from there to Kota Kinabalu, or you can go to Ranau and catch another bus to Sandakan.

Poring has limited accommodation and no canteen (you can eat at the small restaurant opposite the park entrance, or you can take your own food and cook it yourself). At the time of writing, the accommodation consists of a hostel (with a kitchen) where a bunk bed will cost you $M10 a night, and five or six chalets that are being built just up the road from the hostel. The chalets will probably cost around $M150 per night during the week, or $M200 or more at weekends and public holidays. All accommodation must be booked in advance through the Sabah Parks office in Kota Kinabalu.

When to visit

Since Poring is situated at an altitude of 520 m (1700 feet), it is a much warmer place than the park hq. The humidity can be particularly bad during the monsoon season (October to January), but there are always the baths to jump into at the end of a hard day's birding! And yes, there's cold water as well as hot. The downside is that the baths attract large crowds - if possible, go to Poring in the middle of the week rather than at the weekend.

Other attractions

The lowland dipterocarp rainforest at Poring supports a wealth of wildlife, but as usual many of the inhabitants can be difficult to see. During the day you could come across Maroon Langurs (Red Leaf Monkeys) and Bornean Gibbons, and you'll probably see many colourful butterflies and a variety of reptiles. At night, with the aid of a powerful torch or a spotlight, you might find a Colugo (Flying Lemur), a Slow Loris or a Western Tarsier, all of which are quite common in the area.

36 Sepilok
Forest Reserve
Sabah

It is probably fair to say that the Orang-utan is one of Borneo's premier wildlife attractions. Perhaps more than any other animal, this splendid primate evokes images of hot steamy jungle resounding with the wild whoopings of distant apes and the fantastic calls of hidden birds. That said, it is inconceivable that anyone would leave Sabah without paying a visit to Sepilok Forest Reserve, the best place in Borneo to see semi-wild Orang-utans in their natural habitat.

The reserve consists of 4530 ha of pristine lowland dipterocarp forest, and is the site of an Orang-utan rehabilitation centre run by the Sabah Forest Department. The centre cares for young Orang-utans that have been rescued after having been illegally kept as pets, and the animals are released into the reserve's wild Orang-utan population once they have learned to fend for themselves.

Although best known for its 'men of the forest', Sepilok supports most of the mammal species characteristic of Sabah's lowland forests, including the Maroon Langur (Red Leaf Monkey) and the Bornean Gibbon, both of which you've a fair chance of seeing. Needless to say there are birds too, among them a host of sought-after species - for example, Chestnut-necklaced (Scaly-breasted) Partridge, Little Green Pigeon, Bay Owl, Blue-banded and Banded Kingfisher, Great Slaty Woodpecker, Giant, Garnet, Blue-headed and Hooded Pitta, Bornean Wren-Babbler, Black-throated Wren-Babbler, Fluffy-backed Tit-Babbler, Chestnut-capped Thrush, Bornean Blue Flycatcher and Bornean Bristlehead.

Good birdwatching areas

Sepilok is not the easiest of places to explore; there are a number of walking tracks, but visitors are not generally permitted to wander around unescorted. The trick is to get to the reserve early in the day, before the crowds arrive to see the Orang-utans being fed (this takes place twice a day - mid morning and mid afternoon). If you talk to the head ranger, and explain that you've come from the other side of the world to birdwatch at Sepilok, you should have no difficulty gaining access to the forest outside the normal opening times. As well, this is one of the few reserves in Sabah where the rangers (or the head ranger at least) know a lot about birds. At the time of writing the head ranger is Sylvia Alsisto; she is very helpful and can tell you the best spots for birds like pittas and the Bornean Bristlehead.

There are two main walking tracks in the reserve - a short, circular nature trail that takes about half an hour to complete, and a much longer trail that runs for four kilometres or so through rainforest to a patch of mangroves on the edge of Sandakan Bay. Both trails start from near the education centre, and the walk to Sandakan Bay will take you about four hours (there and back). At present, most of the other tracks in the reserve are overgrown and poorly signposted; there are plans to upgrade and extend the track system, however, and this should be done by the time this book is published. You can get a map showing the walking trails from the visitor centre; also, ask for a copy of *A Checklist of the Birds of Sepilok,* a 30-page booklet containing much useful information.

Sepilok Forest Reserve is bounded on three sides by oil palm, cocoa and rubber plantations, interspersed with small market gardens and areas of scrub and secondary forest. The diverse habitats support a wide variety of birds, and you can enjoy often excellent birding along the many narrow roads that run through the area. For instance, the road leading into the reserve from the main Ranau to Sandakan highway is lined with rambutans and other fruit trees, and this is usually a good place for species like sunbirds, spiderhunters and flowerpeckers. As well, close to the road there are several small wetlands that are worth checking for Cinnamon Bittern, White-breasted Waterhen, Pintail Snipe, Lesser Coucal and Stork-billed Kingfisher. Dusky and Chestnut Munias can be found in the long grass and scrub, while flocks of Long-tailed Parakeets and Blue-rumped Parrots are frequently seen passing overhead.

On the whole, the country around Sepilok offers rather more opportunities for birdwatching than does the reserve; for one thing, the birds are much easier to see in the open scrub and plantations than in the shadowy confines of the rainforest. For best results you should stay overnight close to Sepilok - at Uncle Tan's, see Access and accommodation - and get out first thing in the morning.

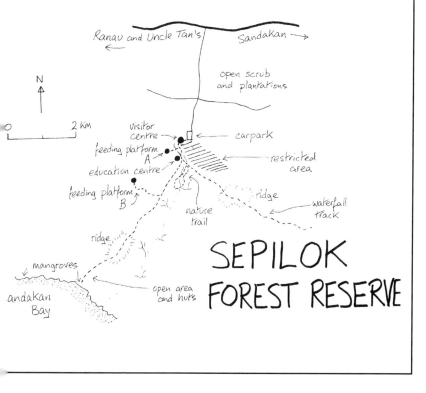

Birds

Open areas, overhead:
- ☐ Brahminy Kite
- ☐ Crested Serpent-Eagle
- ☐ Malaysian Eared Nightjar
- ☐ Edible-nest Swiftlet
- ☐ White-bellied (Glossy) Swiftlet
- ☐ Brown Needletail
- ☐ Silver-rumped Swift
- ☐ Blue-throated Bee-eater
- ☐ Barn Swallow m
- ☐ Pacific Swallow
- ☐ Philippine Glossy Starling
- ☐ Eurasian Tree-Sparrow

Wetlands:
- ☐ Little Heron
- ☐ Cinnamon Bittern
- ☐ White-breasted Waterhen
- ☐ Common Sandpiper m
- ☐ Pintail Snipe m
- ☐ Stork-billed Kingfisher

Gardens, plantations, secondary growth:
- ☐ Pink-necked Pigeon
- ☐ Spotted Dove
- ☐ Long-tailed Parakeet (also overhead)
- ☐ Blue-rumped Parrot (also overhead)
- ☐ Blue-crowned Hanging Parrot (also forest edge)
- ☐ Plaintive Cuckoo
- ☐ Greater Coucal
- ☐ Lesser Coucal (also wetlands)
- ☐ Dollarbird (also forest edge)
- ☐ Yellow-vented Bulbul
- ☐ Olive-winged Bulbul (also forest edge)
- ☐ Magpie Robin
- ☐ Ashy Tailorbird
- ☐ Rufous-tailed Tailorbird
- ☐ Yellow-bellied Prinia
- ☐ Pied Fantail
- ☐ Brown-throated Sunbird
- ☐ Red-throated Sunbird
- ☐ Olive-backed Sunbird
- ☐ Crimson Sunbird
- ☐ Little Spiderhunter
- ☐ Orange-bellied Flowerpecker
- ☐ Scarlet-backed Flowerpecker
- ☐ Dusky Munia*
- ☐ Chestnut Munia

Forest (including mangroves):

☐ Crested Goshawk
☐ White-fronted Falconet* (edges)
☐ Chestnut-necklaced (Scaly-breasted) Partridge
☐ Little Green Pigeon
☐ Large Green Pigeon
☐ Green Imperial Pigeon
☐ Green-winged (Emerald Dove) Pigeon
☐ Hodgson's Hawk-Cuckoo
☐ Indian Cuckoo
☐ Banded Bay Cuckoo
☐ Violet Cuckoo
☐ Drongo Cuckoo
☐ Raffles' Malkoha
☐ Chestnut-breasted Malkoha
☐ Collared Scops-Owl
☐ Brown Hawk-Owl
☐ Brown Wood-Owl
☐ Grey-rumped Treeswift (edges and clearings; also overhead)
☐ Diard's Trogon
☐ Scarlet-rumped Trogon
☐ Blue-eared Kingfisher (along streams; also in plantations and secondary growth near pools of water)
☐ Oriental Dwarf Kingfisher
☐ Collared Kingfisher
☐ Red-bearded Bee-eater
☐ Bushy-crested Hornbill (all hornbills also overhead)
☐ Wreathed Hornbill
☐ Rhinoceros Hornbill
☐ Gold-whiskered Barbet
☐ Red-throated Barbet
☐ Blue-eared Barbet
☐ Brown Barbet
☐ Rufous Piculet
☐ Rufous Woodpecker
☐ Crimson-winged Woodpecker
☐ Checker-throated Woodpecker
☐ Banded Woodpecker
☐ Olive-backed Woodpecker
☐ Buff-rumped Woodpecker
☐ Buff-necked Woodpecker
☐ White-bellied Woodpecker
☐ Grey-and-Buff Woodpecker
☐ Maroon Woodpecker
☐ Orange-backed Woodpecker
☐ Black-and-Red Broadbill (along streams)
☐ Banded Broadbill
☐ Black-and-Yellow Broadbill
☐ Garnet Pitta
☐ Blue-headed Pitta*

- [ ] Black-winged Flycatcher-shrike
- [ ] Scarlet Minivet
- [ ] Green Iora
- [ ] Common Iora (mainly mangroves)
- [ ] Lesser Green Leafbird
- [ ] Greater Green Leafbird
- [ ] Puff-backed Bulbul
- [ ] Cream-vented Bulbul
- [ ] Red-eyed Bulbul (especially edges)
- [ ] Spectacled Bulbul
- [ ] Grey-cheeked Bulbul
- [ ] Yellow-bellied Bulbul
- [ ] Hairy-backed Bulbul
- [ ] Streaked Bulbul
- [ ] Bronzed Drongo (edges)
- [ ] Greater Racket-tailed Drongo
- [ ] Dark-throated Oriole
- [ ] Asian Fairy-Bluebird
- [ ] Black Magpie
- [ ] Slender-billed Crow
- [ ] Black-capped Babbler
- [ ] Short-tailed Babbler
- [ ] White-chested Babbler (especially streams)
- [ ] Ferruginous Babbler
- [ ] Horsfield's Babbler
- [ ] Moustached Babbler
- [ ] Sooty-capped Babbler (edges)
- [ ] Scaly-crowned Babbler
- [ ] Rufous-crowned Babbler
- [ ] Striped Wren-Babbler
- [ ] Chestnut-rumped Babbler
- [ ] Black-throated Babbler
- [ ] Chestnut-winged Babbler
- [ ] Striped Tit-Babbler (edges; also secondary growth)
- [ ] Brown Fulvetta
- [ ] White-rumped Shama
- [ ] White-crowned Forktail
- [ ] Flyeater
- [ ] Grey-chested Flycatcher
- [ ] Large-billed Blue Flycatcher
- [ ] Mangrove Blue Flycatcher
- [ ] Spotted Fantail
- [ ] Black-naped Monarch
- [ ] Rufous-winged Flycatcher
- [ ] Asian Paradise-Flycatcher
- [ ] Mangrove Whistler
- [ ] Hill Myna
- [ ] Plain Sunbird
- [ ] Ruby-cheeked Sunbird
- [ ] Purple-naped Sunbird (along streams)

☐ Copper-throated Sunbird (mainly mangroves)
☐ Grey-breasted Spiderhunter
☐ Yellow-breasted Flowerpecker
☐ Yellow-rumped Flowerpecker* (especially edges)

Difficult-to-find or rare species:
☐ Oriental Darter
☐ Great-billed Heron
☐ Storm's Stork
☐ Eurasian (Crested) Honey-Buzzard
☐ Bat Hawk (try in the vicinity of the visitor centre
  towards dusk)
☐ White-bellied Sea-Eagle
☐ Grey-faced Buzzard m
☐ Rufous-bellied Eagle
☐ Changeable Hawk-Eagle
☐ Wallace's Hawk-Eagle
☐ Crested Wood-Partridge
☐ Great Argus
☐ Thick-billed Pigeon
☐ Cinnamon-headed Pigeon (mainly mangroves; may be
  easier to find in scrub and plantations)
☐ Moustached Hawk-Cuckoo
☐ Black-bellied Malkoha
☐ Red-billed Malkoha
☐ Short-toed Coucal
☐ Bay Owl
☐ Reddish Scops-Owl
☐ Barred Eagle-Owl
☐ Asian Palm-Swift
☐ Whiskered Treeswift
☐ Red-naped Trogon
☐ Cinnamon-rumped Trogon
☐ Blue-banded Kingfisher
☐ Banded Kingfisher
☐ Rufous-collared Kingfisher
☐ White-crowned Hornbill
☐ Black Hornbill
☐ Oriental Pied Hornbill
☐ Helmeted Hornbill
☐ Malaysian Honeyguide
☐ Common Goldenback
☐ Great Slaty Woodpecker
☐ Grey-capped Woodpecker
☐ Dusky Broadbill
☐ Green Broadbill
☐ Giant Pitta (has been seen along the waterfall track)
☐ Hooded Pitta (especially win)
☐ Large Wood-shrike
☐ Lesser Cuckoo-shrike

- [ ] Fiery Minivet
- [ ] Black-headed Bulbul
- [ ] Grey-bellied Bulbul
- [ ] Buff-vented Bulbul
- [ ] Crow-billed Drongo m
- [ ] Crested Jay
- [ ] Velvet-fronted Nuthatch
- [ ] Chestnut-backed Scimitar-Babbler
- [ ] Bornean Wren-Babbler*
- [ ] Black-throated Wren-Babbler* (try the track to Sandakan Bay)
- [ ] Rufous-fronted Babbler
- [ ] Grey-headed Babbler
- [ ] White-necked Babbler
- [ ] Fluffy-backed Tit-Babbler
- [ ] White-bellied Yuhina
- [ ] Siberian Blue Robin m
- [ ] Rufous-tailed Shama
- [ ] Chestnut-capped Thrush
- [ ] Arctic Warbler m
- [ ] Middendorf's Warbler m
- [ ] Dark-necked Tailorbird
- [ ] Asian Brown Flycatcher m
- [ ] Narcissus Flycatcher m
- [ ] Rufous-chested Flycatcher
- [ ] Pale Blue Flycatcher
- [ ] Bornean Blue Flycatcher*
- [ ] Grey-headed Flycatcher
- [ ] Maroon-breasted Flycatcher
- [ ] White-breasted Woodswallow
- [ ] Brown Shrike m
- [ ] Tiger Shrike m
- [ ] Bornean Bristlehead* (has been seen on the ridge along the first part of the waterfall track)
- [ ] Chestnut-cheeked (Violet-backed) Starling m (scrub and plantations; try along the entrance road)
- [ ] Purple-throated Sunbird
- [ ] Thick-billed Spiderhunter
- [ ] Long-billed Spiderhunter
- [ ] Spectacled Spiderhunter
- [ ] Yellow-eared Spiderhunter
- [ ] Scarlet-breasted Flowerpecker
- [ ] Yellow-vented Flowerpecker

Access and accommodation

Sepilok reserve is about 25 km from Sandakan via the main road to Ranau.
You can get there by public transport from Sandakan - go to the bus stand
on the waterfront and take the bus marked 'Sepilok Batu 14', which will
take you right into the reserve's carpark. (Some buses marked 'Sepilok'
don't go to the reserve; if in doubt, ask the driver.) Buses leave every hour
or so and the trip takes about 45 minutes.

The only accommodation close to the reserve is Uncle Tan's, a well-known establishment on the Ranau to Sandakan road about four kilometres west of the turn-off to Sepilok. Uncle Tan's is a cheap and cheerful place; you can get a room for less than $M20 a night, including breakfast and evening meal. It would be wise to book accommodation in advance (Uncle Tan's is a favourite destination for backpackers) - write to PO Box 620, Sandakan 90007, Sabah, or 'phone 089-669516. As well as a guesthouse, Uncle Tan runs a jungle camp that he'll take you to for a price, and from time to time he arranges trips to Turtle Islands Park (see the next two sites in this book). For a few dollars a day you can hire a mountain bike from Uncle Tan, a great way to get around the local area.

If you don't stay at Uncle Tan's you'll have to go to Sandakan where there is a wide range of accommodation.

When to visit

Most of the birds at Sepilok are residents, making this a good place to visit year round. The rainforest will be hot and steamy whenever you go, although the humidity is of course worse during the monsoon season (October to January) than at other times of the year. If possible, avoid weekends when the reserve is usually crowded: and remember to take along plenty of insect repellent - the mosquitoes here are man-eaters!

Other attractions

The feeding of the Orang-utans is what most people come to see, and despite it being a tourist event it is an experience not to be missed. The animals are fed at two sites - feeding platform A is just a five-minute walk from the visitor centre, while platform B is located deep in the forest, some 30 minutes from the visitor centre. Needless to say you have to pay to see the Orang-utans being fed; a ticket to one of the feeding sessions will cost you about $M10, but it is worth paying a little extra and getting a ticket to both platform A and platform B. At feeding site A most of the Orang-utans are young animals still in the early stages of rehabilitation, whereas those that visit site B are older and virtually self-sufficient.

Maroon Langurs and Bornean Gibbons are quite common in the reserve (look for them along the edge of the restricted area - see map), and Pig-tailed and Long-tailed Macaques frequent the forest edge near the carpark. If you make it to the huts near the end of the walk to Sandakan Bay you could get a surprise - several observers have seen two large pythons there! Visitor facilities at Sepilok include an information centre and a cafeteria.

37 Uncle Tan's Jungle Camp   Sabah

With ecotourism a growth industry in Borneo, it's refreshing to find people like Uncle Tan who, so far at least, are resisting the temptation to over-exploit the region's vast appeal to wildlife watchers. Having earned a considerable reputation among the many hundreds of foreign visitors who use his guesthouse each year, Uncle Tan now spends more and more time taking tour groups to his jungle camp on the lower reaches of the Kinabatangan River, south of Sandakan. If you want to experience something of the real Borneo, well away from the usual tourist haunts, this is the place to go.

The birding around the camp is generally excellent. Storm's Stork is almost a certainty, while other regulars include Oriental Darter, Lesser and Grey-headed Fish-Eagle, Buffy Fish-Owl, and at least four species of hornbill - Wreathed, Black, Oriental Pied and Rhinoceros. In addition to birds, the area holds large numbers of the rare Proboscis Monkey, as well as Orang-utans, Bornean Gibbons and Hose's Langurs (Grey Leaf Monkeys).

Good birdwatching areas

You'll start seeing wildlife the moment you get into the boat that takes you down river to the jungle camp. Watch the river edge for darters, night-herons, storks, fish-eagles, kingfishers, hornbills, monkeys (you should see hundreds of Proboscis), Orang-utans and otters.

In the camp area there are a number of tracks leading into the surrounding forest, as well as trails to and around several of the five or six ox-bow lakes that lie nearby. There are also a number of hides and observation platforms that are particularly good at night (take a powerful torch). Uncle Tan's guides will take you for boat trips along the river - be sure to go on at least one, and arrange to leave first thing in the morning when the birding is best and the tropical sun is still low.

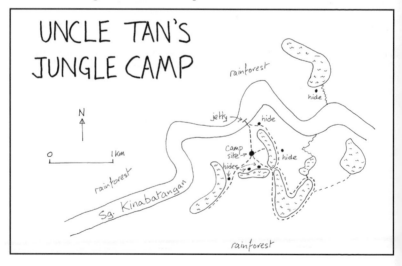

Birds

Open areas, overhead:
- [ ] Eurasian (Crested) Honey-Buzzard
- [ ] Bat Hawk (especially at dusk)
- [ ] Brahminy Kite
- [ ] White-bellied Sea-Eagle
- [ ] Greater Coucal (edges)
- [ ] Malaysian Eared Nightjar
- [ ] Mossy-nest (Uniform) Swiftlet
- [ ] White-bellied (Glossy) Swiftlet
- [ ] Brown Needletail
- [ ] Grey-rumped Treeswift (edges and clearings)
- [ ] Blue-throated Bee-eater
- [ ] Dollarbird (edges)
- [ ] Barn Swallow m
- [ ] Pacific Swallow
- [ ] Magpie Robin
- [ ] Ashy Tailorbird (edges)
- [ ] Rufous-tailed Tailorbird (edges)
- [ ] Yellow-bellied Prinia
- [ ] Pied Fantail (edges)
- [ ] Philippine Glossy Starling
- [ ] Little Spiderhunter (edges)
- [ ] Scarlet-backed Flowerpecker (edges)
- [ ] Dusky Munia*

Rivers and lakes:
- [ ] Oriental Darter (one of the more common waterbirds)
- [ ] Little Heron
- [ ] Great Egret
- [ ] Little Egret m
- [ ] Storm's Stork (this is one of the most reliable sites in Malaysia for this species)
- [ ] Lesser Fish-Eagle (look along the Sg. Kinabatangan for this and the next species)
- [ ] Grey-headed Fish-Eagle
- [ ] White-breasted Waterhen
- [ ] Wood Sandpiper m
- [ ] Common Sandpiper m
- [ ] Buffy Fish-Owl
- [ ] Common Kingfisher (especially win)
- [ ] Blue-eared Kingfisher
- [ ] Oriental Dwarf Kingfisher (also forests)
- [ ] Stork-billed Kingfisher
- [ ] Black-capped Kingfisher m
- [ ] Black-and-Red Broadbill
- [ ] Straw-headed Bulbul

Forests:

☐ Jerdon's Baza (try the edges of the quieter river backwaters)
☐ Crested Serpent-Eagle
☐ Crested Goshawk
☐ Chestnut-necklaced (Scaly-breasted) Partridge
☐ Crested Fireback
☐ Little Green Pigeon
☐ Green Imperial Pigeon
☐ Blue-crowned Hanging Parrot (especially edges)
☐ Raffles' Malkoha
☐ Chestnut-breasted Malkoha
☐ Brown Wood-Owl
☐ Scarlet-rumped Trogon
☐ Bushy-crested Hornbill (all hornbills also overhead)
☐ Wreathed Hornbill
☐ Black Hornbill
☐ Oriental Pied Hornbill
☐ Rhinoceros Hornbill
☐ Red-throated Barbet
☐ Blue-eared Barbet
☐ Brown Barbet
☐ Rufous Piculet
☐ Crimson-winged Woodpecker
☐ Great Slaty Woodpecker
☐ White-bellied Woodpecker
☐ Black-and-Yellow Broadbill
☐ Black-winged Flycatcher-shrike
☐ Common Iora (edges)
☐ Greater Green Leafbird
☐ Red-eyed Bulbul (edges)
☐ Hairy-backed Bulbul
☐ Greater Racket-tailed Drongo
☐ Asian Fairy-Bluebird
☐ Slender-billed Crow
☐ Velvet-fronted Nuthatch
☐ Black-capped Babbler
☐ White-chested Babbler (especially along streams)
☐ Sooty-capped Babbler (edges)
☐ Scaly-crowned Babbler
☐ Chestnut-winged Babbler
☐ Striped Tit-Babbler (edges)
☐ White-rumped Shama
☐ Large-billed Blue Flycatcher
☐ Malaysian Blue Flycatcher (especially along streams)
☐ Black-naped Monarch
☐ Asian Paradise-Flycatcher
☐ Hill Myna
☐ Ruby-cheeked Sunbird
☐ Purple-naped Sunbird (especially along streams)

Difficult-to-find or rare species:
- ☐ Great-billed Heron
- ☐ Black-crowned Night-Heron
- ☐ Rufous-bellied Eagle
- ☐ Wallace's Hawk-Eagle
- ☐ Great Argus
- ☐ Cinnamon-rumped Trogon
- ☐ Wrinkled Hornbill
- ☐ Helmeted Hornbill
- ☐ Greater Goldenback
- ☐ Blue-headed Pitta*
- ☐ Hooded Pitta (especially win)
- ☐ Ashy Minivet m
- ☐ Fluffy-backed Tit-Babbler
- ☐ White-bellied Yuhina
- ☐ Bornean Blue Flycatcher*
- ☐ Spectacled Spiderhunter

Access and accommodation

You will, of course, need to arrange your trip through Uncle Tan (see site 36 for the address), but he only takes small groups - usually 8 to 10 people - at a time so that you may have to wait a few days or so for a place. Transport to and from the camp is by minibus and boat, while the accommodation consists of a collection of wooden huts with mattresses and mosquito nets. Uncle Tan charges about $M150 for the return trip to the camp, plus around $M20 a day for meals and accommodation. If you have time it's worth staying for three or four days.

When to visit

Although most of the best birds here are residents, you could pick up some interesting migrants if you go between September and March. For much of the year it rains mostly at night, but afternoon downpours are common during the monsoon season (October to January).

Other attractions

As well as those already mentioned, you could see mammals such as Slow Loris, Long-tailed Macaque, Giant Squirrel, Plain Pygmy Squirrel, Teledu (Malay Badger), Hairy-nosed Otter, Malay Civet, Bay Cat, Bearded Pig, Mouse-Deer, Banteng and much more. Also, this is as likely a place as any for Asian Elephant and, perhaps, Sumatran Rhinoceros. Spotlighting at night will greatly increase the number of mammals you'll see - and don't forget to take along a mammal guide.

38 Turtle Islands Park
Sabah

Protecting a group of three small islands - Selingaan, Gulisan and Bakkungan Kechil - Turtle Islands Park lies some 40 km north of Sandakan, in the Sulu Sea close to the Philippines border. Green and Hawksbill turtles are what most people go to the park to see: the Green Turtle, the more common of the two, is a frequent visitor to P. Selingaan, while Hawksbill Turtles breed mostly on P. Gulisan.

Although the park's birdlife is not especially rich the area does have some avian attractions, and if you visit between late August and early November (which is the time when Green Turtles are most plentiful) you have a good chance of seeing a variety of migrants, including interesting species like Brown Hawk-Owl.

Good birdwatching areas

You will not have many choices about where to birdwatch - you'll be restricted to birding during the boat trip from Sandakan (this can take up to three hours) and you'll probably spend most of your time on the second largest island, P. Selingaan (8 ha), the site of the park's information centre, staff quarters, visitor accommodation and main turtle hatchery. Much of the original vegetation on the islands has been cleared to make way for coconut groves, but on Selingaan in particular there are still some pockets of mangrove, as well as the attractive yellow-flowered *Sophora* and the silvery, furry leaved *Tournefortia*.

Birds

Seabirds and shorebirds:
☐ Brown Booby (mainly Dec-May)
☐ Great Frigatebird m
☐ Lesser Frigatebird m
☐ Little Heron
☐ Common Sandpiper m
☐ Grey-tailed Tattler m
☐ Ruddy Turnstone m
☐ Red-necked Phalarope m (plentiful at times, for
    example Sept-Nov; look out for Red [Grey] Phalarope as well)
☐ Common Black-headed Gull m (vagrant)
☐ Whiskered Tern m
☐ Bridled Tern
☐ Little Tern
☐ Great Crested Tern m
☐ Lesser Crested Tern m

Landbirds:
☐ Brahminy Kite
☐ White-bellied Sea-Eagle
☐ Tabon (Megapode) Scrubfowl (unlikely but possible -
    there is an old record [1973] of a single bird on P. Selingaan)
☐ Spotted Dove
☐ Green-winged (Emerald Dove) Pigeon (should be easy to find)

☐ Common Koel (especially Sept-Mar)
☐ Brown Hawk-Owl (a winter visitor in small numbers;
  should be easy to find during daylight)
☐ Grey Nightjar m
☐ White-throated Needletail m (flying over, especially Oct-Dec)
☐ Collared Kingfisher
☐ Yellow-vented Bulbul
☐ Arctic Warbler m
☐ Pied Fantail
☐ Philippine Glossy Starling
☐ Brown-throated Sunbird
☐ Olive-backed Sunbird
☐ Orange-bellied Flowerpecker

Access and accommodation

If you don't arrange your trip through Uncle Tan (see site 36) you should
go to the harbour area at Sandakan and ask around for a charter boat. A
boat should be easy to get (there are usually some Indonesian boat owners
hanging around the waterfront looking for work), but be prepared to do
some hard bargaining. If there are two or three of you, the boat trip to the
islands and back should cost around $M120 per person (make sure the
boatman returns to collect you at the end of your stay).

   Accommodation on P. Selingaan consists of several furnished chalets;
the overnight rate is $M30 per person, and accommodation must be
booked in advance through the Sabah Parks office, 9th floor, Wisma Khoo,

TURTLE ISLANDS PARK

N
↑

P. Selingaan
Turtle Islands → Park
P. Gulisan

Philippines
P. BakKungan Kechil

Sepilok Forest Reserve
Sandakan

Kota Kinabalu
Sandakan Bay

Lahad Datu

Sulu Sea

0   20 KM

Jalan Tiga, Sandakan, 'phone 089-273453 (the postal address is PO Box 768, Sandakan 90008, Sabah). Alternatively, you can book accommodation through Sabah Parks in Kota Kinabalu (for the address see site 31). You will need a permit to visit the park (getting one is just a formality), and there is a restaurant on P. Selingaan where you can get inexpensive meals and basic supplies.

When to visit

Although some individuals of both species of turtle come ashore to lay their eggs all year round, breeding among Green Turtles reaches a peak between August and October, which coincides with the best time for migrant birds. Hawksbill Turtles breed mainly from February to April. Remember that during the north-east monsoon season - October to February - you may not be able to reach the islands because of rough seas. The driest months and calmest seas occur from March to July.

Other attractions

In addition to turtle-watching and birding, Turtle Islands Park offers excellent snorkelling - and it's a really great place to relax away from the crowded towns on the mainland. Just imagine walking along an empty beach under a full moon, with the waves lapping gently at your feet - paradise!

39 Danum Valley
Conservation Area   Sabah

As you drive through many parts of northern Sabah, particularly the area between Kota Kinabalu and Sandakan, you can't help but feel deeply saddened by what you see. On hillsides that were once covered in dense rainforest only stumps and isolated trees remain, while here and there, in the less accessible steep-sided gullys for example, patches of lush tropical vegetation stand as reminders of what used to be. Fortunately, in south-eastern Sabah the situation is not so grim, thanks largely to the work of the Sabah Foundation.

The Danum Valley Conservation Area, consisting of about 438 square kilometres of primary lowland and hill dipterocarp forest, is situated along the upper Segama River near the town of Lahad Datu. An increasingly popular destination among birders, Danum Valley is the site of a field centre managed by the Sabah Foundation for the benefit of resident and visiting researchers; as well, the Foundation is upgrading accommodation in the area so as to generate more income by attracting larger numbers of ecotourists.

More than 230 bird species have been recorded at Danum, making it one of the best places in Sabah for lowland birds. Among the highlights are 10 Bornean endemics - you have a good chance of seeing White-fronted Falconet, Blue-headed Pitta and Yellow-rumped Flowerpecker for example, and there's a fair chance you'll see Blue-banded Pitta, Bornean and Black-throated Wren-Babbler, Bornean Blue Flycatcher and Bornean Bristlehead. Other sought-after species at Danum include Bat Hawk, Chestnut-necklaced (Scaly-breasted) Partridge, Crested Wood-Partridge, Crested Fireback, Bulwer's Pheasant (also an endemic), Great Argus, Buffy Fish-Owl, Large and Javan Frogmouth, hornbills (seven species, including Wrinkled), Malaysian Honeyguide, Giant Pitta and Chestnut-naped Forktail.

Good birdwatching areas

You should plan on spending three or four days at Danum, which will give you time to explore along the excellent trail system around the field centre as well as along the access road. The two trails closest to the field centre - the nature trail and the Sg. Palum Tambun Trail - provide a useful introduction to the area; both are less than a kilometre long, and the Sg. Palum Tambun Trail in particular is good for partridges, Crested Fireback, kingfishers, bulbuls, babblers and Chestnut-naped Forktail.

Starting at the footbridge over the Sg. Segama, the Main Trail West takes you through an area of undisturbed lowland forest where many of Danum's special birds can be found, including Long-billed Partridge, Great Argus, trogons, Banded and Rufous-collared Kingfisher, barbets, woodpeckers, broadbills, pittas and wren-babblers. The first couple of kilometres of the Main Trail West provide some of the best birding at Danum, as do the many short paths that branch off it between the footbridge and the Elephant Ridge Trail. For hill forest inhabitants, such as the Blue-banded Pitta, you should try the Rhino Ridge Trail, a 7 km circuit to the south of the Main Trail West.

Birds

Open areas, overhead:
- [ ] Bat Hawk (best looked for at dusk)
- [ ] Crested Serpent-Eagle
- [ ] Japanese Sparrowhawk m
- [ ] Pink-necked Pigeon (edges)
- [ ] Buffy Fish-Owl (can be seen at night feeding on insects that are attracted to lights around the field centre)
- [ ] Malaysian Eared Nightjar
- [ ] White-bellied (Glossy) Swiftlet
- [ ] Brown Needletail
- [ ] Silver-rumped Swift
- [ ] Barn Swallow m
- [ ] Pacific Swallow
- [ ] Common Iora (edges)
- [ ] Magpie Robin
- [ ] Ashy Tailorbird (edges)
- [ ] Rufous-tailed Tailorbird (edges)
- [ ] Dark-sided Flycatcher m (especially forest clearings)
- [ ] Scarlet-backed Flowerpecker (edges)

Ground, lower storey:
- [ ] Chestnut-necklaced (Scaly-breasted) Partridge (try the nature trail and the Sg. Palum Tambun Trail first thing in the morning for this and the next two species)
- [ ] Crested Wood-Partridge
- [ ] Crested Fireback
- [ ] Great Argus (seen regularly along the Main Trail West)
- [ ] White-breasted Waterhen
- [ ] Green-winged (Emerald Dove) Pigeon
- [ ] Greater Coucal (edges)
- [ ] Collared Scops-Owl (also middle storey)
- [ ] Scarlet-rumped Trogon (also middle storey)
- [ ] Blue-eared Kingfisher (try the Sg. Palum Tambun Trail)
- [ ] Oriental Dwarf Kingfisher
- [ ] Rufous-collared Kingfisher
- [ ] Rufous Piculet (also middle storey)
- [ ] Rufous Woodpecker (also middle storey)
- [ ] Buff-necked Woodpecker (also middle storey)
- [ ] Black-and-Red Broadbill (also middle storey; usually near water)
- [ ] Garnet Pitta (easily the most common lowland pitta here)
- [ ] Blue-headed Pitta* (widespread and quite common)
- [ ] Banded Pitta
- [ ] Straw-headed Bulbul (along streams and rivers)
- [ ] Olive-winged Bulbul (edges)
- [ ] Grey-cheeked Bulbul (also middle storey)
- [ ] Yellow-bellied Bulbul
- [ ] Black-capped Babbler
- [ ] Short-tailed Babbler
- [ ] White-chested Babbler (along streams and rivers)

DANUM VALLEY CONSERVATION AREA

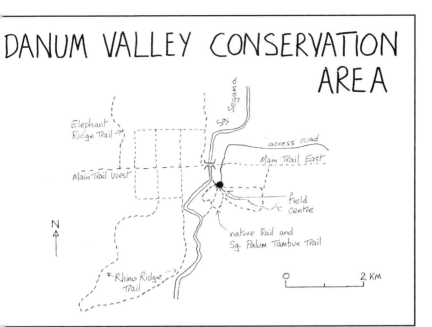

☐ Ferruginous Babbler (also middle storey)
☐ Horsfield's Babbler (also middle storey)
☐ Moustached Babbler (also middle storey)
☐ Sooty-capped Babbler (especially edges)
☐ Scaly-crowned Babbler (also middle storey)
☐ Rufous-crowned Babbler (also middle storey)
☐ Grey-headed Babbler
☐ Chestnut-rumped Babbler
☐ Black-throated Babbler
☐ Chestnut-winged Babbler
☐ Striped Tit-Babbler
☐ Siberian Blue Robin m (especially along streams)
☐ White-rumped Shama
☐ Chestnut-naped Forktail (along the Sg. Palum Tambun Trail)
☐ Dark-necked Tailorbird
☐ Grey-chested Flycatcher
☐ Rufous-tailed Flycatcher (also middle storey; try the
    Rhino Ridge Trail)
☐ Rufous-chested Flycatcher
☐ White-tailed Flycatcher
☐ Malaysian Blue Flycatcher (along streams and rivers)
☐ Grey-headed Flycatcher (also middle storey)
☐ Spotted Fantail (also middle storey)
☐ Rufous-winged Flycatcher
☐ Ruby-cheeked Sunbird (also middle storey)
☐ Purple-naped Sunbird (along rivers and streams)

☐ Crimson Sunbird (also middle storey)
☐ Little Spiderhunter (edges; also middle storey)
☐ Grey-breasted Spiderhunter (also middle storey)
☐ Yellow-breasted Flowerpecker (also middle storey)
☐ Orange-bellied Flowerpecker (also middle storey)
☐ Dusky Munia* (edges)

Middle storey, canopy:
☐ Crested Goshawk
☐ White-fronted Falconet* (perches conspicuously in high bare branches; try along the access road)
☐ Thick-billed Pigeon
☐ Little Green Pigeon
☐ Blue-crowned Hanging Parrot (also overhead)
☐ Hodgson's Hawk-Cuckoo (also lower storey)
☐ Indian Cuckoo
☐ Banded Bay Cuckoo
☐ Violet Cuckoo
☐ Drongo Cuckoo
☐ Black-bellied Malkoha
☐ Chestnut-bellied Malkoha
☐ Raffles' Malkoha
☐ Chestnut-breasted Malkoha
☐ Grey-rumped Treeswift (also open areas)
☐ Whiskered Treeswift (edges)
☐ Diard's Trogon (also lower storey)
☐ Banded Kingfisher (also lower storey)
☐ Red-bearded Bee-eater
☐ Bushy-crested Hornbill (all hornbills also overhead)
☐ Black Hornbill
☐ Rhinoceros Hornbill
☐ Gold-whiskered Barbet
☐ Red-crowned Barbet
☐ Red-throated Barbet
☐ Yellow-crowned Barbet
☐ Blue-eared Barbet
☐ Brown Barbet
☐ Crimson-winged Woodpecker
☐ Checker-throated Woodpecker
☐ Banded Woodpecker
☐ Buff-rumped Woodpecker
☐ Great Slaty Woodpecker
☐ Maroon Woodpecker (also lower storey)
☐ Orange-backed Woodpecker
☐ Banded Broadbill (especially along the Rhino Ridge Trail)
☐ Black-and-Yellow Broadbill
☐ Green Broadbill
☐ Black-winged Flycatcher-shrike
☐ Lesser Cuckoo-shrike
☐ Scarlet Minivet
☐ Green Iora

☐ Lesser Green Leafbird
☐ Greater Green Leafbird
☐ Blue-winged Leafbird
☐ Black-headed Bulbul
☐ Cream-vented Bulbul
☐ Red-eyed Bulbul
☐ Spectacled Bulbul (also lower storey)
☐ Hairy-backed Bulbul (also lower storey)
☐ Buff-vented Bulbul (also lower storey)
☐ Streaked Bulbul
☐ Bronzed Drongo (edges; often along rivers)
☐ Greater Racket-tailed Drongo
☐ Dark-throated Oriole
☐ Asian Fairy-Bluebird
☐ Crested Jay (also lower storey)
☐ Black Magpie
☐ Slender-billed Crow (favours riverside forest)
☐ Flyeater
☐ Arctic Warbler m
☐ Large-billed Blue Flycatcher (also lower storey)
☐ Black-naped Monarch (also lower storey)
☐ Asian Paradise-Flycatcher
☐ Hill Myna
☐ Plain Sunbird
☐ Red-throated Sunbird
☐ Yellow-eared Spiderhunter
☐ Scarlet-breasted Flowerpecker
☐ Yellow-rumped Flowerpecker* (edges)
☐ Everett's White-eye

Difficult-to-find or rare species:
☐ Great-billed Heron
☐ Eurasian (Crested) Honey-Buzzard
☐ Rufous-bellied Eagle
☐ Changeable Hawk-Eagle
☐ Wallace's Hawk-Eagle
☐ Peregrine Falcon
☐ Long-billed Partridge (try the Main Trail West)
☐ Bulwer's Pheasant* (the Rhino Ridge Trail is perhaps
  the best spot for this seldom-seen species)
☐ Large Green Pigeon
☐ Jambu Fruit-Dove
☐ Green Imperial Pigeon
☐ Moustached Hawk-Cuckoo
☐ Brush (Rusty-breasted) Cuckoo
☐ Red-billed Malkoha
☐ Short-toed Coucal (favours riverside forest)
☐ Bay Owl
☐ Reddish Scops-Owl
☐ Barred Eagle-Owl
☐ Brown Hawk-Owl

- ☐ Brown Wood-Owl
- ☐ Large Frogmouth
- ☐ Javan Frogmouth
- ☐ Red-naped Trogon
- ☐ Cinnamon-rumped Trogon
- ☐ Blue-banded Kingfisher
- ☐ White-crowned Hornbill (try the Rhino Ridge Trail)
- ☐ Wrinkled Hornbill
- ☐ Wreathed Hornbill
- ☐ Helmeted Hornbill
- ☐ Malaysian Honeyguide
- ☐ Olive-backed Woodpecker
- ☐ White-bellied Woodpecker
- ☐ Grey-capped Woodpecker
- ☐ Dusky Broadbill
- ☐ Giant Pitta (Danum is probably the best place in East Malaysia for this elusive species)
- ☐ Blue-banded Pitta* (favours bamboo thickets; try along the Rhino Ridge Trail)
- ☐ Blue-winged Pitta (especially win)
- ☐ Hooded Pitta (especially win)
- ☐ Large Wood-shrike
- ☐ Bar-bellied Cuckoo-shrike
- ☐ Black-and-White Bulbul
- ☐ Scaly-breasted Bulbul
- ☐ Grey-bellied Bulbul
- ☐ Puff-backed Bulbul
- ☐ Finsch's Bulbul
- ☐ Hook-billed Bulbul
- ☐ Velvet-fronted Nuthatch
- ☐ Temminck's Babbler (try the Rhino Ridge Trail)
- ☐ Chestnut-backed Scimitar-Babbler
- ☐ Bornean Wren-Babbler* (look in the vicinity of the Main Trail West for this and the Black-throated Wren-Babbler)
- ☐ Striped Wren-Babbler
- ☐ Black-throated Wren-Babbler*
- ☐ Grey-throated Babbler
- ☐ White-necked Babbler
- ☐ Fluffy-backed Tit-Babbler
- ☐ Brown Fulvetta
- ☐ White-bellied Yuhina
- ☐ Malaysian Rail-Babbler
- ☐ Rufous-tailed Shama
- ☐ White-crowned Forktail
- ☐ Chestnut-capped Thrush
- ☐ Asian Brown Flycatcher m
- ☐ Verditer Flycatcher
- ☐ Narcissus Flycatcher m
- ☐ Blue-and-White Flycatcher m
- ☐ Pale Blue Flycatcher

☐ Hill Blue Flycatcher
☐ Bornean Blue Flycatcher*
☐ Maroon-breasted Flycatcher
☐ Tiger Shrike m
☐ Bornean Bristlehead* (try the Rhino Ridge Trail)
☐ Scarlet Sunbird
☐ Thick-billed Spiderhunter
☐ Long-billed Spiderhunter
☐ Spectacled Spiderhunter
☐ Yellow-vented Flowerpecker

Access and accommodation

You can get to Lahad Datu from Kota Kinabalu either by bus or by air
(Malaysia Airlines fly there regularly; the one-way fare is about $M100).
The bus trip from Kota Kinabalu takes almost a full day and costs around
$M25; alternatively, there are regular minibuses to Lahad Datu from
Sandakan (the fare is about $M15). From Lahad Datu it's 70 km or so to the
Danum Valley; there's a minibus that goes to the field centre on Mondays,
Wednesdays and Fridays from the Sabah Foundation office in the
Hapseng Building, Lahad Datu. The return fare is $M60, and there's a
$M15 fee to get into the conservation area.

Accommodation at the field centre consists of a resthouse and a hostel
where overnight charges are $M45 per person and $M30 per person
respectively. As well, visitors will soon be able to stay at a jungle lodge
that is being built in the northern part of the conservation area. Meals will
cost you an additional $M30 a day, or you can take your own food and
cook for yourself.

When to visit

Since the Danum Valley is well off the tourist track you are unlikely to
encounter large numbers of people at any time of the year.
Accommodation in the area is limited, however, thus you should inquire
about the availability of rooms before going there - contact the Sabah
Foundation office in Lahad Datu. (If you get stranded, there are at least 10
hotels in Lahad Datu.) Virtually all of the special birds at Danum are
residents, but for migrants - flycatchers for example - you should visit
between about October and March.

Other attractions

Situated as it is within the largest area of primary lowland rainforest
remaining in Sabah, the Danum Valley supports a rich array of mammals,
at least some of which are harder to find elsewhere. Among those to look
out for are treeshrews, bats, squirrels (including Red Giant Flying Squirrel
and Thomas's Flying Squirrel, the latter being a Bornean endemic), civets
(Malay and Common Palm Civet for example), Clouded Leopard, Leopard
Cat, Flat-headed Cat, Asian Elephant, Bearded Pig and deer. Primates are
well represented, with Western Tarsier, Maroon Langur (Red Leaf
Monkey), Bornean Gibbon and Orang-utan all being seen regularly. The
lucky few may catch a glimpse of the rare endemic Bay Cat, or the
endangered Sumatran Rhinoceros.

40 Tawau Hills Park   Sabah

Situated in the south-eastern corner of Sabah, some 25 km from the town of Tawau, the Tawau Hills Park was established in 1979 to protect the water catchment for nearby towns and villages. The park covers an area of about 28 000 ha, and the rugged volcanic terrain within its borders contrasts markedly with the mainly flat countryside to the south and west of the reserve.

Although agricultural estates - namely oil palm, rubber and cocoa plantations - dominate much of the surrounding area, there are quite extensive stands of hill dipterocarp forest in the park as well as a few patches of lowland forest (unfortunately, almost all of the forest below 500 m was logged before the reserve was established). Steep-sided ridges run through the park, and there are a number of lofty peaks; G. Magdalena, close to the reserve's northern boundary, is the highest at 1310 m (4300 feet).

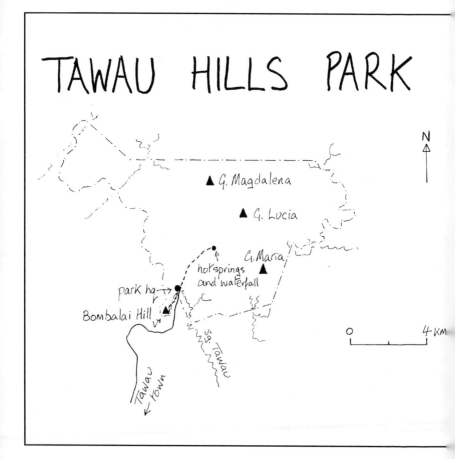

Good birdwatching areas

Tawau Hills is not as well developed as some of the other parks in Sabah and, as yet, there are only a few trails in the reserve, the main ones being a three-hour walk to some hot springs and a waterfall to the north of the park headquarters, and a 30-minute walk to Bombalai Hill (530 m [1740 feet]), which lies just south of the park hq. Birding along the trails can be quite rewarding, especially early in the day; also, there are some old logging tracks north of the park hq that warrant exploration (take care not to get lost). The nearby agricultural estates, while not especially inviting, hold at least some birds that you are unlikely to find within the reserve and may even produce a few surprises.

Birds

Among the more interesting species recorded in the Tawau Hills area are Rufous-bellied Eagle, White-fronted Falconet*, Blue-breasted Quail, Ferruginous (Wood) Partridge (G. Magdalena), Crimson-headed Partridge*, Watercock, Pintail Snipe m, Swinhoe's Snipe m, Mountain Imperial Pigeon, Common Koel (mostly win), Collared Owlet, Diard's Trogon (has been found in plantations), Malaysian Honeyguide (like the trogon, has been recorded in plantations), Speckled Piculet (G. Magdalena), Scaly-breasted Bulbul, Finsch's Bulbul (said to be quite common in cocoa plantations), Black-hooded Oriole, Bornean Wren-Babbler* (may still occur, though in the last twenty years its habitat has been greatly reduced), Maroon-breasted Flycatcher (may still occur), Chestnut-cheeked (Violet-backed) Starling m, Scarlet Sunbird, Thick-billed Spiderhunter, Everett's White-eye and Pygmy White-eye* (G. Magdalena).

Access and accommodation

Since Tawau town is too far from Kota Kinabalu for you to get there by road comfortably in a day, it is best to go via either Sandakan or Lahad Datu. (You may be able to fly from Kota Kinabalu to Tawau - the town has an airport - check with Malaysia Airlines.) The eight-hour bus trip from Sandakan costs about $M25 (there's at least one bus a day), while the three-hour journey from Lahad Datu costs around $M10 (you'll find plenty of minibuses going between Tawau and Lahad Datu). Once you reach Tawau you'll either have to hitch the last 25 km to the park hq, or take a taxi.

There is no accommodation at the reserve but you may be permitted to camp; contact the park ranger on 01-810676 (or the Sabah Parks office in Sandakan on 089-273453) and inquire beforehand. Although Tawau town has plenty of hotels, budget accommodation is hard to find - expect to pay $M40-50 a double.

When to visit

With its waterfalls, hot springs and natural swimming pools, Tawau Hills Park is a magnet for local residents - if possible, don't go at weekends or during holiday periods. As is generally the case throughout Sabah, it can be very wet from about October to January; usually, the driest months are March, April and May.

Other attractions

Although degraded as a result of logging, the forests at Tawau Hills are still quite rich in dipterocarps and other trees. Here and there, towering buttressed trunks hung with thick woody lianas provide a glimpse of what Sabah's lowland forests looked like at one time. On the higher ground the vegetation is less disturbed, and orchids and epiphytes are abundant, while in a few places, above about 1000 m, there are patches of dense, damp moss forest.

Mammals are not all that plentiful and are shy, but you could encounter small groups of Long-tailed Macaques and Maroon Langurs (Red Leaf Monkeys); Orang-utans formerly occurred in the area, but they have been hunted to local extinction. Other, more rarely seen mammals include civets, Clouded Leopard and Leopard Cat, while squirrels include Giant and Prevost's (the latter is reasonably common).

41 Pulau Sipadan   Sabah

Pulau Sipadan lies in the Celebes Sea, about 80 km east of Tawau. With an area of little more than 4 ha, Sipadan is one of the smallest islands off Sabah's east coast, yet despite its size it offers some of the best scuba diving in Borneo - divers from all over the world go there for the spectacular variety of marine life. Although it's a bird sanctuary the island is, of course, too small to support many species; nevertheless, the combination of superb coral, turtles, and the chance of a few good birds makes this a destination well worth visiting.

Good birdwatching areas

Sipadan is easy enough to explore; you can walk right around the island in well under an hour. As is usually the case with such sites, getting to the island can be half the fun - as you leave the mainland, watch for shorebirds in the vicinity of Semporna (see Access and accommodation) and keep your eyes peeled for seabirds once you get a short distance offshore.

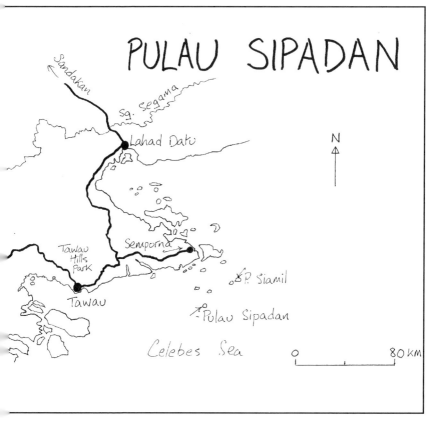

Birds

Species to look for around Semporna, on the way to and from Sipadan, and on the island itself include Brown Booby (mainly Dec-May), Great Frigatebird m, Lesser Frigatebird m, Great-billed Heron, Pacific Reef-Egret, Lesser Adjutant (has been reported breeding near Semporna), Bridled Tern, Little Tern, Great Crested Tern m, Lesser Crested Tern m, Grey Imperial Pigeon (may occur on Sipadan - certainly worth looking out for), Pied Imperial Pigeon (this and the next species were common on Sipadan at one time), Metallic Wood-Pigeon, Javanese (Island) Turtle-Dove (worth watching for - has been recorded on P. Siamil off Semporna) and Nicobar Pigeon.

Access and accommodation

To get to P. Sipadan from Tawau, make your way by minibus or taxi to Semporna (the journey takes around two hours and costs between $M5 and $M20), then you'll have to charter a boat to take you the 30 km or so to the island (expect to pay about $M100 per person for the return boat trip; it could cost more, however, if there are less than three or four people in your group).

As an alternative to making your own arrangements to visit Sipadan, you could go there on an organised tour; for example, Borneo Divers & Sea Sports, 4th floor Wisma Sabah, Jalan Lima Belas, Kota Kinabalu ('phone 088-425080) will take you - for a price! - and will provide diving and other equipment. Borneo Divers also provide meals and accommodation at their own resthouse on the island; if you don't go with a tour group, remember to take along all your food as well as camping equipment.

When to visit

The best time for snorkelling and scuba diving is March through to July; in the north-east monsoon season, between about October and February, you may not be able to reach Sipadan because of rough seas. If you can, avoid weekends when the island is often crowded with day trippers.

Other attractions

Sipadan sits on a limestone pinnacle that rises almost vertically from the ocean floor some 600 m below. All round the island there are underwater caverns, cliffs and overhangs, while close to its shores you can snorkel over coral in shallow water swarming with colourful fish. As well, from about August to October fair numbers of Green Turtles visit Sipadan to dig their nest holes in the island's sandy beaches.

42 Crocker Range National Park

Sabah

Although it is one of the largest reserves in Malaysia, the Crocker Range National Park (140 000 ha) merits only a relatively brief mention because it has no visitor facilities as yet, and because access to much of the area is difficult. Furthermore, most (if not all) of the park's special birds can be found more easily at other sites in East Malaysia - at nearby Kinabalu National Park for instance. Nevertheless, since the reserve isn't all that far from Kota Kinabalu you may decide to pay it a visit, if only to see something of Sabah's colourful rural life (the scenic Tambunan Valley for example, with its terraced rice fields and groves of bamboo, lies along the eastern edge of the park).

Crocker Range National Park protects the forest-clad ridges that extend along Sabah's west coast, from the Kota Kinabalu-Ranau road southwards almost to the Sarawak border. Much of the park lies below 1500 m (4900 feet); G. Alab (1964 m - 6450 feet), the highest point in the range, is just outside the reserve's north-western boundary. Although the lowlands around the park are almost entirely given over to agriculture, the slopes within its boundaries support extensive stands of hill dipterocarp forest, while on the highest ridges drifting mists create ideal conditions for dense moss forest rich in rhododendrons, orchids and pitcher plants.

Good birdwatching areas

As mentioned, access to the park is limited. There are, however, two roads running through the reserve, the main one being the Kota Kinabalu to Tambunan highway, which crosses the range via the Sinsuran Pass. The pass lies at 1670 m (about 5500 feet), making it a good place to look for montane birds. For hill forest species try the lower slopes to the west and east of the pass, or go further south and try along the road that runs westwards across the range from Keningau. Lowland species are best looked for in the vicinity of the Sg. Padas, near Tenom at the southern end of the park.

Birds

The Sinsuran Pass is situated at roughly the same altitude as the Kinabalu National Park headquarters, and as might be expected many bird species are common to both areas. Species to look for in the vicinity of the pass include Red-breasted Partridge*, Crimson-headed Partridge*, Mountain Imperial Pigeon, Large Hawk-Cuckoo, Mountain Scops-Owl, Orange-breasted Trogon, Mountain Barbet*, Golden-naped Barbet*, Black-throated Barbet*, Long-tailed Broadbill, Bar-winged Flycatcher-shrike, Grey-chinned Minivet, Black-crested Bulbul, Flavescent Bulbul, Ochraceous Bulbul, Ashy Bulbul, Black-and-Crimson Oriole, Short-tailed Magpie, Mountain Wren-Babbler*, Grey-and-Brown (Sunda) Laughingthrush, White-browed Shrike-Babbler, Yellow-breasted Warbler, Mountain Leaf-Warbler, Mountain Tailorbird, Short-tailed Bush-Warbler*, Snowy-browed Flycatcher, Little Pied Flycatcher, White-throated Fantail, Bornean Mountain Whistler*, Whitehead's Spiderhunter*, Black-sided Flowerpecker and Pygmy White-eye*.

Access and accommodation

If you have your own transport, the best plan is to spend two or three days exploring the area, stopping at promising spots like the Sinsuran Pass. You'll find hotels at Keningau and Tenom (and probably elsewhere) - don't forget to take along a good map, and watch out for potholes and rocks along some sections of the road. If you don't have a car, you can take a minibus or a taxi from Kota Kinabalu to the Sinsuran Pass, birdwatch all day, then return to KK in the evening (it's about 35 km from KK to the pass; minibuses travel the route every morning on their way to Tambunan and Keningau).

When to visit

Since the upper levels of the range are delightfully cool at any time of the year, a day in the mountain air at the Sinsuran Pass will renew your enthusiasm for the rigours of lowland birding.

Other attractions

Apart from Tambunan, which is located in attractive surroundings between the hills of the Crocker Range and the lower slopes of G. Trus Madi, the most pleasant town in the region is Tenom, a busy agricultural centre on the Sg. Padas. Provided it is still running, it's well worth taking the train from Tenom to Beaufort and back; the line goes through the southern part of the Crocker Range via the Sg. Padas gorge, and in places dense jungle forms a canopy over the narrow track.

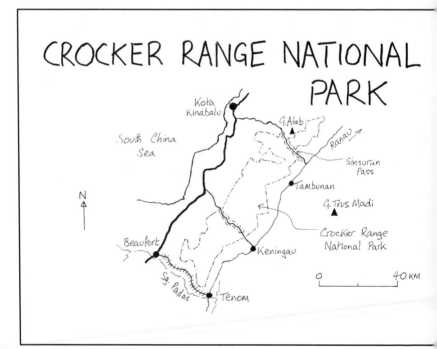

Birds of Malaysia

The order and names used in this list essentially follow King *et al.* (*A Field Guide to the Birds of South-East Asia*, Collins, London, 1975) and Lekagul and Round (*A Guide to the Birds of Thailand*, White Lotus, Bangkok, 1991). Alternative English names in widespread use are given in brackets.

Key to checklist

W	West (Peninsular) Malaysia
E	East Malaysia (Sabah, Sarawak)
w	vagrant West Malaysia
e	vagrant East Malaysia
r	resident
m	migrant
rm	occurs as both a resident and a migrant
x	extinct
*	endemic (to West Malaysia or Borneo)
lo	lowland (mostly below about 500 m [1500 feet])
hi	highland (mostly above about 1000 m [3000 feet])
su	submontane (mostly between about 300 and 1000 m [900 and 3000 feet])
wa	has a wide altitude range

Terms like common, fairly common etc. are not used, but the number of sites that a species is listed for gives a clue to its abundance.

Bird	Scientific name	Region	Status
☐ Little Grebe 2, 23	*Tachybaptus ruficollis*	We	r
☐ Streaked Shearwater	*Calonectris leucomelas*	wE	m
☐ Bulwer's Petrel 24, 27	*Bulweria bulwerii*	WE	m
☐ Swinhoe's Storm-Petrel	*Oceanodroma monorhis*	we	m
☐ Wilson's Storm-Petrel	*Oceanites oceanicus*	w	m
☐ Red-billed Tropicbird	*Phaethon aethereus*	w	m
☐ Eastern White Pelican	*Pelecanus onocrotalus*	W	m
☐ Spot-billed Pelican	*Pelecanus philippensis*	w	m
☐ Masked Booby	*Sula dactylatra*	We	r
☐ Red-footed Booby 21	*Sula sula*	wE	m
☐ Brown Booby 31, 32, 38, 41	*Sula leucogaster*	WE	r
☐ Great Cormorant 32	*Phalacrocorax carbo*	wE	m
☐ Little Black Cormorant	*Phalacrocorax sulcirostris*	e	m
☐ Little Cormorant 20, 23	*Phalacrocorax niger*	We	m
☐ Oriental Darter 30, 33, 36, 37	*Anhinga melanogaster*	x E	r
☐ Christmas Frigatebird 24, 33	*Fregata andrewsi*	WE	m
☐ Great Frigatebird 38, 41	*Fregata minor*	E	m

☐ Lesser Frigatebird 21, 24, 27, 32, 33, 38, 41	*Fregata ariel*	WE	m
☐ Great-billed Heron 21, 24, 27, 36, 37, 39, 41	*Ardea sumatrana*	x E	r
☐ Grey Heron 9, 10, 15, 33	*Ardea cinerea*	WE	r
☐ Purple Heron 2, 10, 11, 23, 33	*Ardea purpurea*	WE	rm
☐ Little Heron 2, 3, 9, 10, 11, 12, 15, 16, 19, 21, 22, 24, 25, 27, 30, 31, 32, 33, 36, 37, 38	*Butorides striatus*	WE	rm
☐ Chinese Pond-Heron 2, 10, 11, 12, 15, 19, 24, 33	*Ardeola bacchus*	WE	m
☐ Javan Pond-Heron 15	*Ardeola speciosa*	w E	m
☐ Cattle Egret 2, 11, 19, 24, 33	*Bubulcus ibis*	WE	m
☐ Pacific Reef-Egret 9, 15, 19, 21, 24, 27, 31, 32, 41	*Egretta sacra*	WE	r
☐ Chinese Egret 9, 12, 15, 27	*Egretta eulophotes*	WE	m
☐ Great Egret 9, 10, 15, 27, 33, 37	*Egretta alba*	WE	rm
☐ Intermediate (Plumed) Egret 10, 15, 19, 27, 33	*Egretta intermedia*	WE	m
☐ Little Egret 9, 10, 12, 15, 27, 33, 37	*Egretta garzetta*	WE	m
☐ Black-crowned Night-Heron 12, 15, 19, 33, 37	*Nycticorax* *nycticorax*	WE	r
☐ Rufous Night-Heron 33	*Nycticorax caledonicus*	E	r
☐ Malayan Night-Heron 8, 19, 22, 30, 33	*Gorsachius melanolophus*	WE	m
☐ Yellow Bittern 2, 10, 11, 15, 24, 33	*Ixobrychus sinensis*	WE	rm
☐ Schrenck's Bittern 2, 3, 15	*Ixobrychus eurhythmus*	WE	m
☐ Cinnamon Bittern 2, 3, 10, 11, 15, 24, 33, 36	*Ixobrychus cinnamomeus*	WE	rm
☐ Black Bittern 8, 15, 20, 23, 33	*Dupetor flavicollis*	WE	m
☐ Eurasian (Great) Bittern	*Botaurus stellaris*	w	m
☐ Milky Stork 9, 15	*Ibis (Mycteria) cinerea*	W	r
☐ Painted Stork	*Ibis (Mycteria)* *leucocephalus*	x	m
☐ Woolly-necked Stork	*Ciconia episcopus*	w	m
☐ Storm's Stork 22, 25, 30, 36, 37	*Ciconia stormi*	WE	r
☐ Lesser Adjutant 9, 10, 15, 27, 33, 41	*Leptoptilos javanicus*	WE	r
☐ Black-headed Ibis 33	*Threskiornis* *melanocephalus*	xe	m

Common Name	Scientific Name			
White-shouldered (Black) Ibis	*Pseudibis davisoni*	e	m	
Glossy Ibis	*Plegadis falcinellus*	e	m	
White Spoonbill	*Platalea leucorodia*	e	m	
33				
Lesser (Treeduck) Whistling-Duck	*Dendrocygna javanica*	WE	r	
2, 11, 19, 33				
Wandering Whistling-Duck	*Dendrocygna arcuata*	e	m	
Northern (Common) Pintail	*Anas acuta*	we	m	
Common Teal	*Anas crecca*	w	m	
Mallard	*Anas platyrhynchos*	e	m	
33				
Eurasian Wigeon	*Anas penelope*	we	m	
33				
Garganey	*Anas querquedula*	WE	m	
2, 11, 12, 33				
Northern Shoveler	*Anas clypeata*	we	m	
12, 33				
Tufted Duck	*Aythya fuligula*	we	m	
33				
Cotton Pygmy-Goose	*Nettapus coromandelianus*	WE	r	
2, 23				
White-winged Duck	*Cairina scutulata*	x		
Osprey	*Pandion haliaetus*	WE	m	lo
7, 15, 20, 22, 23, 25, 27, 31				
Jerdon's Baza	*Aviceda jerdoni*	wE	rm	lo
10, 28, 29, 30, 37				
Black Baza	*Aviceda leuphotes*	WE	m	lo
1, 3, 4, 7, 8, 10, 12, 18, 19, 22, 26				
Eurasian (Crested) Honey-Buzzard	*Pernis ptilorhyncus*	WE	rm	wa
2, 3, 4, 5, 7, 8, 10, 11, 13, 14, 17, 18, 22, 25, 29, 30, 35, 36, 37, 39				
Bat Hawk	*Machaerhamphus alcinus*	WE	r	lo
19, 22, 25, 28, 30, 36, 37, 39				
Black-shouldered Kite	*Elanus caeruleus*	WE	r	lo
2, 10, 11, 15, 16, 19, 23, 33				
Black Kite	*Milvus migrans*	We	m	lo
10, 11, 12				
Brahminy Kite	*Haliastur indus*	WE	r	lo
1, 2, 3, 7, 8, 9, 10, 11, 12, 15, 16, 19, 21, 24, 27, 28, 30, 31, 32, 33, 36, 37, 38				
White-bellied Sea-Eagle	*Haliaeetus leucogaster*	WE	r	lo
2, 7, 9, 10, 12, 15, 16, 19, 20, 21, 24, 27, 31, 32, 33, 36, 37, 38				
Lesser Fish-Eagle	*Icthyophaga nana*	WE	r	lo
22, 23, 25, 30, 37				
Grey-headed Fish-Eagle	*Icthyophaga ichthyaetus*	WE	r	lo
19, 20, 21, 22, 23, 27, 31, 37				
White-rumped Vulture	*Gyps bengalensis*	we	m	lo
Long-billed Vulture	*Gyps indicus*	w	m	lo
Red-headed Vulture	*Sarcogyps calvus*	w	r	lo
Short-toed Eagle	*Circaetus gallicus*	w	m	lo

☐ Crested Serpent-Eagle	*Spilornis cheela*	WE	r	wa

3, 4, 5, 6, 7, 8, 9, 10, 12, 13, 14, 15, 16, 17, 18, 19, 20, 22,
23, 24, 25, 26, 27, 28, 29, 30, 34, 35, 36, 37, 39

☐ Kinabalu (Mountain)	*Spilornis*			
Serpent-Eagle*	*kinabaluensis*	E	r	hi

30, 34, 35

☐ Western Marsh-Harrier	*Circus aeruginosus*	w	m	lo
☐ Eastern Marsh-Harrier	*Circus spilonotus*	WE	m	lo

10, 11, 12, 15, 19, 33

☐ Hen (Northern) Harrier	*Circus cyaneus*	wE	m	lo

33

☐ Pied Harrier	*Circus melanoleucos*	WE	m	lo

11, 33

☐ Japanese Sparrowhawk	*Accipiter gularis*	WE	m	wa

1, 2, 3, 5, 7, 8, 10, 12, 17, 18, 22, 24, 25, 27, 29, 33, 35, 39

☐ Besra	*Accipiter virgatus*	wE	rm	su

30, 34, 35

☐ Northern Sparrowhawk	*Accipiter nisus*	e	m	wa
☐ Crested Goshawk	*Accipiter trivirgatus*	WE	r	lo

1, 3, 4, 7, 8, 19, 20, 22, 23, 25, 26, 27, 28, 29, 30, 35, 36, 37, 39

☐ Chinese Goshawk	*Accipiter soloensis*	WE	m	wa

6, 7, 17, 19, 22, 35

☐ Shikra	*Accipiter badius*	W	m	lo
☐ Grey-faced Buzzard	*Butastur indicus*	WE	m	lo

2, 3, 7, 16, 19, 35, 36

☐ Common Buzzard	*Buteo buteo*	w	m	lo
☐ Black Eagle	*Ictinaetus malayensis*	WE	r	wa

6, 14, 17, 18, 22, 30, 34

☐ Greater Spotted Eagle	*Aquila clanga*	W	m	lo

11

☐ Steppe Eagle	*Aquila nipalensis*	w	m	lo

11

☐ Imperial Eagle	*Aquila heliaca*	w	m	lo

11

☐ Booted Eagle	*Hieraaetus pennatus*	w	m	lo

11

☐ Rufous-bellied Eagle	*Hieraaetus kienerii*	WE	rm	wa

5, 6, 13, 14, 17, 18, 22, 25, 34, 35, 36, 37, 39, 40

☐ Changeable Hawk-Eagle	*Spizaetus cirrhatus*	WE	r	wa

2, 3, 5, 7, 8, 10, 13, 16, 17, 18, 19, 20, 22, 23,
25, 26, 29, 30, 34, 35, 36, 39

☐ Blyth's Hawk-Eagle	*Spizaetus alboniger*	WE	r	su

5, 6, 13, 14, 17, 18, 22, 24, 30, 34, 35

☐ Wallace's Hawk-Eagle	*Spizaetus nanus*	WE	r	lo

22, 25, 26, 28, 30, 36, 37, 39

☐ Black-thighed Falconet	*Microhierax fringillarius*	WE	r	wa

1, 5, 7, 8, 14, 17, 18, 22, 23, 25, 28, 29, 30

☐ White-fronted Falconet*	*Microhierax latifrons*	E	r	lo

35, 36, 39, 40

☐ Eurasian Kestrel	*Falco tinnunculus*	w e	m	lo

19, 33

☐ Spotted Kestrel	*Falco moluccensis*	e	m	lo
☐ Northern Hobby	*Falco subbuteo*	w	m	lo
☐ Oriental Hobby	*Falco severus*	we	m	lo

35

☐ Peregrine Falcon	*Falco peregrinus*	WE	rm	wa
4, 6, 7, 10, 19, 20, 24, 27, 28, 30, 33, 34, 39				
☐ Tabon Scrubfowl				
(Philippine Scrubfowl; Megapode)	*Megapodius cumingii*	E	r	lo
31, 32, 38				
☐ Long-billed Partridge	*Rhizothera longirostris*	WE	r	wa
6, 13, 20, 22, 25, 26, 39				
☐ Black Wood-Partridge	*Melanoperdix nigra*	WE	r	lo
22, 26, 30				
☐ Blue-breasted Quail	*Coturnix chinensis*	WE	r	lo
2, 16, 30, 33, 35, 40				
☐ Bar-backed (Hill)	*Arborophila*			
Partridge	*brunneopectus*	W	r	hi
6, 14, 17, 18				
☐ Red-breasted Partridge*	*Arborophila hyperythra*	E	r	hi
30, 34, 42				
☐ Chestnut-necklaced				
(Scaly-breasted) Partridge	*Arborophila charltonii*	WE	r	lo
36, 37, 39				
☐ Ferruginous (Wood)				
Partridge	*Caloperdix oculea*	WE	r	wa
5, 13, 22, 40				
☐ Crimson-headed	*Haematortyx*			
Partridge*	*sanguiniceps*	E	r	hi
30, 34, 35, 40, 42				
☐ Crested Wood-Partridge	*Rollulus rouloul*	WE	r	wa
5, 18, 20, 22, 23, 25, 26, 28, 29, 30, 35, 36, 39				
☐ Crestless Fireback	*Lophura erythrophthalma*	WE	r	lo
22, 25, 26, 28, 29, 30				
☐ Crested Fireback	*Lophura ignita*	WE	r	lo
22, 23, 25, 28, 29, 30, 37, 39				
☐ Bulwer's Pheasant*	*Lophura bulwerii*	E	r	su
30, 39				
☐ Red Junglefowl	*Gallus gallus*	W	r	wa
3, 4, 5, 7, 8, 10, 18, 20, 22, 23, 25				
☐ Mountain	*Polyplectron*			
Peacock-Pheasant*	*inopinatum*	W	r	hi
6, 14, 17, 22				
☐ Malaysian Peacock-Pheasant	*Polyplectron malacense*	WE	r	lo
22, 26				
☐ Crested Argus	*Rheinardia ocellata*	W	r	su
22				
☐ Great Argus	*Argusianus argus*	WE	r	wa
18, 20, 22, 25, 26, 29, 30, 35, 36, 37, 39				
☐ Green Peafowl	*Pavo muticus*	x		
☐ Barred Buttonquail	*Turnix suscitator*	W	r	lo
2, 3, 7, 15, 16, 19, 23				
☐ Sarus Crane	*Grus antigone*	x		
☐ Water Rail	*Rallus aquaticus*	e	m	
☐ Slaty-breasted Rail	*Rallus striatus*	WE	r	
2, 3, 7, 10, 33				
☐ Red-legged Crake	*Rallina fasciata*	WE	rm	
2, 15, 22, 23, 35				
☐ Slaty-legged Crake	*Rallina eurizonoides*	W	m	
19, 23				

☐ Baillon's Crake 2, 11	*Porzana pusilla*	We	m
☐ Ruddy-breasted Crake 2, 10, 15, 33	*Porzana fusca*	We	rm
☐ Band-bellied Crake 22	*Porzana paykullii*	WE	m
☐ White-browed Crake 2, 23, 33	*Porzana cinerea*	WE	r
☐ White-breasted Waterhen 1, 2, 3, 7, 10, 11, 12, 15, 16, 17, 18, 19, 21, 22, 23, 24, 30, 33, 36, 37, 39	*Amaurornis phoenicurus*	WE	r
☐ Watercock 2, 10, 11, 24, 33, 40	*Gallicrex cinerea*	WE	rm
☐ Common Moorhen 2, 33	*Gallinula chloropus*	WE	r
☐ Purple Swamphen 2, 33	*Porphyrio porphyrio*	WE	r
☐ Eurasian Coot 33	*Fulica atra*	e	m
☐ Masked Finfoot 8, 15, 22, 23, 25	*Heliopais personata*	W	m
☐ Pheasant-tailed Jacana 23, 25	*Hydrophasianus chirurgus*	W	m
☐ Bronze-winged Jacana	*Metopidius indicus*	w	r
☐ Greater Paintedsnipe 2, 10, 11, 33	*Rostratula benghalensis*	WE	rm
☐ Grey-headed Lapwing	*Vanellus cinereus*	we	m
☐ Red-wattled Lapwing 11, 19	*Vanellus indicus*	W	r
☐ Grey Plover 9, 10, 12, 15	*Pluvialis squatarola*	WE	m
☐ Asian (Lesser) Golden Plover 2, 9, 10, 11, 12, 15, 19, 33	*Pluvialis fulva*	WE	m
☐ Little Ringed Plover 2, 3, 10, 11, 15, 19, 24, 33	*Charadrius dubius*	WE	m
☐ Kentish Plover 9, 10, 11, 12, 19, 33	*Charadrius alexandrinus*	WE	m
☐ Malaysian Plover 9, 12, 19, 24, 27, 33	*Charadrius peronii*	WE	r
☐ Long-billed Plover	*Charadrius placidus*	w	m
☐ Mongolian Plover 9, 10, 12, 15, 19, 27, 31, 32, 33	*Charadrius mongolus*	WE	m
☐ Greater Sand-Plover 9, 10, 12, 15, 19, 27, 31, 32, 33	*Charadrius leschenaulti*	WE	m
☐ Oriental Plover 2, 11, 33	*Charadrius veredus*	WE	m
☐ Eurasian Curlew 9, 10, 12, 15, 27	*Numenius arquata*	WE	m
☐ Whimbrel 9, 10, 12, 15, 27, 31, 32, 33	*Numenius phaeopus*	WE	m
☐ Little Curlew 33	*Numenius minutus*	E	m
☐ Eastern Curlew 9, 10, 27	*N. madagascariensis*	WE	m
☐ Black-tailed Godwit 9, 10, 11, 12, 15, 27	*Limosa limosa*	WE	m

☐ Bar-tailed Godwit	*Limosa lapponica*	WE	m
9, 10, 15, 27, 33			
☐ Spotted Redshank	*Tringa erythropus*	WE	m
27			
☐ Common Redshank	*Tringa totanus*	WE	m
9, 10, 12, 15, 19, 27, 31, 32, 33			
☐ Marsh Sandpiper	*Tringa stagnatilis*	WE	m
9, 10, 11, 12, 15, 27, 33			
☐ Common Greenshank	*Tringa nebularia*	WE	m
2, 9, 10, 11, 12, 15, 24, 27, 33			
☐ Nordmann's Greenshank	*Tringa guttifer*	We	m
9, 10, 12, 27			
☐ Green Sandpiper	*Tringa ochropus*	WE	m
11, 33			
☐ Wood Sandpiper	*Tringa glareola*	WE	m
2, 10, 11, 15, 19, 33, 37			
☐ Terek Sandpiper	*Xenus cinereus*	WE	m
9, 10, 12, 15, 27, 31			
☐ Common Sandpiper	*Actitus hypoleucos*	WE	m
2, 3, 10, 11, 12, 15, 16, 19, 21, 22, 24, 25, 27, 30, 31, 32, 33, 36, 37, 38			
☐ Grey-tailed Tattler	*Heteroscelus brevipes*	WE	m
12, 15, 24, 27, 31, 32, 38			
☐ Ruddy Turnstone	*Arenaria interpres*	WE	m
10, 12, 15, 27, 31, 32, 33, 38			
☐ Asian Dowitcher	*Limnodromus semipalmatus*	WE	m
9, 10, 12, 15, 27			
☐ Pintail Snipe	*Gallinago stenura*	WE	m
2, 3, 10, 11, 16, 19, 33, 36, 40			
☐ Swinhoe's Snipe	*Gallinago megala*	WE	m
11, 25, 33, 40			
☐ Common Snipe	*Gallinago gallinago*	WE	m
2, 10, 11, 33			
☐ Eurasian Woodcock	*Scolopax rusticola*	w	m
☐ Red Knot	*Calidris canutus*	WE	m
9, 10, 15, 27, 33			
☐ Great Knot	*Calidris tenuirostris*	WE	m
9, 15, 27, 33			
☐ Sanderling	*Calidris alba*	WE	m
10, 33			
☐ Little Stint	*Calidris minuta*	w	m
10, 15			
☐ Rufous-necked Stint	*Calidris ruficollis*	WE	m
9, 10, 11, 12, 15, 27, 31, 33			
☐ Temminck's Stint	*Calidris temminckii*	we	m
11, 33			
☐ Long-toed Stint	*Calidris subminuta*	WE	m
2, 10, 11, 15, 33			
☐ Sharp-tailed Sandpiper	*Calidris acuminata*	wE	m
☐ Dunlin	*Calidris alpina*	w	m
☐ Curlew Sandpiper	*Calidris ferruginea*	WE	m
9, 10, 11, 12, 15, 27, 33			
☐ Spoon-billed Sandpiper	*Eurynorhynchus pygmaeus*	w	m
10			

☐ Broad-billed Sandpiper 9, 12, 15, 27	*Limicola falcinellus*	WE	m
☐ Ruff 11, 12, 15, 27	*Philomachus pugnax*	we	m
☐ Black-winged Stilt 33	*Himantopus himantopus*	wE	m
☐ Red-necked Phalarope 9, 27, 31, 32, 38	*Phalaropus lobatus*	wE	m
☐ Red (Grey) Phalarope 27, 31, 38	*Phalaropus fulicarius*	e	m
☐ Crab Plover 9	*Dromas ardeola*	w	m
☐ Great (Beach) Thick-knee 27, 31, 32	*Esacus magnirostris*	E	r
☐ Oriental Pratincole 2, 11, 33	*Glareola maldivarum*	WE	m
☐ Australian Pratincole	*Stiltia isabella*	e	m
☐ Pomarine Jaeger	*Stercorarius pomarinus*	we	m
☐ Parasitic Jaeger	*Stercorarius parasiticus*	we	m
☐ Common Black-headed Gull 9, 38	*Larus ridibundus*	we	m
☐ Brown-headed Gull 9, 12, 15, 16	*Larus brunnicephalus*	W	m
☐ Whiskered Tern 11, 12, 15, 27, 33, 38	*Chlidonias hybrida*	WE	m
☐ White-winged Tern 2, 9, 10, 11, 12, 15, 27, 33	*Chlidonias leucopterus*	WE	m
☐ Gull-billed Tern 9, 10, 12, 15, 27	*Gelochelidon nilotica*	WE	m
☐ Caspian Tern 9	*Hydroprogne caspia*	W	m
☐ Common Tern 9, 10, 12, 15, 19	*Sterna hirundo*	WE	m
☐ Roseate Tern 21, 24, 27, 31, 32, 33	*Sterna dougallii*	WE	r
☐ Black-naped Tern 10, 15, 21, 24, 27, 31, 32, 33	*Sterna sumatrana*	WE	r
☐ Bridled Tern 19, 21, 24, 27, 31, 32, 38, 41	*Sterna anaethetus*	WE	r
☐ Sooty Tern 27	*Sterna fuscata*	we	m
☐ Little Tern 2, 9, 10, 12, 15, 27, 31, 32, 33, 38, 41	*Sterna albifrons*	WE	rm
☐ Saunders' Tern	*Sterna saundersi*	w	m
☐ Great Crested Tern 9, 10, 15, 21, 24, 27, 31, 32, 33, 38, 41	*Sterna bergii*	WE	m
☐ Lesser Crested Tern 9, 12, 15, 27, 31, 32, 33, 38, 41	*Sterna bengalensis*	WE	m
☐ Chinese Crested Tern	*Sterna zimmermanni*	e	m
☐ Brown (Common) Noddy	*Anous stolidus*	WE	r
☐ White-capped Noddy	*Anous minutus*	E	m
☐ Yellow-vented Pigeon 13, 14, 17	*Treron seimundi*	W	r	hi
☐ Wedge-tailed Pigeon 6, 13, 14, 17, 18, 22	*Treron sphenura*	W	r	hi

☐ Thick-billed Pigeon	*Treron curvirostra*	WE	r	wa
1, 4, 5, 7, 8, 13, 14, 16, 18, 19, 22, 25, 29, 30, 35, 36, 39				
☐ Cinnamon-headed Pigeon	*Treron fulvicollis*	WE	r	lo
10, 15, 24, 27, 31, 33, 36				
☐ Little Green Pigeon	*Treron olax*	WE	r	lo
8, 15, 16, 19, 22, 23, 25, 26, 29, 30, 36, 37, 39				
☐ Pink-necked Pigeon	*Treron vernans*	WE	r	wa
1, 2, 3, 4, 7, 8, 10, 15, 16, 18, 19, 21, 22, 23,				
24, 26, 27, 28, 29, 30, 31, 33, 35, 36, 39				
☐ Orange-breasted Pigeon	*Treron bicincta*	W	r	lo
☐ Large Green Pigeon	*Treron capellei*	WE	r	wa
19, 20, 22, 23, 26, 29, 30, 36, 39				
☐ Black-naped Fruit-Dove	*Ptilinopus melanospila*	E	r	lo
☐ Jambu Fruit-Dove	*Ptilinopus jambu*	WE	r	wa
5, 8, 13, 18, 20, 22, 23, 24, 25, 26, 29, 30, 35, 39				
☐ Green Imperial Pigeon	*Ducula aenea*	WE	r	lo
18, 19, 21, 22, 24, 25, 27, 31, 35, 36, 37, 39				
☐ Grey Imperial Pigeon	*Ducula pickeringi*	E	r	lo
31, 32, 41				
☐ Pied Imperial Pigeon	*Ducula bicolor*	WE	r	lo
16, 19, 21, 24, 27, 31, 32, 41				
☐ Mountain Imperial Pigeon	*Ducula badia*	WE	r	hi
6, 13, 14, 17, 18, 22, 30, 34, 35, 40, 42				
☐ Metallic Wood-Pigeon	*Columba vitiensis*	E	r	lo
32, 41				
☐ Grey Wood-Pigeon	*Columba argentina*	E	r	lo
☐ Rock Dove (Pigeon)	*Columba livia*	WE	r	lo
☐ Barred Cuckoo-Dove	*Macropygia unchall*	W	r	hi
6, 14, 17, 18				
☐ Little Cuckoo-Dove	*Macropygia ruficeps*	WE	r	hi
6, 13, 14, 17, 18, 22, 30, 34, 35				
☐ Ruddy (Red)	*Macropygia*			
Cuckoo-Dove	*emiliana (phasianella)*	E	r	su
30, 34, 35				
☐ Javanese (Island)	*Streptopelia*			
Turtle-Dove	*bitorquata*	E	r	lo
41				
☐ Spotted Dove	*Streptopelia chinensis*	WE	r	wa
1, 2, 3, 7, 10, 11, 12, 15, 16, 17, 19, 24, 30, 33, 36, 38				
☐ Peaceful Dove	*Geopelia striata*	WE	r	lo
1, 2, 3, 4, 7, 10, 11, 15, 16, 19				
☐ Green-winged Pigeon				
(Emerald Dove)	*Chalcophaps indica*	WE	r	wa
3, 4, 5, 7, 8, 13, 16, 19, 20, 21, 22, 23, 24, 25,				
26, 27, 28, 29, 30, 31, 32, 33, 34, 35, 36, 38, 39				
☐ Nicobar Pigeon	*Caloenas nicobarica*	WE	r	lo
19, 21, 24, 32, 41				
☐ Blue-naped Parrot	*Tanygnathus lucionensis*	E	r	lo
☐ Red-breasted Parakeet	*Psittacula alexandri*	w	r	lo
☐ Long-tailed Parakeet	*Psittacula longicauda*	WE	r	lo
2, 7, 8, 10, 11, 15, 23, 25, 26, 36				
☐ Blue-rumped Parrot	*Psittinus cyanurus*	WE	r	lo
7, 22, 23, 25, 26, 36				
☐ Blue-crowned				
Hanging Parrot	*Loriculus galgulus*	WE	r	wa
3, 4, 5, 6, 7, 8, 13, 18, 20, 22, 23, 25, 26, 28, 29, 30, 35, 36, 37, 39				

☐ Chestnut-winged Cuckoo	*Clamator coromandus*	WE	m	lo
1, 2, 8, 10, 12, 19, 23, 30, 35				
☐ Large Hawk-Cuckoo	*Cuculus sparverioides*	WE	rm	hi
6, 14, 17, 18, 22, 30, 34, 42				
☐ Moustached Hawk-Cuckoo	*Cuculus vagans*	WE	r	lo
4, 22, 30, 36, 39				
☐ Hodgson's Hawk-Cuckoo	*Cuculus fugax*	WE	rm	lo
18, 19, 21, 22, 24, 25, 29, 30, 31, 35, 36, 39				
☐ Indian Cuckoo	*Cuculus micropterus*	WE	rm	lo
4, 5, 7, 8, 19, 20, 22, 23, 25, 26, 29, 30, 35, 36, 39				
☐ Oriental Cuckoo	*Cuculus saturatus*	WE	rm	hi
6, 13, 14, 17, 18, 22, 30, 34				
☐ Banded Bay Cuckoo	*Cacomantis sonneratii*	WE	r	lo
4, 7, 8, 18, 23, 25, 28, 30, 35, 36, 39				
☐ Plaintive Cuckoo	*Cacomantis merulinus*	WE	r	lo
2, 3, 7, 10, 16, 19, 23, 25, 27, 29, 30, 33, 35, 36				
☐ Brush (Rusty-breasted) Cuckoo	*Cacomantis sepulcralis*	WE	r	lo
. 4, 5, 7, 8, 10, 20, 22, 23, 24, 25, 26, 28, 30, 31, 35, 39				
☐ Asian Emerald Cuckoo	*Chrysococcyx maculatus*	w	rm	wa
☐ Violet Cuckoo	*C. xanthorhynchus*	WE	rm	lo
5, 7, 8, 22, 23, 25, 26, 27, 28, 29, 30, 35, 36, 39				
☐ Horsfield's Bronze-Cuckoo	*Chrysococcyx basalis*	e	m	lo
☐ Malayan (Little)				
Bronze-Cuckoo	*Chrysococcyx minutillus*	WE	r	wa
7, 10, 16, 35				
☐ Gould's (Rufous)				
Bronze-Cuckoo	*Chrysococcyx russatus*	E	r	lo
☐ Drongo Cuckoo	*Surniculus lugubris*	WE	rm	lo
4, 5, 7, 8, 16, 18, 19, 20, 22, 23, 25, 26, 27, 28, 29, 30, 35, 36, 39				
☐ Common Koel	*Eudynamys scolopacea*	WE	rm	lo
1, 2, 3, 7, 10, 15, 18, 19, 21, 32, 38, 40				
☐ Black-bellied Malkoha	*Phaenicophaeus diardi*	WE	r	lo
8, 22, 25, 28, 29, 30, 35, 36, 39				
☐ Chestnut-bellied Malkoha	*Phaenicophaeus*			
	sumatranus	WE	r	lo
4, 5, 8, 10, 15, 20, 22, 23, 25, 26, 27, 28, 29, 30, 35, 39				
☐ Green-billed Malkoha	*Phaenicophaeus tristis*	W	r	hi
6, 7, 13, 14, 17, 18				
☐ Raffles' Malkoha	*Phaenicophaeus*			
	chlorophaeus	WE	r	lo
4, 5, 8, 16, 20, 22, 23, 25, 26, 29, 30, 35, 36, 37, 39				
☐ Red-billed Malkoha	*Phaenicophaeus*			
	javanicus	WE	r	lo
5, 8, 13, 18, 20, 22, 23, 25, 26, 28, 29, 30, 35, 36, 39				
☐ Chestnut-breasted	*Phaenicophaeus*			
Malkoha	*curvirostris*	WE	r	lo
4, 5, 8, 10, 16, 18, 19, 20, 22, 23, 24, 25, 26,				
27, 28, 29, 30, 35, 36, 37, 39				
☐ Sunda Ground-Cuckoo	*Carpococcyx radiceus*	E	r	lo
30				
☐ Short-toed Coucal	*Centropus rectunguis*	WE	r	lo
22, 25, 26, 30, 36, 39				
☐ Greater Coucal	*Centropus sinensis*	WE	r	lo
1, 2, 7, 10, 15, 16, 18, 19, 22, 23, 25, 27, 30, 33, 35, 36, 37, 39				
☐ Lesser Coucal	*Centropus bengalensis*	WE	r	wa
2, 3, 7, 10, 11, 15, 16, 19, 22, 23, 33, 34, 35, 36				

Common Name	Scientific Name			
☐ Barn Owl	*Tyto alba*	W	r	lo
10, 11, 16, 23				
☐ Bay Owl	*Phodilus badius*	WE	r	wa
7, 15, 19, 22, 25, 26, 27, 30, 36, 39				
☐ White-fronted Scops-Owl	*Otus sagittatus*	W	r	lo
22, 26				
☐ Reddish Scops-Owl	*Otus rufescens*	WE	r	wa
18, 22, 25, 26, 28, 29, 30, 34, 35, 36, 39				
☐ Mountain Scops-Owl	*Otus spilocephalus*	WE	r	hi
6, 13, 14, 17, 18, 22, 30, 34, 42				
☐ Oriental (Common) Scops-Owl	*Otus sunia*	W	m	wa
7, 19, 22, 25				
☐ Collared Scops-Owl	*Otus lempiji*	WE	r	lo
1, 2, 3, 5, 7, 8, 10, 13, 16, 18, 19, 20, 22, 23, 24, 25, 27, 28, 29, 30, 35, 36, 39				
☐ Rajah Scops-Owl	*Otus brookei*	E	r	hi
30				
☐ Mantanani Scops-Owl	*Otus mantananensis*	E	r	lo
☐ Barred Eagle-Owl	*Bubo sumatranus*	WE	r	lo
1, 5, 6, 7, 8, 18, 22, 23, 25, 26, 28, 35, 36, 39				
☐ Dusky Eagle-Owl	*Bubo coromandus*	x		
☐ Brown Fish-Owl	*Ketupa zeylonensis*	W	r	lo
☐ Buffy Fish-Owl	*Ketupa ketupu*	WE	r	lo
8, 10, 15, 22, 27, 30, 37, 39				
☐ Collared Owlet	*Glaucidium brodiei*	WE	r	hi
6, 14, 17, 18, 22, 30, 34, 40				
☐ Brown Hawk-Owl	*Ninox scutulata*	WE	rm	lo
1, 4, 7, 13, 19, 22, 25, 26, 28, 30, 31, 32, 35, 36, 38, 39				
☐ Spotted Wood-Owl	*Strix seloputo*	W	r	lo
16, 26				
☐ Brown Wood-Owl	*Strix leptogrammica*	WE	r	wa
13, 22, 26, 29, 30, 36, 37, 39				
☐ Short-eared Owl	*Asio flammeus*	we	m	wa
19				
☐ Large Frogmouth	*Batrachostomus auritus*	WE	r	lo
22, 26, 28, 29, 30, 39				
☐ Dulit Frogmouth*	*Batrachostomus harterti*	E	r	su
☐ Gould's Frogmouth	*B. stellatus*	WE	r	lo
22, 23, 25, 26, 28, 29				
☐ Pale-headed Frogmouth	*B. poliolophus*	E	r	su
☐ Javan Frogmouth	*Batrachostomus javensis*	WE	r	lo
22, 25, 26, 39				
☐ Sunda Frogmouth	*Batrachostomus cornutus*	E	r	lo
27				
☐ Malaysian Eared Nightjar	*Eurostopodus temminckii*	WE	r	wa
5, 8, 13, 16, 20, 22, 23, 25, 26, 27, 28, 30, 35, 36, 37, 39				
☐ Great Eared Nightjar	*Eurostopodus macrotis*	W	r	wa
☐ Grey Nightjar	*Caprimulgus indicus*	WE	m	wa
13, 14, 18, 19, 24, 38				
☐ Large-tailed Nightjar	*Caprimulgus macrurus*	WE	r	lo
1, 2, 3, 4, 7, 8, 10, 11, 15, 16, 18, 19, 22, 23, 26, 27, 32, 33, 35				
☐ Savanna Nightjar	*Caprimulgus affinis*	E	r	lo
☐ Bonaparte's Nightjar	*Caprimulgus concretus*	E	r	lo
☐ Giant Swiftlet	*Collocalia gigas*	WE	r	wa
6, 13, 17				

☐ Edible-nest Swiftlet	*Collocalia fuciphaga*	WE r	lo
1, 2, 7, 8, 13, 16, 24, 27, 31, 36			
☐ Black-nest Swiftlet	*Collocalia maxima*	WE r	lo
21, 24, 28, 30			
☐ Mossy-nest (Uniform)	*Collocalia*		
Swiftlet	*vanikorensis*	E r	lo
28, 30, 37			
☐ Himalayan Swiftlet	*Collocalia brevirostris*	W m	wa
2, 6, 11, 13, 17, 19			
☐ White-bellied	*Collocalia*		
(Glossy) Swiftlet	*esculenta*	WE r	wa
1, 2, 3, 4, 5, 6, 7, 8, 10, 13, 14, 17, 18, 20,			
22, 23, 25, 27, 28, 29, 30, 33, 34, 35, 36, 37, 39			
☐ White-throated	*Hirundapus*		
Needletail	*caudacutus*	WE m	wa
13, 27, 28, 38			
☐ White-vented	*Hirundapus*		
Needletail	*cochinchinensis*	W m	wa
6, 13, 17, 19, 22, 25			
☐ Brown Needletail	*Hirundapus giganteus*	WE rm	wa
4, 5, 7, 8, 13, 14, 16, 17, 18, 19, 20, 22, 23, 25,			
30, 33, 34, 35, 36, 37, 39			
☐ Silver-rumped Swift	*Rhaphidura leucopygialis*	WE r	wa
4, 5, 6, 8, 14, 16, 20, 22, 23, 25, 26, 27, 28, 30, 35, 36, 39			
☐ Fork-tailed Swift	*Apus pacificus*	WE m	wa
3, 4, 5, 6, 7, 8, 10, 12, 13, 14, 17, 19, 20, 21, 22, 23, 24, 25, 30, 33			
☐ House Swift	*Apus affinis*	WE r	wa
1, 2, 3, 4, 5, 6, 7, 8, 10, 11, 14, 15, 16, 17, 18, 19, 22, 23, 24, 27			
☐ Asian Palm-Swift	*Cypsiurus balasiensis*	WE r	lo
1, 2, 3, 7, 10, 16, 18, 19, 20, 22, 23, 25, 33, 35, 36			
☐ Grey-rumped Treeswift	*Hemiprocne longipennis*	WE r	wa
1, 3, 4, 5, 6, 7, 8, 13, 16, 20, 22, 23, 25, 27,			
28, 29, 30, 35, 36, 37, 39			
☐ Whiskered Treeswift	*Hemiprocne comata*	WE r	lo
4, 5, 8, 20, 22, 23, 25, 28, 29, 30, 35, 36, 39			
☐ Red-naped Trogon	*Harpactes kasumba*	WE r	lo
4, 5, 8, 22, 23, 25, 26, 28, 29, 30, 36, 39			
☐ Diard's Trogon	*Harpactes diardii*	WE r	lo
4, 8, 22, 23, 25, 26, 28, 29, 30, 35, 36, 39, 40			
☐ Whitehead's Trogon*	*Harpactes whiteheadi*	E r	hi
30, 34			
☐ Cinnamon-rumped Trogon	*Harpactes orrhophaeus*	WE r	lo
22, 25, 26, 30, 34, 35, 36, 37, 39			
☐ Scarlet-rumped Trogon	*Harpactes duvaucelii*	WE r	wa
4, 5, 8, 20, 22, 23, 25, 26, 27, 28, 29, 30, 35, 36, 37, 39			
☐ Orange-breasted Trogon	*Harpactes oreskios*	WE r	su
5, 6, 13, 14, 17, 18, 19, 22, 25, 30, 34, 35, 42			
☐ Red-headed Trogon	*Harpactes erythrocephalus*	W r	hi
6, 13, 14, 17, 18			
☐ Common Kingfisher	*Alcedo atthis*	WE rm	lo
2, 3, 8, 9, 10, 12, 15, 16, 18, 19, 20, 21, 22, 24, 25, 33, 37			
☐ Blue-eared Kingfisher	*Alcedo meninting*	WE r	lo
4, 8, 19, 22, 25, 26, 27, 28, 29, 30, 36, 37, 39			
☐ Blue-banded Kingfisher	*Alcedo euryzonia*	WE r	lo
5, 22, 23, 25, 28, 29, 30, 35, 36, 39			

☐ Oriental Dwarf Kingfisher	*Ceyx erithacus (rufidorsus)*	WE	rm	lo
4, 5, 7, 8, 15, 19, 21, 22, 23, 25, 26, 27, 28, 29, 30, 31, 35, 36, 37, 39				
☐ Brown-winged Kingfisher	*Pelargopsis amauroptera*	W	r	lo
19				
☐ Stork-billed Kingfisher	*Pelargopsis capensis*	WE	r	lo
10, 11, 15, 16, 18, 22, 23, 27, 30, 33, 36, 37				
☐ Banded Kingfisher	*Lacedo pulchella*	WE	r	wa
4, 8, 13, 18, 19, 22, 25, 26, 28, 29, 30, 34, 36, 39				
☐ Ruddy Kingfisher	*Halcyon coromanda*	WE	rm	lo
5, 8, 15, 19, 24, 25, 31				
☐ White-throated Kingfisher	*Halcyon smyrnensis*	W	r	lo
1, 2, 3, 4, 7, 8, 9, 10, 11, 12, 15, 16, 18, 19, 22, 23, 25				
☐ Black-capped Kingfisher	*Halcyon pileata*	WE	m	lo
2, 3, 7, 8, 9, 10, 12, 15, 16, 19, 22, 23, 24, 25, 27, 30, 37				
☐ Sacred Kingfisher	*Halcyon sancta*	e	m	lo
☐ Collared Kingfisher	*Halcyon chloris*	WE	rm	lo
7, 9, 10, 12, 15, 16, 19, 21, 24, 27, 31, 32, 33, 36, 38				
☐ Rufous-collared Kingfisher	*Halcyon concreta*	WE	r	lo
4, 22, 23, 25, 26, 28, 29, 30, 35, 36, 39				
☐ Chestnut-headed Bee-eater	*Merops leschenaulti*	W	r	lo
16, 19				
☐ Blue-tailed Bee-eater	*Merops philippinus*	WE	rm	lo
2, 3, 4, 7, 8, 10, 11, 12, 15, 16, 18, 19, 23				
☐ Blue-throated Bee-eater	*Merops viridis*	WE	rm	wa
1, 2, 3, 4, 5, 6, 7, 8, 10, 11, 13, 14, 15, 16, 18, 19, 20, 22, 23, 25, 27, 33, 35, 36, 37				
☐ Red-bearded Bee-eater	*Nyctyornis amictus*	WE	r	wa
5, 6, 7, 13, 18, 22, 23, 25, 28, 29, 30, 35, 36, 39				
☐ Indian Roller	*Coracias benghalensis*	W	r	lo
21, 22				
☐ Dollarbird	*Eurystomus orientalis*	WE	rm	lo
1, 3, 7, 8, 10, 12, 15, 18, 19, 20, 22, 23, 24, 25, 26, 27, 29, 30, 32, 33, 36, 37				
☐ Hoopoe	*Upupa epops*	we	m	lo
33				
☐ White-crowned Hornbill	*Berenicornis comatus*	WE	r	wa
4, 13, 14, 18, 22, 25, 28, 30, 31, 34, 35, 36, 39				
☐ Bushy-crested Hornbill	*Anorrhinus galeritus*	WE	r	wa
5, 6, 13, 18, 20, 22, 23, 25, 28, 29, 30, 35, 36, 37, 39				
☐ Wrinkled Hornbill	*Rhyticeros corrugatus*	WE	r	lo
18, 22, 25, 30, 37, 39				
☐ Wreathed Hornbill	*Rhyticeros undulatus*	WE	r	wa
5, 6, 13, 14, 18, 19, 20, 22, 25, 30, 34, 35, 36, 37, 39				
☐ Black Hornbill	*Anthracoceros malayanus*	WE	r	lo
8, 22, 23, 25, 26, 27, 28, 29, 30, 35, 36, 37, 39				
☐ Oriental Pied Hornbill	*Anthracoceros albirostris (convexus)*	WE	r	lo
4, 8, 11, 19, 20, 22, 23, 25, 27, 30, 31, 32, 36, 37				
☐ Rhinoceros Hornbill	*Buceros rhinoceros*	WE	r	wa
5, 6, 13, 14, 18, 20, 22, 23, 25, 30, 34, 35, 36, 37, 39				
☐ Great Hornbill	*Buceros bicornis*	W	r	wa
6, 13, 14, 18, 19, 22				

☐ Helmeted Hornbill	*Rhinoplax vigil*	WE	r	wa
5, 6, 13, 14, 18, 22, 23, 25, 30, 34, 35, 36, 37, 39				
☐ Fire-tufted Barbet	*Psilopogon pyrolophus*	W	r	hi
6, 14, 17, 18				
☐ Lineated Barbet	*Megalaima lineata*	W	r	lo
21				
☐ Gold-whiskered Barbet	*Megalaima chrysopogon*	WE	r	wa
4, 5, 6, 8, 13, 18, 22, 25, 26, 30, 34, 35, 36, 39				
☐ Red-crowned Barbet	*Megalaima rafflesii*	WE	r	lo
4, 5, 8, 22, 23, 25, 26, 27, 28, 29, 30, 35, 39				
☐ Red-throated Barbet	*Megalaima mystacophanos*	WE	r	lo
13, 18, 20, 22, 23, 25, 28, 29, 30, 35, 36, 37, 39				
☐ Golden-throated Barbet	*Megalaima franklinii*	W	r	hi
6, 14, 17, 18, 22				
☐ Black-browed Barbet	*Megalaima oorti*	W	r	hi
6, 14, 17, 18, 22				
☐ Mountain Barbet*	*Megalaima monticola*	E	r	hi
30, 34, 42				
☐ Yellow-crowned Barbet	*Megalaima henricii*	WE	r	wa
5, 13, 18, 22, 25, 30, 35, 39				
☐ Golden-naped Barbet*	*Megalaima pulcherrima*	E	r	hi
30, 34, 42				
☐ Blue-eared Barbet	*Megalaima australis*	WE	r	wa
4, 5, 6, 8, 13, 18, 20, 22, 23, 25, 26, 27, 28, 29,				
30, 33, 35, 36, 37, 39				
☐ Black-throated Barbet*	*Megalaima eximia*	E	r	hi
30, 34, 42				
☐ Coppersmith Barbet	*Megalaima haemacephala*	W	r	lo
1, 2, 3, 7, 8, 10, 16, 18				
☐ Brown Barbet	*Calorhamphus fuliginosus*	WE	r	wa
4, 5, 6, 8, 13, 18, 20, 22, 23, 25, 26, 27, 28, 29,				
30, 35, 36, 37, 39				
☐ Malaysian Honeyguide	*Indicator archipelagicus*	WE	r	lo
22, 26, 27, 30, 35, 36, 39, 40				
☐ Speckled Piculet	*Picumnus innominatus*	WE	r	hi
14, 17, 18, 22, 40				
☐ Rufous Piculet	*Sasia abnormis*	WE	r	wa
5, 13, 22, 23, 25, 26, 29, 30, 35, 36, 37, 39				
☐ Rufous Woodpecker	*Micropternus brachyurus*	WE	r	wa
1, 2, 3, 7, 8, 13, 16, 18, 22, 23, 25, 26, 28, 29,				
30, 34, 35, 36, 39				
☐ Laced Woodpecker	*Picus vittatus*	W	r	lo
3, 7, 9, 10, 15, 19				
☐ Grey-headed Woodpecker	*Picus canus*	W	r	hi
17, 22				
☐ Greater Yellownape	*Picus flavinucha*	W	r	hi
6, 14, 17				
☐ Crimson-winged Woodpecker	*Picus puniceus*	WE	r	wa
3, 4, 5, 6, 7, 8, 13, 18, 20, 22, 23, 25, 26, 28,				
29, 30, 34, 35, 36, 37, 39				
☐ Lesser Yellownape	*Picus chlorolophus*	W	r	hi
6, 14, 17, 18				
☐ Checker-throated Woodpecker	*Picus mentalis*	WE	r	wa
4, 5, 8, 22, 25, 26, 30, 34, 35, 36, 39				
☐ Banded Woodpecker	*Picus miniaceus*	WE	r	wa
1, 3, 7, 18, 22, 25, 26, 30, 34, 35, 36, 39				

☐ Common Goldenback 1, 3, 7, 8, 10, 15, 16, 18, 22, 23, 26, 27, 36	*Dinopium javanense*	WE	r	lo
☐ Olive-backed Woodpecker 22, 25, 26, 30, 35, 36, 39	*Dinopium rafflesii*	WE	r	wa
☐ Bamboo Woodpecker 5, 6, 13, 22	*Gecinulus viridis*	W	r	wa
☐ Buff-rumped Woodpecker 5, 6, 8, 13, 18, 20, 22, 23, 25, 26, 28, 29, 30, 31, 35, 36, 39	*Meiglyptes tristis*	WE	r	lo
☐ Buff-necked Woodpecker 4, 5, 7, 8, 16, 20, 22, 23, 25, 26, 28, 29, 30, 35, 36, 39	*Meiglyptes tukki*	WE	r	wa
☐ Great Slaty Woodpecker 8, 19, 20, 22, 25, 26, 30, 36, 37, 39	*Mulleripicus pulverulentus*	WE	r	lo
☐ White-bellied Woodpecker 20, 22, 23, 25, 26, 27, 31, 36, 37, 39	*Dryocopus javensis*	WE	r	lo
☐ Grey-capped Woodpecker 1, 7, 16, 18, 26, 27, 34, 35, 36, 39	*Picoides canicapillus*	WE	r	lo
☐ Brown-capped Woodpecker 10, 12, 15, 27, 33	*Picoides moluccensis*	WE	r	lo
☐ Grey-and-Buff Woodpecker 4, 5, 8, 13, 22, 23, 25, 26, 30, 36	*Hemicircus concretus*	WE	r	wa
☐ Bay Woodpecker 6, 14, 17	*Blythipicus pyrrhotis*	W	r	hi
☐ Maroon Woodpecker 4, 5, 13, 18, 20, 22, 23, 25, 26, 28, 29, 30, 34, 35, 36, 39	*Blythipicus rubiginosus*	WE	r	wa
☐ Orange-backed Woodpecker 4, 8, 22, 23, 25, 26, 28, 29, 30, 34, 35, 36, 39	*Chrysocolaptes validus*	WE	r	lo
☐ Greater Goldenback 10, 19, 37	*Chrysocolaptes lucidus*	WE	r	lo
☐ Dusky Broadbill 5, 13, 18, 22, 23, 25, 28, 30, 34, 35, 36, 39	*Corydon sumatranus*	WE	r	wa
☐ Black-and-Red Broadbill 4, 5, 22, 23, 25, 28, 29, 30, 35, 36, 37, 39	*Cymbirhynchus macrorhynchus*	WE	r	lo
☐ Banded Broadbill 4, 5, 8, 13, 22, 23, 25, 26, 28, 29, 30, 35, 36, 39	*Eurylaimus javanicus*	WE	r	wa
☐ Black-and-Yellow Broadbill 4, 5, 8, 18, 20, 22, 23, 25, 26, 28, 29, 30, 35, 36, 37, 39	*Eurylaimus ochromalus*	WE	r	lo
☐ Silver-breasted Broadbill 6, 13, 14, 17, 18	*Serilophus lunatus*	W	r	su
☐ Long-tailed Broadbill 6, 14, 17, 18, 22, 30, 34, 42	*Psarisomus dalhousiae*	WE	r	hi
☐ Green Broadbill 4, 5, 13, 20, 22, 23, 25, 26, 28, 29, 30, 35, 36, 39	*Calyptomena viridis*	WE	r	lo
☐ Hose's Broadbill* 30, 34, 35	*Calyptomena hosei*	E	r	su
☐ Whitehead's Broadbill* 30, 34	*Calyptomena whiteheadi*	E	r	hi
☐ Rusty-naped Pitta 6, 14, 18	*Pitta oatesi*	W	r	hi
☐ Giant Pitta 22, 25, 36, 39	*Pitta caerulea*	WE	r	lo
☐ Blue-banded Pitta* 30, 35, 39	*Pitta arquata*	E	r	su
☐ Fairy Pitta 28, 29	*Pitta nympha*	E	m	wa

Common Name	Scientific Name			
☐ Blue-winged Pitta	*Pitta moluccensis*	WE	rm	wa
3, 4, 7, 8, 14, 18, 19, 22, 23, 25, 32, 34, 39				
☐ Mangrove Pitta	*Pitta megarhyncha*	We	r	lo
10, 15, 19				
☐ Garnet Pitta	*Pitta granatina*	WE	r	lo
22, 23, 25, 26, 28, 29, 30, 36, 39				
☐ Blue-headed Pitta*	*Pitta baudi*	E	r	lo
28, 29, 30, 36, 37, 39				
☐ Hooded Pitta	*Pitta sordida*	WE	rm	lo
5, 14, 18, 22, 23, 25, 26, 28, 29, 30, 36, 37, 39				
☐ Banded Pitta	*Pitta guajana*	WE	r	wa
22, 23, 25, 26, 34, 35, 39				
☐ Oriental Skylark	*Alauda gulgula*	e	m	lo
☐ Sand Martin	*Riparia riparia*	WE	m	lo
2, 33				
☐ Dusky Crag-Martin	*Hirundo concolor*	w	m	wa
☐ Barn Swallow	*Hirundo rustica*	WE	m	wa
1, 2, 3, 4, 5, 6, 7, 8, 10, 11, 12, 13, 15, 16, 17, 18, 19, 20, 23, 24, 25, 26, 27, 30, 33, 34, 36, 37, 39				
☐ Pacific Swallow	*Hirundo tahitica*	WE	r	wa
1, 2, 3, 4, 5, 6, 7, 8, 10, 11, 13, 15, 16, 17, 18, 19, 20, 21, 22, 23, 24, 25, 26, 27, 28, 29, 30, 31, 32, 33, 34, 36, 37, 39				
☐ Red-rumped Swallow	*Hirundo daurica (striolata)*	WE	rm	wa
2, 4, 7, 8, 11, 13, 18, 19, 20, 23				
☐ Asian House-Martin	*Delichon dasypus*	WE	m	wa
6, 7, 13, 17, 18, 34				
☐ Bar-winged Flycatcher-shrike	*Hemipus picatus*	WE	r	hi
5, 6, 13, 17, 18, 22, 25, 30, 34, 42				
☐ Black-winged Flycatcher-shrike	*Hemipus hirundinaceus*	WE	r	lo
4, 8, 22, 23, 25, 27, 28, 29, 30, 35, 36, 37, 39				
☐ Large Wood-shrike	*Tephrodornis virgatus*	WE	r	wa
4, 5, 7, 8, 13, 15, 22, 23, 25, 29, 30, 35, 36, 39				
☐ Large (Black-faced) Cuckoo-shrike	*Coracina novaehollandiae*	W	r	hi
6, 14, 17, 18, 22				
☐ Sunda (Large) Cuckoo-shrike	*Coracina larvata*	E	r	hi
30, 34				
☐ Bar-bellied Cuckoo-shrike	*Coracina striata*	WE	r	lo
20, 22, 24, 25, 27, 29, 30, 35, 39				
☐ Lesser Cuckoo-shrike	*Coracina fimbriata*	WE	r	wa
5, 17, 18, 20, 22, 23, 25, 26, 27, 30, 35, 36, 39				
☐ Pied Triller	*Lalage nigra*	WE	r	lo
1, 2, 3, 7, 10, 11, 15, 16, 27, 31, 32, 33				
☐ Black-breasted Triller*	*Chlamydochaera jefferyi*	E	r	hi
30, 34				
☐ Ashy Minivet	*Pericrocotus divaricatus*	WE	m	wa
1, 7, 8, 13, 16, 19, 22, 25, 26, 27, 37				
☐ Fiery Minivet	*Pericrocotus igneus*	WE	r	wa
22, 25, 27, 36				
☐ Grey-chinned Minivet	*Pericrocotus solaris*	WE	r	hi
6, 14, 17, 18, 22, 30, 34, 42				

Common name	Scientific name			
☐ Scarlet Minivet	*Pericrocotus flammeus*	WE	r	wa
4, 5, 8, 13, 14, 20, 22, 23, 25, 26, 27, 30, 36, 39				
☐ Green Iora	*Aegithina viridissima*	WE	r	lo
4, 5, 8, 19, 20, 22, 23, 24, 25, 27, 28, 29, 30, 35, 36, 39				
☐ Common Iora	*Aegithina tiphia*	WE	r	lo
1, 2, 3, 7, 10, 15, 16, 18, 22, 26, 27, 28, 30, 31, 32, 33, 35, 36, 37, 39				
☐ Great Iora	*Aegithina lafresnayei*	W	r	wa
5, 23, 25				
☐ Lesser Green Leafbird	*Chloropsis cyanopogon*	WE	r	lo
4, 5, 8, 22, 23, 25, 26, 28, 29, 30, 35, 36, 39				
☐ Greater Green Leafbird	*Chloropsis sonnerati*	WE	r	lo
5, 8, 13, 22, 23, 25, 27, 28, 29, 30, 35, 36, 37, 39				
☐ Blue-winged Leafbird	*Chloropsis cochinchinensis*	WE	r	wa
4, 5, 6, 8, 13, 18, 20, 22, 23, 25, 26, 29, 30, 34, 35, 39				
☐ Orange-bellied Leafbird	*Chloropsis hardwickii*	W	r	hi
6, 14, 17, 18				
☐ Straw-headed Bulbul	*Pycnonotus zeylanicus*	WE	r	lo
3, 4, 5, 7, 8, 16, 22, 23, 25, 27, 28, 29, 30, 33, 35, 37, 39				
☐ Black-and-White Bulbul	*Pycnonotus melanoleucos*	WE	r	wa
22, 25, 26, 29, 30, 35, 39				
☐ Black-headed Bulbul	*Pycnonotus atriceps*	WE	r	lo
5, 7, 13, 16, 18, 19, 20, 22, 25, 26, 28, 29, 30, 33, 35, 36, 39				
☐ Black-crested Bulbul	*Pycnonotus melanicterus*	WE	r	hi
5, 6, 13, 14, 17, 18, 22, 34, 42				
☐ Scaly-breasted Bulbul	*Pycnonotus squamatus*	WE	r	su
5, 13, 19, 22, 25, 30, 35, 39, 40				
☐ Grey-bellied Bulbul	*Pycnonotus cyaniventris*	WE	r	lo
4, 5, 8, 13, 16, 20, 22, 23, 25, 26, 28, 30, 36, 39				
☐ Red-whiskered Bulbul	*Pycnonotus jocosus*	W	r	lo
3, 7, 16				
☐ Puff-backed Bulbul	*Pycnonotus eutilotus*	WE	r	lo
22, 25, 26, 30, 36, 39				
☐ Stripe-throated Bulbul	*Pycnonotus finlaysoni*	W	r	wa
5, 6, 13, 14, 17, 19, 20, 22, 23, 26				
☐ Nieuwenhuis's Bulbul	*Pycnonotus nieuwenhuisi*	E	r	lo
☐ Flavescent Bulbul	*Pycnonotus flavescens*	E	r	hi
30, 34, 42				
☐ Yellow-vented Bulbul	*Pycnonotus goiavier*	WE	r	wa
1, 2, 3, 4, 6, 7, 8, 10, 11, 12, 15, 16, 17, 18, 19, 20, 22, 23, 26, 27, 30, 31, 32, 33, 34, 35, 36, 38				
☐ Olive-winged Bulbul	*Pycnonotus plumosus*	WE	r	lo
1, 3, 4, 5, 7, 8, 10, 15, 16, 18, 19, 22, 23, 24, 25, 26, 27, 28, 29, 30, 31, 33, 35, 36, 39				
☐ Streak-eared Bulbul	*Pycnonotus blanfordi*	W	r	lo
☐ Cream-vented Bulbul	*Pycnonotus simplex*	WE	r	lo
4, 5, 8, 20, 22, 23, 25, 26, 27, 28, 29, 30, 31, 35, 36, 39				
☐ Red-eyed Bulbul	*Pycnonotus brunneus*	WE	r	lo
4, 5, 8, 16, 18, 19, 20, 22, 23, 24, 25, 27, 28, 29, 30, 33, 35, 36, 37, 39				
☐ Spectacled Bulbul	*Pycnonotus erythropthalmos*	WE	r	lo
3, 4, 5, 8, 20, 22, 23, 25, 26, 28, 29, 30, 35, 36, 39				
☐ Finsch's Bulbul	*Criniger finschii*	WE	r	lo
5, 22, 25, 30, 39, 40				

☐ Ochraceous Bulbul	*Criniger ochraceus*	WE r	hi
6, 13, 14, 17, 18, 19, 22, 30, 34, 42			
☐ Grey-cheeked Bulbul	*Criniger bres*	WE r	lo
4, 5, 20, 22, 23, 25, 28, 29, 30, 34, 35, 36, 39			
☐ Yellow-bellied Bulbul	*Criniger phaeocephalus*	WE r	lo
4, 5, 20, 22, 23, 25, 26, 28, 29, 30, 35, 36, 39			
☐ Hook-billed Bulbul	*Setornis criniger*	E r	lo
30, 39			
☐ Hairy-backed Bulbul	*Hypsipetes criniger*	WE r	lo
4, 5, 8, 20, 22, 23, 24, 25, 26, 28, 29, 30, 35, 36, 37, 39			
☐ Buff-vented Bulbul	*Hypsipetes charlottae*	WE r	lo
4, 5, 8, 22, 23, 25, 30, 36, 39			
☐ Mountain Bulbul	*Hypsipetes mcclellandii*	W r	hi
6, 14, 17, 18, 22			
☐ Streaked Bulbul	*Hypsipetes malaccensis*	WE r	lo
5, 22, 25, 27, 30, 35, 36, 39			
☐ Ashy Bulbul	*Hypsipetes flavala*	WE r	wa
4, 5, 6, 13, 14, 17, 18, 22, 25, 28, 30, 34, 42			
☐ Black Drongo	*Dicrurus macrocercus*	W m	lo
11, 24			
☐ Ashy Drongo	*Dicrurus leucophaeus*	WE rm	wa
7, 8, 9, 10, 12, 15, 19, 24, 30, 34			
☐ Crow-billed Drongo	*Dicrurus annectans*	WE m	wa
4, 7, 8, 15, 16, 19, 22, 23, 27, 28, 29, 30, 33, 35, 36			
☐ Bronzed Drongo	*Dicrurus aeneus*	WE r	wa
5, 6, 8, 13, 18, 20, 22, 23, 25, 26, 27, 28, 29, 35, 36, 39			
☐ Lesser Racket-tailed Drongo	*Dicrurus remifer*	W r	hi
6, 14, 17, 18, 22			
☐ Spangled Drongo	*Dicrurus hottentottus*	E r	hi
30, 34			
☐ Greater Racket-tailed Drongo	*Dicrurus paradiseus*	WE r	lo
1, 3, 4, 5, 7, 8, 13, 16, 18, 19, 20, 22, 23, 24,			
25, 26, 27, 28, 29, 30, 35, 36, 37, 39			
☐ Dark-throated Oriole	*Oriolus xanthonotus*	WE r	lo
4, 5, 22, 23, 25, 26, 28, 29, 30, 35, 36, 39			
☐ Black-naped Oriole	*Oriolus chinensis*	WE rm	lo
1, 2, 3, 4, 7, 10, 11, 12, 15, 16, 18, 19, 22, 24			
☐ Black-hooded Oriole	*Oriolus xanthornus*	WE r	lo
19, 40			
☐ Black Oriole*	*Oriolus hosei*	E r	hi
☐ Black-and-Crimson Oriole	*Oriolus cruentus*	WE r	hi
6, 14, 17, 18, 30, 34, 42			
☐ Asian Fairy-Bluebird	*Irena puella*	WE r	wa
4, 5, 6, 13, 16, 18, 19, 20, 22, 23, 25, 27, 29, 30, 35, 36, 37, 39			
☐ Crested Jay	*Platylophus galericulatus*	WE r	lo
13, 22, 23, 25, 26, 28, 29, 30, 35, 36, 39			
☐ Short-tailed Magpie	*Cissa thalassina*	E r	hi
34, 42			
☐ Green Magpie	*Cissa chinensis*	WE r	hi
6, 13, 14, 17, 18, 22, 34			
☐ Sunda (Malaysian) Treepie	*Dendrocitta occipitalis*	E r	hi
30, 34			
☐ Racket-tailed Treepie	*Crypsirina temia*	xe r	lo
☐ Black Magpie	*Platysmurus leucopterus*	WE r	lo
5, 7, 8, 20, 22, 23, 25, 26, 28, 29, 30, 35, 36, 39			

Common Name	Scientific Name			
House Crow	*Corvus splendens*	W	r	lo
1, 2, 3, 7, 10, 16				
Slender-billed Crow	*Corvus enca*	WE	r	lo
22, 25, 26, 30, 35, 36, 37, 39				
Large-billed Crow	*Corvus macrorhynchos*	WE	r	wa
2, 3, 4, 5, 6, 7, 8, 11, 13, 15, 16, 17, 18, 19, 22, 23, 24				
Great Tit	*Parus major*	WE	r	lo
10, 15, 27				
Sultan Tit	*Melanochlora sultanea*	W	r	su
5, 13, 14, 17, 18, 22, 25				
Velvet-fronted Nuthatch	*Sitta frontalis*	WE	r	wa
4, 5, 6, 13, 18, 22, 23, 25, 27, 29, 30, 34, 35, 36, 37, 39				
Blue Nuthatch	*Sitta azurea*	W	r	hi
6, 14, 17, 18, 22				
Puff-throated Babbler	*Pellorneum ruficeps*	W	r	wa
19				
Black-capped Babbler	*Pellorneum capistratum*	WE	r	lo
4, 8, 20, 22, 23, 25, 26, 28, 29, 30, 35, 36, 37, 39				
Buff-breasted Babbler	*Trichastoma tickelli*	W	r	hi
6, 14				
Temminck's Babbler	*Trichastoma pyrrhogenys*	E	r	su
30, 34, 39				
Short-tailed Babbler	*Trichastoma malaccense*	WE	r	lo
4, 5, 8, 16, 19, 20, 22, 23, 25, 26, 28, 29, 30, 35, 36, 39				
White-chested Babbler	*Trichastoma rostratum*	WE	r	lo
22, 23, 25, 27, 28, 29, 30, 31, 35, 36, 37, 39				
Ferruginous Babbler	*Trichastoma bicolor*	WE	r	lo
22, 23, 25, 30, 35, 36, 39				
Horsfield's Babbler	*Trichastoma sepiarium*	WE	r	lo
5, 22, 25, 27, 30, 35, 36, 39				
Abbott's Babbler	*Trichastoma abbotti*	WE	r	lo
1, 3, 7, 10, 16, 19, 20, 22, 23, 25, 27				
Black-browed Babbler	*Trichastoma perspicillatum*	E	r	lo
Moustached Babbler	*Malacopteron magnirostre*	WE	r	lo
4, 5, 13, 19, 20, 22, 24, 25, 26, 29, 30, 31, 35, 36, 39				
Sooty-capped Babbler	*Malacopteron affine*	WE	r	lo
22, 23, 25, 26, 28, 29, 30, 35, 36, 37, 39				
Scaly-crowned Babbler	*Malacopteron cinereum*	WE	r	lo
5, 20, 22, 23, 25, 26, 27, 28, 30, 36, 37, 39				
Rufous-crowned Babbler	*Malacopteron magnum*	WE	r	lo
4, 5, 19, 20, 22, 23, 25, 26, 28, 29, 30, 35, 36, 39				
Grey-breasted Babbler	*Malacopteron albogulare*	WE	r	lo
22, 25, 26, 30				
Large Scimitar-Babbler	*Pomatorhinus hypoleucos*	W	r	hi
6, 14, 18, 22				
Chestnut-backed Scimitar-Babbler	*Pomatorhinus montanus*	WE	r	su
5, 6, 13, 18, 22, 25, 28, 30, 34, 35, 36, 39				
Bornean Wren-Babbler*	*Ptilocichla leucogrammica*	E	r	lo
30, 36, 39, 40				
Striped Wren-Babbler	*Kenopia striata*	WE	r	lo
22, 25, 28, 30, 35, 36, 39				
Large Wren-Babbler	*Napothera macrodactyla*	W	r	lo
22, 23, 25, 26				

☐ Black-throated Wren-Babbler* 30, 36, 39	*Napothera atrigularis*	E	r	lo
☐ Marbled Wren-Babbler 6, 13, 14, 18	*Napothera marmorata*	W	r	hi
☐ Streaked Wren-Babbler 6, 14, 17, 18, 22, 24	*Napothera brevicaudata*	W	r	hi
☐ Mountain Wren-Babbler* 30, 34, 42	*Napothera crassa*	E	r	hi
☐ Eye-browed Wren-Babbler 6, 13, 14, 22, 25, 30, 34	*Napothera epilepidota*	WE	r	su
☐ Pygmy Wren-Babbler 6, 14, 17, 18, 22	*Pnoepyga pusilla*	W	r	hi
☐ Rufous-fronted Babbler 4, 5, 13, 14, 22, 25, 30, 35, 36	*Stachyris rufifrons*	WE	r	su
☐ Golden Babbler 6, 14, 17, 18, 22	*Stachyris chrysaea*	W	r	hi
☐ Grey-throated Babbler 6, 13, 14, 16, 17, 18, 22, 24, 25, 30, 34, 35, 39	*Stachyris nigriceps*	WE	r	su
☐ Grey-headed Babbler 4, 5, 18, 20, 22, 25, 28, 29, 30, 35, 36, 39	*Stachyris poliocephala*	WE	r	lo
☐ Chestnut-rumped Babbler 22, 25, 26, 28, 29, 30, 35, 36, 39	*Stachyris maculata*	WE	r	lo
☐ White-necked Babbler 22, 25, 26, 30, 36, 39	*Stachyris leucotis*	WE	r	lo
☐ Black-throated Babbler 4, 8, 22, 25, 26, 28, 29, 30, 35, 36, 39	*Stachyris nigricollis*	WE	r	lo
☐ Chestnut-winged Babbler 19, 22, 24, 25, 26, 27, 28, 29, 30, 35, 36, 37, 39	*Stachyris erythroptera*	WE	r	lo
☐ Striped Tit-Babbler 4, 5, 6, 7, 8, 10, 13, 16, 18, 19, 20, 22, 23, 25, 27, 30, 31, 32, 33, 35, 36, 37, 39	*Macronous gularis*	WE	r	wa
☐ Fluffy-backed Tit-Babbler 4, 8, 22, 25, 26, 28, 30, 35, 36, 37, 39	*Macronous ptilosus*	WE	r	lo
☐ Grey-and-Brown (Sunda) Laughingthrush 30, 34, 42	*Garrulax palliatus*	E	r	hi
☐ Black Laughingthrush 6, 13, 14, 30, 34	*Garrulax lugubris*	WE	r	hi
☐ Chestnut-capped Laughingthrush 6, 14, 17, 18, 22, 30, 34	*Garrulax mitratus*	WE	r	hi
☐ Hwamei 3	*Garrulax canorus*	W	r	lo
☐ Chestnut-crowned Laughingthrush 6, 14, 17, 18, 22	*Garrulax erythrocephalus*	W	r	hi
☐ Silver-eared Mesia 6, 14, 17, 18, 22	*Leiothrix argentauris*	W	r	hi
☐ Cutia 6, 14, 17, 18	*Cutia nipalensis*	W	r	hi
☐ White-browed Shrike-Babbler 6, 14, 17, 18, 22, 30, 34, 42	*Pteruthius flaviscapis*	WE	r	hi
☐ Black-eared Shrike-Babbler 6, 14, 17, 22	*Pteruthius melanotis*	W	r	hi

☐ White-hooded Babbler 13, 14	*Gampsorhynchus rufulus*	W	r	hi
☐ Blue-winged Minla 6, 14, 17, 18	*Minla cyanouroptera*	W	r	hi
☐ Chestnut-tailed Minla 6, 17, 22	*Minla strigula*	W	r	hi
☐ Rufous-winged Fulvetta 6, 14, 17, 18, 22	*Alcippe castaneceps*	W	r	hi
☐ Brown Fulvetta 5, 20, 22, 25, 26, 30, 35, 36, 39	*Alcippe brunneicauda*	WE	r	su
☐ Mountain Fulvetta 6, 14, 17, 18, 22	*Alcippe peracensis*	W	r	hi
☐ Long-tailed Sibia 6, 14, 17, 18, 22	*Heterophasia picaoides*	W	r	hi
☐ White-bellied Yuhina 4, 5, 13, 18, 19, 20, 22, 25, 30, 34, 35, 36, 37, 39	*Yuhina zantholeuca*	WE	r	su
☐ Chestnut-crested (Babbler) Yuhina* 30, 34, 35	*Yuhina everetti*	E	r	su
☐ Malaysian Rail-Babbler 22, 25, 26, 28, 30, 39	*Eupetes macrocerus*	WE	r	lo
☐ Lesser Shortwing 6, 14, 17, 18, 22	*Brachypteryx leucophrys*	W	r	hi
☐ White-browed Shortwing 30, 34	*Brachypteryx montana*	E	r	hi
☐ Siberian Rubythroat	*Luscinia calliope*	we	m	wa
☐ Rufous-headed Robin 17	*Luscinia ruficeps*	w	m	hi
☐ Siberian Blue Robin 3, 4, 5, 7, 8, 19, 22, 23, 25, 26, 28, 29, 30, 35, 36, 39	*Luscinia cyane*	WE	m	wa
☐ Orange-flanked Bush-Robin	*Tarsiger cyanurus*	e	m	hi
☐ Magpie Robin 1, 2, 3, 4, 5, 6, 7, 8, 10, 11, 13, 15, 16, 17, 18, 19, 20, 22, 23, 24, 25, 27, 29, 30, 31, 32, 33, 35, 36, 37, 39	*Copsychus saularis*	WE	r	wa
☐ White-rumped Shama 4, 5, 7, 8, 16, 18, 19, 20, 21, 22, 23, 24, 25, 26, 27, 28, 29, 30, 35, 36, 37, 39	*Copsychus malabaricus*	WE	r	lo
☐ Rufous-tailed Shama 22, 25, 26, 28, 29, 30, 35, 36, 39	*Copsychus pyrropygus*	WE	r	lo
☐ White-tailed Robin 14, 17, 18	*Cinclidium leucurum*	W	r	hi
☐ Chestnut-naped Forktail 5, 6, 13, 18, 20, 22, 25, 28, 29, 30, 35, 39	*Enicurus ruficapillus*	WE	r	lo
☐ Slaty-backed Forktail 6, 14, 17, 18, 22	*Enicurus schistaceus*	W	r	hi
☐ White-crowned Forktail 22, 28, 29, 30, 34, 35, 36, 39	*Enicurus leschenaulti*	WE	r	wa
☐ Stonechat 2, 11, 33	*Saxicola torquata*	We	m	lo
☐ Pied Bushchat	*Saxicola caprata*	e	m	lo
☐ Northern Wheatear	*Oenanthe oenanthe*	e	m	lo
☐ White-throated Rock-Thrush 18	*Monticola gularis*	w	m	wa

Species	Scientific name			
☐ Blue Rock-Thrush 19, 34	*Monticola solitarius*	WE	rm	wa
☐ Sunda Whistling Thrush 30, 34, 35	*Myophonus glaucinus*	E	r	su
☐ Malayan Whistling Thrush* 6, 14, 17	*Myophonus robinsoni*	W	r	hi
☐ Blue Whistling Thrush 17, 19, 22	*Myophonus caeruleus*	W	r	wa
☐ Chestnut-capped Thrush 22, 28, 35, 36, 39	*Zoothera interpres*	WE	r	lo
☐ Orange-headed Thrush 14, 18, 19, 22, 35	*Zoothera citrina*	WE	rm	wa
☐ Siberian Thrush 6, 13, 14, 15, 17, 18, 22	*Zoothera sibirica*	We	m	wa
☐ Everett's Thrush* 30, 34	*Zoothera everetti*	E	r	hi
☐ Scaly Thrush	*Zoothera dauma*	we	m	wa
☐ Island Thrush (Mountain Blackbird) 34	*Turdus poliocephalus*	E	r	hi
☐ Eye-browed Thrush 5, 6, 7, 14, 15, 17, 18, 19, 22, 34	*Turdus obscurus*	WE	m	wa
☐ Flyeater 1, 3, 4, 5, 7, 10, 12, 15, 16, 19, 22, 24, 25, 26, 28, 30, 35, 36, 39	*Gerygone sulphurea*	WE	r	lo
☐ Chestnut-crowned Warbler 6, 14, 17, 18	*Seicercus castaniceps*	W	r	hi
☐ Yellow-breasted Warbler 6, 17, 22, 30, 34, 42	*Seicercus montis*	WE	r	hi
☐ Yellow-bellied Warbler 5, 6, 13, 22, 30, 34, 35	*Abroscopus superciliaris*	WE	r	su
☐ Dusky Warbler 10, 15	*Phylloscopus fuscatus*	w	m	lo
☐ Inornate Warbler 7, 13, 16, 17, 18, 19, 25	*Phylloscopus inornatus*	W	m	wa
☐ Arctic Warbler 1, 2, 3, 4, 5, 6, 7, 8, 10, 12, 13, 15, 16, 19, 21, 22, 23, 25, 27, 30, 33, 35, 36, 38, 39	*Phylloscopus borealis*	WE	m	wa
☐ Two-barred (Greenish) Warbler	*Phylloscopus plumbeitarsus*	w	m	lo
☐ Pale-legged Leaf-Warbler 19, 22	*Phylloscopus tenellipes*	w	m	wa
☐ Eastern Crowned Warbler 4, 5, 7, 8, 13, 18, 19, 22, 23, 25, 26	*Phylloscopus coronatus*	W	m	wa
☐ Mountain Leaf-Warbler 6, 14, 17, 18, 22, 30, 34, 42	*P. trivirgatus*	WE	r	hi
☐ Thick-billed Warbler	*Acrocephalus aedon*	w	m	wa
☐ Clamorous Reed-Warbler	*Acrocephalus stentoreus*	E	m	lo
☐ Great (Oriental) Reed-Warbler 2, 10, 11, 12, 15, 33	*Acrocephalus arundinaceus*	WE	m	lo
☐ Black-browed Reed-Warbler 2, 11	*Acrocephalus bistrigiceps*	W	m	lo
☐ Pallas's (Grasshopper) Warbler 2, 11, 12, 15, 17, 19, 33	*Locustella certhiola*	WE	m	lo

☐ Middendorf's Warbler	*Locustella ochotensis*	E	m	lo	
36					
☐ Lanceolated Warbler	*Locustella lanceolata*	WE	m	lo	
2, 11, 15, 17					
☐ Striated Warbler	*Megalurus palustris*	E	r	lo	
33					
☐ Common Tailorbird	*Orthotomus sutorius*	W	r	wa	
1, 2, 3, 4, 5, 6, 7, 8, 10, 15, 16, 17, 18, 19, 22, 23, 25					
☐ Dark-necked Tailorbird	*Orthotomus atrogularis*	WE	r	wa	
3, 4, 5, 6, 7, 8, 10, 13, 15, 16, 17, 18, 19, 20, 21, 22, 23, 24, 25, 26, 28, 29, 36, 39					
☐ Ashy Tailorbird	*Orthotomus ruficeps*	WE	r	lo	
2, 7, 10, 12, 15, 16, 19, 23, 27, 28, 30, 31, 33, 35, 36, 37, 39					
☐ Rufous-tailed Tailorbird	*Orthotomus sericeus*	WE	r	lo	
22, 25, 27, 30, 31, 33, 35, 36, 37, 39					
☐ Mountain Tailorbird	*Orthotomus cuculatus*	WE	r	hi	
6, 14, 17, 18, 22, 30, 34, 42					
☐ Rufescent Prinia	*Prinia rufescens*	W	r	wa	
5, 7, 8, 13, 20					
☐ Yellow-bellied Prinia	*Prinia flaviventris*	WE	r	wa	
2, 3, 7, 10, 11, 12, 15, 16, 17, 19, 22, 23, 30, 33, 35, 36, 37					
☐ Hill Prinia	*Prinia atrogularis*	W	r	hi	
22					
☐ Zitting Cisticola	*Cisticola juncidis*	W	r	lo	
2, 10, 11, 15, 19					
☐ Mountain (Sunda) Bush-Warbler	*Cettia vulcania*	E	r	hi	
30, 34					
☐ Short-tailed Bush-Warbler*	*Cettia whiteheadi*	E	r	hi	
30, 34, 42					
☐ Kinabalu Friendly (Bush) Warbler*	*Bradypterus accentor*	E	r	hi	
34					
☐ Fulvous-chested Flycatcher	*Rhinomyias olivacea*	E	r	lo	
30, 33, 35					
☐ Brown-chested Flycatcher	*Rhinomyias brunneata*	W	m	lo	
☐ Grey-chested Flycatcher	*Rhinomyias umbratilis*	WE	r	lo	
22, 25, 26, 27, 28, 30, 31, 35, 36, 39					
☐ Rufous-tailed Flycatcher	*Rhinomyias ruficauda*	E	r	su	
30, 34, 39					
☐ White-browed Flycatcher	*Rhinomyias gularis*	E	r	hi	
30, 34					
☐ Dark-sided Flycatcher	*Muscicapa sibirica*	WE	m	wa	
5, 8, 13, 22, 30, 32, 34, 35, 39					
☐ Grey-streaked Flycatcher	*Muscicapa griseisticta*	E	m	wa	
31					
☐ Asian Brown Flycatcher	*Muscicapa latirostris*	WE	m	wa	
1, 2, 3, 5, 6, 7, 8, 10, 13, 16, 17, 18, 19, 22, 23, 30, 34, 35, 36, 39					
☐ Brown-streaked Flycatcher	*Muscicapa williamsoni*	W	r	lo	
7					
☐ Ferruginous Flycatcher	*Muscicapa ferruginea*	WE	m	wa	
2, 4, 13, 14, 17, 18, 22, 34, 35					

☐ Verditer Flycatcher 5, 6, 13, 18, 22, 25, 30, 35, 39	*Muscicapa thalassina*	WE	r	su
☐ Indigo Flycatcher 30, 34	*Muscicapa indigo*	E	r	hi
☐ Yellow-rumped Flycatcher 1, 2, 3, 5, 7, 8, 15, 18, 19, 26	*Ficedula zanthopygia*	W	m	lo
☐ Narcissus Flycatcher 8, 26, 35, 36, 39	*Ficedula narcissina*	WE	m	lo
☐ Mugimaki Flycatcher 6, 13, 14, 17, 18, 19, 22, 27, 34	*Ficedula mugimaki*	WE	m	wa
☐ Red-throated Flycatcher 19	*Ficedula parva*	We	m	wa
☐ Rufous-browed Flycatcher 6, 14, 17, 18, 22	*Ficedula solitaris*	W	r	hi
☐ Snowy-browed Flycatcher 6, 17, 22, 30, 34, 42	*Ficedula hyperythra*	WE	r	hi
☐ Rufous-chested Flycatcher 5, 22, 23, 25, 30, 34, 35, 36, 39	*Ficedula dumetoria*	WE	r	su
☐ Little Pied Flycatcher 6, 14, 17, 18, 22, 30, 34, 42	*Ficedula westermanni*	WE	r	hi
☐ Blue-and-White Flycatcher 5, 13, 18, 22, 30, 34, 35, 39	*Cyanoptila cyanomelana*	WE	m	su
☐ Large Niltava 6, 14, 17, 18, 22	*Niltava grandis*	W	r	hi
☐ Rufous-vented Niltava 17	*Niltava sumatrana*	W	r	hi
☐ White-tailed Flycatcher 5, 25, 30, 34, 39	*Cyornis concreta*	WE	r	su
☐ Pale Blue Flycatcher 5, 13, 22, 25, 30, 36, 39	*Cyornis unicolor*	WE	r	su
☐ Blue-throated Flycatcher 22, 26	*Cyornis rubeculoides*	W	m	lo
☐ Hill Blue Flycatcher 5, 6, 13, 14, 17, 18, 22, 30, 34, 35, 39	*Cyornis banyumas*	WE	rm	su
☐ Bornean Blue Flycatcher* 30, 34, 35, 36, 37, 39	*Cyornis superba*	E	r	wa
☐ Large-billed Blue Flycatcher 27, 28, 29, 30, 36, 37, 39	*Cyornis caerulata*	E	r	lo
☐ Malaysian Blue Flycatcher 4, 22, 27, 28, 29, 30, 35, 37, 39	*Cyornis turcosa*	WE	r	lo
☐ Tickell's Blue Flycatcher 5, 18, 19, 22	*Cyornis tickelliae*	W	r	lo
☐ Mangrove Blue Flycatcher 10, 15, 27, 31, 36	*Cyornis rufigastra*	WE	r	lo
☐ Pygmy Blue Flycatcher 14, 17, 18, 22, 30, 34	*Muscicapella hodgsoni*	WE	r	hi
☐ Grey-headed Flycatcher 4, 5, 13, 14, 18, 22, 25, 26, 30, 34, 35, 36, 39	*Culicicapa ceylonensis*	WE	r	wa
☐ White-throated Fantail 6, 14, 17, 18, 22, 30, 34, 42	*Rhipidura albicollis*	WE	r	hi
☐ Spotted Fantail 5, 18, 22, 23, 25, 28, 29, 30, 34, 35, 36, 39	*Rhipidura perlata*	WE	r	wa
☐ Pied Fantail 1, 2, 3, 7, 10, 12, 15, 16, 18, 19, 23, 27, 28, 30, 31, 32, 33, 35, 36, 37, 38	*Rhipidura javanica*	WE	r	lo

Species	Scientific name			
Black-naped Monarch	*Hypothymis azurea*	WE	r	wa
4, 5, 8, 19, 20, 22, 23, 25, 26, 27, 28, 29, 30, 31, 32, 35, 36, 37, 39				
Maroon-breasted Flycatcher	*Philentoma velatum*	WE	r	lo
5, 13, 22, 28, 29, 30, 35, 36, 39, 40				
Rufous-winged Flycatcher	*Philentoma pyrhopterum*	WE	r	lo
4, 5, 8, 18, 20, 22, 23, 25, 26, 28, 29, 30, 35, 36, 39				
Japanese Paradise-Flycatcher	*Terpsiphone atrocaudata*	We	m	wa
7, 26				
Asian Paradise-Flycatcher	*Terpsiphone paradisi*	WE	rm	wa
4, 5, 7, 8, 13, 16, 18, 20, 22, 23, 25, 26, 27, 28, 29, 30, 35, 36, 37, 39				
Bornean Mountain Whistler*	*Pachycephala hypoxantha*	E	r	hi
30, 34, 42				
Mangrove Whistler	*Pachycephala cinerea*	WE	r	lo
9, 10, 12, 15, 19, 21, 27, 31, 36				
White Wagtail	*Motacilla alba*	wE	m	lo
27, 33				
Grey Wagtail	*Motacilla cinerea*	WE	m	wa
3, 5, 6, 7, 13, 14, 16, 17, 18, 19, 20, 22, 24, 25, 29, 30, 31, 33, 34, 35				
Yellow Wagtail	*Motacilla flava*	WE	m	lo
2, 3, 10, 11, 24, 27, 30, 33				
Forest Wagtail	*Dendronanthus indicus*	WE	m	wa
4, 7, 8, 10, 15, 16, 18, 19, 22, 24, 25, 33				
Olive Tree-Pipit	*Anthus hodgsoni*	WE	m	wa
6, 17, 18				
Richard's Pipit	*Anthus novaeseelandiae*	WE	r	wa
2, 3, 6, 7, 10, 11, 16, 17, 19, 25, 27, 33				
Red-throated Pipit	*Anthus cervinus*	WE	m	lo
11, 24, 33				
Petchora Pipit	*Anthus gustavi*	E	m	lo
33				
White-breasted Woodswallow	*Artamus leucorhynchus*	WE	r	lo
10, 11, 27, 31, 32, 33, 36				
Brown Shrike	*Lanius cristatus*	WE	m	wa
1, 2, 3, 5, 6, 7, 8, 10, 11, 13, 15, 16, 17, 18, 19, 21, 23, 24, 27, 33, 36				
Tiger Shrike	*Lanius tigrinus*	WE	m	wa
1, 2, 3, 4, 5, 6, 7, 8, 10, 13, 16, 18, 19, 22, 25, 27, 31, 36, 39				
Long-tailed Shrike	*Lanius schach*	WE	r	lo
2, 23				
Bornean Bristlehead*	*Pityriasis gymnocephala*	E	r	lo
36, 39				
Philippine Glossy Starling	*Aplonis panayensis*	WE	r	lo
1, 2, 3, 7, 8, 10, 11, 15, 16, 18, 19, 21, 23, 24, 26, 27, 30, 31, 32, 33, 36, 37, 38				
Chestnut-cheeked (Violet-backed) Starling	*Sturnus philippensis*	wE	m	lo
7, 36, 40				
White-shouldered Starling	*Sturnus sinensis*	we	m	lo
24				
Purple-backed Starling	*Sturnus sturninus*	We	m	lo
2, 3, 7, 10, 16, 21				
Common Myna	*Acridotheres tristis*	WE	r	wa
1, 2, 3, 7, 8, 10, 11, 15, 16, 17, 18, 19, 20, 22, 23, 24				

☐ Jungle Myna — *Acridotheres fuscus* — W   r   lo
2, 3, 7, 10, 11, 15, 18

☐ White-vented Myna — *Acridotheres javanicus* — W   r   lo
2, 3, 16

☐ Crested Myna — *A. cristatellus* — WE   r   lo
16

☐ Golden-crested Myna — *Ampeliceps coronatus* — w   r   lo

☐ Hill Myna — *Gracula religiosa* — WE   r   lo
7, 8, 15, 16, 19, 20, 22, 23, 24, 25, 27, 28, 29, 30, 31, 36, 37, 39

☐ Plain Sunbird — *Anthreptes simplex* — WE   r   lo
4, 5, 20, 22, 23, 26, 27, 29, 30, 36, 39

☐ Brown-throated Sunbird — *Anthreptes malacensis* — WE   r   lo
1, 3, 4, 7, 10, 11, 12, 15, 16, 18, 19, 20, 22, 24,
27, 28, 30, 31, 32, 33, 35, 36, 38

☐ Red-throated Sunbird — *Anthreptes rhodolaema* — WE   r   lo
22, 25, 27, 30, 31, 36, 39

☐ Ruby-cheeked Sunbird — *Anthreptes singalensis* — WE   r   lo
4, 5, 8, 10, 16, 19, 20, 22, 23, 25, 26, 27, 28,
29, 30, 35, 36, 37, 39

☐ Purple-naped Sunbird — *Hypogramma hypogrammicum* — WE   r   lo
4, 5, 8, 22, 23, 25, 26, 28, 29, 30, 35, 36, 37, 39

☐ Purple-throated Sunbird — *Nectarinia sperata* — WE   r   lo
16, 19, 24, 25, 31, 35, 36

☐ Copper-throated Sunbird — *Nectarinia calcostetha* — WE   r   lo
10, 12, 15, 16, 19, 21, 27, 31, 32, 36

☐ Olive-backed Sunbird — *Nectarinia jugularis* — WE   r   lo
9, 10, 12, 15, 16, 19, 24, 27, 31, 32, 33, 35, 36, 38

☐ Black-throated Sunbird — *Aethopyga saturata* — W   r   hi
6, 14, 17, 18, 22

☐ Crimson Sunbird — *Aethopyga siparaja* — WE   r   lo
16, 19, 27, 28, 29, 30, 35, 36, 39

☐ Scarlet Sunbird — *Aethopyga mystacalis* — WE   r   su
5, 17, 18, 20, 22, 23, 25, 30, 34, 35, 39, 40

☐ Little Spiderhunter — *Arachnothera longirostra* — WE   r   wa
1, 3, 4, 5, 6, 7, 8, 10, 13, 16, 17, 18, 20, 22,
23, 25, 26, 27, 28, 29, 30, 35, 36, 37, 39

☐ Thick-billed Spiderhunter — *Arachnothera crassirostris* — WE   r   lo
22, 25, 30, 35, 36, 39, 40

☐ Long-billed Spiderhunter — *Arachnothera robusta* — WE   r   wa
5, 13, 18, 22, 25, 28, 29, 30, 35, 36, 39

☐ Spectacled Spiderhunter — *Arachnothera flavigaster* — WE   r   lo
1, 3, 7, 8, 22, 25, 26, 34, 35, 36, 37, 39

☐ Yellow-eared Spiderhunter — *Arachnothera chrysogenys* — WE   r   wa
5, 16, 20, 22, 23, 28, 29, 30, 35, 36, 39

☐ Grey-breasted Spiderhunter — *Arachnothera affinis* — WE   r   lo
5, 13, 16, 20, 22, 23, 25, 26, 28, 29, 30, 35, 36, 39

☐ Streaked Spiderhunter — *Arachnothera magna* — W   r   hi
6, 13, 14, 17, 18

☐ Whitehead's Spiderhunter* — *Arachnothera juliae* — E   r   hi
30, 34, 42

☐ Scarlet-breasted Flowerpecker — *Prionochilus thoracicus* — WE   r   lo
22, 25, 27, 28, 29, 30, 36, 39

☐ Yellow-breasted Flowerpecker — *Prionochilus maculatus* — WE   r   wa
4, 5, 6, 13, 20, 22, 25, 26, 27, 28, 29, 30, 35, 36, 39

☐ Yellow-rumped Flowerpecker*   *Prionochilus xanthopygius*   E r lo
    29, 30, 35, 36, 39
☐ Crimson-breasted   *Prionochilus*
  Flowerpecker   *percussus*   WE r lo
    4, 5, 7, 8, 16, 18, 20, 22, 23, 24, 25, 26, 35
☐ Thick-billed Flowerpecker   *Dicaeum agile*   W r wa
    22
☐ Brown-backed Flowerpecker   *Dicaeum everetti*   WE r lo
☐ Yellow-vented Flowerpecker   *Dicaeum chrysorrheum*   WE r wa
    5, 6, 13, 22, 23, 25, 30, 35, 36, 39
☐ Orange-bellied Flowerpecker   *Dicaeum trigonostigma*   WE r wa
    4, 5, 6, 7, 8, 16, 19, 20, 22, 23, 24, 25, 27, 28,
    29, 30, 31, 32, 35, 36, 38, 39
☐ Plain Flowerpecker   *Dicaeum concolor*   WE r lo
    16, 22, 23, 25, 35
☐ Black-sided Flowerpecker   *Dicaeum monticolum*   E r hi
    30, 34, 42
☐ Scarlet-backed Flowerpecker   *Dicaeum cruentatum*   WE r lo
    1, 2, 3, 4, 7, 10, 16, 18, 19, 20, 22, 23, 24, 27,
    31, 32, 35, 36, 37, 39
☐ Buff-bellied Flowerpecker   *Dicaeum ignipectus*   W r hi
    6, 14, 17, 18, 22
☐ Oriental White-eye   *Zosterops palpebrosa*   WE r lo
    7, 10, 15, 16, 24, 27
☐ Black-capped White-eye   *Zosterops atricapilla*   E r hi
    30, 34
☐ Everett's White-eye   *Zosterops everetti*   WE r wa
    4, 5, 6, 13, 17, 18, 20, 22, 23, 25, 35, 39, 40
☐ Javan White-eye   *Zosterops flava*   E r lo
☐ Mangrove White-eye   *Zosterops chloris*   E r lo
☐ Pygmy White-eye*   *Oculocincta squamifrons*   E r hi
    34, 40, 42
☐ Mountain Black-eye*   *Chlorocharis emiliae*   E r hi
    30, 34
☐ Eurasian Tree-Sparrow   *Passer montanus*   WE r wa
    1, 2, 3, 7, 8, 10, 11, 15, 16, 17, 18, 19, 20, 22,
    23, 25, 27, 29, 30, 31, 33, 36
☐ Plain-backed Sparrow   *Passer flaveolus*   W r lo
    10, 16, 19
☐ Baya Weaver   *Ploceus philippinus*   W r lo
    2, 3, 7, 10, 11, 16, 19
☐ Red Avadavat   *Amandava amandava*   WE r lo
    11
☐ Pin-tailed Parrotfinch   *Erythrura prasina*   WE r wa
    5, 6, 13, 22
☐ Tawny-breasted Parrotfinch   *Erythrura hyperythra*   WE r hi
    17, 18, 30, 34
☐ Java Sparrow   *Padda oryzivora*   WE r lo
    16
☐ White-rumped Munia   *Lonchura striata*   W r wa
    2, 5, 6, 8, 10, 15, 16, 19, 20, 21, 22, 23, 24, 25
☐ Dusky Munia*   *Lonchura fuscans*   E r lo
    27, 28, 29, 30, 31, 33, 35, 36, 37, 39
☐ White-bellied Munia   *Lonchura leucogastra*   WE r lo
    4, 11, 22, 25, 30

☐ Scaly-breasted Munia	*Lonchura punctulata*	W	r	wa
1, 2, 3, 4, 7, 10, 11, 16, 17, 18, 19, 23				
☐ Chestnut Munia	*Lonchura malacca*	WE	r	lo
2, 10, 16, 33, 35, 36				
☐ White-headed Munia	*Lonchura maja*	W	r	lo
2, 7, 8, 10, 16				
☐ Brown Bullfinch	*Pyrrhula nipalensis*	W	r	hi
6, 14, 17, 22				
☐ Chestnut-eared Bunting	*Emberiza fucata*	w	m	lo
11				
☐ Little Bunting	*Emberiza pusilla*	E	m	wa
33				
☐ Yellow-breasted Bunting	*Emberiza aureola*	We	m	lo
11				

Mammals of Malaysia

Key to checklist
W   West (Peninsular) Malaysia
E   East Malaysia (Sabah, Sarawak)
*   endemic (to the Malay Peninsula or Borneo)

☐ Moonrat (Gymnure)	*Echinosorex gymnurus*	WE
☐ Lesser Gymnure	*Hylomys suillus*	WE
☐ Eastern (Short-tailed) Mole	*Talpa micrura*	W
☐ House Shrew	*Suncus murinus*	WE
☐ Black Shrew*	*Suncus ater*	E
☐ Savi's Pygmy Shrew	*Suncus etruscus*	WE
☐ South-east Asian White-toothed Shrew	*Crocidura fuliginosa*	WE
☐ Sunda Shrew	*Crocidura monticola*	WE
☐ Himalayan Water Shrew	*Chimarrogale himalayica*	WE
☐ Pentail Treeshrew	*Ptilocercus lowii*	WE
☐ Common Treeshrew	*Tupaia glis*	WE
☐ Lesser Treeshrew	*Tupaia minor*	WE
☐ Ruddy Treeshrew*	*Tupaia splendidula*	E
☐ Mountain Treeshrew*	*Tupaia montana*	E
☐ Slender Treeshrew*	*Tupaia gracilis*	E
☐ Painted Treeshrew*	*Tupaia picta*	E
☐ Striped Treeshrew*	*Tupaia dorsalis*	E
☐ Large Treeshrew	*Tupaia tana*	E
☐ Smooth-tailed Treeshrew*	*Dendrogale melanura*	E
☐ Colugo (Flying Lemur)	*Cynocephalus variegatus*	WE
☐ Geoffroy's Rousette	*Rousettus amplexicaudatus*	WE
☐ Bare-backed Rousette	*Rousettus spinalatus*	E
☐ Large Flying Fox	*Pteropus vampyrus*	WE
☐ Island Flying Fox	*Pteropus hypomelanus*	WE
☐ Short-nosed Fruit Bat	*Cynopterus brachyotis*	WE
☐ Greater Short-nosed Fruit Bat	*Cynopterus sphinx*	W
☐ Horsfield's Fruit Bat	*Cynopterus horsfieldi*	WE
☐ Tailless Fruit Bat	*Megaerops ecaudatus*	WE
☐ Dayak Fruit Bat	*Dyacopterus spadiceus*	WE
☐ Spotted-winged Fruit Bat	*Balionycteris maculata*	WE
☐ Black-capped Fruit Bat	*Chironax melanocephalus*	WE
☐ Grey Fruit Bat	*Aethalops alecto*	WE
☐ Dusky Fruit Bat	*Penthetor lucasii*	WE
☐ Cave Nectar Bat	*Eonycteris spelaea*	WE
☐ Greater Nectar Bat	*Eonycteris major*	E
☐ Long-tongued Nectar Bat	*Macroglossus minimus*	WE
☐ Lesser Sheath-tailed Bat	*Emballonura monticola*	WE
☐ Greater Sheath-tailed Bat	*Emballonura alecto*	E
☐ Black-bearded Tomb Bat	*Taphozous melanopogon*	WE
☐ Long-winged Tomb Bat	*Taphozous longimanus*	WE
☐ Pouched Tomb Bat	*Taphozous saccolaimus*	WE
☐ Lesser False Vampire	*Megaderma spasma*	WE
☐ Greater False Vampire	*Megaderma lyra*	W
☐ Hollow-faced Bat	*Nycteris javanica*	WE
☐ Intermediate Horseshoe Bat	*Rhinolophus affinis*	WE
☐ Lesser Woolly Horseshoe Bat	*Rhinolophus sedulus*	WE
☐ Trefoil Horseshoe Bat	*Rhinolophus trifoliatus*	WE
☐ Great Woolly Horseshoe Bat	*Rhinolophus luctus*	WE

Common Name	Scientific Name	Distribution
☐ Lesser Brown Horseshoe Bat	*Rhinolophus stheno*	W
☐ Peninsular Horseshoe Bat	*Rhinolophus robinsoni*	W
☐ Glossy Horseshoe Bat	*Rhinolophus refulgens*	W
☐ Least Horseshoe Bat	*Rhinolophus pusillus*	W
☐ Big-eared Horseshoe Bat	*Rhinolophus macrotis*	W
☐ Croslet Horseshoe Bat	*Rhinolophus coelophyllus*	W
☐ Northern Malayan Horseshoe Bat	*Rhinolophus malayanus*	W
☐ Bornean Horseshoe Bat	*Rhinolophus borneensis*	E
☐ Arcuate Horseshoe Bat	*Rhinolophus arcuatus*	E
☐ Acuminate Horseshoe Bat	*Rhinolophus acuminatus*	WE
☐ Philippine Horseshoe Bat	*Rhinolophus philippinensis*	E
☐ Creagh's Horseshoe Bat	*Rhinolophus creaghi*	E
☐ Trident Horseshoe Bat	*Aselliscus stoliczkanus*	W
☐ Dusky Roundleaf Bat	*Hipposideros ater*	WE
☐ Bicolored Roundleaf Bat	*Hipposideros bicolor*	WE
☐ Least Roundleaf Bat	*Hipposideros sabanus*	WE
☐ Ashy Roundleaf Bat	*Hipposideros cineraceus*	WE
☐ Fawn Roundleaf Bat	*Hipposideros cervinus*	WE
☐ Cantor's Roundleaf Bat	*Hipposideros galeritus*	WE
☐ Intermediate Roundleaf Bat	*Hipposideros larvatus*	WE
☐ Diadem Roundleaf Bat	*Hipposideros diadema*	WE
☐ Shield-faced Bat	*Hipposideros lylei*	W
☐ Great Roundleaf Bat	*Hipposideros armiger*	W
☐ Ridley's Roundleaf Bat	*Hipposideros ridleyi*	WE
☐ Malayan Roundleaf Bat*	*Hipposideros nequam*	W
☐ Dayak Roundleaf Bat*	*Hipposideros dyacorum*	E
☐ Cox's Roundleaf Bat*	*Hipposideros coxi*	E
☐ Lesser Tailless Roundleaf Bat	*Coelops robinsoni*	WE
☐ East Asian Tailless Roundleaf Bat	*Coelops frithii*	W
☐ Whiskered Myotis	*Myotis muricola*	WE
☐ Black Myotis	*Myotis ater*	E
☐ Hasselt's Large-footed Myotis	*Myotis hasseltii*	WE
☐ Grey Large-footed Myotis	*Myotis adversus*	WE
☐ Horsfield's Myotis	*Myotis horsfieldii*	WE
☐ Pallid Large-footed Myotis	*Myotis macrotarsus*	E
☐ Ridley's Myotis	*Myotis ridleyi*	WE
☐ Small-toothed Myotis	*Myotis siligorensis*	WE
☐ Large Brown Myotis	*Myotis montivagus*	WE
☐ Narrow-winged Pipistrelle	*Pipistrellus stenopterus*	WE
☐ White-winged Pipistrelle	*Pipistrellus vordermanni*	E
☐ Brown Pipistrelle	*Pipistrellus imbricatus*	W
☐ Dark Brown Pipistrelle	*Pipistrellus ceylonicus*	E
☐ Red-brown Pipistrelle*	*Pipistrellus kitcheneri*	E
☐ Javan Pipistrelle	*Pipistrellus javanicus*	WE
☐ Least Pipistrelle	*Pipistrellus tenuis*	WE
☐ Woolly Pipistrelle	*Pipistrellus petersi*	E
☐ Coppery Pipistrelle*	*Pipistrellus cuprosus*	E
☐ Thick-thumbed Pipistrelle	*Glischropus tylopus*	WE
☐ Narrow-winged Brown Bat	*Philetor brachypterus*	WE
☐ Least False Serotine	*Hesperoptenus blanfordi*	WE
☐ Tomes' False Serotine	*Hesperoptenus tomesi*	WE

☐ False Serotine	*Hesperoptenus doriae*	WE
☐ Greater Bamboo Bat	*Tylonycteris robustula*	WE
☐ Lesser Bamboo Bat	*Tylonycteris pachypus*	WE
☐ Yellow House Bat	*Scotophilus kuhlii*	WE
☐ Lesser Tube-nosed Bat	*Murina suilla*	WE
☐ Bronzed Tube-nosed Bat	*Murina aenea*	WE
☐ Hutton's Tube-nosed Bat	*Murina huttoni*	W
☐ Orange Tube-nosed Bat	*Murina cyclotis*	WE
☐ Gilded Tube-nosed Bat*	*Murina rozendaali*	E
☐ Hairy-winged Bat	*Harpiocephalus harpia*	E
☐ Hardwicke's Woolly Bat	*Kerivoula hardwickii*	WE
☐ Clear-winged Woolly Bat	*Kerivoula pellucida*	WE
☐ Small Woolly Bat	*Kerivoula intermedia*	WE
☐ Least Woolly Bat	*Kerivoula minuta*	WE
☐ Papillose Woolly Bat	*Kerivoula papillosa*	WE
☐ Painted Bat	*Kerivoula picta*	W
☐ Whitehead's Woolly Bat	*Kerivoula whiteheadi*	E
☐ Frosted Groove-toothed Bat	*Phoniscus jagorii*	E
☐ Gilded Groove-toothed Bat	*Phoniscus atrox*	WE
☐ Large Bent-winged Bat	*Miniopterus magnater*	WE
☐ Common Bent-winged Bat	*Miniopterus schreibersi*	WE
☐ South-east Asian (Medium) Bent-winged Bat	*Miniopterus medius*	WE
☐ Lesser Bent-winged Bat	*Miniopterus australis*	E
☐ Free-tailed Bat	*Tadarida mops*	WE
☐ Wrinkle-lipped Bat	*Tadarida plicata*	WE
☐ Naked Bat	*Cheiromeles torquatus*	WE
☐ Slow Loris	*Nycticebus coucang*	WE
☐ Western Tarsier	*Tarsius bancanus*	E
☐ Silvered (Langur) Leaf Monkey	*Presbytis cristata*	WE
☐ Banded (Langur) Leaf Monkey	*Presbytis melalophos*	WE
☐ Dusky (Spectacled) Leaf Monkey (Langur)	*Presbytis obscura*	W
☐ Hose's Langur* (Grey Leaf Monkey)	*Presbytis hosei*	E
☐ Maroon Langur (Red Leaf Monkey)	*Presbytis rubicunda*	E
☐ White-fronted Langur* (Leaf Monkey)	*Presbytis frontata*	E
☐ Proboscis Monkey*	*Nasalis larvatus*	E
☐ Long-tailed (Crab-eating) Macaque	*Macaca fascicularis*	WE
☐ Pig-tailed Macaque	*Macaca nemestrina*	WE
☐ Stump-tailed Macaque	*Macaca speciosa*	W
☐ Agile Gibbon	*Hylobates agilis*	WE
☐ White-handed (Lar) Gibbon	*Hylobates lar*	W
☐ Siamang (Black Gibbon)	*Hylobates syndactylus*	W
☐ Bornean Gibbon*	*Hylobates muelleri*	E
☐ Orang-utan	*Pongo pygmaeus*	E
☐ Pangolin (Scaly Anteater)	*Manis javanica*	WE
☐ Giant Squirrel	*Ratufa affinis*	WE
☐ Prevost's Squirrel	*Callosciurus prevostii*	WE
☐ Kinabalu Squirrel*	*Callosciurus baluensis*	E
☐ Plantain Squirrel	*Callosciurus notatus*	WE
☐ Black-banded Squirrel	*Callosciurus nigrovittatus*	W

☐ Bornean Black-banded Squirrel*	*Callosciurus orestes*	E
☐ Grey-bellied Squirrel	*Callosciurus caniceps*	W
☐ Mountain Red-bellied Squirrel	*Callosciurus flavimanus*	W
☐ Ear-spot Squirrel*	*Callosciurus adamsi*	E
☐ Horse-tailed Squirrel	*Sundasciurus hippurus*	WE
☐ Slender Squirrel	*Sundasciurus tenuis*	WE
☐ Low's Squirrel	*Sundasciurus lowii*	WE
☐ Jentink's Squirrel*	*Sundasciurus jentinki*	E
☐ Brooke's Squirrel*	*Sundasciurus brookei*	E
☐ Red-bellied Sculptor Squirrel*	*Glyphotes simus*	E
☐ Himalayan Striped Squirrel	*Tamiops macclellandii*	W
☐ Three-striped Ground Squirrel	*Lariscus insignis*	WE
☐ Four-striped Ground Squirrel*	*Lariscus hosei*	E
☐ Red-cheeked Ground Squirrel	*Dremomys rufigenis*	W
☐ Bornean Mountain Ground Squirrel*	*Dremomys everetti*	E
☐ Shrew-faced Ground Squirrel	*Rhinosciurus laticaudatus*	WE
☐ Black-eared Pygmy Squirrel	*Nannosciurus melanotis*	E
☐ Plain Pygmy Squirrel*	*Exilisciurus exilis*	E
☐ Whitehead's Pygmy Squirrel*	*Exilisciurus whiteheadi*	E
☐ Tufted Ground Squirrel*	*Rheithrosciurus macrotis*	E
☐ Selangor Pygmy Flying Squirrel*	*Petaurillus kinlochii*	W
☐ Hose's Pygmy Flying Squirrel*	*Petaurillus hosei*	E
☐ Lesser Pygmy Flying Squirrel*	*Petaurillus emiliae*	E
☐ Horsfield's Flying Squirrel	*Iomys horsfieldi*	WE
☐ Black Flying Squirrel	*Aeromys tephromelas*	WE
☐ Thomas's Flying Squirrel*	*Aeromys thomasi*	E
☐ Temminck's Flying Squirrel	*Petinomys setosus*	WE
☐ Vordermann's Flying Squirrel	*Petinomys vordermanni*	WE
☐ Whiskered Flying Squirrel	*Petinomys genibarbis*	WE
☐ Grey-cheeked Flying Squirrel	*Hylopetes lepidus*	WE
☐ Red-cheeked Flying Squirrel	*Hylopetes spadiceus*	WE
☐ Smoky Flying Squirrel	*Pteromyscus pulverulentus*	WE
☐ Red Giant Flying Squirrel	*Petaurista petaurista*	WE
☐ Spotted Giant Flying Squirrel	*Petaurista elegans*	WE
☐ Large Bamboo Rat	*Rhizomys sumatrensis*	W
☐ Hoary Bamboo Rat	*Rhizomys pruinosus*	W
☐ House Rat	*Rattus rattus*	WE
☐ Malaysian Field (Wood) Rat	*Rattus tiomanicus*	WE
☐ Ricefield Rat	*Rattus argentiventer*	WE

☐ Polynesian Rat	*Rattus exulans*	WE
☐ Norway Rat	*Rattus norvegicus*	WE
☐ Summit Rat	*Rattus baluensis*	E
☐ Annandale's Rat	*Rattus annandalei*	W
☐ Bowers' Rat	*Rattus bowersii*	W
☐ Muller's Rat	*Sundamys muelleri*	WE
☐ Mountain Giant Rat	*Sundamys infraluteus*	E
☐ Dark-tailed Tree Rat	*Niviventer cremoriventer*	WE
☐ Long-tailed Mountain Rat	*Niviventer rapit*	WE
☐ Chestnut Rat	*Niviventer fulvescens*	W
☐ White-bellied Rat	*Niviventer niviventer*	W
☐ Brown Spiny Rat	*Maxomys rajah*	WE
☐ Red Spiny Rat	*Maxomys surifer*	WE
☐ Malayan Mountain Spiny Rat*	*Maxomys inas*	W
☐ Mountain Spiny Rat*	*Maxomys alticola*	E
☐ Chestnut-bellied Spiny Rat*	*Maxomys ochraceiventer*	E
☐ Small Spiny Rat*	*Maxomys baeodon*	E
☐ Whitehead's Rat	*Maxomys whiteheadi*	WE
☐ Long-tailed Giant Rat	*Leopoldamys sabanus*	WE
☐ Grey Tree Rat	*Lenothrix canus*	WE
☐ Asian House Mouse	*Mus castaneus*	WE
☐ Ricefield Mouse	*Mus caroli*	W
☐ Common Pencil-tailed Tree-Mouse	*Chiropodomys gliroides*	WE
☐ Large Pencil-tailed Tree-Mouse*	*Chiropodomys major*	E
☐ Grey-bellied Pencil-tailed Tree-Mouse*	*Chiropodomys muroides*	E
☐ Marmoset Rat	*Hapalomys longicaudatus*	W
☐ Monkey-footed Rat	*Pithecheir melanurus*	W
☐ Ranee Mouse*	*Haeromys margarettae*	E
☐ Common (Malayan) Porcupine	*Hystrix brachyura*	WE
☐ Thick-spined Porcupine*	*Thecurus crassispinis*	E
☐ Long-tailed Porcupine	*Trichys fasciculata*	WE
☐ Brush-tailed Porcupine	*Atherurus macrourus*	W
☐ Dhole (Asian Wild Dog)	*Cuon alpinus*	W
☐ Sun Bear	*Helarctos malayanus*	WE
☐ Yellow-throated Marten	*Martes flavigula*	WE
☐ Malay Weasel	*Mustela nudipes*	WE
☐ Ferret-Badger	*Melogale personata*	E
☐ Teledu (Malay Badger)	*Mydaus javanensis*	E
☐ Hairy-nosed Otter	*Lutra sumatrana*	WE
☐ Smooth Otter	*Lutra perspicillata*	WE
☐ Eurasian (Common) Otter	*Lutra lutra*	W
☐ Oriental Small-clawed Otter	*Aonyx cinerea*	WE
☐ Malay Civet (Tangalung)	*Viverra tangalunga*	WE
☐ Large Indian Civet	*Viverra zibetha*	W
☐ Large Spotted Civet	*Viverra megaspila*	W
☐ Little Civet	*Viverra malaccensis*	W
☐ Banded Linsang	*Prionodon linsang*	WE
☐ Common Palm Civet	*Paradoxurus hermaphroditus*	WE
☐ Masked Palm Civet	*Paguma larvata*	WE
☐ Binturong (Bearcat)	*Arctictis binturong*	WE
☐ Small-toothed Palm Civet	*Arctogalidia trivirgata*	WE

☐ Banded Palm Civet	*Hemigalus derbyanus*	WE
☐ Hose's Civet*	*Hemigalus hosei*	E
☐ Otter-Civet	*Cynogale bennettii*	WE
☐ Short-tailed Mongoose	*Herpestes brachyurus*	WE
☐ Collared Mongoose	*Herpestes semitorquatus*	E
☐ Hose's Mongoose*	*Herpestes hosei*	E
☐ Indian Grey Mongoose	*Herpestes edwardsii*	W
☐ Small Indian Mongoose	*Herpestes auropunctatus*	W
☐ Javan Mongoose	*Herpestes javanicus*	W
☐ Tiger	*Panthera tigris*	W
☐ Leopard (Panther)	*Panthera pardus*	W
☐ Clouded Leopard	*Neofelis nebulosa*	WE
☐ Leopard Cat	*Felis bengalensis*	WE
☐ Marbled Cat	*Felis marmorata*	WE
☐ Flat-headed Cat	*Felis planiceps*	WE
☐ Temminck's Cat	*Felis temmincki*	W
☐ Bay Cat*	*Felis badia*	E
☐ Dugong	*Dugong dugon*	WE
☐ Asian Elephant	*Elephas maximus*	WE
☐ Malay Tapir	*Tapirus indicus*	W
☐ Asian Two-horned (Sumatran) Rhinoceros	*Dicerorhinus sumatrensis*	WE
☐ Wild Pig	*Sus scrofa*	W
☐ Bearded Pig	*Sus barbatus*	WE
☐ Lesser Mouse-Deer	*Tragulus javanicus*	WE
☐ Greater Mouse-Deer	*Tragulus napu*	WE
☐ Barking Deer (Red Muntjac)	*Muntiacus muntjak*	WE
☐ Bornean Yellow Muntjac*	*Muntiacus atherodes*	E
☐ Sambar Deer (Rusa or Payau)	*Cervus unicolor*	WE
☐ Javan Rusa	*Cervus timorensis*	E
☐ Gaur	*Bos gaurus*	W
☐ Banteng (Tembadau)	*Bos javanicus*	WE
☐ Serow	*Capricornis sumatraensis*	W